A Bowl of Cherries

Jules Legal

◆ FriesenPress

Suite 300 - 990 Fort St
Victoria, BC, V8V 3K2
Canada

www.friesenpress.com

Cover Image by Stephen Meehan
Author Photo by Gladys Legal

ISBN
978-1-5255-5228-1 (Hardcover)
978-1-5255-5229-8 (Paperback)
978-1-5255-5230-4 (eBook)

1. Biography & Autobiography, Personal Memoirs

Distributed to the trade by The Ingram Book Company

A BOWL OF
CHERRIES

To: ~~Dorothy~~

Jules Legal

Introduction

"Life is just a bowl of cherries." The line may not mean much in today's world, and it didn't impress me much when I first heard it as a kid, back in the early 1940s. To me, it was just a simple little ditty I kept hearing over the radio, and I never thought to ask the meaning. And then, I heard adults use the line in casual conversation. I took it to mean: "Don't be worried. You mustn't take life so seriously." And confusingly, sometimes the expression was used to remind one another of how beautiful life can be. After all, what could be more beautiful than a bowl of cherries?

Life was no bowl of cherries for my grandparents, though, when they first arrived in Manitoba in the late 1800s. It remains hard for me to understand how they even survived, let alone how they went on to raise large families in the harsh scrublands of south-eastern Manitoba.

My parents, when they married, were determined to fashion a more comfortable life; one that wasn't totally consumed with putting bread on the table and stomping out fires. They dared to dream of simple pleasures, a new car perhaps, a nice home, maybe a family of their own one day.

Just when they thought they had it made; the Great Depression hit, and it would turn their world upside down. However, it didn't deter them from raising a family—five kids—in the end.

I freely admit that I probably got more than my share of attention, perhaps because I was firstborn, perhaps because I was always getting into trouble. "That kid!" Mom would say. "If he doesn't kill himself, he'll kill me. Just look at my white hair." Somehow I survived the ongoing ventures, and Mom's hair just kept getting whiter.

The Second World War brought an end to the Depression, but those turbulent war years brought their own set of challenges—tragedies, too, when yet another loved one died on the battlefields of Europe. Life on the home front carried on and the radio kept playing, "Life Is Just a Bowl of Cherries."

Somehow, our growing family made it through the countless challenges and the occasional calamity. Luck, perhaps? I prefer to believe that our "luck" was largely due to my parents' ingenuity, their industrious nature, and their readiness to pull up stakes and move to a new location whenever they felt there were better options elsewhere.

We lived in nine different homes as I was growing up. Each came with its own cast of characters and each played a unique role on an ever-evolving stage. I'm an old man now—"an old codger," some would say—yet the stories still reside in the far reaches of my mind where they remain fresh and true. And yes, I still believe that life is just a bowl of cherries.

TABLE OF CONTENTS

CHAPTER 1
This New Land, 1892-1924

AUGUSTE AND HERMANCE

My dad has taken me to a small clearing surrounded by dense willows and sparse scrub poplar. There are pools of standing water everywhere. If he hadn't pointed it out, I doubt that I would have noticed anything unnatural about this particular place, but sure enough, there appears to be a low, rectangular mound of rotting wood that has yet to be absorbed by the saturated soil. The only indication of life comes from a chorus of noisy frogs vigorously proclaiming their lust.

"This is where I was raised," Dad tells me. "This is all that remains of the cabin your grandfather built in 1902, the year I was born." A flood of emotions well up as I try to fathom what it must have been like, living here in this "almost swamp." Having only known my grandparents in their later years, when they lived a relatively comfortable life, makes it that much harder to imagine how these frail, gentle souls from a faraway land could have raised a large family in a tiny log cabin with mud for a floor.

Knowing that my grandparents and their children called this place home for over ten years, I expect some evidence, some objects to prove that someone actually lived here. After all, a family struggled to put food on the table, to keep warm in winter, but there are no clues to indicate how they managed. Other abandoned farms I have seen included remnants of buildings, rusting machinery, even modest luxury items that hinted at moments of leisure. Apart from that mound of rotting wood there is nothing, not even a piece of garbage. However, the site does give context to the stories my grandmother would relate whenever someone expressed interest.

Here it is, 1950, almost fifty years later, and the surrounding area has barely changed. Fewer people live here now, confirming in my mind the futility of trying to farm in this land of rocks and swamps. I can imagine that an ascetic hermit trying to get away from civilization may have been able to eke a sparse existence here, but I remain incredulous that anyone would have had the nerve to raise a large family in this unlikely place. I pester my dad with a barrage of questions, but he is unable to answer the key one: "What were they thinking?"

By now the mosquitoes are so thick we must retreat to the sanctuary of our vehicle. Dad expertly negotiates the jeep around the large puddles and deep ruts that define the trail. He deems this a "pretty good road," much better than the mud track he remembers only a few decades ago where, sometimes, even the horses could get stuck.

Dad and I are headed for Vita, Manitoba, where we shall be working together this summer. There's another swamp to drain, another road to build. He doesn't push it, but I know Dad would like for me to take over his excavation business one day. How hard he laboured to bring it to this point. "Didn't it serve our family well?" he reminds me. I've worked with him several summers now, enough to know that this is not what I want to be doing for a living, but I'm looking forward to spending precious time with him. This shall be the perfect opportunity to learn more about his early life. Just how did the boy raised in utter poverty in this "almost swamp" become the complex, confident man I'm proud to call my Dad?

Gabriel was the name given him by his parents, but everyone calls him Gaby. It seems a bit unfair that he should have to put up with this silly name that implies being too talkative when in truth he is a man of few words. I did not inherit this quality, and so whenever just the two of us are together I get to do most of the talking. I look upon my dad as my human encyclopaedia who never seems to tire of answering my ceaseless questions, no matter how silly they may be. When I am not asking questions, I shamelessly use him as a sounding board for my observations, opinions, and random ideas that burst forth like popcorn on a hot stove.

Dad is reluctant to talk much about his boyhood. There is little mention of life's simple joys. "Didn't you play games," I ask, "like baseball or hockey? Didn't you go horseback riding?"

"No time for frills like that," he shrugs. There is no mention of family outings, entertainment, or travel—just school and the obligatory attendance at church every Sunday. Those early years, the years that he remembers, were totally consumed with never-ending work, but he doesn't complain. "That's just the way life was in those days," he says, with no hint of bitterness or regret.

With a bit of prodding, Dad goes on to fill me in on some of his memories and impressions of growing up in this family that must have been the object of more than their share of local curiosity. I'm sure there were neighbours who wondered just what on earth were those two bumbling, impractical, people from France doing in these backwoods, having too many children and occasionally having to rely on neighbours to survive?

"Your grandparents weren't alone," Dad assures me. "Extreme hardships were the norm during those early pioneering years. Today, there may be few signs of prosperity, but there is no obvious poverty," he points out.

"So, what brought settlers here in the first place?" I ask.

"I guess the land was cheap." After a long pause, he continues, "You have to keep in mind that by the early-1890's, when your grandparents came to Canada, most of the good, arable land was taken, but the Canadian government kept encouraging newcomers to come and try their hand at homesteading."

As I look around the islands of farmed land strewn with rocks, I get the impression that it wouldn't take long for the scrub poplar and willows to take over and return this land to its natural state, leaving few signs anyone had ever lived here.

I'm sure Dad senses that I am still mystified as to why this unlikely couple from a faraway land with no homesteading skills came to set down roots in such a foreboding place. As we drive on, Dad, who is usually a man of few words, goes on to explain in more detail the circumstances that brought my grandparents to Canada.

He confirms bits of tantalizing rumours I had overheard as a boy, whispers that Grandpa had attended a Catholic seminary in Nantes, France where he studied to be a priest. Just before his ordination, he left his home and family and came to Canada. Why he made this momentous move that would forever alter his life and the lives of hundreds of his descendants remains mostly mystery. A few clues have trickled down through the years, and relatives from France have added their own juicier bits.

One story suggests that just as his hometown of St. Lyphard was preparing to welcome back their native son, expecting that one day he would be their priest, Auguste had a revelation—an epiphany, some might call it. It suddenly struck him that once he left the big city of Nantes, he would never be able to enjoy a normal family life. There would be a profoundly different relationship with the friends he grew up with. He would forever be stuck in this gloomy, austere village where the rest of his life would be severely proscribed. "I can't say I blame him," observed one of my French cousins. "Catholic priests must take a vow of celibacy. How much fun could that be?" he chuckled.

Once the momentous decision was made, Auguste had few options. He had to leave. He had to leave the country of his birth. He had to leave everyone he ever knew and loved. And so, like many Bretons before him, he set his sights on Canada. He crossed the channel to

England where he worked at various jobs until he was able to get a job as a deckhand on a cattle boat to Canada.

Somewhere along the way he heard about the Klondike and how hundreds of adventurous men were scrambling around the mountains and rivers of the Yukon looking for gold. This intrigued Auguste. He knew nothing about prospecting, or mining, or how much money it would take—just to get started.

His cash only took him as far as Winnipeg, where his fluency in languages enabled him to get a job as a teacher in La Rochelle, a tiny community near St. Pierre Manitoba. Dreams of the Klondike would have to be put on hold.

Around the same time, a family from another part of France was regretting their decision to come to Canada. Like many Europeans, they were victims of shameless government propaganda that promised cheap land and boundless opportunities in the "New West." The Baron family bought into this dream, expecting that the proceeds from their holdings near Foucherans in the foothills of the Alps would buy them hundreds of acres of rich farmland in the wilds of Canada.

When they arrived in 1892, much of the good land was occupied and they eventually found themselves in southeastern Manitoba where marginal land was still available at a reasonable price. Like many Europeans, they were totally unprepared for the brutal Manitoba winters and all the hardships facing early pioneers. They toughed it out for a few years, but soon the Baron family was making plans to move to Oregon.

As they prepared to embark on another long journey, an unexpected complication emerged. Their daughter Hermance, had met this schoolteacher in St. Pierre, and their interest in each other could not be ignored. Her parents were totally dismayed. Their headstrong daughter, not yet sixteen, was prepared to abandon her family for this older man with a mysterious past.

"I am not going to Oregon," she declared. "Auguste and I are getting married, and he will look after me."

Questions arose. Teaching was a respectable profession. Why was Auguste Legal, this learned scholar, stuck in this primitive backwoods school? Would he ever be able to provide for their daughter, who had led a comfortable, sheltered life up to now? How would she manage with no family to support her? These were all questions without answers for the distraught Baron family.

For his part, Auguste Legal must have been extremely excited at the prospect of marrying this beautiful young woman. Life would certainly be different after all those years of reclusive study in the austere, celibate, seminary in Nantes, France. He appeared completely unconcerned about how he would provide for the two of them when his tiny salary barely covered his own personal expenses.

They were married in 1895. Shortly after, the rest of the Baron family boarded a train in Winnipeg and headed west to Oregon. It was a tearful farewell for the Baron family, knowing it was unlikely they would ever be together again. Hermance and her younger sister, Juliette, were especially close, and years later Juliette came back to Manitoba to be with her beloved sister for a brief period. One of her brothers, Jules Baron, was quite elderly when he paid a short visit to Manitoba, but Hermance never saw her parents or the rest of her sisters and brothers again.

How foreign it must have felt to be a newly married woman in this small, mostly Métis community of La Rochelle. What a far cry from the life Hermance had enjoyed as a young girl in the comfortable little town of Foucherans near Dôle in eastern France. She would learn through the years that her family, the Barons, were doing well in Oregon and they missed her. Auguste continued to teach while Hermance had their first child, Augustine, in 1896.

Through numerous letters, Juliette pleaded with her sister to join them in Oregon, but Hermance, having a husband with a small but steady income, could not afford the fare—and besides, another child was on the way. She would have to make the best of her situation, a situation that would become ever more challenging in the years to come.

Perhaps it was inevitable that Auguste Legal would grow tired of teaching primary grades to rural children; after all, he was fluent in French, Greek, Latin, and English, as well as numerous lofty subjects that were all part of academic life at the seminary in Nantes.

Why did he not apply to teach at the prestigious Collège de Saint-Boniface? No doubt he would have had ample credentials, but no; he decided he would try his hand at farming, a vocation of which he knew nothing, on a piece of land that was practically worthless.

How Auguste could have lured his beautiful young bride into this trap of poverty and unspeakable hardship is another of those unfathomable mysteries that cause people to shake their heads in puzzlement.

Auguste and Hermance Legal went on to have sixteen children, most of whom also had large families. When relatives in France learned of the progeny stemming from Auguste and Hermance, they were incredulous. Why so many children, they wondered, when much smaller families had been the norm for generations throughout France?

With a bit of prodding, Dad goes on to fill me in on some of his memories and impressions of growing up in this odd family. Was he aware that the Legal's were the object of more than their share of local curiosity? *Just what on earth are those, impractical, bumbling people, doing in these back woods:* a common question among the gossips?

"It was hard for your Grandma, especially those early years, when the children were too young to help with everyday chores," Dad continues. "Your Grandpa just didn't seem overly concerned about his responsibilities as a father, and so it fell upon your Grandma to take care of the cooking, clothing, education, health, religious discipline, and countless other chores involved in bringing up children. All the while she also had to keep a watchful eye for potential injuries and everyday hazards."

Dad relates the oft-told story of when the family went picking wild berries in the surrounding woods. "I guess all of us should have kept a closer eye out for each other, but your Grandma blames herself for having dropped her guard for one regretful moment. Young Marcel, her seventh child, strayed from the group and disappeared in the dense bush. Initially, the family was confident they would find Marcel on their own, but as darkness approached, panic set in and neighbours were notified. Eventually hundreds of volunteers from miles around joined the search, combing every inch of bush and swamp. As the days and nights passed with no sign of the little boy, hopes faded and cruel speculation grew."

How could such a young boy survive the cold nights with light clothing and no food or water? This was the question on everyone's mind. With millions of ravenous mosquitoes relentlessly sucking the lifeblood from his body, when could he rest? When could he sleep?

One particularly insensitive volunteer related the story of a man who was lost in the bush for over a week and finally drowned himself as a preferred alternative to the bugs. Another told of a hunter who was lost for two weeks and went completely mad before he was rescued. There was even talk of hungry bears in the area. The thought of little Marcel succumbing to some horrific fate was almost too much to imagine.

Each day a trickle of volunteers dropped out of the search, convinced that the little boy could not possibly be alive after all this time. Family and close neighbours continued the search, despite an ever-growing sense of dread.

"The local priest conducted a special mass, beseeching the Virgin Mary to help searchers find the lost boy. The torrents of prayers offered up provided little solace for your poor Grandmother, who was on the verge of total collapse."

And then, miracle of miracles, little Marcel was found. He had spent three days and three nights in the bush, and though he survived the ordeal, he was somehow 'changed.' He spoke of a beautiful lady who wrapped him in her long, blue gown and held him close.

The devout who had been praying non-stop since the beginning were ecstatic. Obviously, the Blessed Virgin had intervened and protected little Marcel from harm. Another Mass was dedicated, offering heartfelt gratitude to the Virgin Mary for having spared the little boy.

"Wow!" I exclaim. "How come there isn't a statue or a church built to commemorate this miracle, like when the Virgin Mary appeared to those young girls at Lourdes, or to the children of Fatima?"

Dad is strangely silent as I leave him to discern whether I am being sincere. Does he sense my thinly veiled skepticism?

Finally, he relents. "You know, at the time nobody doubted for a moment that your uncle Marcel was saved by the Blessed Virgin. Through the years that followed, there was a lot of talk, a lot of talk . . ." he repeats, barely audible, as he trails off. Now Dad is strangely silent. I'm left to wonder: *Is he going to elaborate on the nature of the 'talk'? Is he reliving painful memories from long ago? Time to change the subject.*

"So, tell me more about Grandpa," I urge. "What was his life like before he came to Canada?" Dad immediately perks up and appears eager to share his version of the father he knew.

Curiously, Dad seems to know almost nothing about his father's life in France. From an early age, though, he was keenly aware that Auguste was the butt of gentle ridicule for his incompetence as a farmer. Dad could handle that. What bothered him was the idle gossip swirling through the community that Auguste was just not interested in his family. "He seems to live in a world of his own, they would say, and isn't it a shame that his poor wife and kids have to do all the work?"

Dad disputes this. "Your Grandfather worked hard, and he was a good father," he insists. "Yes, he was a 'little different.' It didn't help that he spoke French with an impeccable Parisian accent. Local folk considered it kind of snooty, especially those from Québec, who spoke a dialect called *Joual.*"

According to Dad, *Joual* was a crude, unsophisticated language with mostly French-sounding words but many with unknown origin.

"Your grandfather could read multiple languages, including Greek and Latin," Dad boasts. "After Sunday Mass, just for practice, he would converse in Latin with the local priest. Most of the time, though, he spoke very little; he wasn't much for small talk. However, on the rare occasion an educated, fellow countryman would visit, Auguste could revert to that passionate student from Nantes, debating the cause and the carnage of the French Revolution while recognizing the democratic merits that followed. He would sometimes quote wisdoms from the great philosophers in their original language of Greek or Latin without realizing that few could understand."

I can see how this might have annoyed the locals, whose education would have been minimal or sometimes non-existent. Having a learned scholar in their midst just didn't make sense.

What good was all that education, anyway? What brought him here, in the first place? All of these quirks just added to the mystique of the man.

Although Dad respected and admired his father's academic accomplishments, he didn't share in Auguste's passion for philosophical pondering. Dad dropped out of school after grade 8. Despite this disparity in education, they were much alike in many ways. Both were fearless risk-takers and never seemed to worry about potential consequences. Neither saw the need to acquire material comforts, and both were indifferent to their status within the community.

I can now better appreciate how traits, genetically handed down from father to son, could explain what motivated Dad to embark on new ventures and the occasional folly. To hell with personal discomforts, or the embarrassment that might follow. If you don't aspire to be wealthy or to make a name for yourself, you can afford to try risky options. That way, I guess you can just live day by day and accept whatever life has to offer without a lot of concern about the outcome.

Throughout my childhood, Dad often reminded the rest of us in the family what a fine, rich life we lived—but then, he wouldn't have recognized poverty or failure if it were staring him in the face. I suspect that is how Grandpa coped with all those hungry kids that kept popping up and needing to be fed. As for the mosquito-infested swamp that Grandpa tried making into a farm, perhaps it wasn't much worse than the rather austere land in Bretagne, France, where he grew up in the village of St. Lyphard.

Around 1914, the Legal family moved to a nearby cluster of homes that was slowly growing into a modest village. "Saltel," they called it. Bit by bit, the older children in the ever-expanding Legal family took over the farm chores, and slowly a level of comfort and security replaced the mind-numbing poverty that drove my grandmother to despair.

Around this time, Auguste took an interest in civic affairs, serving as a school trustee for a time. He also served several terms as municipal councillor for the area and acted as local representative in provincial business. By all accounts, he was well respected as a community leader despite his questionable skills as a family provider.

Although he wasn't particularly devout, it is my understanding that Auguste was instrumental in organizing the construction of the local Catholic Church in Saltel. He suggested naming the church "Ste. Geneviève" after the patron saint of Paris. The local priest promoted the idea and went through the process of making it official.

The general area was also irreverently known as "'Pôche aux Lièvre" (a bag of rabbits), supposedly because wild bush rabbits were so plentiful that hunters could count on filling a bag with rabbits whenever they chose to. Could this be the reason that Auguste sought to have the name of the village changed from Saltel to Ste. Geneviève, or was it simply to match the name of the church?

Eventually, my grandfather became postmaster of Ste. Geneviève, affording him a tiny income. More importantly, it gave him a reason to be absolved from all further farm and household chores.

Auguste may not have been very industrious or ambitious, but to his credit, his was a gentle soul who treated everyone with respect and kindness. He harboured few bad habits and his needs were extremely modest. The only luxury reserved for his personal indulgence was a daily apple, which he kept in his private cache in the root cellar, under the floorboards.

When Dad mentions Grandpa's little box of apples it triggers a memory—a faint memory that is suddenly awakened. The rest of the family had all gone to church, and Grandpa stayed behind to look after me. I was aware of Grandpa's little box of apples. Not knowing that they were strictly for him, I asked if I could have one.

"Mais oui, mon cher garçon, but before I let you have one, you must promise that you will eat the whole apple and not waste any."

Grandpa was known for his fastidious frugality, which continued long after it could politely be called a survival imperative. It must have impressed this kindly old man when I revealed to him what was left of the bare core which had not an edible morsel left.

"Bon garçon, bon garçon," he repeated as he patted the top of my head.

Dad is incredulous. "How can you remember that minor event? You weren't even three years old." I add a few more details that the story has unlocked from my brain, and he admits they all sound authentic. If he still doubts my word, he doesn't say.

I want to understand what compelled Dad to leave his family at the unthinkable age of fourteen. He is reluctant to attribute any particular reason, and he certainly would not blame anyone for prompting his move. I am left to speculate, but as we talk, the story of his boyhood becomes clearer.

I try to imagine what life was like on the Legal farmstead once the family had moved out of that primitive log cabin in the swamp. It sounds like a wonderful new chapter is about to unfold. The new house has a wood floor, it has an upstairs, decent windows; it even has two doors. The older kids have taken over the farm chores and there are plenty of hands to look after household duties. Grandma is pleased that she now has neighbours close by, and best of all, the church is only a five-minute walk down the road.

It would be nice to believe that the worst of those horrendous hardships for Grandma was now over. It should be a time to relax, to enjoy her growing family, but she cannot escape the realities that haunt her.

Her husband continues to retreat ever deeper into his private world. His interest in the family seems more remote. Even births, which occur with predicable regularity, have become routine. Could it be that Hermance has also moved into her own private world?

Despite having a large and growing family of her own, Hermance still aches with longing for her childhood family, her loving parents, her brothers and sisters—people so dear, but unlikely to ever be reunited. She learns through occasional letters that the Baron family have fashioned a comfortable life in their new home in Oregon, but she doubts that it can compare to the charming little village they left behind in Eastern France. "Why did they move?" she wonders. "Didn't they have it all?"

Throughout the years, Hermance often spoke longingly of her childhood, describing the bountiful orchards, and the lush farms with fat, contented animals. She remembers the profusion of beautiful flowers everywhere, and in the distance, the mysterious Swiss Alps, which turned white in winter. She remembers their beautiful home in Foucherans, that perfect little village, near the ancient city of Dôle, and she would remind people that Dôle was the birthplace of the famous Louis Pasteur who transformed the world's understanding of disease and who developed the first vaccines.

In her later years, when all her children had grown and were on their own, Grandma was persuaded to be interviewed on radio. She told of the hardships she endured as a young mother trapped in the bush with a seemingly indifferent husband and no parental family to help or offer comfort.

She described in detail the oppressive heat of summers with clouds of buzzing mosquitoes followed by the bitter cold of winter and all the challenges and discomforts this entailed.

I try to imagine the burden of responsibility that weighed heavily upon my grandma day after day. How did she survive the ordeal and pain of childbirth? How stressful it must have been in this primitive part of the world, where medical care meant a precarious ten-mile trip to Ste. Anne by horse-drawn carriage or sled. How did she cope with the tragedies of babies who died at childbirth? I am reminded of one story in particular.

It was early March 1902. Grandma was about to deliver her fourth child. There had been problems with a previous delivery that resulted in a stillbirth. She was determined that her next baby would not be born in that primitive cabin with no medical backup.

Sparse as it was, she wanted this birth to take place at the modest little hospital in Ste. Anne, some ten miles away. The snow had begun to melt but was still too deep for horse and carriage, so Grandpa was forced to transport her by sleigh.

While crossing Rivière des Petits Poissons, the horse and sleigh broke through the ice. Auguste quickly jumped into the freezing water, grabbed the halter of the terrified horse, and persuaded it to finish crossing the waist-deep creek. They continued on to Ste. Anne hospital where Gabriel—my father—was born without incident.

Decades later, Grandma still looked upon this ordeal with both dread and relief. What if she had been thrown into that ice-cold water? Would she or the baby have survived? What if the water had been deeper—would her husband have survived? Would the horse have survived? What if she was forced to give birth alone in that tiny open sleigh? Meanwhile, Grandpa took it all in stride, never admitting that there was ever any danger and quite pleased with how it all turned out.

Slowly, it dawns upon me that Dad's leaving the family home wasn't so mysterious after all. It probably came as no surprise to his mother, either. Gabriel was a precocious child. "That boy, he always had a mind of his own," she would freely tell people, without divulging how hard it was to bend him to her wishes.

She knew full well that neighbours had noticed that Gabriel skipped Sunday Mass too often but were too polite to ask why. It was only a matter of time before the priest would confront her and demand to see Gabriel in regular attendance. There was no point in asking Auguste to intervene; by now his fatherly authority had withered to insignificance—and besides, Auguste also skipped mass from time to time.

Dad did not agonize over leaving his family and setting off on his own. There was no single, compelling reason. The idea just popped into his head one day, and bit-by-bit, over the summer of 1916, it became firmly implanted in his mind.

It occurs to me that his independent, somewhat reckless spirit wasn't much different from his parents. Didn't they too defy common wisdom? Didn't they disregard their parent's expectations? I admire their boldness, but I do not share their cool determination. Dad was only fourteen when he left his family home. I have just turned sixteen, and still I can't imagine leaving my family.

As we bounce along in the open jeep, I reflect upon the stories Dad has shared with me. How great it would be to talk with my grandparents, now that I have some understanding of their past. What fascinating, courageous characters were Auguste and Hermance. I deeply regret that we had such a distant relationship. Still, I feel a warm familiarity and think of them often with renewed respect and profound admiration.

"Hermance and Auguste"   Source: family photo

GABRIEL

By 1916, when Gabriel left home, railway companies had spread their steel tentacles across most of the arable land in Western Canada. Grain elevators and related infrastructure followed close behind. The rich, virgin soil produced bumper crops of every type, and the West held the promise of becoming Canada's breadbasket.

Coincidentally, steam-driven tractors were fast replacing horses and ox teams. Ingenious mechanical marvels like, sheave binders and threshing machines were making it possible for fewer people to harvest more and more grain. There was a hitch, however. The short growing season meant that crops had to be harvested in a hurry, and despite all the new-fangled machinery, when it came to harvesting crops, it still required plenty of muscle power, both animal and human.

Every able-bodied person, from young children to frail old folk, pitched in to get the precious crops off the fields in time to avoid early frosts, late rains, and those dreaded hailstorms. How devastating it must have been when a hard-working farm family could only watch in helpless anguish as their bountiful crop got wiped out in a single summer storm.

Complicating the operation of this vast enterprise was the fact that Canada was at war, and thousands of young men were overseas, fighting and dying in the muddy trenches of Europe. Farm families struggled to cope with the relentless, backbreaking work. Neighbours helped each other unstintingly, but still it was not enough.

Newspapers across Canada were filled with "HELP WANTED" ads, promising good wages and, just as importantly, good food. Men of all ages came forth to work on "*les battages*," (the harvest) grateful for the opportunity to make a bit of cash and eat a hearty meal. Gabriel was one of these men—if you can call a fourteen-year-old a man. So, in the late summer of 1916, Gaby, as he was known to his friends, boarded an open rail car in Winnipeg and headed west.

He ended up at a typical 160-acre mixed farm near the Saskatchewan border and was immediately put to work. His first job was pitching sheaves of wheat onto a horse-drawn wagon as it moved along at a steady pace. Workers following on foot were expected to load the wagon, no matter the speed. The driver was often a young kid or an old man. Sometimes, a woman or girl could be the driver, if they weren't totally occupied with food preparations. When the wagon was full to capacity, the ripened sheaves were delivered to a mysterious mechanical monster called a threshing machine or a 'thrashing machine' as some preferred to call it.

This marvel of engineering gobbled up sheaves of grain as fast as men could pitch them into the maws of the hungry beast. From there, they disappeared into a complex array of drums, shakers, and blowers where the grain was separated from their stalks. Precious, clean grain came pouring out of a spout near the bottom while the straw was blown from a long pipe onto a pile that grew to resemble a small mountain as the days wore on.

Typically, the threshing machine was driven by a long flat belt connected to the flywheel of a wheezing, cantankerous steam tractor positioned some distance away. A common observation held that for every hour spent in useful labour, these early machines required an hour of service or repair.

This often meant a welcome rest for the hired help, but Gabriel's curiosity compelled him to observe closely and to help the service crew whenever possible. In turn, his intuitive mechanical skills were soon appreciated, and he was asked to join the service crew. This was the moment when Gaby recognized that he much preferred mechanical work to farm labour.

Near the end of September, the harvest was complete, work crews from out East returned home, and the frenetic activity of the past month slowed to a more normal pace. Gaby wasn't in a hurry to go home. He knew full well that his siblings were managing the farm just fine without him. If he did go home, he would likely have little say and would end up doing menial chores like cleaning the barn and carrying endless pails of water from the well to the thirsty animals. And then there were those dreaded Sundays in church.

By now, his English had improved and so had his confidence. Near the end of the harvest, he approached the kindly farmer who had hired him at the outset. "Could you use an extra hand for a few more months?" Gaby suggested. "I could help with machinery repair and whatever chores need doing."

The elderly gentleman, a recent immigrant from England, seemed intrigued with the idea. "Trouble is, my wife won't share the house with farm hands," he reluctantly admitted.

"There's the bunkhouse," Gaby reminded him.

"No, it wouldn't do when the weather gets cold, and I don't want to heat it all winter," declared the farmer. "Besides, I couldn't afford to pay you the wage you've been getting during harvest."

"No problem," Gaby persisted, "you pay me what you think I'm worth, and I would be happy to sleep in the barn with the livestock."

And so, Gaby spent the winter, working long days, learning new skills, and doing his best to survive on the strange food concocted by the prim English lady who ruled the house.

Gaby found it quite agreeable sleeping with the horses and cows. They made few demands, and as long as they had enough to eat and drink, there was never a complaint. Free time was spent reading, mostly technical stuff, and of course it was all in English. He learned the intricacies and quirks of steam-powered engines, but what intrigued him most was this emerging new technology called the "internal combustion engine" and how it was transforming society.

Although he was well treated, by spring Gaby knew there was no future for him on the farm, and so with the farmer's blessing and a letter of recommendation he packed his bag and headed for Winnipeg. There wasn't much to show for all those months of hard work, but he did manage to save a few dollars, and he could now read and speak English better than any of his siblings. He was only fifteen, but he was determined to prove that he didn't just survive those long, lonely months away from home; he had become a man.

He was supremely confident that he could make his way in that big sophisticated city called Winnipeg. He would prove to all that he was a hard-working, independent young man who could fashion a whole new life for himself. It would in no way resemble that dull, familiar one most of his childhood friends seemed content to follow.

Gaby remained short in stature, but his body had grown into a muscular powerhouse with seemingly limitless stamina. He knew since the harvest that he could keep up his end of any physical task with the biggest and the strongest of grown men, but he was no longer content to accept any mundane backbreaking work. His next job would have to be one that would satisfy his thirst for adventure, and it had to pay a decent wage.

While the war in Europe raged on, businesses in Manitoba were desperate for skilled workers, so Gaby was able to try his hand at all sorts of jobs. With his mechanical knowledge, his various skills, and his strong work ethic, Gaby could afford to be selective.

The Great War ended November 11, 1919—at least, the open hostilities ceased. Thousands of soldiers were coming home, eager to get on with their lives. No longer was there a shortage of human brawn, but this commodity was becoming less valued as machines were replacing workers in all walks of life.

With the return of servicemen and women to civil life, the demand for consumer goods appeared insatiable. It followed that entrepreneurs eagerly took up the challenge of manufacturing stuff for the masses, spawning thousands of new enterprises and jobs. For the next ten years, our young country boomed with a spirited energy that many believed would go on forever.

The internal combustion engine that made possible military tanks and the aeroplane rendered the horse obsolete as a tool of war. Now this "infernal" combustion engine, as some people called them, was threatening to displace the horse in civil life as well. Technology was changing rapidly. The mighty steam engine, which seemed so all-powerful a few years earlier, gave way to the more efficient gasoline engine, to be followed soon after by the diesel engine. Steam would continue to power locomotives and ships for a time, but by 1920, virtually every truck, every car, and every tractor was driven by a gasoline or diesel engine. Gaby was determined to embrace this new mechanical age and to become as proficient as possible in all related technologies.

A multitude of opportunities lay before him. Gaby could have carved out a comfortable living at any number of jobs, but he chose heavy construction, with land drainage and road construction as his specialty. It's not too hard to imagine how this would appeal to a young man like Gaby. What a sense of power he must have felt as a skilled bulldozer operator, moving more earth in one day than a dozen teamsters and their horses.

Gaby would be the first to admit that operating a bulldozer didn't require a lot of skill. The real challenge was to keep that pricey machine operating with minimal down time. These early machines may have looked robust, but in fact, they were rather fragile. Breakdowns were common, particularly in the hands of a careless operator lacking that all-important "light touch." The need to be gentle was re-enforced by requiring the operator to repair the machine he had broken. As often as not, repairs had to be carried out in the open, no matter the weather, no matter the bugs. "Time is money," was the adage, often heard on construction sites. If the boss determined that an operator was logging up too much downtime, he could be out of a job in a flash.

During the 1920s, a new revolutionary machine appeared on the scene. It was called a dragline, it too was powered by an internal combustion engine, and its utility was immediately recognized by the heavy construction industry. The dragline evolved from the heavy, cumbersome steam shovel commonly used in the mining industry. This new, more versatile machine would prove particularly invaluable for land drainage and road construction through difficult terrain.

From the moment Gaby saw his first dragline, he was hooked. It was love at first sight, so impressed was he with the genius of its design. He determined that this mechanical marvel would become central to his life's work. No other machine could come close to its versatility. It could dig a ditch through swamps or just about any type of terrain for that matter. At the same time, with a skilled operator at the controls, it could deposit the freshly dug earth to create that all-important access road or onto a truck to be hauled away. Gaby found the versatility of this wonder machine totally fascinating, and it perfectly suited his personality.

At the end of a typical construction season, Gaby could look back on his work with satisfaction, knowing that more farms were now protected from flooding and more people now had a decent road that gave them year-round access to the comforts of civilized society. With his dragline, he had drained another swamp, he had created new roads, and it felt good to realize that he had contributed to the quality of people's lives.

How he wished that his work could carry on throughout the year. What a pity that construction season in Manitoba was so short. Work would not begin again until late spring, when melt water had subsided and frost was out of the ground. Over a hard winter, frost might penetrate four feet deep, delaying the dragline season until early June, and depending on snow levels, it could be over by November. What to do with all that time in between?

Gaby was not one to sit idle for long. If he could not find a decent alternate job, he could always find work in bush camps, cutting trees with an axe and handsaw and hauling endless cords of wood with horses. Life in these bush camps was hard, but the camaraderie and good humour that prevailed made it all bearable.

During the 1920s, Gaby learned that mechanization was making mining in Manitoba and Northern Ontario an exciting new possibility. It wasn't always a profitable enterprise, but since the war's end, there was no shortage of prospectors, convinced that they could one day strike it rich, and a few of them did. More often, though, their findings led to further exploration that required heavy drilling equipment and supporting infrastructure. This in turn led to another job opportunity.

Transportation to these remote sites was typically over ice roads that could only be travelled by tractor train in the winter. These early tractor trains consisted of several heavy-duty sleds pulled by a single crawler-type tractor. Everyone knew that driving such a train through the swamps and over ice-covered lakes was fraught with danger, but of equal dread was suffering a breakdown along the trail.

Gaby felt well suited for this challenging work. It held the promise of new adventures, and the pay was good. There wasn't much he couldn't fix, and if he had to spend a night or two in the bush, well, that didn't bother him one bit. After all, he always had his "Five Star" eiderdown sleeping bag. He knew it could keep him warm down to minus 40 degrees.

Rarely would Gaby talk about his early work experiences, but there was one in particular that stood out in his mind—one that almost took his life.

The events played out somewhere near Lac St. Joseph in Northwest Ontario. He had been hauling supplies to a remote drilling camp all winter. Spring was approaching, but the drillers desperately needed one more trainload to complete the season. Gaby knew the ice was getting weak in spots, but he agreed to try.

He was on the last leg of the trip, only a couple of hours from camp, and the most worrisome stretch was approaching. Ahead was a shallow lake where he knew the ice was thinning and getting weaker by the day. Whenever possible, he stayed close to shore where the water was less deep, but the strength of the ice was harder to read. He remembered times when certain small areas might remain open all winter. Of course, he gave wide berth to these "hot spots," as some drivers called them. Other times, these hot spots could freeze over with thin ice, supporting a layer of snow and looking the same as any other part of the lake. Gaby had made a mental map of these deadly traps along his route, but there was no telling when a new one might pop up.

Gaby was always on the lookout for subtle depressions in the snow, a wisp of water vapour, animal tracks, and other telltale signs that spelled danger. Sometimes it was just a powerful "gut feeling" that he couldn't explain. *Best not ignore these feelings*, Gaby told himself. It may not warrant a change of course; just be focused and stay alert, pay close attention to any change to the constant creaking coming from the sleds as they glide over the hard-packed snow and glare ice. Listen for sharp cracks even though the roar from the engine drowns out the smaller ones.

It was during one of those inexplicable moments when Gaby sensed danger ahead. Time to resort to that cautionary procedure used by every tractor train driver whenever the ice was questionable. It involved unhitching the tractor from the sleds and reconnecting it at a distance with a long logging chain. That way, weight on the ice is better distributed, but more importantly, the heavy tractor would likely sink before the sleds, giving the operator a better chance of surviving a crash through the ice. At least that was the theory.

Steering was accomplished with long leather straps attached to the clutches, much like teamsters use to control their horses from a distance. Gaby did one more thing: He attached a thin rope to the engine's ignition system.

Years later, Gaby remembers the moment well. The sun was setting, and he idly speculated that it would be dark by the time he reached camp. He was getting mighty hungry. Hopefully there would be hot food waiting for him at the cookhouse.

He was grateful that there was no wind and the temperature was mild for late March. And then . . . *CRACK!* A rifle shot? But there was no rifle. Water began filling the ruts in the ice road. The tractor chugged on through the slush. For a silly moment, he thought it strange that the tractor had stopped sinking. Maybe, just maybe, it might carry on to firm ice, and he could continue the journey just like he had on all those other trips throughout the winter.

The water got deeper, slowly at first, until it became obvious that a miracle was not about to happen. He killed the engine and watched with fascination as the tractor slowly sank, steaming water swirling around the tracks, the engine covers, and over the seat he had been sitting on just a little earlier.

Not until his sled pitched forward and cold water started filling his boots, did he recognize that his life was in peril. He'd best not hesitate; his very survival was at stake. With water swirling all around, Gaby jumped from the sled, landing just short of firm ice. He doesn't recall how, but he managed to scramble onto solid footing with his upper body still dry.

Taking a moment to survey the situation, the impression that struck him first was how eerily quiet it was. More slowly, it dawned upon him how lucky he was to be alive. He took note that part of the tractor was still visible, and he immediately began assessing the possibility of a salvage operation.

Gaby knew there was a sturdy team of horses in camp that could be dispatched when it became obvious that he was late. It would take less than two hours, but with darkness approaching, quite possibly they would wait until morning. Meanwhile, his wet wool pants were getting stiff with ice. His boots felt awfully heavy. Camp was a ten-mile trek, and soon it would be dark; he'd best get moving. As he jogged towards camp, he noticed the temperature falling dramatically, and this made him happy. *The colder the better*, he thought. *Let the ice thicken and strengthen.* By the time he reached camp, he had developed a plan on how he would rescue this precious tractor.

Over the next several days, the valiant horses were worked to their limit, transporting tons of supplies from the still accessible sleds. They were a willing team, but they could only haul a fraction of the load the tractor had drawn. It took many trips, ten exhausting miles each way. Now, only the tractor remained, its vertical exhaust pipe serving as a monument to the cold, dead machine resting on the bottom of the lake.

Early one bright morning, a dozen men from the drill crew set out with Gaby, along with a sled full of tools and supplies. The cook had prepared pots of warm food, enough for a long day, and there was a sack of oats for the horses.

While Gaby dismantled much of the engine, the rest of the crew built two large log tripods, which they placed over the tractor. By late afternoon, they were ready to haul away on the multi-ton chain hoists. Hopefully, they could lift the machine from its watery grave without breaking new ice. If that worked, the plan was to lay a bed of logs under the tracks and to keep fashioning a moveable corduroy road until the tractor was on solid footing.

When Gaby removed the spark plugs, he was relieved to see that water had not reached the cylinders, and he was pleased with himself for having the foresight to kill the engine before the tractor went down. He meticulously dried all the critical components, including the dozens of intricate parts that make up the carburetor. He drained the oil and heated it over a fire before pouring it back into the crankcase, while a helper kept heating the intake manifold with a blowtorch. Everyone held their breath, most still doubting that the engine would start. Gaby positioned the crank into that strategic position of arc. Without fanfare he jerked up on the hand crank. The big Caterpillar engine obediently roared into life, just as Gaby knew it would.

■ ■ ■

I am so grateful that I was able to persuade my dad to share a few such stories from his youth. It wasn't easy. He simply was not a natural-born storyteller. The ice road story was the exception. Once he got started, he appeared to relish relating the details of this marvellous adventure that could have so easily taken his life. I would have liked to hear how he felt after that ordeal. Did it traumatize him? Did it deter him from doing the same work the following winter? Not very likely; instead he relates with some amusement what a "pain in the ass" it was jogging the ten miles back to camp after his dip in the lake—how he had to stop occasionally to break up the ice that formed over his frozen pants, and what a nuisance it was having to pee when the buttons on his fly were frozen. No mention of trauma or fear. He certainly was never boastful, but he did admit that as a young man he was pretty tough. The telling of that ice road venture awakened another memory that had him chuckling.

He was in his early twenties and working with a few friends in a small bush camp one winter. It had started to snow before going to bed, and when he awoke it was still snowing. Almost three feet, he figures. This made cutting wood pretty much impossible, so it was decided to wrap it up for the season. Besides, spring was just around the corner.

The crew had packed up their gear, the horses were hitched and all piled onto the sled for the long ride home. With the deep snow they knew it would be slow going, but nobody was prepared for what came next. The horses advanced a few steps, but when the snow reached their bellies they refused to budge another step. Other teamsters might have reached for a whip, but Gaby and his workmates considered their horses good friends. They couldn't do that. So they coaxed and cajoled, pulling the horses by their halters. The horses would advance a few steps and stop. Gaby suggested they break trail on foot, ahead of the horses. To everyone's surprise, the horses followed. It would be a long gruelling ordeal, wading through the deep snow but it appeared to be the only way. Of course it required two people, one for each horse, and Gaby was happy to do his part. His trail-breaking partner had to drop out after a mile or so and another took his place. And so they alternated all the way home. Meanwhile, Gaby went the whole way without being spelled.

As he relates the story he acknowledges the seemingly boundless physical energy he possessed when he was young. He attributes this stamina to pure luck. I am more impressed with his mental toughness. How many would have undertaken that final run across weakening ice? How many would have dared to conduct the salvage of a tractor at the bottom of a remote lake so late in the season? I know I wouldn't. But then I also recognize that I certainly wouldn't be raising a large family in the mosquito-infested bush and swamps of southeastern Manitoba, either.

"Ice road tractor train"   Source: public domain

OLIVIER AND AMANDA

I barely got to know my mom's father, and here we are on a cold day in January, attending his funeral. Like everyone in church this sombre day in 1951, I feel sad. Oh, he led a good life, and he lived long—almost ninety, my grandfather. It's the sinking feeling that I barely got to talk to him that bothers me. I don't think I even called him "Grandpa." I'm seventeen now, old enough to understand that I had the opportunity a few years back, and I blew it.

I remember the scene: this grey-haired old man, sitting ramrod-straight in his wicker wheelchair, looking all-knowing and at peace with himself. We each mumbled something—I'm not sure what—then stared into each other's eyes. Mom always said I had eyes like her dad, but that's not what was going through my mind.

Where was this robust, muscular man Mom told me about with big, well-worn hands; "Gauthier hands," she called them. The shock of seeing what time and wear had done to him was taking too long for my mind to process. And I wanted to ask about that neat wicker wheelchair with two large wheels in front and tiny casters at the back. I guess either one of us could have, should have, said more, but we didn't, and now it's too late.

It was different with my mom's mother. Although Amanda was younger than Olivier, she looked older, so very old, shrivelled and bent, the colour of weak tea. We were introduced once, but she barely looked up and I detected no spark. So it came as no surprise when I learned of her death a short while later. I remember the funeral, but not much more.

The church is packed, this beautiful little church in Ste. Geneviève that marked countless milestones along the road of life for so many people. It's the church where my parents were married.

The priest begins the requiem mass and reads prescribed passages from the holy book. He drones on and on in Latin, arms outstretched, and I don't understand a thing—not the gestures, not the ritual, not the language. This is the cue for my wayward brain to tune out and let it wander where it will.

It takes me to that epic journey some eight years back when our family travelled by car from St. Catharines, Ontario, to the back woods of southeastern Manitoba. It was 1943, in the middle of World War II. Not the best of times to be travelling, but Mom got word her elderly parents were not well, and she longed to see them again. She also saw it as an opportunity for us kids to meet my grandparents, my aunts and uncles, and countless cousins—all strangers to me and my siblings. Meanwhile, Dad was eager to explore the final link of the highway that would connect Canadians from coast to coast by road.

It took us a whole week to make that slow trip along a rough and lonely road, still unfinished in many places. I enjoyed the journey. It was mostly fun, but there were long stretches that were not. Mom filled in these boring bits with stories from her youth, and I kept pestering her to tell us more, especially those early years before trucks and cars took over the sweaty labour that willing horses had performed since early history.

Mom was the youngest of thirteen children. She didn't get to witness first-hand the tough early years when her parents must have struggled to make their way in this new land, but with so many brothers and sisters to remind her, she had a pretty good idea.

"My parents were married in Matane, Québec, in 1885," she began. "They had two children before moving to Ste. Anne, Manitoba, in 1889. Over time, four of my father's brothers and several sisters joined them in Ste. Anne, and settled into various communities nearby."

Mom admits she grew up barely knowing her aunts and uncles, and there were far too many cousins to keep track of. It got even more complicated when these cousins married and moved on to greener pastures. It was enough to know that whenever she came across another Gauthier, she could be quite certain they were related, and if they took the time, they could trace their common ancestors back to Québec, back to the Gaspé. Over the years, I would find out more about our ancestors. I learned that the Gauthier clan trace their heritage back multiple generations to a common ancestor named Bernard Gontier. Records show that he sailed from France to Québec around 1665. There are now thousands of people who carry his name and his genes—maybe not his name exactly, because somewhere along the way the original name Gontier became Gauthier and has remained so to this day.

Whether every Gauthier is a direct descendant of Bernard Gontier is debatable and of minor consequence to me. I find it remarkable enough that I am but one descendant from this huge prolific family scattered across North America.

More intriguing to me is the environment that shaped my grand-parents. What compelled them to leave their familiar home? What prepared them to thrive in this sparse new land in Manitoba where others struggled and often failed?

Out of curiosity, I visited the region from where my grandparents came. Perhaps clues would unfold.

I learned that at least one Gauthier settled in the St. Jerome de Matane area of la Gaspésie at some period in the early 1800s.

The Gaspé, as the area is commonly called today, is a large penin-sula jutting eastward from Québec City into the Gulf of St. Lawrence. While this region may not have an abundance of commercial resources, it is famous for its rugged beauty, its countless streams and wooded hills. Some Québécois regard the Gaspé as a poor cousin, sort of an appendage to greater Québec.

The Mi'kmaq, the original peoples who lived here countless cen-turies before, were reputed to be friendly and helpful to those "hairy ones" who first landed on their shores in the early 1600s. At least they didn't forcibly try to stop the foreigners who chose to make the Gaspé their homeland too.

There evolved a mix of many cultures including French, Irish, English, Scots, and other minorities, and it's safe to say the Mi'kmaq added to this complicated mélange as well. Today, ethnic labels don't mean much to most people and I firmly believe that this is a good thing.

My mother, Nadia, always knew that she was of mixed blood, but I wasn't aware of what this implied during my formative years. She doesn't know whether her dad, Olivier Gauthier, would con-sider himself of "pure laine," (pure wool) but she knows that her mom, Amanda Fillion, retained a measure of Indian ancestry, most likely Mi'kmaq.

Nadia remembers her mom relating Indian tales and superstitions. Amanda often warned her children to beware of mysterious tricksters who did nasty things to people for no particular reason. Mom under-stood these to be cautionary tales, a warning to avoid dangers and to explain bad luck when bad things happen—pretty harmless stuff, as far as Nadia was concerned. However, she knew such tales would clash with teachings from the Catholic Church, and so she was wary to pass them along to her family. To her it was no big deal. I like her laissez-faire attitude. Still, I find it kind of intriguing that we share such a rich and diverse heritage.

There must have been some compelling reason for so many of the Gauthier clan to leave the Gaspé in the late 1800s. Unlike the Acadians from an earlier era, they weren't banished from their homes and history doesn't point to any political upheavals that would account for this major move. We do know there was a worldwide depression that peaked around 1897. Perhaps it was just too hard to make a decent living in this sparse land during those hard times.

Whatever the reason, the Gauthiers never looked back. They never complained about their lot in life, and as far as we know, none ever returned to the land of their heritage.

Mom's dad, Olivier, was the respected patriarch of their close-knit family. He found living in Ste. Anne quite agreeable, and so did his lifelong partner, Amanda. A good place to raise a family, they figured.

Olivier had no trouble finding work and took on all sorts of jobs. Carpentry, masonry, blacksmithing, and working on the railroad: it seems there was nothing Olivier couldn't do. He even tried his hand at veterinary services, assisting farm animals with problems, even performing minor surgeries when needed.

By 1906, Olivier and Amanda and their twelve children had outgrown their modest home in Ste. Anne. Perhaps it was time to move on.

Olivier was aware that a few miles to the northeast of Ste. Anne, beyond the rich farmlands, settled years ago, a number of families were taking up government offers of free land. *Free land?* How tempting. It sounded too good to be true. The catch, of course, was that this marginal land was so poor that only the very resourceful and the most determined could make a go of it. The area was mostly scrub bush, swamps, and stones everywhere. Hardships and poverty awaited those who came ill-prepared.

Despite the challenges, a tiny cluster of homes had somehow merged together in this unlikely place. One of the settlers started a general store, and now there was promise of a school to accommodate the many children sprouting up like flowers in springtime. There was even talk of building a church. "Saltel," they called the place. Later, it became Ste. Geneviève. Maybe those settlers weren't so foolhardy after all.

Olivier had his eye on more promising real estate. He had hunted game far afield and knew of an area of higher ground a few miles to the northeast. Although the soil didn't appear much better than around Saltel, at least it was a bit higher and looked more like the familiar land he had left behind in Québec.

When this area was finally surveyed and an access road pushed through, Olivier was quick to claim his 160 acres. Others followed with similar intentions, and when enough of them had settled in this new neck of the woods, they called it Ross.

So in 1906, Olivier and Amanda uprooted their children. They left behind the relative comfort and security of village life in Ste. Anne and embarked on a new challenge, one that would test their ingenuity and their resolve.

Olivier knew that the land was too poor to sustain a proper farm where surplus produce could be sold for cash. And so, Olivier and Amanda and their children set about creating a homestead so diverse that there would be little need for store-bought stuff.

There was wood aplenty on the property, and Olivier knew how to turn trees, stone, and gravel into building materials. He had, through the years, practiced all the skills needed to build many things. Olivier and his boys lovingly crafted a fine new home—the largest in the area—and it would keep their family snug and secure for many years to come. Over time, the Gauthiers continued clearing land, enlarging pastures, hayfields, and gardens. They built barns to shelter an ever-expanding menagerie of horses, cows, pigs, chickens, turkeys, ducks, and even a flock of sheep.

The sheep were to keep the family supplied with wool. During the winter months, the kids were kept busy carding, spinning, and knitting. The boys were encouraged to knit their own socks, mittens, and sweaters too. When it came to working, little distinction was made between boys and girls. Whether it was farm chores, kitchen work, or any of the hundreds of jobs that are part of everyday life, all were expected to pitch in.

The Gauthier homestead was a lively place, with chores starting at dawn and finishing in time for a convivial family dinner. Despite the never-ending work, the Gauthiers always reserved time for a bit of leisure. They played cards and board games, and there was always music. Several of the boys became self-taught musicians, practicing their skills nightly and offering lively music at social functions.

Recognizing a need in the community, Olivier partitioned off a section of their large house and set up a modest store. Amanda and the girls looked after customers while the older boys were kept busy hauling supplies from Ste. Anne or sometimes from Winnipeg, where a trip by horse and wagon could take two days.

Things were becoming a little less hectic as their children grew into adulthood. A couple of the girls were of marriageable age, and one of the boys had already set off on his own. Those early days of hardship were largely behind them now. Life for the Gauthiers promised a measure of welcome leisure.

Then, in 1907, another child came along—an afterthought, some said. They named her Nadia. She remained the youngest, the baby of the family, and there was no denying, she received more than her share of attention.

Nadia's childhood memories are mostly pleasant, at least the ones she chooses to talk about. She was just six, but she remembers clearly that day—the day that would change the lives of all in her family in ways they never could have imagined.

It was around 1913 when survey crews were spotted slashing and thrashing their way through the bush close to the Gauthier farm. When confronted, the workers freely explained their work assignment and were happy to share their version of the politics behind this ambitious project, an undertaking many thought to be impossible.

Following years of debate and scandalous neglect, big-shot politicians finally admitted the city of Winnipeg needed an alternate source of potable water. Existing sources from rivers and wells were often contaminated and almost certainly spreading disease, especially in poor parts of the city. People were dying.

It was determined that the best long-term solution would be to pipe in clean water from one of the many pristine lakes scattered across Eastern Manitoba. Shoal Lake was chosen, in part, because it was said to have an unlimited supply of water so pure that it required no treatment at all. And its elevation was such that gravity alone would propel the precious water over a hundred miles westward into Winnipeg.

Plans called for a massive concrete pipe, large enough to accommodate a booming city far into the future. It would be cast in place and require countless tons of concrete. Hundreds of workers would be involved and construction could take years.

Survey sketches showed the aqueduct passing through the Gauthier property. Far from being alarmed, Olivier saw opportunity. He would be happy to sell a few acres to accommodate the right of way; a bit of cash wouldn't hurt.

Olivier was quick to recognize that this massive undertaking would need a parallel rail line to bring in supplies and workers. He foresaw that this new access line had the potential to change the lives of all who lived along its route.

Olivier was one of the first to benefit when he was hired to lead a work gang laying down track, miles and miles of track. Much of the line ran through muskeg where the base kept shifting and required ongoing maintenance. This became a full-time job. It would now be up to Amanda to run the store, and thankfully, the children were old enough to handle most of the farm chores.

There was great rejoicing in 1919 when sparkling fresh water reached Winnipeg from Shoal Lake. The aqueduct was a monumental success and put Winnipeg on the map as a modern, progressive city. The deadly flu pandemic of 1918 was waning and waterborne illnesses became a thing of the past.

"The Greater Winnipeg Water District Rail Line", as it became known, made access to Winnipeg an easy one-hour ride from Ross. It eliminated that all-day ordeal by horse and wagon for supplies. And what a relief it was knowing that the occasional emergency trip to Winnipeg would no longer require a rough ride by wagon over primitive roads, often awash with mud.

The Gauthiers now enjoyed an even more comfortable life. They could afford decent clothes and the occasional luxury. Olivier even dared to dream that one day he might be able to buy one of those new-fangled contraptions they called a "horseless carriage."

What a blessing to have regular train service for everybody living along the route. It was so much easier to keep the Gauthier store well stocked, and trips to Winnipeg, for whatever reason, became fairly routine.

So nobody thought it was particularly unusual when, one summer's day, Olivier took two of his older boys on such a trip. Everyone assumed he was planning to buy some heavy stuff and would need their muscle. Of course, the boys were pleased to go with Dad. How they loved all the weird and wonderful sights of the city, and they hoped Dad might take them to a restaurant for lunch.

It was an exciting walk from the train station on Plinguet through the messy, smoky, industrial area, on past the stinky stockyards, and down Marion into the heart of St. Boniface. The boys were intrigued by so many people scurrying about—and all those pretty girls riding bicycles; how precarious they looked, balancing on two wheels.

The Gauthier boys grew up hauling all kinds of stuff with horses and wagons, but now there were trucks everywhere. Could this be the new way to haul things? Would they someday replace those hard-working horses they had grown to love? And those noisy, horse-less carriages, spewing smoke as they sped past? Sure, they grabbed people's attention, but somehow they didn't seem as elegant as those showy horses clip-clopping effortlessly along paved streets; fancy buggies in tow. Surely those beautiful rigs could never become obsolete—could they?

Olivier had been to the city many times before. He shared his boys' enthusiasm. Still nothing prepared him for the wild excitement that took over when he took them to an automobile dealership and they could actually sit in one of those vehicles. They took turns behind the wheel, making weird noises and pretending to drive. Their excitement ramped ever higher when a salesman offered to take them for their first ride.

Along a quiet street, the salesman stopped the vehicle. With barely any coaching, Olivier took the wheel and brought the shiny new Model T back to the show room without a problem. Cash moved across a table, papers were signed, and Olivier took possession of his first automobile.

What excitement when this marvellous machine pulled into the farmyard that evening, and what wondrous disbelief when the family realized that Dad was at the wheel.

Nadia remembers the first time they went to church in their new automobile and how smug she felt as people gathered round to gawk and gossip. "How could those Gauthiers afford such a useless luxury?" was the gist of the whispered comments she overheard.

Who could blame the neighbours if they felt a bit envious? After all, it was clear to Nadia that her family was pretty special. Wasn't her dad the smartest, the strongest, and the boldest man in all of Ross? And wasn't her mom equally gifted and wise and loved by all who knew her?

"And now, sadly Amanda and Olivier are both gone," proclaims the priest in language I can understand. Time to rein in my wayward mind and listen. I'm anticipating that he will tell the congregation about my grandparents and the mark they left upon this community. Perhaps he has a heart-warming story to tell about my grandfather, or he may call upon someone to come forward and deliver a poignant eulogy. Instead, he repeats that story from the scriptures, the same old myth I've heard at other funerals. I suppose it's meant to console the grieving family, but I'm tired of it.

"We mustn't dwell too long on Olivier's passing," the priest intones. "Olivier's body may be no more, but rest assured his soul has joined his beloved Amanda in heaven. The two of them are looking down upon us right now and trying to tell us not to feel so sad. They are blissfully happy together, and they are busy. They are busy preparing a new home for all the family. And what rejoicing there will be when all can be together again."

To me, it all sounds pretty silly, but obviously not to everyone. I sense that Mom is struggling to keep her composure, and a number of the older ladies are dabbing away tears.

As we leave the beautiful, little church, I can't help but notice all the cars parked along the main drag, not a horse in sight. I try to imagine my mom as a young girl arriving at this same church in their new Model T, and how proud she felt that day—proud to be a member of the Gauthier clan.

"Olivier Gauthier and Amanda"   Source: family photo

"Ste. Geneviève church"   Source: family photo

NADIA

Nadia grew up, confident that she was her dad's favourite. She sensed that she got more than her share of his attention, and in turn, she was happy to do small favours for him. Without being asked she would fetch his slippers when he retired to his rocking chair after supper, she would fill his pipe with his lovely smelling tobacco and light it, stealing a puff or two in the process. Her brothers called her Daddy's girl. She pretended not to mind the teasing, but she would find ways to pay them back.

A favourite trick was to pin a witty note to the offender's back which would cause others to laugh at the expense of the victim. One time, she pinned a rabbit's tail to one of her brothers' pants in just the right place. He went the whole day without discovering it. Nobody could figure out how she'd managed that. She developed such a reputation for pulling off tricks that she was the first one blamed when strange things happened around the Gauthier household.

When one of her brothers found a dead mouse in his boot, he was convinced Nadia had put it there. Nadia blamed it on the cat. Her mom thought it might be that mythical trickster she often talked about, and her dad suggested the mouse might have just crawled into the boot on its own and died.

"Of course that's what happened," Nadia quickly affirmed. "One whiff of that smelly boot would be enough to kill any beast."

The whole family had a good laugh, but Nadia never admitted to anything and the mystery was never resolved.

A high-spirited kid, Nadia loved to make people laugh and to play tricks that she considered humorous. On one occasion though, one of her tricks nearly ended in tragedy.

It all started with a pitiful old man who lived alone in a tiny cabin a few miles to the north. He eked out a simple living through hunting and trapping. Monsieur Goulet, they called him. There were others like him, lost souls, harmless enough, but cut off from society for one reason or another. They kept to themselves mostly, except Monsieur Goulet.

He was often seen wondering the back roads of Ross where he would wave and shout a hearty "Bonjour!" to people he met along the way. Whenever he spotted neighbours working outdoors, he would approach; "Just to convey my good wishes," he cheerily assured them. Monsieur Goulet was remarkably knowledgeable about many things, and he could be downright charming when he wanted to be.

Moved by polite manners and good grace, neighbours felt compelled to invite him in for supper. "Why, I'd be delighted," was his standard reply and "how timely," he would observe with no one suggesting for a moment that it was deliberately planned.

Nadia certainly never believed it was pure coincidence. It happened all too often. Was it because Monsieur Goulet loved her mom's cooking? Was it because her dad treated Monsieur Goulet with kindness and respect? Or was he simply lonely? Whatever the reason, Nadia thoroughly disliked "that smelly old geezer," never referring to him as Monsieur Goulet.

Mind you, Monsieur Goulet did carry an odour, not a particularly offensive odour but certainly noticeable to Nadia. Lots of old folk seemed to have that aura about them. Most people just learned to ignore it. Not Nadia!

The moment supper was over, she urged her dad to retire to the living room. "I have your pipe and slippers ready, Dad." Everyone knew it was her way of getting Monsieur Goulet out of the kitchen, knowing that her dad's aromatic pipe tobacco would create clouds of smoke that would mask the smell.

One day, with feigned politeness, Nadia offered to fill Monsieur Goulet's pipe. She was careful not to touch the slimy stem. She wouldn't think of putting her lips to his pipe even though it meant missing out on a few more puffs of that sweet smoke. The smelly old geezer could light his own pipe.

She watched from a distance as Monsieur Goulet put the flaming match to the packed tobacco. *How will he react?* she wondered, as he breathed in that deep, sucking breath that would draw the flame down into the tobacco.

CRASH! The pipe went flying noisily to the floor while the burning match dropped onto his lap. Monsieur Goulet frantically gripped the armrests of the chair, unable to extinguish the fire near his crotch. Monsieur Goulet's head shot back, eyes wide open, fixed to the ceiling, feet sticking out, stiff as boards. His face turned red then purple and then chalk white.

"He's having a heart attack!" someone screamed. Everyone rushed to watch with no one knowing what to do and Nadia in a state of panic.

And then Monsieur Goulet began to cough, a feeble effort at first that slowly grew into violent, racking explosions. Olivier thumped his back and Amanda brought him water. Slowly he returned to a calmer state, drawing ever-deeper wheezing breaths and spitting buckets of phlegm into Olivier's spittoon.

Nadia knew exactly what happened. She tearfully confessed to having stuffed talcum powder into Monsieur Goulet's pipe before loading the rest with tobacco. She had no idea it would nearly kill him.

Nadia knew she deserved the severe scolding from her dad. She was totally devastated, and she agonized over how long it would take to return to his good graces.

Monsieur Goulet never uttered a word about his near-death experience. Mind you, it never stopped him from visiting the Gauthiers just as regular as ever.

Each visit was a painful reminder for Nadia. She tried to avoid being in the same room as Monsieur Goulet but she was forced to eat at the same table. Maybe she didn't have to look at him, but she had to put up with his smelly presence. Period!

Oh, how remorseful she felt but also eternally grateful that Monsieur Goulet was still alive. Never again would Nadia play tricks on anybody, and she wondered if her brothers would ever stop reminding her of that near fatal day at the Gauthiers.

CHAPTER 2

Ste. Geneviève, 1924-1937

NADIA AND GABRIEL

Gabriel was barely twenty when he decided to stake out his own parcel of land. It was midway between Ste. Geneviève and Ross. He built a small log cabin in the virgin bush where he lived alone as a bachelor. A wife and family would be nice, but it wasn't yet in his plans.

Although he lived alone, he certainly wasn't a recluse. He visited with his parental family regularly, travelling the few miles to Ste. Geneviève with his new car. More often he was pulled in another direction where a lively, boisterous family seemed to have an innate ability to live well in this marginal land while maintaining that special *"joie de vivre."* It was just part of their nature. Olivier and Amanda welcomed him as one of their own, with the youngest boy, Romeo, becoming his best friend.

How he admired the Gauthiers, who seemed to know how to turn every job into a sort of game where banter and gentle humour was the norm. Gaby experienced little of this in his early years. All he remembers was a life of constant toil with little time for frivolity. His inhibitions rarely allowed him to join in their antics, but he enjoyed being with the Gauthier family no matter the occasion. Whether it was building a barn, fixing machinery, hunting game, or partying, it was always more fun with the Gauthiers.

Meanwhile, Nadia, the youngest in the family, couldn't help but take note of this stocky, quiet, and confident young man. He was so unlike her brothers. He never spoke to her directly, but she suspected that he was watching, so she made sure that she was on her best behaviour whenever he was around. Of course she was too young to entertain any fantasies of romance, or so she told herself. She would bide her time, maybe check out other possibilities.

Time moved on, and boys came calling. None impressed her. When other young ladies started showing an interest in Gabriel, she knew it was time to make her move.

They were married in late summer, 1924. It was a modest wedding, in keeping with the times and customs of the community. Both Nadia and Gabriel came from first-generation pioneering families where most still struggled just to provide the essentials for their large families. An extravagant wedding would have been considered unbecoming even for the few who could manage the expense.

A modern honeymoon was considered even more highfalutin, at least the type where the newlyweds go to a quiet place to be alone together. Such self-indulgence was reserved for the rich and the privileged. Besides the young couple mustn't waste too much time. Facing them was the serious business of preparing for a family that was bound to follow soon enough.

Gabriel did impress his new bride by booking a couple of nights at a fancy hotel in Winnipeg, but that was as far as his plans went. He assumed that they would then live together in his little log cabin. Meanwhile, Nadia had other plans.

For years she had looked on with envy as her older brothers prepared for another winter of working in the bush. The Gauthier boys really looked forward to these ventures. For weeks it was all they talked about. How she would have loved to join them.

Her parents taught life skills to their many children with scant regard to gender. The girls were expected to be adept at every farm chore, while the boys did their part in the kitchen. However there were still a few activities deemed "men only" and so this idea was quickly shot down. That didn't stop her from dreaming. She knew she could work as hard as any man and she could probably put up with discomforts better than most. Maybe this was the opportunity to experience a semblance of what life in a bush camp was all about.

"What if we were to spend the winter in the bush together," she proposed to her new husband, "just the two of us? You could be cutting wood like you've done with my brothers in the past, and I will do the hauling and the cooking."

And, why wouldn't he agree? How could Gabriel pass up such an opportunity? Gabriel loved working in the bush, but he hated cooking, and he hated housekeeping even more. With Nadia in charge, no doubt the quality of food would be far superior to any "men only" camp, and having a warm body to share his bed—well, could camp life get any better?

Nadia was not expecting a particularly romantic honeymoon but rather one that would be memorable, a winter venture they could one day tell their kids about. And if they managed to make a bit of money, well, that would help towards starting their own farmstead.

The Gauthier family bought their daughter and new son-in-law a team of sturdy, chestnut horses from a respected horse ranch north of Ross. People considered a team of horses to be a strange wedding present, but this was exactly what Nadia wanted.

Hers was a high quality team, a gelding and a mare, which worked well together. They were not only perfectly matched in size and strength they also had the same agreeable temperament. Horse specialists maintained that if you wanted to pair up the ideal team you would watch for clues that told you whether the horses liked each other. Such a team could be counted on to put in a good day's work without fuss, and if ever you got stuck or had to call on them to work extra hard, they could be relied upon to give you everything they had. Nadia didn't consider herself to be a horse expert, but she was certain that her team really liked each other.

Nadia had just turned eighteen. Physically she didn't look particularly robust, but she possessed a certain determined toughness that equipped her to take on any job no matter how difficult. During her early life she worked alongside her dad at every farm chore imaginable, from milking cows, to shearing sheep, to pitching manure. They even hunted wild game together. And from her mom she learned all the domestic skills, from spinning wool, to knitting, to sewing, as well as cooking and baking.

Gabriel for his part knew the ways of the bush, and he was familiar with the tools of the trade. He was known for always having the best of equipment and for always keeping his tools sharp and in good repair.

When Gaby and Nadia set out on their winter honeymoon, they knew that between them they had all the skills necessary to live in relative comfort throughout the winter. With a fine team of horses and hundreds of pounds of provisions, they were well equipped to handle whatever nature might throw at them.

Of course just surviving the winter in the bush wasn't good enough for Gabriel; there had to be a practical purpose, as well. He contracted with the paper mill in Pine Falls to buy the wood that he would cut. The mill would supply empty flat cars to a siding along the Greater Winnipeg Water District rail line and then haul away the full ones. Each flat car held about thirty-six cords, and Gabriel estimated that over the winter he could cut enough wood to fill several cars. He would ensure that it was all spruce, tamarack, or jack pine because that is what the mill preferred. Pulpwood fetched a better price than mixed stove wood, but still, after all expenses were factored in, it didn't leave much for wages.

Less predictable was the amount of work required to haul all that wood from the bush to the waiting flat cars. With the cutting area several miles from the railway siding, it took most of one day just to gather and haul a single sled of wood. Each sled would require the handling of a couple hundred logs, and over the winter it could take over one hundred trips to transport all the wood that Gabriel expected to cut. Was it fair or even possible for Nadia and her team to haul those tons and tons of wood to market?

It took no time at all for Nadia to fall in love with her beautiful animals. She marvelled at how strong they were, and how hard they worked with just a few words of encouragement. They were smart, too. They seemed to know when it was time to advance the sled as Nadia loaded another log or two. Even when there wasn't a defined trail, they picked the best route through the tangled brush to avoid getting the sled snagged. At the end of the day Nadia made sure her horses had plenty to eat and drink and that they enjoyed a snug shelter at night.

Camp life became more comfortable as the winter wore on. Nadia had refurbished their crude cabin to make it homier, and she experimented with dishes seldom tasted in a bush camp. Unlike the "men only" camps, she tried to bake something fresh every day. Most often it would be galettes, that staple that substituted for bread in every bush camp. Oatmeal biscuits were a regular favourite, too. Sundays she might bake a cake. Somehow in between her multiple chores she found time to snare a rabbit or two, so there was welcomed fresh meat as well.

Spring came early that year, and the snow-packed trail was getting more difficult with each load. Near the end of a bright sunny day the fully loaded sled slid off the slippery track and tipped over, spilling all the logs in a jumbled pile. Nadia was faced with a dilemma. If she walked back to camp it would be too dark for Gabriel to come to the rescue. They'd have to leave it for morning; a whole day would be lost. She determined she would try to right the heavy sled by herself, reload the scattered wood, and continue on to the siding in the dark. Supper would be late, but she knew that Gaby would be duly impressed and it would be a good note on which to wrap up the season.

When family and friends learned of her accomplishments, they marvelled at her physical strength as well as her grit. No longer would she be regarded as the spoiled brat of the family. She was now a hardened, tough young woman ready to take on any and all challenges that life had to offer.

Once the newlyweds were settled, Gabriel returned to work at heavy construction. His summers were spent like many before, working twelve-hour days when all was going well and sixteen or more hours when the pressure was on. Seven-day weeks were the norm; it was all work, work, work. There wasn't much else to do in a typical construction camp, so Gabriel didn't mind the long hours. Come winter there would be time enough to visit with family and rest up a bit before heading out to the bush.

Meanwhile, Nadia spent that first summer of their marriage alone in the one-room log cabin that had been Gabriel's base those rare times when he wasn't working. She enthusiastically set about furnishing and renovating this bare-bones cabin, transforming it into a cheery little place that Gaby would scarcely recognize. All this effort, however, did little to relieve the loneliness she felt. Not that she was hopelessly isolated; her new home was conveniently located midway between Ross and Ste. Geneviève. She could hitch up her team and be visiting with her parents near Ross in less than an hour. Or she could go to Ste. Geneviève, pick up the mail at the post office, and have lunch with her in-laws. Still, the time was long. This is not how she pictured married life should be.

Gabriel had enjoyed spending winters in the bush, whether it was driving a tractor train over frozen lakes or cutting cordwood. Now that he was married, everything changed. He suggested spending another winter in the bush with Nadia, but she let it be known she was not about to go through such drudgery again. She could take the hard work, but those fourteen to sixteen-hour days were just too much. Now she could appreciate what Gaby meant when he observed that working in the bush meant you had to work twice as hard for half the pay of most other jobs. Besides, she wanted to get a start on that farmstead that she and Gabriel had talked about.

Together they planned to set up a modern, specialized farm, one that would concentrate on raising quality beef. Theirs was to be a cut above the all-too-common farmsteads that could barely feed a family. They had no illusions of becoming rich, but they certainly counted on realizing a decent income.

Others had tried to get beyond that bare-bones subsistence level, but for a variety of reasons it seldom worked out. Gabriel and Nadia should have known that the odds were stacked against them, so what compelled them to try? Perhaps they were simply responding to the same independent urge their parents must have felt when they began their particular way of life—or was it something else? Most farmers can attest that there's a certain appeal to this age-old vocation called farming. Could it be that comforting sense of security that comes from knowing that the farm, no matter how modest, could conceivably sustain the family no matter what was happening in the outside world?

Gabriel was not about to embark on such an ambitious venture in a timid fashion. Throughout his bachelor years he had accumulated quite a decent nest egg. He could afford to build a huge barn to house quality breeding stock. He could afford the very latest in labour-saving machinery, and there was enough in reserve to carry the farm for a time, if at first it wasn't profitable.

Nadia brought to the partnership her life experience and an abiding love of animals, and she was eager to invest her boundless energy and enthusiasm. The farm was mainly her idea, and she was prepared to take on the bulk of the work.

The farm was moderately successful for a few years, but then as the Depression took hold, it became obvious that this way of life didn't pay much better than cutting wood, and it left absolutely no time for leisure. It became increasingly clear that the farm was just too much for her alone, but Gaby was reluctant to give up his customary summer work. The pay was just too good.

Nadia had hoped that Gaby would see the farm as an alternative to his beloved construction work, but she knew that come spring it would be hard to hold him back. They would spend another long lonely summer apart, and she was left with all the farm work and all the responsibilities—not the sort of life she had bargained for when they first married. Now that the farm was well established she continued to wonder: why couldn't Gaby just stay home?

And then, an unexpected complication came along that would persuade Gaby to do just that. Nadia was pregnant. The baby was expected in April. Nadia made it clear; she was not going to spend the coming summer alone with her first child.

"Nadia and Gabriel"   Source: family photo

A BRIGHT NEW WORLD

From an early age I was told that April 22, 1934, was a very special day for my parents. They were married almost ten years and had pretty much given up any hope of having a child. Now that long-awaited baby was finally here, and he would change their lives in ways they could never have imagined. They were prepared to accommodate all of his earthly needs and most of his wants—even for the rest of their lives, if it came to that. However, they took on more, much more. They taught through gentle guidance, but mostly he was left to his own devices and they indulged his whims and passions a fulsome measure beyond parental responsibility.

. . .

I came into this world right in the middle of the Great Depression. Life was really tough for a lot of Canadians, especially for those trying to eke a living from the parched earth of the western prairies. In Eastern Manitoba, where we lived, it was much the same, except it was not as dry—and besides, this region was always poor, so the downturn wasn't considered quite as serious. Of course, I was blissfully unaware of this calamity that caused so much hardship for so many people. I knew nothing of the challenges facing my parents, nor did I appreciate all the critical decisions they would have to make over the years in order to provide for our family.

Before summer's end, both Mom and Dad reluctantly agreed that their dream farm had failed to live up to their expectations. Time to put it up for sale. It was a bad time to be selling. It seems nobody had any money, and credit wasn't cheap. They might have to hang on to the farm a while longer, but there were ready customers for the livestock.

It was a sad day to see them all trucked away. Perhaps the farm would sell more easily now. Meanwhile that little log cabin Gabriel had built would still be home.

Nobody remembers who came up with the idea, but one day a young couple came by, asking if they could celebrate their coming wedding in the loft of the now-empty barn. After climbing the steep narrow stairs, guests remarked how pleasantly surprised they were at what a lovely space this was. There was not a hint of manure; only the faint, pleasant perfume of hay and seasoning wood. Some marvelled at how sturdily it was built. It looked nothing like any barn they had ever seen. By all accounts the wedding was enjoyed by all, with many observing what a perfect place it would be to hold dances on a regular basis.

And so, the idea for transforming this spacious hayloft into a rustic country dance hall was now embraced by both Mom and Dad. Of course, it needed a proper entrance with a set of stairs, separate from the barn below. A stage would be needed for the musicians. There was the small detail that the floor was rough sawn lumber, too rough for dancing; after all, it was originally meant for storing hay. Dad smoothed the entire dance area with a hand plane, one board at a time—a challenging task that would be unthinkable to most people. Too frugal to buy readymade furniture, Dad set about building tables and benches. Nothing too fancy; after all, this was still a barn. With Mom's creative decorating, the loft was now transformed. They were open for business, and people came.

In this less developed part of the country, nearly everyone still travelled by horse-drawn vehicles. What to do with your horses when you were visiting for any length of time, especially in the winter? Well, that problem was neatly taken care of when patrons came to party at the Legal's new dance hall. It featured indoor parking for horses. Since the ground floor of the barn was originally built for livestock, it was the perfect place for guests to park their horses while they partied upstairs. Free hay and oats kept the animals comfortable while they waited patiently for their masters.

The dance hall was a huge success—too successful, it turns out. On Saturday nights, people would come from miles around to party and have a good time. There was never a shortage of musicians, and of course, home brew was the common drink. However, something else was happening that no one could have predicted. It seems church attendance at Ste. Geneviève dropped dramatically, and the priest was none too happy.

We'll never know if was the priest himself, some self-righteous soul, or maybe just a disgruntled party-pooper, but police got wind of this den of debauchery and decided to raid the place.

At first the police said they were just checking for a dance hall permit, and that would have been a minor oversight, easily correctable, but the police noticed something else. It was the open presence of home-brewed whiskey that caught their attention. In the end, it was the threat of being charged with bootlegging that persuaded my parents to close up this perfect place where people could put aside their troubles during the depths of the Depression.

They never expressed bitterness about having to shut down this promising enterprise, but I later learned that this was just one more thing that kept my parents from embracing the Catholic Church. Besides, Mom wanted to try her hand at running a general store, just like her parents had years before. She reasoned that once the store was established there would be plenty of work for the two of them, and Dad wouldn't have to be away all summer working on construction. That was the plan, but as so often happens in life, things didn't quite work out that way. Building and stocking the store used up most of their savings and proved to be more complicated than expected.

The store was finally open for business in early 1936, and people came—many just to visit and to socialize. With so much unemployment, few could afford anything but the bare essentials. Subsistence farmers often required credit to bridge the gap between "cream cheques," as locals called their meagre income. The store also extended credit to those who may have had good intentions but were unemployed and held faint hope of finding a job—perhaps when the Depression ended? Surely these hard times can't last forever . . . can they?

In the midst of these troubled times, my sister Juliette was born. She was a colicky baby and demanded Mom's full attention while I was left in the hands of multiple babysitters.

Years later, each of these babysitters felt the need to remind me what a challenge it was to keep me entertained and to keep me out of trouble. All of them had amusing stories to tell, but I was left to wonder if their experiences were pleasant ones, or if I was just a hassle.

Mom sure had her hands full, and Dad knew this, but after only a year in business he felt there was no other option. Come spring, he had to find a construction job and bring in some much-needed cash.

Dad was in for a shock. He knew construction work was slowing down, but he had no idea that it could come to a complete halt. Now, for the first time in his life he was out of work. He had been proud of the fact that since he left his parental home over twenty years ago he could always find a job, but he soon learned that not much was happening anywhere in Manitoba, so he was forced to start looking farther afield.

While people in Manitoba, Saskatchewan, and Alberta were getting desperate, it wasn't until the mid-thirties that things started slowing down out East. In Ontario the drought wasn't nearly as severe, and relatively speaking, most were managing quite well. For nearly a century, migration had been westward. It was now shifting into reverse as prairie people began moving east. Dad got caught up in this search for jobs, and so on a spring day in 1937 he bought a one-way train ticket to Toronto, not knowing what to expect.

Meanwhile, Mom was left to manage the store on her own. As a source of income the store was no substitute for the dance hall, but over time it became the meeting place for the people of Ste. Geneviève and the nearby community of Ross. That suited Mom just fine. She loved to talk and to share stories.

Some of these stories became legends that carried on for years. One that I heard often was centred around the time when her wayward boy defied death, twice in one week, causing her to age by at least ten years, she swore.

Remember when Gaby was out East? She would begin. *He left me to look after the store, and me alone with two little kids. Remember how hot it was that summer? Well, one day I was nursing Juliette; she was still a baby, you know, and oh, she sure was a handful.*

Now Jules, he was just three, and I had to keep an eye on him too. That kid was always getting into trouble. So I got little Marie, you know, Ava's oldest daughter, to help with the chores and to babysit when I was real busy. Well, she was supposed to be outside looking after Jules when she came in and calmly told me that Jules had just fallen off the porch and he wouldn't get up. Thinking that he was probably playing some game, I wasn't too concerned, but I went outside and there he was, on the ground, white as starch and foaming at the mouth.

Well, you can imagine my panic. I just started screaming and yelling at Marie to tell me what happened. Marie was crying. It took a while to get the full story. "I don't know," she blubbered, "Jules just drank a cup of some stuff and then he fell down."

Thank god, the neighbours came over and together we figured that he must have opened the tap on the coal oil drum and helped himself to a drink—you know, the coal oil that everybody uses for their lamps.

All the way to the hospital I tried to open his mouth, but his teeth were clamped tight, tight like a steel trap. He was turning blue and he started convulsing. I was sure he was going to die. But, the good doctor—remember Doctor Savoie in Ste. Anne? Well, somehow he was able to pry Jules' mouth open and forced him to vomit. They kept him in the hospital overnight, and by the next day he was fine, except that his breath smelled like coal oil for days. Whenever people asked him why he drank that awful stuff, he always gave the same simple answer: "because I was thirsty."

That same week, I sent Marie outside to start the laundry. We didn't have a washing machine in those days. We always washed our clothes outside in the summer, you know. Well! . . . Marie couldn't have been outside five minutes when she came running into the store screaming, "Jules fell in the water and I can't see him, I think he drowned."

My god, I didn't know what she was talking about, we don't have a lake around here, you know. But, this sounded serious. I ran out expecting the worst. I was sure Jules must be dead. Well! . . . You know how hot it was that summer. There was my happy little guy jumping up and down in the soapy water and having a good time. I guess he just wanted to cool off. How he climbed up that table and into that big tin tub I just don't know.

Over the years she repeated the story to anyone who would listen, and she always ended with the line: "That kid! If he doesn't kill himself, he'll kill me. I bet I've aged at least ten years. Just look at my white hair."

■ ■ ■

Mom's general store never did make a profit, and as the Depression wore on, people got farther behind on their credit accounts. The store began losing money, which meant it would be a hard sell if it were to be put on the market. Running the store must have been a painful thing during this period. Mom was dealing with desperate people who had no means to pay for groceries and of course she couldn't refuse them credit. How long could she keep the store going while watching family assets dwindle? The answer came by letter in early June. Dad wrote to announce that he had found a job. "Pack up the kids and join me in St. Catharines," the terse note read. Mom would have preferred to check out this new place before moving, but it seems women didn't have much say in these affairs, and besides, that long train ride would cost money. There was no mention of what to bring, and no hint of how long we might be staying in Ontario. As for the house and contents, Dad left it up to Mom to decide. It was also up to her to do something with the store, all he would say was, "just get rid of that money pit."

And so, Mom dutifully began the complicated process of selling the store and what was left of the inventory. "Everything has to go," wrote Dad and that included all the household effects they had accumulated during those twelve-plus years together. Shipping by train was just too costly.

The most difficult part for Mom would be saying goodbye to the close-knit family she grew up with and the many neighbours, customers, and friends she had come to know. She fully expected to return one day, but there was no telling when that might be.

A month passed. Almost nothing had sold. There was such a scarcity of cash in the community that it was becoming obvious that practically everything would have to be given away. Mom was totally stressed and feeling depressed when another letter came from Dad. This time he sounded more optimistic—excited, even. He had found another job, this one as a dragline operator constructing the 'Queen Elizabeth Way'. Once again, he was employed in the line of work he loved and he was quite certain that it would carry on for several years.

It was now clear; our family's move, east just might be for a long period. Mom no longer needed to agonize over what to do. It was time to put her familiar life behind her. Slowly she convinced herself that a bright new world was just a train ride away. St. Catharines, here we come.

"Jules"   Source: family photo

"Nadia's store"   Source: family photo

CHAPTER 3
Port Dalhousie, 1937–1939

LAKEPORT ROAD

It's a hot summer day and a small group of relatives have come to see us off at the grand CNR railway station in Winnipeg. Mom is carrying baby sister Juliette, and I follow while trying to take in the bewildering sights and sounds that surround me. I feel very small in this crowded, cavernous building where a booming voice keeps interfering with our family farewells. I know that soon we will be with my dad, and I miss him. Somewhere along the way, the picture-perfect blue lakes and endless green forests start to lose their appeal. My initial excitement turns to boredom, then impatient anticipation as the plodding steam engine chugs its way slowly along the endless tracks: *clickety-clack, clickety-clack, clickety-clack.*

At long last, we arrive at the railway station in St. Catharines, and I can hardly contain my excitement. I quickly spot my dad. He is smiling, my mom is smiling, and I am satisfied knowing that everything will be just fine.

Mom had warned me that people in St. Catharines would be speaking English; still, I'm unprepared to hear so many strangers carrying on conversations that I can't quite understand. I'm three years old, and during my short life, I have enjoyed the undivided attention of my parents, my grandparents, numerous aunts and uncles, countless cousins, and several babysitters. Not surprisingly, I learned to talk at any early age, and according to my mom, I've been conversing quite well with adults since I was two. Naturally, I speak French, but I can also understand some English, having learned from customers that came to Mom's store. I will have to learn this new language real quick. At the moment, I am totally absorbed by this fascinating place, and I share my parent's enthusiasm in discovering fresh wonders at every turn.

Mom came from a large, close-knit family where she was the youngest and was used to having lots of people around. Left behind are loving parents, sisters, brothers, aunts and uncles, and countless cousins, and she misses them.

Mom recognizes that Dad won't be leaving his newfound Eden anytime soon, so she sets about trying to entice family and friends to come out East. In her letters to relatives in Manitoba, she paints vivid pictures of the good life in her adopted city. She sends dozens of photos taken with her little Kodak Brownie. If she can't return to Manitoba for some time, she is determined to create a rich new life for our small family and she would encourage others to follow.

She paints word pictures of the big, blue lake next door. "Lake Ontario is so wide you can't see the other side, she says, and the water is so clear you could probably drink it. The shoreline has sandy beaches that go on forever, and everywhere you look, there are inviting green parks with picnic tables. Just two blocks from our apartment, there's an amusement park that's open all year. And, when you come you'll have to ride the merry-go-round. It costs only a nickel, and kids can ride for as long as they want."

In one of her letters, Mom describes her first trip by electric streetcar to downtown St. Catharines, where everything is up to date. "There are hundreds of stores and shops, all with clean windows where you can buy anything you can imagine. The streets bustle with hundreds of shiny cars. You'll never see a dirty one here," she boasts.

She shamelessly extols the charms of her tidy little city for its diversity and general feeling of prosperity, while disparaging Winnipeg for its dusty frontier feel. "Remember all the horse manure and the hoards of hungry flies?" she reminds them. "Even in the outskirts of St. Catharines, you never need rubber boots, because no matter where you walk, there is no fear of stepping in manure. There just isn't any garbage or mud around here either," she tells people back home, "only green grass, lots of flowers, and clean cement sidewalks."

A steady stream of relatives appear at our door, some more welcome than others. It goes without saying that they will be staying at our house for a while, and it's unlikely that they shall contribute anything towards groceries. Mom and Dad don't seem to mind. They know full well how tough things are in Manitoba and how difficult it must have been just to buy train tickets. Most are looking for work, and I suspect they also want to see first-hand what Mom has described in her letters. A few ask good-naturedly, "Where are those gold-paved streets you talked about?"

First to arrive from Manitoba is an exuberant young man who speaks good English and makes friends easily. He has curly blond hair, and I suppose that explains why most people call him Curly. His name is Midas Pelletier, but I am to call him Uncle. He is engaged to Dad's sister, Aunt Adrienne, who is expected to join us when she finishes teaching school in Ste. Geneviève. Uncle Midas and Aunt Adrienne plan to marry and settle nearby once they find jobs.

Although I faintly remember my Uncle Midas from earlier days, he was but one of many relatives, and in my mind, he did not stand out. Here in Port Dalhousie, I have only one uncle, and he becomes very special.

Our first apartment is in a big, unpainted wood building on Lakeport Road, across from the old Welland Canal and the abandoned ship lock. There's a long climb up a wooden staircase on the outside of the building. Mom likes the private entrance because it offers a measure of privacy in this multi-family building. The apartment is small and a bit shabby, but it has running water and electricity: luxuries Mom could only dream of in Manitoba.

"The best thing about this place," she tells visitors, "No more trips to the outhouse," flushing the toilet to prove her point.

Through the large front window, we enjoy a marvellous view of the old Welland Canal, Lock One. A short walk takes us to the harbour, where all sorts of boats are tied up. I particularly enjoy watching as they come and go: fishing boats, pleasure boats, and tugboats pulling barges. This is such neat stuff. Oh, how I would love to ride on one of those boats. Mom shares my enthusiasm for the boats, but she also loves to explore all the fascinating sights in Port Dalhousie.

Sometimes we walk to the other side of the canal across from what appears to be a bridge, and I am intrigued by the waterfall under the bridge. Mom doesn't seem to know what all the crumbling concrete and rusty steel is all about.

One day, I talk my dad into visiting this neat place, just the two of us. When we get to the middle of the bridge he explains, "Not so long ago, this wasn't just a bridge; it was a key part of the Welland Canal. A bunch of such locks made it possible for boats to travel from Lake Ontario to Lake Erie, which is pretty far from here, and Lake Erie is at a much higher level. How do you suppose those boats climbed up those hills to get to Lake Erie?" he asks, pointing in the direction of the Henley Rowing Club.

I try picturing boats with giant legs or maybe huge wheels clambering up those distant slopes, but I know that can't be. Dad points to the remnants of giant gates leading to the Lake. "At one time, those gates could be swung open and closed just like a set of doors. Now picture another set of identical gates located where we are standing. By opening and closing the gates at just the right time, a boat can be raised or lowered by the changing water levels, depending which direction they want to go."

On our way back, I notice a rusty old boat that is completely out of the water. It's resting on some kind of frame. I wonder aloud. "What it's doing there?"

"That's a dry dock," Dad explains, "much like a service garage for cars, only this one is for boats. Boats enter the enclosure through those big gates, just like a car coming into a garage. Then the gates are closed and all the water is pumped out, leaving the boat high and dry. That's why they call it a dry dock. Workers can now get at the hull, the part that would normally be underwater, and fix it or maybe just paint it. Looks like this one could use a paint job."

Just below our apartment, dad parks his big old Reo on the street, and I watch while he tinkers away. It seems that boats and cars often need fixing, and I shall have to learn how to fix things too, but right now I am more interested in learning to drive.

While Dad tinkers away, I climb into the car and position myself where he sits when he drives. I may not be able to reach the pedals with my feet, but by standing on the front seat, I can grip the steering wheel and have a clear view through the windshield. I'm turning the steering wheel back and forth while trying to imitate the sound of the engine. It doesn't take much of a leap in my mind to make the fantasy real.

I'm cruising along a familiar roadway, past ripening fruit orchards and busy fruit stands. I guide the car smoothly past miles of green parkway, luxurious homes, and through the town of Niagara-on-the-Lake. All the while, I am describing to my passengers the various sites, just like Dad does when he takes another visitor from Manitoba on a tour.

Of course, driving a car involves more than just steering, so I must shift gears as well. I push and pull the floor-mounted shifter back and forth, side to side, and *WHOA!* Did I feel the car move just now? But how could that be? The engine isn't running. I've got to investigate this. I abandon the driving game and concentrate on the gearshift. There seems to be a special position of the shifter, where if I wait a short time, the car moves a tiny bit. When I pull the gearshift back, it stops. I push the shifter forward to this special place; wait a few moments, and sure enough the car moves. I pull the gearshift back; the car stops. Oh, this is fun. I want to show Dad what I've just discovered. I wonder if he knows about this magical thing. I look around, but I don't see him.

I continue to operate the gearshift, back and forth, the Reo creeping ahead a few inches each time. Hey, now I don't have to wait with the shifter in that special place any more; the car rolls in short spurts down the hill when I push the gearshift to that special spot and stops as soon as I pull it back. This is becoming more fun all the time. As the speed builds, the shifter gets harder to move. The car is rolling faster down the hill, and uh-oh, I can't move the shifter anymore. It seems to be stuck.

A neighbour spots me, and I can see she's laughing. I guess she's oblivious to any danger as the car veers towards the canal with me still proudly gripping the steering wheel, enjoying the ride.

The rest of the story I heard from my mom, who repeated the incident many times to every relative and neighbour for years afterward:

Me and Gaby, we were sitting in the kitchen, having a cup of tea with Midas Pelletier—you know, Curly, the guy who married Gaby's sister, Adrienne. Well, we were just talking, everything seemed fine. Curly is looking out the window when all of a sudden, without saying a word, he explodes from the kitchen table. Gaby and me, we try to follow, not knowing what the hell is going on. By the time we got down the stairs—you know those steep stairs just outside the apartment. Well Curly was running like crazy towards this car. Oh my God, I suddenly realized that was our Reo! Is somebody trying to steal it?

Gaby yells, "Jules is in the car!" He starts running, and I start screaming. The car is headed straight for the canal, and I'm paralyzed. All I can do is watch. I was sure my little boy was going to be killed. It was like a bad dream, every-thing was in slow motion. Gaby was way behind. I knew he couldn't catch up to the car in time, but he was still running. The car was going faster and faster, but it looked like Curly might be catching up. The car is only a few feet from the canal when Curly jumps onto the running board. You know those handy things the old cars used to have to make it easier to get in and out? I thought, my God! He's too late, they're both going over. Then I see Curly reaching into the car through the side window. I thought he was going to pull Jules out. What's keeping him? I wondered. He seems to be taking forever. Too late, too late—I cover my eyes, expecting to hear a loud splash. When I look again, there's Curly with Jules in his arms, Gaby is just getting to the scene, and the old Reo is stopped a couple of feet from the edge of the canal.

"Did you ever see that canal along Lakeport?" Mom asks, even when she knows the listener has never been anywhere near. "There's a flimsy little railing along the edge," she explains. "Of course that heavy car would've crashed right through the thing, and there's a twenty-foot drop to the water below. So even if Jules would have survived the drop, for sure he would have drowned. He doesn't know how to swim, you know. I don't think Curly does either, and I can tell you, me and Gaby sure can't. Gaby tells me, Jules is alive because of the superior quality of that 1931 Reo. You see, when Curly reached in through the window, he pulled real hard on the emergency brake, and that's what stopped the car. Gaby says most cars only have flimsy parking brakes which wouldn't be strong enough to stop that big car once it got rolling.

"I guess Curly knew that, too. Just the week before, Gaby was explaining to everyone that his 1931 Reo was the first model to have hydraulic brakes and how they work so much better than regular brakes. Curly, he always liked our old Reo. Why Gaby didn't use those fancy hydraulic brakes when he parked the car, I'll never know. I just know that he sure did after that."

Over the years, Mom repeated the story to anyone who would listen, making it sound like it happened just yesterday. Sometimes, depending who she was telling the story to, she might end it with the now-familiar line: "That kid! If he doesn't kill himself, he'll kill me. I bet I've aged at least ten years. Just look at my white hair."

"1931 Reo"   Source: public domain

THE BEACH HOUSE

Early fall. The tourists are all gone, and Port Dalhousie returns to a quieter pace; it's a good time to explore the neighbourhood. Mom takes sister Juliette and me for long walks while Dad is at work.

One day as we stroll along the deserted beach she spots a "FOR RENT" sign on one of the cottages near the beach. This vine-covered cottage on Gary Road is nestled at the foot of a steep cliff, a stone's throw from the main beach. It couldn't be more picturesque. Mom dares to dream that maybe, just maybe, we could live in this cute, cozy cottage, at least for a while. By the time Dad comes home she has made enquiries, and yes, he agrees the rent is affordable, and so we move into this modest little beach house on Lake Ontario.

Port Dalhousie beach was known as the best on Lake Ontario. Even before the Queen Elizabeth was finished, hundreds of visitors from miles around came from as far away as Toronto to enjoy the pristine white sand and the pure clear waters.

Swimmers were encouraged to use the huge wooden change houses set back a short distance from the beach. At the entrance you were forced to walk through a shallow metal tub containing a blue coloured liquid. I don't know if it was meant to sterilize your feet before venturing onto the beach or perhaps before you changed back into your street clothes. I suppose it could have served both purposes. In any case it really impressed upon me that this was a special place and deserved respect.

There was never a hint of garbage, but on our walks along the beach Mom always brought along a garden rake that she used to look for coins and other treasures left behind by recent sunbathers.

This famous beach that attracted so many people just a few weeks ago is deserted now, and the merry-go-round is boarded up for the winter.

Our beautiful, unobstructed view of the lake comes with a price that was not apparent in the summer. Cold damp winds routinely penetrate the flimsy little building after picking up speed and moisture from the stormy waters of Lake Ontario, rendering the cottage cold and clammy.

There is no furnace, not even a proper stove. The electric heater is just not up to the job, and although the kitchen "hot plate" helps, it's never enough. It now becomes clear why the rent is so cheap, but Mom doesn't complain. She simply bundles up us kids and we spend hours browsing in the warm stores and shops of Port Dalhousie.

Returning home one afternoon we pass a bunch of young boys playing on the steps leading down to the beach. Several of them are close to my age, and they invite me to join them. Even though we don't always understand each other we get along just fine.

Most days my new buddies come by my place and I am free to join them. Mom doesn't worry too much. What could go wrong?

To grow up in Port Dalhousie is just about the most perfect place, especially if you're a boy with a few good buddies and plenty of freedom. There are countless fascinating places to explore and I am introduced to all sorts of new games.

One of these games is racing our toy cars down the concrete curbs that border the multi-level steps that lead from the beach to the top of the hill. Since my buddies all live in the neighbourhood above, we must climb these steps several times a day. Coming down we sometimes slide on our bums along the concrete curbs. The slope is such that you could only slide if the concrete is very dry and sometimes you have to pull with your heels to assist the sliding. One day I got the idea of pouring sand from the beach onto the curbs.

Wow! Now we can speed down to the bottom in less than a minute. We spend the rest of the afternoon sliding down the curbs and then racing back up, pouring fresh sand at every level.

My buddies think this is pretty cool, and I feel real good for having come up with the idea. Mom never did figure out how I could wear through the seat of my pants in one afternoon.

Good-natured roughhousing seems to come naturally to young boys. My friends and I are no exception. It might start with a simple shove, then push back, and soon it turns into a friendly but serious wrestling match. To an outsider it may look like we are just rolling in the grass, but we are testing each other's strength, our agility, and our stamina. One of the boys has an older brother who seems to know a lot about wrestling, and he teaches us proper techniques and strategies and he stresses the importance of speed. I am small for my age and I recognize that I must master all these tricks, and I must be very fast if I am to hold my own with the bigger kids.

Wrestling becomes my favourite sport, especially when I learn that with speed and the right techniques I can pin down a kid much bigger than me. We are careful never to hurt each other physically, but egos get bruised from time to time.

One rainy day, Dad takes me to the local garage at the corner of Lock and Main to buy a couple of tires for the Reo. I have never been in a car garage before, partly I suspect because Dad fixes his own car outdoors in the lane by our house. On a typical Sunday, Dad is either working on the Reo or someone else's car. I sense that people regard him as a genius because there isn't a thing that he can't fix.

As we enter the garage I take in the smell of oil and rubber, and I love it. I love the whole atmosphere. All the neat tools and strange new stuff intrigue me and I have all sorts of questions to ask. One of the workers volunteers to keep an eye on me while Dad goes outside with the boss to check out some tires.

The mechanic suggests it would be great fun if I would hide in this large cardboard box and pretend it's a secret fort and my dad would have to look for me when he returned. I can't say whether he wants to entertain me, or if he just wants me out of the way, but yes, this sounds like fun. My new friend cuts a small hole on one side of the box to act as a window, then lowers me into the box and piles weights on top.

It wasn't long before I became tired of this game, and I called out for my new friend to let me out. Silence! I look around through the fist-sized hole. No one! Where did everybody go? Did they forget about me? But wait. There on a table within easy reach is the knife that was used to cut that small hole. With the knife, I go on to create an exit door.

As I step out, there is cheering and loud laughter. It seems the men were waiting to see what I would do. They are duly impressed that I had cut not just any escape hole but that I have carefully cut three sides of the box, creating a perfect rectangle while leaving the vertical edge of the box to act as a hinge for my newly created door. I have no idea why this is so funny, but it feels good to get all that attention, especially in front of my dad.

Early spring: Still too cold to go swimming but warm enough to open the Port Dalhousie amusement park and all the rides. Most popular is the merry-go-round with beautifully painted wooden animals that go round and round, seemingly forever while an organ plays on. It costs only a nickel so I get to ride often. This ride appeals to kids of all ages, but some adults like it too. Even though it's still cold I must ride that merry-go-round as soon as it opens.

I especially like riding the lion. To me that magnificent animal is alive, and together we travel through the mysterious, vine-covered jungles of Africa. My lion was wild when I first met him, but I have tamed him. He is now my friend and my slave, and he will carry me into secret places no human has ever been. I have no fear; after all, my lion is King and will scare off the most ferocious beasts with just a growl. Even the biggest elephants make way for our wanderings.

Much as I love riding my lion, this spring I plan on trying something different. I want to ride a wild horse. So this time I just pat the mane of my faithful lion and I go on to choose the wildest-looking horse, and of course it must be black.

This spirited horse not only goes round and round, but also through some clever mechanism goes up and down at the same time, just like the real untamed horses do when they try to buck their rider off their back.

I can understand why little kids must be accompanied by an adult; it does look a bit dangerous. Of course, that can't be fun. I don't consider myself a little kid, so I quickly mount when the attendant isn't looking. With my cowboy hat and shiny new cap pistol, maybe he won't notice that my feet don't quite reach the stirrups.

The music begins, and slowly all the animals come alive. My beautifully carved horse with nostrils flaring suddenly becomes a wild stallion that tries his best to buck me off. But how is that possible? After all, I am not just any cowboy. I am also an expert rodeo rider who can hang onto the reins with just one hand and shoot my gun with the other, and I wouldn't hesitate to shoot any varmint who gave me trouble.

All of my buddies also have cap pistols and they introduce me to a game they call "Cowboys and Indians." It always involves a lot of shooting and a lot of noise. I don't remember much about the rules, but I do remember being very intrigued by the clever mechanism that works just like a real revolver—at least that's what I figure. The black powder cap is in the form of little blisters along a roll of stiff red paper that automatically advances with every pull of the trigger. Pulling the trigger all the way also causes a hammer to hit the black powder blister, resulting in a loud pop and blue smelly smoke that stings when it creeps up my nose.

In the middle of a particularly intense battle we run out of ammunition. A truce is called and all the "cowboys" and all the "Indians" must go to buy a new supply of ammunition. We come to the intersection of Lock and Main, where Dad bought tires for the Reo a few weeks before. I can't understand why we aren't crossing. Being impatient and seeing no cars, I start running across the street. I am almost across when my buddies start yelling like crazy. Recognizing I've done something wrong, I start running back and WHAM! I'm hit by a car and I end up somewhere under the chassis. The driver is a grey-haired old gentleman who is in a panic, convinced that he has just killed a little kid.

The rest is a blur. I remember a lump on my head that was pretty sore. The doctor said I had a broken collarbone. He taped my arm tight to my body to prevent movement while it was healing.

The part I do remember vividly came weeks later when it came time to remove those yards and yards of sticky white tape and how it pulled out all the hair on my arm. That was far more painful than the break itself.

The grey-haired old gentleman came by our house a few days after the accident and presented me with a beautiful toy car. He was ever so pleased to see me up and about and I suspect much relieved that my parents did not blame him for the accident.

Before he left, Mom made a point of telling him this wasn't Jules' first brush with death, and she worried it wouldn't be his last. And so, it became another story for my mom to tell and retell over the years, and another reason for her hair to turn white.

"Merry-go-round"   Source: family photo

CHAPTER 4
Gregory Road, 1939 –1941

MR. BURTON

I knew that our stay at that cute little cottage by the beach wasn't meant to last. Still, it was kind of sad when it came time to leave. Summer was just around the corner, the owners of the place would soon be reclaiming their little piece of paradise, and our family would have to find another place to call home. Mom was hoping that it would be somewhere in Port Dalhousie. "It has that small-town feel," she says, "yet it's just a streetcar ride from downtown St. Catharines."

Everyone loves this charming little town by the Lake. I also feel that Port Dalhousie is the most perfect place to be. I could live here forever. I shall miss the beach, the merry-go-round, and all the boats, but most of all I shall miss my buddies. I sure hope there'll be other boys to play with where we're going.

Dad has rented an old, two-story house from a Mr. Burton, an elderly farmer who recently moved to a newer house next door. Mr. Burton's farm fronts onto a narrow country lane called Gregory Road. It's only a few miles from St. Catharines, but it appears quite rural. Dad takes us on a tour of the area in the old Reo. He points out that typically vineyards and peach orchards would dominate such an area, and he wonders why they haven't yet taken over this charming countryside. Mom seems to like what she sees, and I am really excited by all the farm animals grazing in green pastures.

I have just turned five, and Mom speculates that Mr. Burton must be at least seventy. Unlikely as it may seem, we become real good friends even though Mr. Burton is old enough to be my grandfather. There are no playmates nearby, so I adopt Mr. Burton as my buddy. I follow him around like a faithful puppy and ask hundreds of questions. Mr. Burton doesn't seem to mind; I tell myself that he enjoys teaching me things. For the next two years, this wondrous farm would become the centre of my universe.

Dad figures that Mr. Burton originally came from England, because he speaks with the same accent as that kindly farmer who gave him his first job when he was fourteen. Dad's old boss never spoke a word of French, and it becomes clear that Mr. Burton isn't about to either, so I try not to slip too many French words into our conversations. Each day I learn new words, sometimes silly ones that don't make sense, and sometimes curse words that Mr. Burton lets fly on a regular basis. I am determined to become real good at speaking English, but I must learn to separate the naughty words from the proper "King's English."

Mr. Burton doesn't just teach me English. Bit by bit, he fills me in on the intricacies of farming and how one type of farming can be totally different from another. He marvels at how hard the first settlers must have worked to clear the land, and how resourceful they had to be just to survive. "Just take a look at that wild, old-growth forest down the road," Mr. Burton declares. He makes it sound like that was a bad thing. "At one time, the entire area looked like that."

Meanwhile I'm thinking how neat it would be if it was all wild and wooded, and what a wonderful home it would be for all kinds of animals. "Do Indians live in that forest?" I ask.

Mr. Burton doesn't answer, but he goes on to explain how the early settlers tamed the wilderness and improved upon nature, making this the finest real estate in the world. "It was a nicer country in those early years, but now there are too many roads, too many buildings, too many vineyards, and too many orchards sprouting up everywhere. All the beautiful little farms with their well-managed woodlots are gone."

"What's a woodlot?" I ask. Mr. Burton goes on to explain how early settlers always set aside a few acres of their farm for a woodlot. "A properly managed woodlot is a precious thing, and at the same time, it can be a thing of beauty. Just a few acres can go on supplying prime heating and cooking fuel for generations. The wise manager was always on the lookout for dead or diseased trees, which he would put aside for firewood while keeping in mind that certain trees might make good lumber for buildings and furniture. Rarely would he cut a healthy tree. Mind you," stressed Mr. Burton, "there are exceptions. If an over-mature tree was casting too much shade over younger trees with growth potential, that tree might be sacrificed and turned into lumber or firewood. This wasn't common and would be carried out with great reluctance. Then, there are some trees that only a fool would ever consider cutting," Mr. Burton firmly declares as he launches into a passionate lecture on the utility of each tree species and how some serve more than one purpose. "Take the Black walnut, for example: Did you notice those big leafy trees lining the driveway by your house? They're not just there to provide shade in the summer, you know. Those are Black walnut trees, and they are more than 150 years old. This fall, you'll be able to pick all the nuts you can eat. Just don't let your dad drive over them," he warns.

"Now, if we were to wait another hundred years, these walnut trees may start to die from old age, but a responsible person would not burn them, and we certainly wouldn't bury them like we do dead people, no indeed. Even after they die, the walnut wood can be transformed into fine furniture which could easily last hundreds more years."

Mr. Burton points to a row of equally huge trees further along the road. "Those were obviously planted by someone with a sweet tooth," he says. "They're called sugar maple, and they are also over a hundred years old." Mr. Burton goes on to describe how in the fall, the leaves turn from green to yellow to orange, and finally, bright red, because of their high sugar content.

"So, do the leaves taste like candy?" I ask. Mr. Burton laughs and promises that next spring he'll take me to a maple syrup farm where they harvest the sap and we can sample some real maple candy.

Mr. Burton points out a solitary, giant tree across the road from our house. "That's a hickory," he says. "Must be a couple of hundred years old, and still produces bushels of tasty nuts every year. Don't be too surprised, though, if the owner decides to cut it down. After all, that tree is getting mighty old, and it will surely die one day. Before the wood starts to deteriorate, it will be harvested and used for making furniture, axe handles, hockey sticks, baseball bats, and all sorts of tool handles. Hickory is probably the toughest wood in the world," says Mr. Burton.

I'm more interested in the nuts. "Do you suppose I could pick some of those nuts?" I ask.

Mr. Burton laughs. "Good luck with that, boy; that big old tree is impossible to climb, and there isn't a ladder in all of Ontario tall enough to reach them nuts. If you really want some, you'll have to wait till later this fall and keep a sharp watch for the squirrels. They'll pick them for you." Mr. Burton smiles, knowing I am doubtful but too shy to challenge him.

Finally, he relents and goes on to explain, "Most city squirrels just collect as many nuts and acorns as they can fit in their cheeks, which means they would have to climb that tall tree many times to fill their larder for the winter. Our country squirrels are smarter than that. They wait until the nuts are nearly ripe and then they'll knock down a whole bunch before they fall to the ground on their own. Sometimes they'll leave the nuts on the ground for a couple of days for the husks to dry. That's when you take your little basket and pick them real quick, before they call all their friends. You wouldn't want an army of angry squirrels chasing after you, would you boy?" I'm left to wonder if there is some truth to the story. I know my dad really loves hickory nuts, and I like them too, so come fall I'll have to find out for myself.

I learn from Mr. Burton that those years before he bought this place, his was one of those diverse little farms that could sustain a family with all the essentials for a healthy life—perhaps not in luxury, but with a decent level of comfort. I am fascinated to hear Mr. Burton describe life in those early days before tractors and modern farm machinery. I find myself sharing his love of the way people lived, how resourceful they had to be, and just how independent they were of the chaotic world around them. I don't mind at all that Mr. Burton repeats his stories, especially since fresh details are added from time to time.

"Yessiree," Mr. Burton starts, "the typical farm family maintained at least one team of horses to work the land, to haul heavy loads, and for general transportation. Dairy products formed a big part of the family diet, so they would keep a few milking cows, and of course every farm always had chickens for eggs and a couple of hogs for meat."

While Mr. Burton's farm may not fit his definition of that perfect little farm that he admires so much, he does maintain a few features that give him a measure of precious independence. Mr. Burton is proud of the fact that he has never tasted a store-bought egg. "My ladies," as he calls his hens, "have always produced more eggs than Mrs. Burton can use."

Every day, he gives me a few to take home, and in turn, it becomes my job to keep the feed troughs and water containers full. "A happy hen lays a happy egg," says Mr. Burton.

While their attention is diverted, I collect the eggs without arousing alarm. I marvel at how dumb they are, not to have figured out where their eggs disappear. Sometimes I try to play with them, but my attempts at being friends are completely ignored. I don't much care for chickens, but Mr. Burton seems to love them all. We cannot leave the hen house without bidding, "Good day, ladies, and thank you for the eggs. We'll see you tomorrow."

There are signs that Mr. Burton tried his hand at various types of farming. The dilapidated old barn behind our place was obviously home to generations of dairy cows. It now stores hundreds of old wooden crates, which suggest that at one time, fruit was a productive side crop as well. There are remnants of apple and cherry trees that have long passed their prime. What fruit they produce is mostly left to the birds.

Like the fruit trees, Mr. Burton freely admits that he has also passed his prime. He may no longer have what it takes to operate a dairy business or to maintain a productive fruit orchard, so he has planted acres of strawberries and raspberries, and he puts up a sign for "U-pickers" to do the harvesting. Mr. Burton has generously given our family permission to pick all the strawberries and raspberries we want, and Mom makes jars and jars of jam.

One day, Mr. Burton plucks two small, rose-coloured apples that seem to have escaped the birds and the worms. He hands me one and we munch away on the tasty treat. "Notice anything different?" he asks.

"Well, it does taste really good," I offer.

"You're right," says Mr. Burton, "these apples are sweeter than all the other varieties, and because of the extra sugar, they can withstand a bit of frost. They're called 'snow whites.' Keep an eye out for these little beauties after the trees have lost their leaves. There can be snow on the ground, and these apples could still be perfectly good to eat. This is my favourite apple," declares Mr. Burton. "Just look at the meat of this apple," he continues, "notice how white it is. Unlike a lot of apples, these don't have a hint of green, that's why they call them snow whites."

I'm left to wonder. What has meat got to do with apples? Does "snow white" mean that these apples are white as snow on the inside, or is there some connection to the story of Snow White eating that poisoned apple? Sometimes this English language sure can be confusing.

Mr. Burton keeps a bright red tractor locked up in one of his sheds. I would love to see it working, but since we moved here, I have yet to see it turn a wheel. Ever since Mr. Burton's son Bob moved off to "greener pastures," it has been gathering dust.

"How come you don't use it anymore?" I ask.

"Because my lovelies don't like that tractor," he tells me. "After all, they want to feel useful too." Mr. Burton loves his horses and he treats them as you would trusted friends. Lady and Godiva are the names he has given these huge Clydesdales. When he wants their attention, he calls out "Lady, Godiva," but when he is talking about them, he refers to them as his "Lovelies".

Mr. Burton spends hours grooming and fussing over his Lovelies. While he's brushing their coats, it's my job to feed Lady and Godiva a few apples and carrots.

"Remember, hold the carrots in the palm of your hand, not with your fingers," Mr. Burton cautions. Their sharp teeth would chomp right through those tiny fingers of yours, just like they were carrots. Look what happened to me when I was a boy," he says as he holds up his hand with a missing finger. I would love to know how he lost that finger. I suspect he is teasing again, so I don't ask.

I just love following Mr. Burton as he tends to the hundreds of jobs involved in running his fascinating little farm. I'm often allowed to participate or at least play some small role in doing the chores. There is however one complex routine where I must stand back and let Mr. Burton and his Lovelies go through a ritual that I suspect they have performed thousands of times. It involves the complicated procedure of harnessing up Lady and Godiva when it's time to work the land or haul some heavy load. Today they shall be cultivating the asparagus crop to loosen the soil and to kill invasive weeds, and I am eager to watch and to marvel.

The routine is always the same. The big gentle giants are led, one at time, to the "tack room," where the elaborate leather harnessing is stored. With some effort, Mr. Burton throws what seems like a messy pile of straps, buckles, and hardware onto Lady's broad back. He then methodically untangles the complicated heap of leather and buckles while hooking up heavy-duty straps and chains to the machine or wagon he'll be using.

"Why do you always start with Lady?" I ask.

"Because she is the oldest, and she knows she's boss, and besides, it's just more respectful," reasons Mr. Burton.

I might not have noticed, but Mr. Burton draws my attention to subtle clues that clearly indicate both horses are ready and eager to work. They nod their heads downward as Mr. Burton lifts the collar over their ears and down onto their big broad shoulders. They seem to know when it's time to lift their huge, hairy hoofs when the traces are not quite right.

Mr. Burton suggests I pay close attention. "Just look at the twinkle in their eyes." I look carefully but I cannot detect twinkles. Is Mr. Burton teasing again or am I just not observant enough? I had watched other men working their "teams," as they called them, but none were as smart as Lady and Godiva. Normally, Mr. Burton would steer his Lovelies by tugging gently on the reins, but today he'll require both hands to manipulate the wheeled cultivator close to the fragile asparagus stalks. As they approach the end of each row, Mr. Burton yells, "Gee," and his two Lovelies turn to the right in a perfect arc. When he yells, "Haw," they turn to the left. Could it be that these two plodding, sweaty beasts might understand English as good as me?

Late in the afternoon, the cultivator gets tangled in a maze of tree roots that have encroached onto the tilled soil. Mr. Burton asks me to go back to the shop and fetch him a spade. It's a long walk back to the farmyard, but of course I would be happy to do anything Mr. Burton asks of me. After all, Mr. Burton has taken the time to teach me the names of the machines stored in their houses, which he calls sheds, and the names of the tools neatly organized in the most intriguing of all the buildings, the shop. To a kid who has never seen a farm before, this is awfully neat stuff.

What the heck is a spade? I wonder. I wait for Mr. Burton to explain, but he is busy fussing with the cultivator while Lady and Godiva stand patiently swishing at flies with their tails. "Well, go on, boy, fetch me that spade." I detect a hint of impatience in his voice, so off I go without quite knowing what he means, but I have a plan.

I decide to make a detour to our house and ask my mom to explain what kind of tool is a spade, then I shall run to the shop, get the spade, and hurry back to Mr. Burton, who no doubt will thank me and tell me what a good boy I am. I know that a spade must be a tool, but to my great frustration, my mom insists a spade is a type of playing card.

What to do? Do I go back and confess my ignorance, and then what? Without pointing to a spade, how would Mr. Burton describe it to me? Even if he could, that would mean yet another trip, and it's so very, very, hot out there. What to do? In the end, I stay home, praying that Mr. Burton won't be angry with me.

By the next morning, my guilt is such that I know I must apologize to Mr. Burton. I find him in the barn, grooming his "Lovelies." Before I can begin my apology, Mr. Burton greets me in his usual cheery manner. "Good morning, Laddie. Lady and Godiva are waiting for you."

Sure enough, they seem to be greeting me. They are making soft, snuffling noises with their nostrils. I'm sure they are saying, "Good morning, Jules, and hurry up with our treats." You know, I think I can see that twinkle in their eyes that Mr. Burton talks about.

And so, another wondrous day begins, and I'm thinking, *I really like Lady and Godiva, and I just love Mr. Burton, what a kind and patient man.*

"Clydesdale horses"   Source: Adobe stock #89839692

MY BUDDY CLAIRE

We'd been living on Gregory Road for some time when a Mrs. Brown came by with her daughter Claire. "Welcome to the neighbourhood," greets Mrs. Brown, and the two moms start chatting like they've known each other for years.

Claire doesn't utter a word and never leaves her mother's side. She's a cute little girl with light brown, almost blond, hair. The moms quickly establish that we are both five years old, and they seem to imply that we should play together. It doesn't occur to me that a girl could be a play buddy, so I hesitate to invite her into my world. We glance at each other shyly, neither of us making any attempt at conversation during the entire visit.

A few days later, Mrs. Brown drops by again. She has a favour to ask. "I have to run some errands," says Mrs. Brown. "Could you look after Claire for an hour or so?"

So now it seems I have no choice; I must show Claire around and keep her occupied while my mom continues with her chores. I've never played with a girl before. I wonder: *Just what do girls do?* Maybe we could wrestle, but . . . judging by her scrawny little arms and slightly bowed legs, it would be no contest—besides, would a girl want to wrestle in a dainty dress that would likely get torn in minutes? Probably not a good idea! Why she doesn't just play with my sister Juliette, I'm not sure. Maybe Claire considers her too young, or maybe she senses that Juliette wouldn't be much fun. I know I don't much care for my sister, especially when she whines and tattles on me at every opportunity. I swear she's never happier than when she tattles to Mom that I am doing something she thinks is bad. "Hey, Mom, Jules didn't close the screen door! Hey, Mom, Jules stole a cookie! Hey, Mom, Jules is making faces at me!"

"So, Claire, do you like cherries?" I ask.

"Sure do," she says.

"We have our own cherry tree in the front yard," I boast. "We could climb it and eat as many as we want."

During the season, I would often spend an hour or more in that big beautiful tree, eating luscious cherries until I was full, and then I would pick a bowl for the rest of the family. As the cherries became scarcer, I had to climb higher and farther along slender branches, increasing the risk of falling but improving my climbing skills.

I demonstrate to Claire how to jump straight up with all your might, then grab the lowest branch and haul yourself up. I proceed to a comfortable branch to wait for Claire. She barely got started and, uh-oh, down she falls!

I sure wasn't prepared for all the commotion that followed. Poor Claire, she must be really hurt. Turns out, one knee is slightly bruised, and her dress is a little torn, but she has to make a big production of it. Only after my mom has washed and bandaged her knee and only after a cookie or two and a lot of comforting does Claire quit crying. Whew! Are all girls such sissies?

When Mrs. Brown arrives, Claire runs to tell her mom what happened, and the crying starts all over again. Through her tears, she relates how Jules forced her to climb that big mean tree and she has never climbed a tree before. Completely forgotten are the cherries I picked for her in my efforts to make her forget her accident. Girls!

After a week or so, Claire is back with her mom, and it seems all is forgotten. This time, I suggest we visit my mom's garden where we can pick peas. "They are especially good when they are not too ripe, and you can eat the whole pod," I tell her. Her mom and my mom agree that would be a great idea. What could possibly go wrong?

We barely get started, and suddenly, there is this blood-curdling scream. Claire has spotted a snake and she is paralyzed with fear. "Just stay still," I tell her. "The snake is just sunning itself and won't bother you, I promise." Normally I would just pick it up by the tail and toss it over the fence, but this snake is huge—bigger than any I've ever seen.

I am reminded of an incident with a snake a few months before. It happened when I was helping my mom in the garden, and she suddenly shouted in alarm, *"Snake . . . watch out!"*

I didn't know what she meant at first; to me, snakes were just another plaything. Mr. Burton's son, Bob, demonstrated how if you grabbed a snake by the tail and held it at arm's length, it couldn't bite you, and besides, Bob says snakes are good critters to have around the farm because they love to eat mice, and . . . it seems there's always too many mice.

My mom has other ideas. "Go to the woodpile and bring me the splitting axe quick," she commands. Upon my return, I offer to pick up the snake to show her how harmless they are, but too late. Mom grabs the axe, and with deadly aim, cuts the poor snake in half with one blow. She tells me that some snakes are poisonous, and besides, there are just too many snakes around here.

Maybe there are too many snakes, and who knows, maybe this one that has Claire terrified just might be poisonous. The powerful urge to save the "damsel in distress" convinces me the situation calls for action. I make a hasty, fateful decision. I grab the garden hoe, confident it will serve as a weapon just as lethal as that splitting axe Mom had used on that other poor snake.

I attack the snake that has Claire terrified, but the hoe just bounces off its scaly skin. Is this snake super tough, or maybe the hoe is just dull? The poor thing is obviously injured and writhing in weird patterns towards Claire. Her screams are piercing as I continue to pound the snake with the hoe. I deal it harder blows, and yet it continues to writhe around, and I wonder if this snake is just indestructible.

Claire's mom comes running, her enormous breasts swinging wildly as if they have a life of their own. Now she sees the snake and tries to calm her hysterical daughter. "It's alright, Claire, Mommy will save you," she says soothingly. Mrs. Brown hesitates for a moment, then putting aside her own fears, scoops up Claire and runs from the garden. Meanwhile, my mom appears on the scene, splitting axe in hand, and without saying a word, deals the snake one mighty blow. As we leave the garden, I note that the two halves of the giant snake are left to die separately, bleeding and squirming amongst the peas.

Another week goes by, and once again Mrs. Brown comes by to visit, and of course Claire is with her. Sensing that her daughter wants to leave her clutches, Mrs. Brown tightens her ample grip around Claire's tiny wrist. "Mom, I want to play with Jules," Claire pleads in a pitiful voice. With dire warnings and a multitude of cautions, Claire is allowed to join me.

As we leave the house, I assure Claire there are no snakes where I plan to take her, and I cross my fingers that my credibility shall not be put to the test. Being careful to avoid the vegetable garden, I lead her by a circuitous route to the back of the property. She follows gingerly through a maze of old vegetable crates and tall weeds, glancing nervously from side to side.

Pulling aside a large burlap bag that serves as a door, I invite Claire to enter my secret fort. "No one else has ever been here," I tell her. "Promise you won't tell anyone."

"What do you do in here?" she asks as she timidly steps inside.

"This is where I come when I want to hide from my sister, and this is where I keep my treasures."

I show her glass jars with holes punched in the tops. "If you look carefully, hiding amongst the leaves are some of the neatest worms and bugs you could possibly imagine. See that stick? Watch what happens when I poke it a little."

"Wow, it moves," says Claire in astonishment.

"Mr. Burton says that, by being very still, the stick insect keeps from being eaten by birds."

Another jar has a colourful little frog that I found under a board. It seems quite content to just sit there among the green leaves, its tiny white throat pulsing slowly as it breathes.

Claire pays scant attention to all these marvels, but finally something catches her interest. "What's all this stuff?" she asks, pointing to some utensils I had borrowed from Mom's kitchen.

I explain to Claire how you can take fresh raspberries and push them through a window screen stretched over this pot and you end up with delicious juice. "Would you like to make some?" I ask. To my delight, Claire is intrigued.

Off we go towards Mr. Burton's raspberry patch. Earlier in the week, Mr. Burton told me that the peak of the raspberry season was over, the pickers from the city have left, but there are still lots of berries.

We have nearly filled our containers when I notice Claire squatting between the rows of raspberry canes. "Are you tired, Claire?" I ask.

"Just having a pee," she replies. What the heck? *Why would anybody need to squat to pee*, I wonder, but sure enough a wet puddle is growing at Claire's feet. I have never seen such a thing. I was vaguely aware that girls were built different than boys, but come to think of it, I never saw a girl pee before. Claire doesn't seem to mind when I ask to have a closer look. All I see is a small crease between her legs.

"Hey, where's your pee thing?" I ask. "I have a special little thing to make pee with," I tell her.

"Only boys have a penis," she explains.

I think back to all the times my buddies have stopped to pee. As far as I could tell, they all had a pee thing just like me, and we could all pee standing up. All you had to do was find a reasonably private place and undo the buttons on your pants. You could even aim the stream at some object. It might be a stone, a leaf, or maybe a bug. I offer to demonstrate to Claire this better system, but she doesn't seem at all interested.

In the process of making raspberry juice, Claire spills some over the front of her dress. I am relieved to learn that she doesn't seem too concerned. Surprisingly, Claire's mom doesn't seem upset either, once she is satisfied that it isn't blood. I breathe a sigh of relief as Claire's mom samples a sip of the fresh raspberry juice, neglecting to ask how we had produced it. Seems to me she should be a little curious.

"Jules has a penis just like Daddy," Claire blurts out, "only much smaller." Mrs. Brown and my mom pretend not to hear and go on discussing the various methods of removing raspberry stains.

The last time Claire and I played together, it started innocently enough. We were picking big round burrs at the back of the property and we started to throw them at each other. They sometimes stick to our clothes, but are easy enough to remove. Claire doesn't much care for this game. "We could pack a whole bunch together to make a ball and play catch," I suggest, but after a short while Claire finds this boring too. "Hey, we could make two balls, and if we throw them at the same time towards each other, maybe that would be fun." On the very first throw, the two balls collide in midair and stick together.

"I've had enough of these silly games," says Claire and heads towards the house.

I mould the two balls into one enormous one and impulsively I throw it towards Claire as she walks away. It hits her in the back of the head, and uh-oh, it sticks.

I rush to remove it, but Claire has already started the process and tells me to leave her alone. Her attempts are futile and only serve to entangle her fine, frizzy hair even more. Suddenly she screams and runs back to the house. Now both Mrs. Brown and my mom are desperately trying to remove the burrs and both are scolding me mercilessly. Claire screams ever louder. Mrs. Brown grabs Claire by the arm and they leave in a huff, ignoring my heartfelt apologies.

The next day, Mrs. Brown comes by to drop off some article she had borrowed from my mom. The purposeful walk and the scowl on her face tell me not to even say hello. Claire is under strict orders to remain in the car. As I approach the passenger window, I notice that it is shut tight, even though it must be hot and sweltering in the old car.

Claire flashes her sweet, shy smile but makes no attempt to roll down the window. Thankfully, the burrs are gone, but so too is her hair. The short, fine straw-coloured fuzz remaining looks like the surface of an over-mature peach.

Now that Claire's hair is shorter than mine, she looks a bit like a boy, and for a moment I fantasize that if only she wore pants we could be buddies, maybe have a friendly wrestling match just like we boys used to in Port Dalhousie.

Mrs. Brown returns. She brushes me aside, and with wheels spinning, the old car gathers speed down the driveway. Claire's sweet smile fades as tears stream down her cheeks. She waves goodbye through the rear window, and I respond with the same hopeless gesture until the car dissolves in a cloud of dust down Gregory Road.

A feeling of sadness creeps over me as slowly I realize that this may be the last time that I shall see my buddy Claire.

"Girl with bowl of cherries"   By: Alycia Marsh

THAT BEAUTIFUL TRUCK

Major construction on the Queen Elizabeth Highway was pretty much finished by the summer of 1940, and unfortunately, so was my dad's job as a dragline operator. Mom was hopeful that perhaps now we could move back to Manitoba, the place she still considers home.

"Not so fast," says Dad. "There's still a ton of cleaning up to do and if I had a truck, I could be busy for another year or two, and besides, the money is a whole lot better here than in Manitoba."

Without further discussion, he sells our classy old Reo and buys a brand-new GMC, two-ton dump truck. The cab is bright red, and it comes with a green steel box. Dad takes great delight in showing off the powerful hydraulic system that tips the whole box when you want to dump a load. He describes this feature in such detail, it's almost as though he invented it himself. I think it's the most beautiful truck I have ever seen, and I want to ride in it every chance possible. Mom is not impressed; she wonders why we couldn't have kept the Reo. Even though it was almost ten years old, that big old car still looked classy, and there was plenty of room for our whole family.

Lately there's been a lot of talk about the war, and for the first time, it's starting to affect our family. Work on the Queen E was cut back drastically as Canada got more involved in the war. Dad's hours of work have also been cut. His days are shorter now and he only gets to work four or five days a week. Mom is worried. She manages the money carefully, but after rent and countless other expenses, there is barely enough to make payments on the truck. What to do?

An opportunity comes unexpectedly one day when a neighbour asks Dad if he could haul some fruit to the cannery with his truck. Word gets around and soon Dad is busy most weekends hauling all kinds of stuff. I look forward to the weekends. It's great hanging around with Mr. Burton, but I'd rather be riding around in the truck with my dad. I get to ask all sorts of questions and I learn all kinds of neat things. We meet tons of interesting people and he tells everyone I am his helper. I am only five, so I don't get to do very much.

The best part is when Dad lets me help with the driving. Lately I've been learning how to shift gears with the five-speed transmission. Of course, Dad still steers, and he operates the clutch with his left foot, but I've learned that when he lets up on the accelerator and pushes down on the clutch pedal, it's time to shift. It's easy enough when we first start out. Instructions on the gearshift knob indicate the correct path to move the shifter from first gear to second to third to fourth and sometimes fifth gear. "And don't forget to hesitate for just a second in neutral before shifting into the next gear," Dad keeps reminding me.

Down-shifting, or going to a lower gear as we slow down, is a bit trickier, especially if you forget which gear the transmission was just in, and you can't always tell by looking at the outline on the gearshift knob. Sometimes, Dad has to double clutch. Now, this is real tricky, so I leave that part to him. "Why double clutch?" I ask Dad.

"That's to make sure the gears are properly meshed," he tells me. "If we don't do this quickly and perfectly, the gears will grind, and that's not good for the teeth." I can't quite picture this, especially the teeth part; I don't suppose these teeth look anything like human teeth.

Just when I think I've learned to shift fairly good, Dad tells me it's not always necessary to start out in first gear or "bull low," as he calls it. When we don't have a heavy load, or when the ground is hard and flat, it's perfectly fine to start off in second gear. I also learn that fifth gear is rarely used. That's reserved for travelling down the Queen E with a light load. I've noticed in fifth gear, the noisy engine slows right down and everything becomes quieter. In light traffic, Dad lets me sit on his lap and I actually steer. I can hardly wait for the day when I can drive this beautiful truck all on my own.

■ ■ ■

We've been living in Mr. Burton's old house for over a year now, and although it lacks some comforts, Mom is pleased to have a proper wood stove. To me it looks complicated, but Mom knows how to use it. To heat the house, she burns mostly salvage wood, which might be a bit rotten or damp, but for cooking, she uses only dry, medium-size wood. She adds one or two pieces at a time and constantly adjusts things to control the heat. There's a tiny little door below the firebox and a smoke adjuster on the stovepipe above the stove. Although she is forever fussing with these controls, she can't explain exactly how they work. Shifting pots and pans around the top of the stove is another way of fine-tuning the temperature, she tells me. I learn that when baking a pie or a cake, the oven temperature is especially critical. "So how do you know when the oven heat is just right?" I ask.

"Oh, I can tell by the heat on my face when I open the oven door," she explains.

Wow! This all sounds just as complicated as shifting gears and double clutching on the GMC. My parents are so smart. How will I ever learn all these things?

One morning it occurs to me that Mom is getting kind of fat—or at least, her tummy is starting to look pretty big. Sensing my curiosity, she answers my unasked question. "Soon, Jules, we'll be adding to our family with a baby brother or baby sister, and I'll need you to help me with some of the work around here." I'm not sure how to take this news. I guess that'll be okay. If it's a boy, maybe he'll eventually grow big enough to play with, and if it's a girl, she could become a playmate for Juliette, and that would be a good thing if it keeps her out of my hair. As far as helping Mom, I don't know what she has in mind, but I'm already pretty busy. Every morning, I help Mr. Burton with the chickens. On weekends, I help Dad hauling all kinds of stuff with the dump truck.

"I know you're busy," she agrees, but it sure would be a big help if you could look after the wood box." I'm not sure what she means by that; I had no idea Mom had been splitting and hauling tons of wood to keep that box full. She reminds me that soon the baby will arrive, and she may not have time to keep doing this. Dad figures he's done his part by sawing up the salvage wood from the dump, so it becomes my job to split kindling and lug the wood to the house with my little wagon. I had no idea how much wood that stove went through, especially on laundry day. At times it seems like a full-time job just keeping that darn box full.

. . .

It's late October, and the big day has arrived. Aunt Jeanne comes to stay with us while Mom is in the hospital. It sure is quiet around here when Mom is away. Sure hope she won't be gone too long. My new baby sister is a cute little girl. Alice, we call her. She seldom cries or fusses, but I doubt that we'll ever be close playmates, certainly not if she's anything like sister Juliette. Hopefully, Alice and Juliette will become good buddies, and I can be left to do my own thing.

We are now five in our family, and like Mom predicted, it sure is tight when we all go somewhere in the truck. Mom holds baby Alice on her lap while Juliette and I have to squeeze into the narrow space between my parents. We both hate this. I wonder how we'll manage when we grow bigger? I love this beautiful truck, but I sure wish Dad could have kept our big old Reo.

"1939 GMC dump truck"   Source: public domain

BRANDY BARONS

It's midsummer, peach season, and Dad and I are kept busy hauling lush ripe peaches to the canneries. We also haul culled peaches to the dump. There's no market for overripe or bruised stuff, and they rot in no time, and so less-than-perfect peaches are quickly sorted and thrown out. Still, I'm amazed at how much fruit ends up in the dump. Some of it looks real good, at least to Dad and me. We eat our fill of the better ones and we take some home for Mom and sister Juliette.

You never see a person in our neighbourhood eating a peach, and now I think I know why. Our family is getting pretty tired of them too. Mom runs her own version of a cannery, and she figures we have all the canned peaches we can eat for the next two years. So what to do with the rest?

Seeing all this fruit going to waste really bothers my parents—all the more because of their upbringing in Manitoba, where peaches are an exotic treat that only rich people can afford. Now here we are, fed up with them just like the locals. Mom and Dad are super resourceful. They are always looking for ways to save money and to make improvements to our daily living. "Surely there must be something we can do with them," they reason.

I can't say who thought of it first, but soon, Dad and me are picking up a small pig and Dad fashions a crude pen not far from our house. I've been warned not to consider it a pet because, come fall, she shall be going to piggy heaven. Let's hope the little pig doesn't get tired of peaches, because that is pretty much all she gets to eat for the next month or so.

Summer is drawing to a close, and now Dad and I are hauling grapes, hundreds of crates of grapes from small farms to the big wineries. We also haul tons to the dump.

It's such a shame to see how much is thrown out, and like the peaches, it surprises me how quickly we get tired of eating this lovely fruit as well. Miss Piggy seems quite happy to switch diets. She eats green grapes, red grapes, rotten grapes, vines and all. All summer long she has been feasting, mostly on fruit, and she is growing really fat.

While picking up a load one day, Dad asks the grape farmer why so many grapes get thrown out.

Mr. Santos, a weathered old man from Portugal, admits that he, too, is bothered by this. "Back in Portugal, nothing goes to waste, but here, the wineries are so fussy they demand perfect grapes for their precious wine. Whataya gonna do?" He shrugs. "You like wine?"

I've never seen Dad drinking wine, but it would be impolite not to express some interest. "I love wine," he says with a straight face.

"I tell you what," suggests Mr. Santos. "You take a couple barrels of my grapes, pick out the best stuff, and I'll come to your house and help you make your own wine."

Dad may not be a wine connoisseur, but he recognizes an opportunity, and he's not going to pass up this generous offer.

True to his word, Mr. Santos appears at our house the following Sunday with a well-used grape press and a bunch of other equipment in the back of his beat-up old pickup truck. I watch in fascination as he cranks away, slowly squeezing juice from the grapes, which we pour into a wooden barrel in a corner of the kitchen.

"In sunny Portugal where I come from, says Mr. Santos, "young women crush the grapes with their bare feet."

There's a long silence, but now that he has our full attention, Mr. Santos goes on to describe a fall festival that was celebrated in the village he came from. "Everyone gathers around a big open vat where young woman are busy crushing grapes with their feet. Only young, unmarried women are allowed. They wear special clothes and they wash their feet before they climb into the vat. I remember as a young man cheering the girls on, and everybody singing and laughing and getting drunk."

This all sounds so weird. I have to wonder: *Is he teasing like Mr. Burton does all the time?* Just when I think this must be the end of the story, Mr. Santos adds one more detail.

"You know, there was never any trouble selling that wine, and for a very good price, it was known as lover's wine because the grapes were crushed by the prettiest, single girls in all of Portugal. I don't know why we can't do that here in St. Catharines; after all, we have plenty of fine grapes and plenty of beautiful girls."

I can't think of a good reason either, except maybe girls from St. Catharines might not think it was much fun. I know I wouldn't want to be crushing grapes with my bare feet.

Mr. Santos is not shy about giving directions. He shouts out commands and expects everyone to jump. Mr. Santos even finds jobs for me to do. Luckily, Dad has invited Uncle Midas to lend a hand.

As the barrel in the kitchen fills, Mr. Santos gives detailed instructions on the art of transforming this smelly juice into a tasty wine. "While the juice is fermenting, you got to keep 'her' nice and warm," he warns. "Cover her with a blanket or a nice warm overcoat. I'll be around to visit her in a few days."

I find it a bit weird that this barrel of grape juice seems to have taken on a personality all its own. It sounds like she will require lots of care and attention, and she shall be occupying a corner in Mom's kitchen for quite a while. Mom seems okay with this and has even given her the name "Miss Tameron."

"Uncle Midas doesn't much care for wine, and Dad prefers beer, so who is going to drink all this wine?" Mom wonders. "Mind you, I can't imagine any of it going to waste, either. Dad is too frugal, and besides, a lot of effort went into brewing this juice." Uncle Midas suggests they could build a still and turn it into brandy. Dad quickly agrees, and although he is not familiar with distilling brandy, it couldn't be much different than the stuff they brewed in homemade distilleries in Manitoba.

This all sounds pretty intriguing. I would love to see how it's done, but it seems this secret process is for adult eyes only. No kids are allowed to even peek at all the activity going on in Uncle Midas and Aunt Adrienne's basement. I overheard Mom and Aunty express concern that if word ever got out, the police would raid the place in a flash. They might even send Dad and Uncle Midas to jail. Wow—this sounds pretty serious, no wonder I am not to say a word about it, not even to Mr. Burton.

It is early fall when Mr. Santos pays us a surprise visit. He wants to know how the wine turned out, which of course implies he would like to sample a glass. Dad dips into the nearly empty barrel. Mr. Santos is quick to chastise him for not bottling the mature wine like he was supposed to. He makes a sour face as he sniffs the glass. Reluctantly, he sips a minuscule amount then promptly spits it back into the glass. "This isn't fit to drink," he declares. "What happened to that good stuff we started a few weeks back?"

Dad is clearly embarrassed. He feels badly about disappointing Mr. Santos. Perhaps Dad could have feigned a lapse of memory about the bottling and he could have said that he gave the rest to family and friends. That's what Mom wanted him to say. Instead, he admits that neither he nor uncle Midas are real wine drinkers, so they decided to distil what may have been perfectly good wine into brandy. He offers Mr. Santos a glass and nervously awaits the verdict.

Mr. Santos swirls the home-brewed brandy around in his mouth for what seems an awfully long time. His eyes widen, and a smile crosses his dark, wrinkled face. *"Delicioso!"* he declares. "I want more of this stuff."

Mr. Santos goes on to explain that he has barrels of poor quality wine that he would love to have distilled into brandy. "I know my friends and relatives also have plenty of the same kind of stuff, we will pay good money if you could turn this wine into *delicioso* brandy like yours." Mr. Santos expands upon the possibilities. He would supply the wine and look after the business end of things while Dad could concentrate on producing this most excellent product. "We could become rich," he declares.

Dad is now clearly in a quandary. He has no respect for the law that prohibits home brewing. After all, everybody knows that those laws were passed solely to protect the big distilleries from open competition. It's the strict penalties including jail time that give him pause.

Mom is telegraphing a stern look. She knows Dad very well. She knows that it is not easy for him to pass up what looks like the opportunity of a lifetime. She also knows that to object to this proposal in front of Mr. Santos might have the opposite effect and push Dad into going ahead with this dangerous enterprise.

Finally, Dad gives his answer. He tells Mr. Santos that their homemade still is much too small to handle the volumes being contemplated, and yes, he could fabricate a larger one that could handle any amount, but where would he put it? Not wanting to disappoint Mr. Santos, Dad suggests a possibility. "Suppose I was to build you a still and show you how to use it, then you and your friends could be brewing all the brandy you want."

At first, Mr. Santos seems open to the plan, but as Dad goes on to explain in great detail all the pitfalls of operating a still and a few of the tricks the police use to arrest bootleggers, it becomes clear this whole idea will need a lot more thought. Mr. Santos graciously accepts Dad's gift of a large bottle of brandy, declaring, "We must do this again next year."

Every family gathering that followed would include brandy brewed by Dad and Uncle Midas. As the men savour their golden brew, the conversation inevitably comes around to that intriguing offer from Mr. Santos and all the money they could be making. Aunt Adrienne worries that the temptation still has not gone away. Mom just smiles and tries to reassure her.

"Let those Brandy Barons fantasize all they want," says Mom. "That just ain't gonna happen."

LESSONS FROM GRADE ONE

I was really looking forward to beginning grade one. It would be so exciting learning how to read and write and meeting new friends. I wasn't too concerned that my parents couldn't attend that first day. Mom had arranged for the neighbour's eldest daughter to come by, and together we would walk the half-mile or so to Woodland School. Becky took my hand and off we went down Gregory Road towards that mysterious old-growth forest that seems to bother Mr. Burton.

I find the forest positively enchanting. The trees are just huge. They are like tall, friendly giants, looking down upon all the little creatures who live here and who need protection from the rain and the hot sun. They seem to say "welcome" as we pass under their wide spread arms. I just can't imagine cutting down such a wonder of nature. To me the forest is a magical place that is home to every kind of animal. I picture deer, moose, rabbits, maybe even bears and wolves. Today we see only birds and squirrels who scold as we walk in silence down the narrow trail that wends through the dark woods.

The forest gives way to a grassy field, and beyond is a low white building with green trim and a cedar shingle roof. It blends in perfectly with the natural surroundings. Anticipation grows as we join the crowd of children and adults gathered in front of the school. Finally, the doors open, and Becky, my new friend, whose hand I grip tightly, brings me to the grade one classroom.

I am introduced to Miss Smith, a large, stern-looking woman who is to be my teacher for the coming year—such a contrast to Becky, who is so sweet and quite pretty. I have come to regard her as my substitute mom. Reluctantly, I loosen my grip from Becky's comforting hand and prepare to enter a strange new world.

With scarcely a glance, Miss Smith directs me to stand in line near the back of the room. When all have assembled, Miss Smith orders us to stand at attention and sing with her, "God save the King." I have no idea who this king is and why he needs to be saved.

Next, we are directed to sit at a strange looking piece of furniture that is both a seat and a table but is in fact called a desk. Another new word that I must remember among the many I have heard today. As far as I can tell, no one speaks the language I grew up in. I feel small and alone.

On each desk are pencils and crayons and several books. A pretty blue one called "Dick and Jane" grabs my attention. It has lots of pictures with stories about a boy named Dick and a girl named Jane. They live in a tidy house in a tidy neighbourhood and lead a life that isn't anything like mine. And oh, at the front of the book is a full-page colour picture of that king we were singing about. He looks really important, with lots of medals pinned to his chest.

Soon it is recess, and we are let out to play. I rush outside, eager to make new friends. I am totally unprepared for what happens next. As I approach a group of boys kicking a ball around, one of the bigger kids yells at me, "Get out of here, kid, go play with the girls!"

"But I want to play ball too," I protest. Bobby shoves me to the ground and makes fun of my clothes. I am wearing burgundy shorts with an attached bib and suspenders, a white shirt, and knee-length white stockings. I have no idea what Mom was thinking when she dressed me in this outfit she had lovingly sewn for this special day. Needless to say, I would never wear those clothes again, but Bobby would find new reasons to taunt me.

One day, Bobby pushes me too far. This time anger wells up and dispels my fears, and I strike back with a vengeance. I am surprised at how easy it is to turn the tables. I knock Bobby to the ground—only I go a bit further. Using a few wrestling tricks I had learned in Port Dalhousie, I pin Bobby down and push his face into the dirt. I twist one arm behind his back until he screams with pain. I don't want to hurt Bobby, but it feels good to stand up for myself. Bobby never bullied me again. I vow that from now on, nobody will ever bully me.

The rest of the boys finally accept me, and school actually becomes fun, until one fateful day that shakes my world.

Boys could be bullies, but I was certain that adults could always be counted on to treat you nicely. My naive belief is tested as Miss Smith escorts me to the basement of Woodland School. I can tell by the smell that the concrete floor has been freshly painted, and at first, I am fascinated by the gleaming furnace and bewildering array of pipes and machinery that occupies most of this strange space they call the boiler room. She directs me to a small, dark room and leaves me alone as she locks the door behind her. I try hard not to cry, but I am six years old, and I am scared.

There had been a fire drill and everyone was ordered outside. Mr. Bailey, the principal, addressed all the students and told us what a fine job we did, and as a reward, we were free to run around the school five times before going back to our classrooms. The boys took the opportunity to show the girls how fast we could run, and we challenged them to try and catch us. During the race, my classmate, my friend, who was in front of me, bumped into a parked bicycle and sent it crashing to the ground. The bike belonged to one of the teachers and she was not amused. An enquiry was launched and another girl told the teacher it was Jules who knocked the bike down. I expected my friend to own up to the accident, but he remained silent.

Miss Smith got involved and demanded an apology. I told her it wasn't me but I didn't implicate my friend. I refused to apologize. Her face turned red and she threatened to banish me to the boiler room, but I remained silent. She grabbed my arm and dragged me from the class.

At that moment, I learned that adults could be bullies too. I knew that I could never pin Miss Smith to the ground and twist her arm behind her back. I guess sometimes life just isn't fair and there is nothing you can do about it, and sometimes a friend can let you down.

I don't remember much about grade one, perhaps because I feared and disliked my teacher, but I vividly remember another incident that was a lot more serious. It didn't involve me directly, but it was kind of sad and a bit scary too.

There was this painfully shy kid named Karl. Karl dressed quite poor and never combed his hair. He only spoke when he absolutely had to, and when he did, it was with a strange accent. Karl didn't seem to have any friends. I tried to talk with him a few times, but he wouldn't reply to any of my questions. Eventually, everyone kind of gave up on Karl, and he was left pretty much to himself until one fateful day, for a painful couple of hours, Karl became the centre of attention.

It started when Miss Smith decided to test our reading skills by having each kid read aloud from their "Dick and Jane" book. When it was Karl's turn, he remained silent. Miss Smith approached and immediately scolded Karl for not having his book opened at the right page. As she flipped the pages she noticed something else. "Where is our king?" she shouted. "Where is the picture of King George the sixth?"

After more grilling, Karl tearfully admitted that his father had cut it out from his book.

"Why on earth would he do such a terrible thing?" she demanded in an even louder voice.

Miss Smith left the room, ordering all of us to stay in our seats. A short time later, she returned with Mr. Bailey, the school principal. He quickly checked Karl's "Dick and Jane" book, then ordered Karl to come with him and to bring all his workbooks and school supplies. A short time later, a police car pulled up and took Karl away.

The next day, one of the girls asked, "What happened to Karl? Where did he go?" Miss Smith tried to explain that Canada and England were at war with Germany, and Karl's parents are German and the police will investigate.

This didn't make much sense to me. Mom agreed it was all so sad. Dad didn't say much; he just shook his head and muttered something about the English and their damned wars. I never saw Karl again. I often wonder what happened to him and his family.

I can't say that year at Woodland was a whole lot of fun, but I did learn to read and write and I learned a few other lessons, as well.

"Woodland School"   Source: family photo

THREE BLIND MICE

Ever since I was locked up in that boiler room, I've been feeling kind of glum. I don't like Miss Smith and I probably never will, so it was a nice change one morning to have a cheery, smiley young lady address our class.

"I'm Miss Garland, Mr. Bailey's assistant," she tells us. Of course, everybody knows Miss Garland, and everybody knows that she works with Mr. Bailey—but why is she in our classroom? For a hopeful moment, I let myself believe that Miss Garland is going to make an important announcement, and I get all excited. Maybe she's here to inform us that Miss Smith is resigning, or maybe Miss Smith has some incurable disease and can't teach anymore.

Miss Garland begins by reminding us that Christmas is just around the corner, and for the next few weeks the whole school shall be preparing for the annual Woodland School Christmas concert. Miss Garland says she will be coordinating things, but it's up to each teacher to prepare an exciting, entertaining program. She cannot stress enough that the most important players are the students themselves, and she wants all of us to have lots of fun.

It seems this Christmas concert idea is a pretty big deal at Woodland. It is Mr. Bailey's official policy that every student must perform on stage in some way, no matter how shy or how scared the kid might be. Mr. Bailey considers it part of our education and he expects every teacher to come up with a play, a skit, a song, a recital; whatever it takes to involve every single student. It won't be easy for Miss Smith.

There are forty or so kids in our room, some in grade one, others in grade two. If any has a natural talent, they keep it well hidden. Everyone knows how stern Miss Smith can be, and everyone is aware that she has a temper, so nobody dares to speak out of turn and nobody ever laughs. A few kids are so shy, they can barely read out loud; it is hard to imagine how they will perform.

Miss Smith makes sure that every kid has a costume no matter how minor a role they may play. Parents are pressed into helping, and of course that means mostly the moms. Each is asked to come to the school to receive instructions on what is expected. My mom is told that I am slated to play the part of a mouse from the nursery rhyme, "Three Blind Mice." I don't like the idea one bit, but Mom has already agreed to sew all three mouse costumes and it seems I have no say in the matter.

It's the night of the concert. Excitement is in the air. Every parent is there along with lots of relatives, neighbours, and friends. With such a large audience, I guess it really is a big deal. All the kids are backstage, dressed in their costumes, giggling and laughing and nervous about the part they are about to perform.

First up is a play adapted from the Grimm Brothers' old tale, "Hansel and Gretel." Claire, my buddy from the previous summer, is playing Gretel. I kind of wish I was chosen to be Hansel. I don't know if I would be up to playing this prominent role, but it would be fun traipsing hand in hand with Claire through the fake forest, spreading shiny pebbles and bread crumbs. But here I am stuck in this silly mouse costume along with my buddies, Mickey and Peter, who I suspect aren't any happier than I am.

Maybe I should be grateful. I could be stuck in an even lesser role like the super shy kids who are standing at the back of the stage waiting their turn to participate in the recital of a poem. The poem is used as a filler that allows for a quick change of scenery. In this case, the Hansel and Gretel scene is being replaced with the "Three Blind Mice" scene. These shy kids get to say, "drip, drip, drip," at the end of each verse.

The Icicle and the Sun

An icicle hung on a red brick wall,
And it said to the sun,
"I don't like you at all!"
    Drip! Drip! Drip!
The sun said, "My, you've a saucy tongue.
You should remember,
I'm old and you're young."
    Drip! Drip! Drip!
But the icicle only cried the more,
Though the sun still shone on it
Just as before!
    Drip! Drip! Drip!
Until at the end of the winter's day,
It had cried its poor little self away.
    Drip! Drip! Drip!

The last "drip, drip, drip!" is the cue for the performance to begin. It's time for my mouse buddies and me to make our entrance. We are wearing grey flannel costumes that look suspiciously like long underwear with long tails that drag across the floor. We also have dark sunglasses, just like the ones blind people always wear. Miss Smith is at the piano playing some spooky tune while a chorus sings the words. I don't understand the meaning of this silly story. For one thing, I'd like to know how those poor mice got blind in the first place, and why would the farmer's wife want to cut off their tails? Sounds pretty sick to me.

Three Blind Mice

Three blind mice,
Three blind mice.
See how they run!
See how they run!
They all ran after the farmer's wife,
She cut off their tails with a carving knife.
Did you ever see such a sight in your life
As three blind mice?

Now it's time for the three mice to make their entrance. Mickey leads and I follow with Pete close behind—too close, it turns out. Pete steps on my long tail. It rips right off. Miss Smith is in a panic, her face flush with embarrassment. She orders us back behind the curtains and calls one of the helper moms to fix it.

The delay is not that long, and the audience seems patient enough with just a few people snickering. It's what happens next that still brings a smile whenever I think back to that evening at Woodland School.

According to the nursery rhyme, the mice are supposed to be chasing the farmer's wife. This part is played by a fat girl from grade two named Zelda, and she is running around the stage like crazy. I think she enjoys her part. Meanwhile, the mice stumble around, bumping into walls and tripping over things. Thank goodness we can still see through our dark glasses, or someone could get hurt!

Miss Smith is playing some weird music that keeps getting louder and louder. Suddenly, Zelda has a big fake carving knife, and she is waving it around in big circles. Now the tables are turned and she starts chasing us. We continue to stumble around like idiots. It makes no sense to me.

This goes on far longer than I would like, but the audience seems amused. Eventually, we each get caught by Zelda, who then goes through an exaggerated cutting motion as she removes our tails. In fact, she only has to tug a little and the tail comes off, just as it was designed to. This worked fine with my buddy's costumes, but when Zelda pulls on my tail, it won't let go. Zelda grabs it with two hands and pulls so hard I am knocked off my feet, and still the tail won't come off.

The audience is laughing, but Miss Smith is not amused. She strides purposefully across the stage and rips off my tail, along with a patch of grey flannel and a bunch of heavy-duty safety pins. Now the audience is laughing like crazy and I sense that Miss Smith is getting more furious by the second.

Right after the performance, Miss Smith storms backstage, her homely face livid with rage. "Now stand in that corner and keep still!" she commands. "I don't want you to move, and I don't want to hear a peep from you three for the rest of the evening."

Miss Smith is barely out of the room when the three of us look at each other and break into a fit of giggling that just won't stop. Then Mickey starts stumbling around like we did during the performance, and Pete and I join in—three tailless mice stumbling around, giggling like mad. If anyone was watching, now, they could be excused for asking, "Did you ever see such a sight in your life?"

The rest of the school year passes without incident, and I did learn quite a lot. I passed all the tests, so I guess next year I'll be in grade two, which means I'll be in the same room, and I'll have the same teacher. Unless, of course, something bad happens to Miss Smith.

CHRISTMAS ON GREGORY ROAD

During the night, a sparkling white blanket has settled over my world, and it is absolutely gorgeous. I've never seen anything like it. Everything is buried in a sea of white: the houses, the trees, and the roads have practically disappeared. The weatherman says the snow came from the waters off Lake Ontario and dumped over two feet throughout the entire Niagara region. We don't often get this much snow in St. Catharines, and when we do, it usually melts in a couple days.

Since the wind is now coming from the north and the weather is turning colder, Dad is predicting it will last quite a while.

This will make his job on the Queen E much more difficult, if not impossible. He is not happy. Mom, on the other hand, is positively exuberant. "Now this looks more like a Manitoba winter," she declares. "This year, we are going to do things a little differently. This year, our family is going to celebrate Christmas properly."

Up until now, Christmas wasn't a big deal in our family. I remember last year when we lived in Port Dalhousie, I got a cap gun and a cowboy hat from Santa, and that was about it. Oh sure, we got together with relatives from Manitoba, but family dinners are pretty routine, so the Christmas season wasn't much different from most weekends.

Mom isn't alone in her efforts to celebrate Christmas. The streets in downtown St. Catharines are brightly lit with coloured lights, reminding everyone of the festive season that is fast approaching. Store window displays are filled with luxury products that few can afford.

Many are playing Christmas music and there are crowds of cheery, bustling people everywhere.

Even Gregory Road seems to have more traffic than usual, and I keep hearing the sound of bells tinkling in the distance. Who could be ringing those bells so energetically, and for what purpose?

Finally one day, the mystery is resolved when a handsome, meticulously groomed black horse struts past our house pulling an equally perfect black sleigh with red trim. Onboard is a prosperous-looking couple dressed in furs. They smile and wave as they glide by.

"Gee! That looks like fun. I sure wish we had a horse and sleigh with bells," I tell my parents. Of course I know that you've got to be pretty rich to afford something like that.

It turns out a number of our neighbours have decided to dust off their sleighs—or cutters, as locals call them—and we are treated to a number of pretty horses prancing down Gregory Road. None are quite as classy as that first rig, but they all have bells that make a rhythmic sound just like in the song: "Jingle bells, Jingle bells, Jingle all the way."

This is another sign that Christmas can't be far off.

Dad shakes his head as we watch neighbours go by with their fancy horses. He's certain that none of these horses has ever worked a day in their lives. He can't imagine why anyone would keep a horse purely for fun when there are so many fine cars available. "Everyone should know by now that a car can get you where you want to go, much quicker and cheaper too," he tells us.

I guess Mr. Burton came to that conclusion too. He now owns a car, but he keeps his little cutter and his one-horse buggy safely stored in the machinery shed. "Do you think you'll ever use that cutter again, Mr. Burton?" Secretly I'm thinking how much fun it would be to ride in a one-horse open sleigh, just like in the "Jingle Bells" song.

"I guess there is always that possibility," says Mr. Burton. "If the old Buick gives me too much trouble, I may just trade it in for a horse."

It occurs to me that Mr. Burton already has two horses. *Why not hitch up Lady or Godiva?* I wonder. And then I look more closely at these gentle giants, and it becomes obvious that the dainty little cutter and the flimsy-looking buggy weren't made for Clydesdales. I suspect Mr. Burton would just laugh if I made such a suggestion. I'd better not even mention the thought.

Since that heavy snowfall, Mr. Burton has been working on another kind of sled. It's a big heavy-duty thing that hasn't been used in years, but now with all this snow, he figures it can be put to good use once again. The big sled is certainly not fancy. It has a plain wooden bench for the driver and straw bales along both sides to act as seats for everyone else. "Lady and Godiva need the exercise, and besides they just love to take kids for rides," he says. "Every evening I'll be taking my lovelies through the neighbourhood as long as the snow lasts. Anybody who wants a ride can just hop aboard."

It's early evening, and passengers are waiting along Gregory Road. Everyone seems to know the routine. Lady and Godiva are walking by at a brisk pace, and they won't be stopping, so if you want to get on board you've got to hustle. The sled fills quickly. Over twenty people have piled on, mostly kids but a few adults as well. Everyone is laughing and singing, having a great time, and I can understand why Mr. Burton claims that Lady and Godiva love these hayrides, too.

We leave the main road and head for less travelled farm lanes and forest trails. It's getting dark, and we're beginning to see a crescent moon and millions of stars twinkling. There's just enough light to appreciate that we are in a wonderland of such beauty that it almost takes my breath away.

At times, everyone stops the chatter, the laughter, the singing; all fade to a hush as we take in the magic of it all. During these special moments, I hear the muffled clomping of eight big hoofs on the snow-covered, frozen ground. I hear the calm measured breathing of Lady and Godiva. I want to shout out, "Thank you, thank you, you big hairy beasts!" but I doubt they would understand. I suspect that Mr.

Burton and his passengers wouldn't understand either, so I'll just let that thought pass and express my gratitude in some other way.

. . .

Mom keeps the radio on all day, and lately all they play is Christmas music, so it can get pretty boring. I'm not paying much attention, but I recognize that right in the middle of one of my favourite songs, the radio goes dead. The sudden silence grabs everyone's attention, and I'm thinking the radio must be broken. But wait—there's a crackling noise then a lot of static. The static is getting louder and louder, and now it even gets Dad's attention.

The announcer's voice bursts forth, apologizing for the break in the program and repeats, "Please stand by." He has on the line a reporter from somewhere near the North Pole who has some breaking news about Santa.

Mom turns up the volume as our family gathers around the radio. A tense dialogue unfolds with the local radio announcer speaking loud and clear while the reporter from the North Pole is barely audible. Every time the reporter tries to speak, there is so much static going on in the background that we must strain to hear him.

This exchange goes on for some time. Gradually it emerges that a few minutes ago, the reporter had talked with Santa by two-way radio. Santa informed him that he was headed south with his trusty reindeer where he planned to visit a few chosen towns before delivering presents on Christmas Eve. Unfortunately, a terrible blizzard struck shortly after Santa left his home at the North Pole, and nobody has been able to contact him since. Through the static and the howling wind, we are barely able to make out the reporter's last words—something about concern over Santa's safety, and the possibility that he could be lost in this blinding blizzard where the visibility is zero.

The radio announcer cuts in, "Now, now, no need to worry, boys and girls, I'm sure Santa will be alright; and don't forget, boys and girls, reindeer just love the cold and the snow—after all, they were born and raised in the North, they know their way around. They would never get lost."

I look to my parents, and they nod in agreement. Whew! Maybe the reindeer won't get lost, but still I've got to wonder how Santa is doing in this terrible storm.

The next day, the radio announcer is pleased to inform anxious listeners that the storm near the North Pole is over and contact with Santa has been restored. Santa and his reindeer are back on track and should arrive in St. Catharines on Saturday, just in time for the Christmas parade in downtown St. Catharines.

There's already quite a crowd as we line up to watch the parade on St. Paul Street. It seemed to take forever for Santa to appear.

Christmas bells are ringing louder and louder. I hear a low, deep voice repeating, "Ho! Ho! Ho! Merry Christmas! Ho! Ho! Ho! Merry Christmas! Ho! Ho! Ho! Merry Christmas!"

Finally, there he is, sitting high in his giant red sled, looking happy and fat and ever so jolly. He is throwing handfuls of candies at the crowd. Sister Juliette and I manage to collect our share. This is such fun. I can't remember ever being so excited. Santa is so nice. I'm sure glad he made it through that storm okay.

I can tell those aren't real reindeer pulling his sled. I suspect the real reindeer are resting after that long journey from the North Pole, and besides, they are going to need all their strength to deliver those thousands of presents on Christmas Eve. I can hardly wait.

I'm so grateful for that big snowstorm and all the snow we got, especially now that I know Santa and his reindeer are safe. Everything looks so clean and peaceful and just perfect for Christmas. Everyone we meet seems extra cheery, and people are wishing us "Merry Christmas" everywhere we go. I just can't imagine a place more filled with beauty and good cheer.

The week before Christmas, Mom is busy shopping and decorating the house. This year, for the first time, we will have our own Christmas tree, so Mom sends Dad and me to pick one up at the farmer's market downtown. Dad remembers mowing down hundreds of young spruce trees when he worked on construction, and hundreds more while cutting bush along the water district line in Manitoba. "Now we have to pay good money for this scruffy little thing not even suitable for firewood," he grumbles.

I was surprised to learn that neither Mom nor Dad ever had a Christmas tree in the homes they grew up in. Dad's family didn't even exchange gifts. They went to church a lot, where they celebrated the birth of baby Jesus. I learned that he's been dead a long time, but apparently people still have a birthday party for him every year.

Mom's folks did a lot of feasting and visiting at Christmas and made sure that the kids had fun. Everybody had large families, so there were all kinds of cousins to visit and play with. This was usually the time when kids got new clothes, much of it homemade, like sweaters, toques, stockings, and mittens, but some store-bought stuff too. All the kids could count on getting school supplies like scribblers, crayons, and pencils, and possibly a book or two. The better off folks might buy their kids some toys, and there was never any shortage of sweets. There was no mention of Santa.

Christmas was mainly centred around the kids, Mom recalls but New Year's Eve was reserved for adults. Celebrations started early, with young men making their rounds, visiting and paying respect to their elders. Naturally, wherever they went, they would be offered something to eat and a drink or two. By evening they would be in a jolly mood and eager to party.

After everyone had eaten a simple meal of *cipâte* (a type of meat pie), the instruments came out and music filled the air. There was dancing and singing and drinking until dawn. Kids were free to participate, but they knew this was a party for adults, so they would eventually retreat to the bedrooms to play games or fall asleep wherever they could. As Mom relates these happy memories, it's obvious that she would just love to be back in Manitoba, reconnecting with her huge family. Mind you, a growing number of close relatives have followed my parents to St. Catharines, so things will be livelier this year. They'll all be here Christmas Day, and I'm looking forward to seeing aunts and uncles and cousins I've met only recently.

Mom keeps the radio on the same station all the time where Christmas songs play continually and there is a lot of talk about Santa. Now that I've seen him in person, he has become a hero to me. I want to know everything about him, and I pester my parents with questions. I want to know about Santa's elves at the North Pole. "Do they spend the whole year just making presents for all the kids in the world? What do the reindeer do when they're not driving Santa around? What do reindeer eat?"

Yesterday, our family went to Eaton's to visit Santa, and all the kids got to sit on his lap. He asked everyone what they wanted for Christmas. I told Santa I want a toy dump truck just like Dad's. Santa doesn't know if that's something his elves make, but he'll check.

"Maybe we could send you a picture of the truck," I suggest. Juliette wants a doll and a baby carriage like Mom uses for sister Alice when we go out. Borrrring! I don't know what Santa will bring baby Alice. She doesn't talk yet, and she's too small to play with toys, but I guess Santa will come up with something.

Finally, it's the night before Christmas. I couldn't be more excited, but I'm also kind of worried. It's been melting all day, and there is practically no snow left on Gregory road. "How will Santa's reindeer pull that heavy sleigh if the road is dry?" I ask Mom.

"I wouldn't worry about it," she assures me. "Didn't the weatherman say they were expecting more snow overnight?"

I heard that some kids leave milk and cookies for Santa. I hate milk. "So what if Santa hates milk too?" I question Dad. "What else do you think he would like?"

Dad suggests some of his homemade brandy. "I'll bet Santa would really like that."

Yeah, everybody loves Dad's brandy, what a good idea. "And, do you think his reindeer would like carrots?" I ask. "Well, of course they would. All reindeer love carrots," Dad assures me. Dad spent a lot of time working up north, so he should know.

Sleep just won't come. Mom says Santa may pass by our house if I'm not sleeping. *I'm trying; I'm trying real hard, Mom.* Maybe I could pretend to be asleep, and hopefully he won't notice. I hear the faint sound of sleigh bells in the distance. *Could that be Santa and his reindeer? Oh no! I must fall asleep, I must, I must.*

■ ■ ■

It's almost daylight in my room. What happened to the night? I rush to the window, and it's snowing outside. Oh, happy day! This means Santa's reindeer won't have any trouble pulling that humungous sled, at least not down Gregory Road.

It's awfully quiet. Everyone is still sleeping. Has Santa come yet? I want to check under that Christmas tree so badly, but I better get back to bed. What if he comes and finds me awake? Even if I can't sleep, I must pretend.

I can hear sister Alice starting to fuss. Mom is getting up. I rush to her room, half expecting to be sent back to bed, but no; Dad is getting up too. Is it really morning? Is this finally Christmas morning? I rush to the top of the stairs from where I can see the little table and comfy chair that I arranged for Santa. The carrots are gone, and the brandy glass is empty, and it looks like Santa left a note on the table. Wow! I rush back shouting the happy news. I wake up sister Juliette to tell her, and she gets all excited too.

Without washing or brushing our teeth, we all hurry downstairs. The Christmas tree is all lit up and looking fabulous. Under its branches is a pile of beautifully wrapped presents. Oh, my! Oh my! Oh my! This is going to be the bestest, most wonderful Christmas ever—probably in the whole wide world, I figure.

MOUSE WARS

It's been almost two years since we moved into Mr. Burton's old house, and everyone is real happy living here. So it came as a shock one morning when Mom discovered what looked like a few tiny black seeds in the corner of the kitchen.

"There's a mouse in the house!" Mom yells, getting everyone's attention. Mom absolutely hates mice. It's not that she's scared of them, but just the thought of sharing our house with these "filthy little rodents" turns her right off, and she lets everyone know how annoyed she is. Dad doesn't deny that these are genuine mouse droppings, but he doesn't consider the deposit of a dozen or so little black seeds as cause for alarm. He theorizes that a single mouse could have snuck into the house when the kitchen door was left open, and it was probably very glad to get out at the first opportunity.

A couple of days go by with no sign of droppings, and Mom breathes a little easier. I tend to think that Dad was right. It was likely just an adventurous little guy that came for a visit, looked around, and decided to return to his family.

One morning, Mom is getting bowls from the kitchen cupboard for our daily oatmeal and she lets out a piercing scream. "More mouse shit!" she yells in disgust, "right on the shelf where the dishes are kept." She rewashes all the dishes, the bowls, and all the cups, and piles them on the kitchen table. "That's where they'll stay until you make that cupboard completely mouse-proof," she tells Dad.

Without saying a word, Dad gets his tools out, and I watch as he remounts and adjusts the door hinges and fixes the spring latches that are supposed to keep the doors tightly closed.

A week goes by, and the scene is repeated. The mice have deposited what looks like an identical number of droppings, and Mom's scream is followed by declarations of disgust. The scene matches perfectly that first discovery, only this time the little black seeds are in the cutlery drawer. Mom soaks all the cutlery in bleach and then washes every fork, knife, and spoon in boiling water. I must confess that putting that spoon in my mouth was a little troubling knowing that only an hour ago there could have been mouse poop clinging to it. Out come the tools, only this time Dad must practically rebuild the whole drawer unit.

Mom recognizes that Dad can be slow in following her instructions—that's why she has learned to be self-sufficient and needs no help keeping the house and yard tidy and in good repair. However, I have noticed that when a job requires urgent action, Mom can be a firm taskmaster.

"I want you to go to the store and get some mousetraps," she commands, "at least ten, and while you're at it get some rat poison too." Within minutes, Dad and I take off in the GMC. I guess Dad knows to follow orders when he has to.

Mom immediately goes about setting the traps with cheese, and Dad is busy rebuilding the drawer unit. Mom is grumbling, while Dad seems to be deliberately making as much noise as possible with his sawing and hammering. The air feels a bit frosty; I think I'll go visit Mr. Burton.

Mr. Burton appears surprised when I fill him in on our mouse problem. "Never saw anything resembling a mouse when Mrs. Burton and I lived there," he says. "Mind you, we always had a bunch of cats hanging around the place. I'll bet if you had a cat or two, those mice would soon disappear."

Mr. Burton fills a large pan with cat treats and shakes it around a bit. Instantly, cats appear from the barn, the hen house, and every corner of the barnyard. There must have been at least a dozen of them. I never knew there were so many. "Why don't you take a couple home? I'll bet your Mom would be really pleased, take your pick," he offers.

I know Mom doesn't like cats very much, so I take my time making a selection. I pick a little orange striped one that I kind of like, and I'm hoping Mom will like it too.

I didn't know what to expect when I returned with this little sweetie tucked inside my jacket. To my relief, Mom agrees it's really cute. "It's certainly worth a try," she admits, "but it won't stick around here very long," she predicts. "It'll go right back to Mr. Burton's soon. What's its name?" she asks.

"Mr. Burton calls it a tabby—and oh, Mr. Burton says to feed it sardines and milk, and Tabby will never leave."

Sure enough, Tabby loves sardines and milk and hangs around even though sister Juliette keeps torturing the poor thing. Tabby puts up with being dressed in doll clothes and going for rides in the doll buggy, at least for a while. When she's had enough, Tabby makes her escape and hides in some dark corner where Juliette can't find her.

We've had Tabby for about a week, and so far, so good. There's no sign of mice, until one day, we hear a snap and moments later a god-awful yowling, which could only come from a cat. Tabby is thrashing around the house with a mousetrap clamped tightly to her paw.

Poor Tabby! I manage to catch her, and with Mom's help, I remove the mousetrap. Mom gets scratched quite badly in the process. Mom opens the kitchen door and heaves Tabby outside, all the while cursing like I'd never heard before. "Goddamned cats," she yells. "I never want to see another one around here again."

It didn't help matters that when Dad got home and heard the story, he chastised Mom for leaving a set trap lying around when there's a cat in the house. "I can't believe you would do that," he tells her in an accusatory tone.

"Of course I know that!" she shouts back. "Do you think I'm stupid? I collected all the traps when Jules brought that goddamned cat in the house. I must have missed one."

Now that there is no longer a cat in the house, Mom goes about setting all ten traps, placing them in every room. Juliette gets her special attention. "And, don't you be touching those traps," Mom warns, "and don't try to eat the cheese either, or you could end up out the door just like Tabby."

I'm grateful that Mom doesn't direct her wrath at me, although I'm feeling badly for being the cause of it. I wonder if Tabby is back with her friends, and I wonder if her paw is okay.

One night, when all of us are sleeping, I hear *snap! snap!* in quick succession, and two more mice have met their doom. Mom is ecstatic, and dares to hope that this shall ultimately eliminate the problem. Dad is not so sure. Over the next few weeks, several more mice are sent to mouse heaven, and then days go by with no deadly snaps in the middle of the night and no mouse poop. Mom is not celebrating just yet, but dares to hope that will be the end of this war.

Then early one morning, horror of horrors, Mom lets out a yell, and we all know the mice have paid another visit. We rush to the kitchen. Strewn across the floor is a mess of oatmeal mixed together with mouse poop.

Mom is downright religious about keeping every morsel of food in glass jars or tins with tight-fitting lids. She can't believe that the lid was left off the oatmeal tin. She tests to see if the lid could have been removed by the mice, unlikely as that may seem. Knowing how we all dislike porridge, she doesn't question whether one of us could have left the lid off. Instead, she goes about gathering all ten traps and replaces the bait with peanut butter. Mom reasons that fresh peanut butter might be better than cheese. She freshens the peanut butter every day.

I counted three snaps one night, and some awful squealing that went on for several minutes. I wonder if Mom is feeling sorry for those poor mice. *Not very likely*, I conclude. I'm hoping there'll be no more, but there are. It seems there are always new ones that can't resist the fresh peanut butter and end up being cremated in the cook stove. It's my job to empty the ash drawer, and I notice remnants of their tiny bones among the ashes. I'd like to think that they have gone to a better place like my religious aunt seems to think, but I find this hard to imagine.

So where could they be coming from is the constant question. Dad has refitted both front and back doors to eliminate any space there might have been around the edges, and he has installed really strong springs to ensure that the doors are never left open. The possibility of them coming through an open door probably doesn't count anymore, so Mom has a new theory.

This old farmhouse doesn't have a basement; it doesn't even have a decent foundation, and Mom is convinced that there must be an army of mice living in the shallow space under the house. From there, she pictures mice by the dozen clawing their way between the walls with free access to the interior of the house. I've heard scratching behind the wall of my bedroom, so it's not hard to imagine that Mom could be right.

"I sure wish we had a skunk around here," Mom declares. "Now, if we were in Manitoba, there's no doubt that by now a hungry skunk would have discovered this banquet under the house and we wouldn't have this problem."

Wow! This is amazing. I wonder how many moms would be okay with having skunks living under their floors. I'll bet Mom might even put out the odd can of sardines just to keep them coming back once they cleaned out the mice. I'm pretty sure that skunks like sardines too.

I remember Mr. Burton's son, Bob, telling me that snakes eat mice. I wonder if a snake or two could accomplish the same thing as a skunk, but I know how much Mom hates snakes, so I better not say anything, and I better not suggest how killing that huge snake in the garden last year may be the cause of our mouse problems.

Mom keeps nagging Dad about getting rat poison. She wants to place some under the house, and Dad keeps making excuses. I ask Mr. Burton what he thinks of the idea. Mr. Burton is appalled. "Please tell your Mom she must not do that. I don't want my cats getting into that awful stuff and dying a horrible, painful death."

"I hadn't thought of that," Mom admits, but now she has a new plan and she gets me to help her carry it out.

We gather up a bunch of old jars from a nearby dump and bust them up with a hammer. It is my job to pulverize them into a course powder then Mom mixes a concoction of bacon grease and flour along with the glass powder. We spread the stuff on thin slices of stale bread and place them on a long board. Then we slide the baited board under the house where there are gaps in the rotten skirting. Mom figures the mice won't be able to resist this tasty treat and the glass granules will cause the mice to bleed internally and die. She assures me they will die a painless death.

A couple of days later we pull out the boards and it looks like most of the bread is gone, but the "tasty spread" is left intact. Oh well, it sounded like a good idea.

Mom keeps her traps set with fresh peanut butter and the odd dumb mouse still gets caught, but there hasn't been any obvious mouse poop for quite a while. I figure Mom must be starting to relax by now, but I am wrong.

We have visitors one evening, and one of the guests decides to rearrange some of the furniture—for better seating, I suppose. As he plunks down the old upholstered chair that Dad usually sits in, out pops a mouse. It runs across the living room floor and disappears into thin air. Upon a close examination, it looks like the mouse had been in the process of building a nest deep within the upholstery of the chair.

The guests all laugh, but Mom is totally mortified. She manages to hold it together until all the guests have left before flying into a rage. I have never seen my mom like this before. She picks up the heavy chair that was going to be home to a bunch of baby mice and single-handedly throws it outside. I had no idea my mom was so strong. It was all kind of scary. Dad says nothing.

By the next morning, Mom seems to have calmed down a little, but she issues Dad an ultimatum: "One more sign of a mouse in this house, and I'm moving out. So if you want us to continue living as a family, you better start looking for another place to live, real soon."

Dad makes a feeble attempt at nailing up a few slats to cover the gaps where the floor meets the walls, but he is not making any promises. I think he knows it's all pretty hopeless.

I have a feeling we'll be moving soon—probably right after school breaks for summer holidays. Mom has already started packing, even though we don't have another place just yet. I'm really going to miss Mr. Burton's farm.

I really like Mr. Burton and his lovelies. I love everything about this perfect little farm. I know our family really appreciates all the strawberries, raspberries, and free eggs. Where else could you eat apples right off the trees and gather walnuts along the driveway? Where else would squirrels pick hickory nuts for you? And, most precious, where else could you stuff yourself with luscious sweet cherries and fill a bowl in a few minutes? If it wasn't for the mice, this would be a perfect place to live, almost as good as Port Dalhousie.

A couple of weeks go by with no mention of moving, and I'm wondering and hoping that maybe Mom has had a change of heart; maybe there'll be no more mouse problems, and we can continue living here forever. And then, early one morning, there's an awful wail coming from Mom and Dad's bedroom. I rush to their room. Mom is hugging baby sister Alice, tears streaming down her face. I'm filled with dread, thinking something terrible must have happened to my little sister; maybe she's dead. Dad takes me to Alice's crib. He doesn't have to spell out what happened. Strewn amongst the blankets are bits of rubbery-looking stuff that could only have come from the shredded rubber nipple on Alice's milk bottle. The bottle is empty.

I find myself cursing under my breath. *"Goddamn those mice. I can't wait to get out of this stupid house."*

CHAPTER 5

Concord Avenue, 1941–1943

MY ITALIAN BUDDIES

I finished grade one with very mixed feelings. I did learn to read and write, but Woodland School wasn't the fun place I imagined it would be. So when my parents announced that we were moving, I was sort of glad. At least I wouldn't have to put up with Miss Smith anymore.

I'm really going to miss Mr. Burton and his perfect little farm, especially Lady and Godiva. Mom says, "We'll be back to visit often, and you can be sure that Mr. Burton and his lovelies won't forget you."

Mom is ready to move. She's eager to leave behind that mouse invasion that plagued our family for months. I suspect the main reason we're moving, though, is because Dad's work on the Queen E is finished and so is his reason for buying that beautiful dump truck. As construction work wound down, Dad was hoping to get enough local jobs to keep busy, but now he is ready to throw in the towel. Hauling stuff for local farmers doesn't pay much, and besides, this is mid-1941; the war machine is getting into full swing, so there are other options.

A number of our relatives are making good money at McKinnon's, and Dad was persuaded to apply. Because of the war, there is a shortage of men who are fit for hard work, so he is accepted real quick. His job is in the forge shop, next to the foundry where it's always super

125

hot. All day, he operates a multi-ton drop hammer that can forge an ingot of white-hot steel into almost any shape in a matter of seconds. The air is filthy, the noise is horrendous, and injuries are common. Dad hates his job, but the pay is good, and he recognizes that for the time being it will have to do.

These must have been tough times for my parents. No one knew how long the war would last, and Mom had to put aside any thought of moving back to Manitoba. Perhaps it was time to lay down roots and settle into this strange but comfortable corner of Canada.

Dad used his truck for the last time when we moved from Gregory Road to our new place in a quiet suburb of St. Catharines. He then trades in that beautiful truck for a brand-new 1941 Studebaker Champion. Wow! Our car sure stands out in this neighbourhood. Practically no one owns a car—certainly nothing like our classy-looking Studebaker. I shamelessly show it off to anyone who expresses an interest.

Nearly all our neighbours are Italian, some coming from Italy not so long ago and speaking little English. As far as I can tell, we are the only French family, but there are a few Polish people, so we don't feel totally out of place. Everyone is super friendly, and our family is happy to be moving into this tidy community of strangers.

Ours is a small bungalow on the corner of Concord and Leila. There are several sour cherry trees in our yard, and I'm thrilled that they're about ready for picking. Some find these cherries too tart, but I just love them. Dad says our yard was probably an orchard at one time. "It's a crying shame that precious fruit orchards keep getting mowed down to make way for more new homes," he says. "Where else in Canada does such a variety of fruit grow so plentifully?"

I am so happy that there are lots of boys around my age, and in no time, I am accepted as just another kid in the neighbourhood. A couple doors down Leila Street lives the Marcellus family. Mrs. Marcellus talks real loud, but she's a nice lady. She welcomes us to the neighbourhood by bringing over a huge bowl of spaghetti.

We learn that she has lots of kids, but they don't all live at home. Two of the boys are in the army, and gossip has it that one is in jail. Mrs. Marcellus is quite heavy, some call her fat but not to her face. She seems to sweat a lot, even though she wears loose-fitting dresses with no bra and she is always barefoot. Neighbours whisper that she is probably pregnant again, and they wonder why she would want another kid. After all, the latest one is still in diapers, and besides, they can't afford another kid. We often hear her yelling, sometimes real loud, and although I don't understand Italian, I soon learn the swear words. It seems like most of the scolding is directed at her boy Dino, who is a year younger than me. I like Dino, even though our friendship didn't start out so good.

I'm sitting on the back steps of our new home, sorting through a bunch of marbles and arranging them by size and colour when Dino happens by. "Wanna play alleys?" he asks. I don't know what he means, but before I know it, he digs a small hole in the ground and we are flipping marbles towards it with our thumbs.

The rules are pretty simple; they involve a lot of skill, and you have to make good decisions to win the other guy's marbles. When the round ends, we return each other's marbles, and oh my, this is a lot of fun!

"Wow!" Dino shouts. "I can't believe this is the first time you've played this game, Jules. You're super good at alleys. Wanna play another game?"

"Sure thing," I reply.

"How about we make the game more interesting," suggests Dino. "How about we play keepers this round?"

I reluctantly agree.

Well, one round leads to another, and pretty soon I've won all the marbles and Dino looks sad, and I'm feeling guilty. I offer to return his marbles when Dino says, "Wait a minute—I just found a few more marbles in my other pocket. Just one more round, okay?"

We continue to play for another hour, and now Dino has all the marbles. Slowly, it dawns on me. Dino is much better at this game than I am. He let me win that first round, just to suck me in. I've been fooled. Oh, well . . . I did learn how to play alleys, and I learned a lesson too.

I'm not sure why I hang out with Dino; we really don't have a lot in common. Maybe it's because we both like to explore, or maybe it's because we like to try fun things, even when our parents don't approve.

Smoking is one thing where we don't see eye to eye. Dino goes to a lot of trouble salvaging partially smoked cigarettes from his dad and his older brothers and lights up as soon as we are far enough from the watchful eyes of close neighbours. He offers me a puff, but I refuse.

It seems I have to keep explaining to Dino that smoking a stranger's soggy cigarette butt just does not appeal to me. "Besides, I don't want to get sick again like I did last year," I tell him.

Dino wants to hear more.

"It happened last fall, when people came over to our place to celebrate Thanksgiving," I begin. "After supper, all the men were sitting outside drinking beer and smoking cigars. I asked my dad if I could have a puff of his cigar. Dad says, 'You know, Jules, you're getting to be a pretty big kid; maybe you'd like to try your own cigar?' All the men are laughing. Sure—why not? I'm puffing away, thinking I must look pretty cool. Here I am, seven years old and I can smoke a cigar just like all the men. Well, it didn't take long. I started getting dizzy and feeling like I needed to vomit. Thank god I was able to stagger away to a private place before puking my guts out."

One evening, Dino comes over to my house, and in a hushed voice asks me to follow him. The destination is his Mom's garden shed across the street from where they live. He doesn't want anybody to see us entering the shed, so we approach from the back through a neighbour's yard. We crawl on our hands and knees and open the door just enough to squeeze in. Quietly, we close the door behind us.

Dino pulls out a brand-new pack of cigarettes with a picture of a camel on it. He expertly opens the cellophane wrapper and produces two crisp, white cigarettes and hands me one.

"That's very generous of you, Dino, but I don't want to get sick again, remember?"

"That only happens with cigars," Dino assures me. I didn't think to ask how he would know. Dino's family is too poor to afford cigars, and of course Dino's dad would never let him have a puff of anything, never mind a cigar all to himself.

I must admit this is kind of fun, puffing away trying to look cool, just like those guys you see in tobacco ads. We experiment with holding the cigarette different ways and we flick the ashes in a nonchalant manner just like the cool guys in the movies.

Dino is trying to teach me how to blow smoke rings, when: *CRASH!* The door explodes open, and there's Dino's dad, his eyes round with rage. "I thought the shed was on fire!" he screams, demanding to know where the cigarettes came from.

"Jules gave them to me," Dino stutters, panic written across his face.

Mr. Marcellus turns to me, and I freeze with fear. He picks up the cigarette package, examines it, and in a calmer voice orders, "Get the hell out of here, Frenchy."

The last scene I remember was Dino being lifted off his feet by his hair. I sail over the garden gate without opening it and am safe in my house in a flash. I try to act calm while my heart is thumping like mad. Even with the door closed I can hear poor Dino wailing and crying, and I'm ever so glad I don't have a dad like Mr. Marcellus.

The next day, I'm surprised to see Dino at my house around the usual time, and he wants to go for a walk. We are barely a block away and Dino pulls out a butt and lights up. *Wow, this is one nervy little guy,* I think to myself, *or maybe he's just loves to smoke.* Neither of us talks about the day before.

Between the Marcellus house and our house lives a friendly young couple, the Catalonis. They have a small baby and Mom keeps telling them how cute it is. I think the baby is ugly, so I have to wonder if mom is really serious. I have to agree with Mom, though, when she compliments the Catalonis on their lovely home. "And the yard, how do you keep it so neat? Ours is always so messy."

I know she's talking about my collection of junk that I use to make stuff with, but I don't say anything. The young mother graciously thanks mom but is quick to correct her about the house. Turns out they're just renting the main floor, while the owner is actually the old guy that we often see puttering around outside.

Mr. Sylvester, their landlord, lives in the basement by himself, and he never talks to anyone. He wears patched-up pants that are held up by red rubber suspenders that look suspiciously like there're made from inner tubes.

Like most Italians, Mr. Sylvester spends a lot of time in his garden, but occasionally we see him with his two-wheeled cart loaded with scrap lumber and dead tree branches. He cuts the salvage wood into short lengths with a handsaw and stores them all in perfect piles. Mrs. Catalonis says that Mr. Sylvester collects enough wood to heat the whole house all winter.

Once in a while, I peak through the vine-covered fence that separates our yards, and I take note of another of Mr. Sylvester's habits. Every day around noon, he pours himself a glass of wine and eats his lunch at a small table in a shady spot under a tree. This is always followed by a ritual involving cleaning his quirky corncob pipe and stuffing it with tobacco from a large tin. As the sweet smoke drifts in my direction, I am reminded of that sorry episode in Mrs. Marcellus' garden shed and the germ of an idea takes hold in my mind.

By the next day, this idea has grown into a detailed plan and I share it with Dino. He is so excited that he does a little happy dance and suggests we get started right away.

"Not so fast, Dino. If we are going to make our own corncob pipe, we are going to need a proper corncob. Got any ideas?" I ask.

Dino scratches his head for a moment. "Yeah, I think I do. Remember when we had that smoke in the garden shed? Remember all those big yellow cobs hanging from the ceiling—would one of those work?"

"Yeah, I remember. What the heck are they doing there, all dry and hard? How are you ever going to eat them?"

"There're not for eating, dummy," says Dino, and he goes on to explain how some of the bigger cobs are dried and kept for next year's seeds.

"That's out of the question, then. Your dad would never agree. Why even think about it?"

A couple of days go by. Dino comes over, he's all smiles as he pulls a gorgeous, yellow corn from under his shirt. I don't want to know how he got it. The dry corncob is as hard as wood. It looks like carving out the bowl for the tobacco will be a slow tedious job, but with my new pocketknife it should be possible. I experiment with the various blades on my knife and remove the core material one morsel at a time while Dino looks on.

Tedious as this job is, it's the stem that turns out to be the biggest challenge. The stem of a bought pipe is usually carved from hard wood and has a small hole through its length to carry the smoke from the bowl to your mouth. I'm thinking of using a fresh, maple sapling that has a soft pulpy centre, and I'm hoping to drill a hole all the way through this pulp. Twisting a length of coat hanger back and forth, it works to a certain depth but not deep enough to make a decent stem. I try heating the end of the coat hanger with a candle and plunging the hot wire into the pulp, and to my pleasant surprise the wire penetrates a little deeper. I repeat the process many times and eventually the hole is all the way through, and now we have the makings of a proper stem—just like the one on Mr. Sylvester's pipe.

Dino and I had planned to keep our corncob pipe a secret, but somehow a couple of our buddies have heard about it and they want to be there when we test it for the first time. Pietro knows of a remote spot with no people around. It's quite far, but we want this special occasion to be totally private.

Dino places his hat on the ground, and we huddle around in a tight circle as he dumps his collection of smelly cigarette butts into his sweaty hat. We all lend a hand removing the paper and ashes as best we can.

Since this was my idea, I shall be the first to test it out. I pack the salvaged tobacco into the bowl and tap it down with a small stick, just like Mr. Sylvester. As I hold the match to the tobacco, I'm surprised at how hard I must suck to draw the flame down. I immediately get a lungful of smoke and begin to choke and cough like mad. Dino grabs the pipe and proceeds to smoke it like this is something he's done all his life. He smiles and lets out a whoop and passes it on to the other guys.

The pipe is a huge success. All the guys are excited. My Italian buddies spend the next hour or so smoking, and they don't get sick. They don't even cough. I try a few more puffs, but I recognize this is just not my thing. I'm not sure what happened to the pipe-smoking after that. Some of the boys were planning on collecting cigarettes butts from the streets and sidewalks. Ugh! I just knew it would be a long time before I ever tried smoking again.

A few doors down Concord live the DeLillo family. Mr. and Mrs. DeLillo speak only Italian, but their two boys, Angelo and Cicero, speak pretty good English. Unlike the Marcellus house, their home is super neat and the yard is bursting with flowers and healthy-looking vegetables. Both parents are very strict and keep the boys busy, tending to the garden and all sorts of other chores. Whenever Angelo can get away, he comes to my house and we become good buddies. We are about the same age, and I am pleased to learn that after the summer holidays, we will be starting grade two together at St. Joseph's.

August days are typically hot and muggy in St. Catharines. Outside activities slow down, and even the hard-working Italian mamas stay indoors during the hottest afternoons. Meanwhile, Mr. DeLillo, who works for the City, has to work hard no matter how hot it is. He puts in ten-hour days, six days a week, installing sewer and water pipes with a pick and shovel. Angelo tells me how every day his dad comes home drenched with sweat and totally exhausted. He keeps telling his boys they better do good in school or they could end up just like him. Sundays, Angelo and his brother Cice have to be super quiet while his dad sleeps and rests all day.

After supper, as it cools down, kids from all over the neighbourhood gather in little groups and look around for something to do. Our favourite spot is just across the street from our house where light from a lamppost attracts both moths and the kids who are allowed to be out after dark. Sometimes a whole bunch of kids, including girls, gather under the lamppost and we play hide and seek or team tag. When it's just boys, we play a game that involves kicking around a small ball. It's a lot of fun, and we don't need a lot of space. Sometimes we wrestle, sometimes we just talk.

If we've had an active evening, chances are, someone will suggest that we make a trip to the bakery on Facer Street. Everybody checks their pockets for change, and if we have twelve cents between us we can get a loaf of crusty French bread. We try to time it so the day's last batch is about to come out of the oven. The smell is mouth-watering, and as we wait in line, we know we shall not be disappointed. As soon as we're out the door, the loaf gets ripped apart, so everybody gets a share and it's totally devoured before we get back to our lamppost.

One evening, as we count up our change to see if we have the needed twelve cents, Dino announces that today is his birthday.

"So how come you didn't invite us to your birthday party?" asks Mario.

"We never celebrate birthdays at my house," says Dino. Wow! I can't imagine that.

"But you get a present, don't you?" I ask.

"Nope," says Dino with a sad look on his face. "My dad says we can't afford such things."

"How about a cake? Your mom must bake a cake?" says Angelo.

"Nope," repeats Dino. All the guys are quiet for a while, trying to figure what to say. Everybody knows Dino's family is poor, but I guess nobody realized just how poor they are.

Finally, Pietro announces, "Well it looks like we have our twelve cents, let's head for the bakery."

Angelo asks me to hang back. He has an idea that he wants to run by me, but he doesn't want to share it with the others, at least not yet.

While our buddies are waiting in line for the customary loaf of bread, Angelo and I wander over to the pastry section, near the front of the bakery, trying to look cool.

Just like Angelo predicted, both clerks are busy at the back serving customers, and I watch them from a distance. I feel Angelo behind me doing something with my jacket. Seconds later, I feel a tap on my shoulder. That's the signal for me to cinch up my belt that is around the outside of my jacket. Slowly, ever so casually, we saunter out of the bakery and wait for our buddies outside.

As usual, we polish off the bread within minutes. Everybody is unusually quiet. Maybe we're all thinking of poor Dino. I'm still a bit skeptical that the Marcellus family could be so poor. Couldn't they even acknowledge Dino's birthday? Then again, I remember an incident from a few weeks ago that just astounded me.

Dino and I had been walking down Leila one afternoon, and there, parked on the sidewalk, was Dino's baby sister lying quiet in her stroller, sucking away on her bottle while her mom was digging potatoes from the garden. While I was taking a peek at the baby, Dino snatched the bottle from her little hands, ripped off the nipple, and gulped down the milk. The kid screamed, Dino took off, and I stood frozen like my feet were glued to the sidewalk.

Mrs. Marcellus came charging from the garden, yelling at Dino and throwing potatoes at him as he ran for all he was worth down the sidewalk. "Bad boy! Bad boy!" she kept repeating, and I had to wonder if she meant me or Dino or both of us. I also had to wonder if Dino was so deprived that he couldn't even have a glass of milk at home.

Anyway, Angelo has been walking close behind me, and as we approach our familiar lamppost, I feel that tap on my shoulder. I unbuckle my belt, and just like a magician pulling a rabbit from a hat, Angelo pulls out a gorgeous chocolate cake. The icing is a bit mushed, but it doesn't take away from the joy on Dino's face when he learns that this is his special birthday cake. I'm thinking, *Too bad we don't have candles.*

We sing "Happy Birthday," and Dino looks so happy. As I cut the cake into six equal pieces with my pocketknife, I point out to my buddies that the extra piece is for Dino.

I could be imagining it, but Dino's eyes look a bit watery as he thanks his bestest buddies. But then, my tough little Italian buddy could never admit that those just might be tears he's trying to hide.

"1941 Studebaker"   Source: public domain

SISTER ANNA MARIA

Through the 1940s, the primary school system in Ontario was divided between Catholic and Protestant denominations. It naturally followed that when it came time for me to attend school in St. Catharines, I would be enrolled at St. Joseph's, the only Catholic school in the neighbourhood. Mom had already met with Sister Superior and saw no need to accompany me on my first day. She was satisfied that Angelo, my new buddy, would be coming by, and together we would begin grade two together at St. Joseph's.

Along the way, Angelo fills me in on what to expect. "I'll introduce you to Sister Anna Maria and I'll show you the ropes," he says—whatever that means.

"How come you call her Sister when she isn't really your sister?" I ask.

"I don't know," says Angelo, "but that's what you're supposed to call the nuns, and you better not forget or you could be in trouble."

"So what's she like?" I ask.

"Oh, she's alright," says Angelo. "I think you'll like Sister Anna Maria." I had hoped for a more encouraging response. Is he holding something back? I sure hope Sister Anna Maria won't be as mean and cranky as Miss Smith, the grade one teacher I had at Woodland School.

I had no experience with nuns except for seeing them at Sunday Mass from time to time. I must say, I find those black outfits they wear kind of mysterious, even a bit creepy. I learn that this uniform is called a habit—*another strange word*, I'm thinking. Maybe if I could see their faces, they might look more friendly, but that black veil and those big white collars reveal only a small oval of impersonal expression. At church, they never look around, and the few times I've seen their faces, they have their eyes closed and they seem to be totally absorbed with clutching those strings of beads draped around their waists.

As Angelo and I get closer, I can see that St. Joseph's School is a solid looking, two-story brick building that stands out in this residential neighbourhood of modest homes. I immediately make comparisons with Woodland School, where I completed grade one just a couple months ago. To my mind it would be hard to beat the rustic charm of Woodland School with all those acres of green grass surrounded by a dense forest of giant trees. St. Joseph's has very little grass, and there are no trees at all. It does have plenty of flowers, though, and lush green shrubs. Everything is super tidy and has a freshly scrubbed look about it.

I head for the front entrance when Angelo stops me. "That door is just for big people," he says. "We have to use the side door, the one marked, 'BOYS'."

"Don't girls come to this school?" I ask. Angelo assures me they do, but they have to use the door on the other side of the building, the one marked, "GIRLS." This is weird. I wonder what other surprises await me.

I'm not sure what to expect as we bound up the short flight of stairs to the large foyer that extends the whole length of the school. The outside may be kind of plain, but I am not prepared for the heavenly scene that unfolds.

It's like entering a beautiful church. There are green ferns and flowers everywhere. Pictures of religious scenes line the walls, along with paintings of pious-looking people dressed in weird clothes. I think they're saints or something. They don't interest me much, but they give the impression that this is a special place.

In the centre of the foyer is a small statue of the Virgin Mary with candles burning at her feet. The candles give off an aroma much like the church. A feeling of excitement and anticipation washes over me. It's wonderful just to be in this bright place and to see all those happy faces. I notice that the kids come in all shapes and sizes, and all colours too.

Angelo pulls me away and suggests we go to our classroom; "Maybe Sister Anna Maria will be there."

If I had any misgivings, they are quickly dispelled. Sister Anna Maria greets us with a warm smile, and I'm liking her already. Even the snug-fitting collar and black shawl can't hide the fact that she is very pretty, and she is oh-so young. If it weren't for her black habit, she could easily be mistaken for one of the students.

"I'm so happy to see you, Angelo. I'm so glad to have you back in my class again," she says as she gives him a big hug. Angelo stares at the floor and blushes. *When is he going to introduce me?* I wonder. Sister Anna Maria turns to me. "Welcome to St. Joseph's, Jules. I know we are going to have a good year together." I suspect she's right, but I have to wonder: *How does she know my name?*

A cluster of eager kids gathers around Sister Anna Maria. We follow her upstairs to join the rest of the students. The space here is the same as the foyer downstairs, but not as fancy. There are ferns and flowers and plainer pictures on the walls and a piano at one end.

There's a buzz of excitement, and the noise level gets ever louder as the other sisters enter the room, each with an entourage of admiring students. One of the sisters, the oldest-looking one, raises her arm, and as if by magic, everyone becomes quiet. "I'm Sister Mary Rudolf," she announces. She must be the Sister Superior, I figure. She tells us a little about herself and how she is looking forward to getting to know each of us during the coming year. She introduces the other three sisters one by one and has us all laughing as she warns about the quirks and foibles of each of the nuns and what we can expect from them in the coming year. We sing a few songs and end by singing "O Canada." What happened to "God Save the King"? I much prefer "O Canada."

Back in our homeroom, the seating arrangements are sorted out and now it's time to get down to business. Sister Anna Maria addresses all her students in grades one and two. She starts out by explaining the importance of mutual respect, what it means and what is expected from each of us. She pauses long enough to make eye contact with every kid.

She writes on the blackboard a number of very important rules. "Break a rule and there will be consequences," she promises. I'm thinking, *Holy smokes!* This sister really means business. She's not just a young girl in a nun's habit. Sister Anna Maria is very pretty and oh-so sweet. I quickly fall in love with her, but I soon find out I am not alone.

It's a beautiful, sunny day. All my classmates are playing outside at recess when one of the girls spots Sister Anna Maria coming from the school to join us. She's never done this before. One of the girls shrieks with excitement and the rest all join in. The girls form a circle around our angelic sister, some stroking her habit, and a couple of nervy ones even hold her hand. The boys are shyer, but one thoughtful kid has picked a bunch of dandelions and presents her with a bouquet. I am annoyed that I didn't think of this first, but I fashion a chain necklace that I made from dandelion stems and she drapes it around her neck. By the time the bell rings, signalling the end of recess, Sister Anna Maria is smothered with flowers and dandelion necklaces and shameless love.

So eager am I to please that I excel at everything Sister Anna Maria teaches, getting top marks in every subject. I wish I could have remained in Sister Anna Maria's class forever, but of course that was not to be.

At the end of the school year, my parents are summoned to St. Joseph's to hear first-hand how their kid has performed. Sister Superior sits close by as Sister Anna Maria reads her report, ending with the recommendation that her top student, Jules Legal, be promoted from grade two to grade four. My parents seem a bit confused. Sister Superior intervenes to explain that Sister Anna Maria is recommending that Jules skip grade three and go directly into grade four. She is prepared to accept this recommendation provided it is agreeable with Mom and Dad.

No one asks what I think of skipping a grade. I think I would have been happier if I had to repeat grade two. That way I would have had Sister Anna Maria as my teacher for another year.

"St. Joseph's School"   Source: family photos

GUITAR LESSONS

A smiling young man with a guitar slung over his shoulder appeared at our door one morning. "I just want to play a few songs for you," he says, and before my parents can ask any questions, he begins strumming away. He is obviously quite good, and he sings with such gusto that his performance impresses even my dad. As far as I can tell, Dad has no appreciation for any kind of music. Sometimes he turns off a song my mom and I are listening to, on the radio so he can listen to the news. I'm sure he isn't being insensitive. He just doesn't understand how anyone could waste their time listening to music when it's time for the news.

Maybe he recognizes this flaw in his makeup; maybe he wants to ensure that I do not inherit this shortcoming, so he lets the young man carry on with the real reason he is here.

"Absolutely," the young man asserts. "Every child has the potential to become a great musician. Within a few weeks, with proper lessons, young Jules here could be making beautiful music. Just think how impressed all your friends and relatives will be when they hear him playing the latest songs, and it might even lead to a wonderful career where the pay is good and your hands never get dirty." In our working-class neighbourhood, it is every parent's dream for their child to get a job less menial than their own.

I don't remember my dad asking if this was something I wanted, but I remember the salesman making his final pitch.

"And so, Mr. Legal, if you subscribe to a year's worth of lessons, my boss will allow me to give you a free guitar."

Never one to pass up a deal, my dad signs the contract, and I am committed to an hour of guitar lessons every Saturday for the following year.

The teachers are a cheery husband-and-wife team who do their best to make musicians out of every student, no matter how little innate talent they have to work with. Mrs. Ford is my instructor. Each week, she hands out a new song sheet, expecting us to play it back the following Saturday. This requires at least a couple hours of practice, and I resent the precious time it takes away from playing with my buddies. I particularly resent when my parents are entertaining guests and I am summoned to put on a show. Invariably, my audience loses interest within a minute or two and I know darn well I'm not impressing anyone.

The fact that I learn to read music after just a few lessons really amazes my dad. When he learns that I can write the notes after listening to a new song (never mind what it sounds like), he thinks this is pure genius.

When the year is up, I recognize that I will never be a real musician and I want to quit. "But, you can read music," Dad protests, "and besides, to me you sound pretty good." Dad insists I keep taking lessons, at least for one more year. He sweetens the deal by promising me a quarter each week, which I am free to spend any way I want.

This works out just great. I am always hungry after the morning music lesson, so I use ten cents from my quarter to buy lunch. The menu is always the same. I stand in line near the corner of James and

King where a guy in a truck does a booming business just selling French fries. Loaded with lots of salt and vinegar, they are absolutely delicious.

Then I continue to St. James Street, where there are two movie theatres located close to each other. I just love movies, and sometimes they both look so good that it is agonizing trying to decide which one to see. Saturday afternoon, both charge only fifteen cents, and I am free to park my guitar with the projectionist whichever theatre I choose.

More often I go to the Grenada, where they usually show cowboy movies. Both theatres have an impressive confectionery that is impossible to ignore. At times, I have to use my streetcar dime to indulge my weakness. This means almost an hour's walk home, but when the liquorice craving strikes, it's too powerful to resist.

I had been taking lessons for nearly two years when one Saturday morning, Mr. Ford pops in to listen to our class. He picks out a couple of us and asks that we come see him after the lesson. I suspect that he might want to tell us we are wasting our time and that more lessons would be for naught, but no, quite the opposite. He tells us we are a cut above the other students and asks if we are interested in joining a group of volunteers in a giant string ensemble that he and Mrs. Ford are organizing.

The plan is to travel as a group to various halls and churches and put on a series of Christmas concerts. Proceeds are to go to some worthy charities. Of course we would have to rehearse, and that means giving up Sunday afternoons for as long as it takes to put on a professional performance.

Mom and Dad think this is a wonderful idea, so the following Sunday, I dutifully attend the first rehearsal. I was told there would be about thirty students, but I am shocked to see such big kids. Maybe "kids" is not the right term, because they are mostly teenage boys and girls towering above me, and there is no doubt I'm the smallest in the group.

I am also amazed at the variety of instruments. There are violins, Spanish guitars, steel guitars, mandolins, ukuleles, and even a couple of cellos. I had no idea that Mr. and Mrs. Ford were such versatile musicians. I am struggling to learn just one instrument, and here they are teaching at least six, and now they are attempting to create an orchestra with a bunch of amateur kids—a "string ensemble," Mr. Ford calls it.

During that first rehearsal, we sound just awful. The Fords are ever so patient, but they can also be quite demanding. Bit by bit, we get better. Midway through the afternoon, Mrs. Ford calls a break, and we are treated to hotdogs, cookies, and soft drinks, and Mr. Ford tells us what a fine job we are doing. To my surprise, this is turning out to be lots of fun.

I lost track of how many practices we worked through, but by the end of November, Mr. and Mrs. Ford pronounce us ready to hit the road. We travel by bus to theatres all over the Niagara region and we are well received everywhere we go. We play a wide variety of music, but there is one song in particular that seems to move the audience, some even to tears.

The song expresses the deep emotions that lovers must feel upon reuniting after a long separation. It was made popular by Bing Crosby, but one of our senior students can sing it just as good. While he croons, a lovely young lady performs a solo dance. At the end, they embrace and exchange a long passionate kiss.

It's Been a Long, Long Time

Kiss me once, then kiss me twice, then kiss me once again
It's been a long, long time
Haven't felt like this, my dear, since I can't remember when
It's been a long, long time

You'll never know how many dreams I dreamed about you
Or just how empty they all seemed without you
So kiss me once, then kiss me twice, then kiss me once again
It's been a long, long, time

The grand finale is my favourite, not because it is the last song, but because it features a composition that is meant for the steel guitar. We play softly at first with a moderate tempo, sounding like a typical mellow Hawaiian tune. Gradually we pick up the pace and dramatically increase the volume. At this point, a sexy young dancer bursts onto the stage wearing a fake grass skirt made of shimmery, yellow cellophane and a skimpy top. She has shiny blond hair down to her waist and a lei around her neck and she is barefoot. While our steel guitars furiously play the "Hawaiian War Chant," she dances a fast-paced hula, wriggling her hips like crazy.

Being in the middle of the front row, I am perfectly positioned to fully appreciate her talents. Occasionally, our "Hawaiian Princess" comes so close that her grass skirt brushes against me, and my imagination goes into overdrive. I can easily picture being stranded on a remote Pacific island just the two of us, living happily in a little grass shack and not caring if we are ever rescued.

I struggle with lessons for another year, and I am finally starting to show promise. I'm even beginning to enjoy playing the guitar until one fateful day when . . . everything changes.

Some relatives from out West came by for a visit. Near the end of the evening one of them, who was quite inebriated, suggests that I play the guitar for him. I decline, but he keeps insisting. Finally, my dad steps in and commands, "Jules, play the damned guitar." I refuse. Dad takes the instrument and throws it outside in the snow. I never played another note, and the subject never came up again.

Could I have been another Les Paul? Not very likely, but I guess we'll never know for sure. One thing I do know is that I felt bad about disappointing my dad and wasting all that hard-earned cash.

"Jules and his guitar"   By: Simone Legal

MY BUDDY JACKIE

Jackie was a full-grown fox terrier when I bought him from the pound for $2.50. He was my first dog, and over the next few years, we shared a bond that only a boy and his dog can fully understand.

I had saved all my nickels and dimes, even pennies, for months with the naive belief that this was the only obstacle to my owning a dog of my own. When I had accumulated about $2.00, I shared this yearning with my parents. They were none-too-pleased since, only a few years earlier, our family dog had attacked my sister Juliette, biting her in the face and causing a lot of trouble. Shortly after, it disappeared and was never seen again. Maybe that's why they didn't want to hear about getting another dog.

Ultimately, they relented, but Mom laid down a bunch of conditions. "It's got to be a boy dog. I don't want to be surprised with a bunch of puppies that nobody wants. And he's got to be shorthaired—I don't want some hairy beast shedding bushels of hair all over the place. And you're the one who's going to feed him and water him, and you're the one who's going to clean up when he poops or makes a mess."

It came as quite a shock when I first entered the town animal pound. I'm not sure what I was expecting, but I quickly realized that this was actually a prison for cats and dogs, and the whole place smelled pretty bad. The cats were quiet enough, but the dogs were either barking and jumping crazily at the steel bars or they were slinking at the back of their cages, fearful and silent. There was, however, one that stood out, at least in my eyes. He was black and white, kind of medium-built but muscular and sturdy. Mom liked the idea that he was male and shorthaired.

The attendant told us he was a fox terrier who had arrived just this morning and his name was Jackie. Jackie stood quiet and defiant, unafraid to look me in the eye. I could almost hear him saying, "I don't belong with all those silly dogs. Get me out of here."

It was love at first sight. It didn't occur to me that this wonderful feeling could be so one-sided. As we left the pound, Jackie strained at the leash, trying his best to get away. I was certain all that was needed was to give him good food and shower him with tender loving care and he would soon become part of our family.

After about a week of being kept indoors or tied up outside, I was confident that he no longer harboured any urges to escape. I was wrong. The instant I untied Jackie, he was gone. I ran after him, but it was no use; he could run so much faster, and in seconds, he disappeared around the corner. I was devastated; a feeling of profound sorrow swept over me as I tried to imagine what life would be like if I was never to see Jackie again.

My mom tried consoling me to no avail. Finally, Dad came home, and in his typical calm fashion, assured me there was no problem. All we had to do was go back to the pound and they would still have the particulars of where Jackie used to live, and he was right. I was to witness this remarkable quality in my dad countless times as I grew up.

As we pulled up to the address given by the pound attendant, I had a queasy feeling that there must be a mistake. The ramshackle house was barely visible from the street. In this tidy neighbourhood, it was the only place totally overrun with trees, shrubs, and weeds. Vines engulfed the front porch, and there was no sign of life. Dad stayed in the car as I went to knock at the door. As I stepped onto the porch, my presence was detected immediately and announced by ferocious yet familiar barking. This was indeed the right place.

The waiting was almost unbearable as the only sound came from Jackie's non-stop barking. Finally, a frail, elderly black man opened the door with Jackie continuing to bark in the background. We both tried to hush him, but Jackie kept up the commotion until the old man threatened with his cane. Jackie finally stopped, and the wrinkled old man apologized for the rude reception and introduced himself.

"Thomas Jefferson," he said. "Just call me Tom." He explained that Jackie was normally a good dog and would still be living with him, but his health had gotten real bad, and he felt he could no longer look after him properly. The old man turned his attention and explained to Jackie how he wished it wasn't so, but Jackie couldn't live here no more. "This here boy is your new boss now, and you best be goin' with him." Jackie growled barely audible protestations as my leash was latched to his collar. I thanked Mr. Jefferson profusely and dragged Jackie forcibly to the car.

The following week was hard for both Jackie and me. I was desperate to make Jackie my friend, but it was obvious he wanted to go back to his old home. I kept him confined indoors and treated him with lots of good food and attention. Despite all my efforts, one day, Jackie saw his chance and bolted through the door. This time, though, I knew where he would be. I didn't feel quite as bad as before, but I did wonder: Would Jackie ever let me be his friend?

Since my dad wasn't home, I set off on foot to where I knew Jackie would be. I marvelled at the mysterious powers he must possess to be able to navigate the long, complicated route to his original home in a distant suburb. As I approached the decrepit old house from a different direction than the previous week, the yard no longer looked so foreboding. The profusion of trees, shrubs, and weeds now appeared as a green sanctuary from the burning sun and oppressive heat.

Through a tangle of vines, I spotted Mr. Jefferson with another elderly black man. They were seated at a small table with a jug of lemonade, and sleeping soundly at their feet was Jackie. Mr. Jefferson greeted me warmly and introduced me to his brother George. The moment I uttered a word, Jackie awoke, peered at me, and wagged his tail. I was absolutely thrilled and relieved, for I had visions of Jackie being hostile towards me. Mr. Jefferson pointed to a chair. "Sit yourself down awhile and have a glass of lemonade. Best to give Jackie time to adjust."

I sat for what seemed like an eternity. Finally, Mr. Jefferson took my leash and clipped it to Jackie's collar. Once more he spoke to Jackie in a firm, but gentle tone. "Jackie, you gots to get it through your head that you can't live here no more. You gots a new boss now, and I know that you'll be happy with this here boy. Now go." I thanked Mr. Jefferson and his brother George, and together Jackie and I began our long, hot trek home.

The whole way back, Jackie took every opportunity to pee on every pole and every fire hydrant. I imagined that this was Jackie's way of marking his way home for future reference, just like Hansel and Gretel did with their breadcrumbs. I marvelled at how he could have found his way home the first time, before he'd had the opportunity to mark every pole along the way. I was left to wonder; maybe he had marked every pole and every fire hydrant in St. Catharines and beyond. Quite possibly, he had marked enough places to get him home from any place on earth.

Jackie made no further attempts at returning to his original home, and soon he was aggressively defending our property on Concord and several adjacent neighbours as well. He hated all dogs with a passion, and if any had the nerve to step onto his perceived property, he wasn't content to just growl or bark. He would attack with such ferocity that every dog in the neighbourhood would steer completely clear of Jackie's domain.

One day, I spotted a stranger to the area walking towards our place with a huge Great Dane. Too late—Jackie had spotted this interloper and was already running towards him. To my great relief, he didn't attack immediately as was his custom. I told myself that he recognized this dog was at least five times his own size and perhaps he should be a little careful. The Great Dane was not on leash, and despite the owner's urging to move on, it stopped right in front of our house. Jackie growled menacingly. The hair on his back and around his neck stood stiff, giving it the appearance of a lion's mane. He slowly strutted around the Great Dane who stood stock-still and silent. His owner seemed amused and moved out of the way, likely thinking this little fox terrier was about to get the thrashing of his life. I screamed at Jackie, who was baring his teeth and foaming at the mouth.

I had never seen Jackie like this, and I admit I was scared too. My hope was that Jackie would recognize the folly of taking on this giant and let it go. Then Jackie did something that surprised us all. He slowly strutted under the mid-section of the Great Dane, his hackles scraping the big dog's underbelly. He then proceeded to strut under the big dog's loose, hanging jowls. In a flash, the big dog clamped his teeth around Jackie's neck and hoisted him into the air. He shook Jackie's body as if it were a stuffed toy, and tossed him several feet towards me. Jackie lay still. I was sure he was dead. I bent down to examine him, a mix of emotions washing over me, when suddenly, Jackie stood up and gave himself a shake like he does after a swim. He looked around, blinked a few times, and spotting the Great Dane some distance down the street, he began growling and scrambling to attack. This time I was ready. I grabbed Jackie's collar and hung tight with both hands. The feisty, angry little dog dragged me some distance along the sidewalk and didn't stop struggling until the Great Dane was out of sight.

I took Jackie into the house and fed him his supper, which he ate with great gusto, and then he promptly fell asleep. As I watched over him, my admiration for his fearless bravery was tempered by the realization that Jackie was, after all, just a dog with a poorly developed instinct for survival. If we were to be close buddies like I had planned, I would have to be more vigilant to ensure he didn't get killed.

Over time we became much more than friends. We developed a bond that only a young boy and a dog perfectly suited to one another can understand. We went everywhere together. I can't say Jackie always followed me, because he was usually in the lead and seemed to sense exactly where I planned to go.

Most times he waited when I called him, but I guess some scent trails were just too interesting, and he forged ahead, paying no heed to the rest of the world around him. When I called and tried to stop him, he might turn his head and look at me for a moment; other times he ignored me completely. It became frustratingly obvious that Jackie had a mind of his own. One day something in the distance caught his attention, and despite my frantic yelling, he continued running. As he was disappearing out of sight, my human buddy, Angelo, let go a loud whistle blast and Jackie stopped in his tracks. Not only did he stop, but he also waited obediently until we caught up to him.

I was determined to learn to whistle just like my pal Angelo. Night after night, I would stand in front of a mirror trying hard to tighten my lower lip against my teeth while shaping my tongue into a "V" and letting go with a sharp blast of air, all to no avail. And then, one day, wonder of wonders, a sound came out. I kept practicing in front of that mirror, spraying it with spit and increasing the volume every day until I could whistle almost as loud as Angelo.

My other buddies were envious of our whistling, but Angelo suggested we shouldn't teach them this special skill. This would be our secret signal that only the two of us, as best buddies, would share. We made a pact that if ever one of us got into trouble, that whistle would be the signal for the other to come to the rescue. Since Angelo and I were together most of the time, I can't recall if it ever served its avowed purpose, but it proved invaluable in calling for Jackie.

The moment I finished school at the end of the day, I would sound off with a few powerful whistle blasts, and sure enough, even though home was a couple blocks away, Jackie would appear in a matter of minutes. We rolled around on the ground in a mock fight. I would attempt to pin him down. He would ultimately break free and tug and tear at my clothes, and the fight would end in a draw. A race for home followed, and Jackie always won.

THE KOWALSKI BROTHERS

We've been living on Concord Avenue for over a year now, and although I found no problem making friends with the Italian boys in the neighbourhood, it wasn't so easy for my mom. The Italian ladies are friendly enough, but few could speak English, and of course, no one spoke a word of French. With so little in common, I'm sure our family must appear a bit different, but I really like it here.

A Polish family lives down the street, and they don't seem to fit in the community at all. With their blondish hair and blues eyes, the Kowalski's certainly look different, but it's their quiet, less social nature that seems to bother our Italian neighbours. "What do those people do all day? We never see them outside," they say.

Mom suspects that our family may also be the butt of idle gossip. "Busy-bodies," she calls them. Dad doesn't seem to notice any of this and probably wouldn't care if he did.

Mr. and Mrs. Kowalski have two boys, Joe and Walter. On the rare occasion when my mom or dad has bumped into the brothers, they are always so polite. "Good afternoon, Mr. Legal," they say, or "Good morning, Mrs. Legal, hope you're having a nice day." Mom is impressed.

"How come your Italian buddies never say anything like that?" she asks. "They don't even say 'thank you' when I give them a cookie or a piece of cake."

When the brothers do venture outdoors, they are always together, and they always seem to be in a hurry. I get the impression that they may be a bit scared of the Italian boys, so it comes as a surprise one day when Walter shows up, alone, at my house and asks if I would like to come to his place and meet his parents.

Mr. and Mrs. Kowalski are really nice people, and no sooner am I in the house then they insist that I have lunch with them. The food is a little different from what I'm used to, but it's not bad. Brother

Joe appears, and before Walter can introduce us, he shakes my hand firmly, just like an adult would. Mind you, Joe looks like an adult. He's taller than his dad and just as sturdy looking. His voice is so deep; it's hard to believe he is just fifteen. "So, you're the French kid from down the street," he says knowingly.

Walter, who is about my age, suggests we go downstairs and see their shop. The basement is full of complicated-looking machinery, all well organized and spotless, just like the rest of the house. Exotic woodworking tools hang along one wall, each in its proper place. Walter shows me a couple of professional-looking hockey sticks. "Joe made these," says Walter. Joe shows me the baseball bats he makes on their wood lathe. I am super impressed, and I let Joe know.

"They're not that hard to make," says Joe modestly. "The hard part is getting the right wood. Tomorrow, right after church, me and Walter are going on a hike to the Burgoyne Bush to see what we can find."

"Want to come with us?" suggests Walter. "We'll pack a lunch for you," he adds.

"Can I bring my dog, Jackie?"

And so the next day, the four of us are on our way. Right from the start, I sense this isn't going to be the leisurely, pleasant hike I had in mind. Joe has long legs and he walks really fast. He doesn't seem to care that Walter and I have to regularly break into an awkward trot just to keep up. It's obvious that Joe knows this, but he won't slow down and he won't stop for a break.

After a mile or so, we come to a railway crossing, and parked on the tracks is a freight train with hundreds of boxcars just sitting there. I'm kind of glad, thinking this will give us a break, but that's not how Joe sees it.

"Son of a bitch," he declares. "I'll bet those stupid train operators have stopped for lunch." Without hesitation, he hops over the boxcar coupling to the other side of the tracks.

"Come on, come on," Joe taunts. "We could be here all day." We wait a few minutes and Joe starts yelling again. "If you pussies

153

are too scared to cross over like I did, why don't you crawl under-neath instead?" Walter admits that he's scared, and I'm debating if I should go, but what to do with Jackie? We wait a few more agonizing minutes. "Well, I'm not waiting any longer," Joe declares and starts walking away.

"Wait, wait," shouts Walter, in obvious panic, "I'm coming, I'm coming, Joe." He starts crawling under the boxcar coupling that Joe had jumped over so effortlessly.

Walter gets halfway across when there's a mighty crash followed by a clattering of metal on metal that ripples down the length of the train. The cars start inching ahead, and Walter freezes in a crouched position. "Duck, Walter, duck," Joe orders. And just as the first set of axles are about to hit him in the back of the head, Walter ducks. He lies facedown on the rail bed and puts his hands over his head. The axles go past without harm. *Whew*!

As the train slowly picks up speed, I'm thinking if Walter will just keep his head down and stay put, he'll probably be okay, but that's not what brother Joe has in mind.

"Move it, for Christ's sake, move, move, move it right now!" Joe screams in his deep, powerful voice. Walter finally obeys and starts crawling like mad in the same direction as the train.

"Gimme your arm," Joe commands. "Gimme your arm," he repeats over and over, but Walter is intent on frantically crawling on his hands and knees, ever faster, as the train picks up speed. It's now moving slightly faster than Walter, and the gap between Walter and the next set of wheels is getting shorter. This is all so horrible. Jackie is barking like mad, and brother Joe is yelling louder and louder. Finally, Walter stops crawling and thrusts out his arm over the track. Oh no—in seconds those steel wheels will cut Walter's arm off, or maybe something worse. I can't bear to watch.

I don't know how long my eyes were closed, but I felt compelled to check why Jackie's barking stopped and why Joe is no longer yelling.

Through the intermittent spaces between the wheels, I can make out both Kowalski brothers and I dare to hope that Walter will be okay.

The train seems to take forever, but finally it passes and Jackie and I quickly cross the tracks. Thank god—Walter looks okay, but he is sobbing and shaking like mad. Brother Joe is holding him in his arms and trying to comfort him.

I guess Joe's idea worked. I learned that when Walter finally stuck out his arm, Joe was able to yank Walter out from under the train just before the wheels passed by. Wow! I shudder to think what a horrible tragedy this could have been. I can't remember how long we sat there by the tracks, but eventually Walter quit shaking and sobbing and we were on our way again. Joe is walking slower now, and I am grateful.

The Burgoyne Bush is our destination, but Joe wants to check out the city dump first, "Just to see if there are any treasures to be found," he says.

Jackie has been straining on his leash for some time now, letting me know he wants his freedom. The moment I unclip him, he makes a beeline for a mountain of rotting grass clippings. "From the golf course," Joe figures. Jackie is digging like mad, almost disappearing into the smelly stuff. Finally, he emerges with some poor animal wriggling in his jaws. Jackie shakes his head vigorously and deposits a dead rat at my feet then returns to the pile.

Meanwhile, Joe has climbed to the top of the pile and is jumping up and down yelling like a madman. More rats come out and scurry around aimlessly. "Why don't they just run away?" I wonder. Joe is now busy throwing some lethal weapons that I have never seen before. They slice deep into the rats' bodies, spreading blood all over the place. "Throwing knives," Walter explains. "Joe makes them from used hacksaw blades that Dad brings home from work."

I watch in mute amazement as Jackie and Joe continue killing rats. They seem to be loving every minute of this carnage. How disgusting! Time to pull Jackie away before one of Joe's deadly knives slices into him. "I'm going home," I tell the boys.

"Wait, you haven't seen Burgoyne Bush yet," says Joe. "I'll be right with you. Just have to wipe the blood off my knives." Walter assures me that I will really like Burgoyne Bush, so we wait for Joe to finish his messy business.

On the way there's a sludge pond that we have to check out. "There won't be any rats there," Joe promises. As we approach, I can see why. All around the pond there is not a living thing in sight—not even a blade of grass, only piles of rusty steel littering the barren, yellow ground. The pond itself looks quite neat with clear turquoise coloured liquid that looks mysterious but smells real bad. "Don't touch the water, it's full of acid and poison stuff," Joe warns.

On the way, Joe had spotted an open, shallow steel tank. It looks like an oversize washtub, except that this tub is square, about the size of a kitchen table. He presses Walter and me to help him drag it a couple hundred yards to the pond. Joe wants to launch this rusty piece of junk. "Just to see if it floats," he says.

Of course it floats. Now he proclaims it to be a landing craft like the army uses to land soldiers onto hostile beaches overseas. He jumps into the rusty tank and paddles around the toxic pond, shouting "Geronimo!" I don't know what that means, but it does look like fun and it takes little persuasion for us to join him.

We get only a few feet out into the pond when I realize that this was a really dumb idea. The tank has a small leak, and our boots are getting wet, but that's not my main concern. I notice that the top lip of the tank is only a couple of inches above the waterline. What if we tip?

"Please take me back, Joe," I plead. Joe ignores me. Jackie is tied to a piece of rusty junk on the shore, barking like crazy. I thought he might have more concern for a dog than for me and his little brother. "Jackie is going nuts," I tell him, "please take me back." Walter is shaking with fear, but curiously he says nothing. I'm sure he is also well aware that if we should tip, we'll all be goners. None of us know how to swim, but even if we did, how far would we get in this god-awful stuff?

Walter is shaking real bad, almost as bad as when Joe pulled him out from under that train, and he's beginning to sob. I sure hope he doesn't panic. One wrong move and it's game over. Our eyes are tearing up from the fumes. Joe finally relents and starts paddling back. *Whew!*

As we walk away from this desolate place, I breathe a bit easier. I shudder to think of the kind of death we would have suffered if we had tipped into that sludge pond. I can vividly imagine thrashing around in that acid water, my skin burning like it's on fire. At some point I would run out of breath and be forced to suck in this poison. I feel my heart pounding. I better just quit thinking about it; after all, it's a beautiful day, we are safe, and soon we'll be in the Burgoyne Bush.

Burgoyne Bush does not disappoint; the woods are absolutely lovely, even more beautiful than that forest I used to walk through to get to Woodland School. Best of all, there's a charming little brook making burbling music as it meanders over and around boulders and stones. The water is perfectly clear and we don't hesitate to drink our fill. I am fascinated watching the small fish swimming about in the quieter pools.

We barely finish our lunch before Joe commands, "Let's go, guys." I would like to stay here all day, but I don't object. I know that Joe is intent on finding some suitable wood to make baseball bats. Oh well—I'll be coming back real soon, but certainly not with Joe.

So now Joe wants us to be on the lookout for a particular type of tree. "It's got to be maple," he tells us, "with no knots. Also, I would prefer a slow-growing tree with dense growth rings."

How the heck can you tell a slow-growing tree from a fast-growing one? I don't ask. I will just quietly look around and take in the magic of these beautiful woods.

Late in the afternoon, Joe has found his prize and he whittles it down with his hatchet, just like he's sharpening a humungous pencil. It is a perfectly healthy maple about twice as fat as a baseball bat and almost as tall as our house. A few feet have no knots or branches, so Joe figures he can make at least two bats from this tree. Seems kind of wasteful to me, but I guess there are lots of other trees like it. I want to watch when Joe makes those baseball bats; maybe he'll let me try cutting wood on his lathe. That would be really cool.

We're on our way home, and I'm getting mighty tired. I'll bet Walter is too, but neither of us will admit it. Meanwhile, Joe seems just as energetic as ever, and he wants to show me one more neat place. It's one of the abandoned locks from the old Welland Canal, and I must say it does look interesting, with crumbling concrete and rusting steel machinery, a bit like the one in front of our first apartment in Port Dalhousie. This is another one of those places I want to explore in more detail someday, again without Joe.

Water is rushing through the ancient gates. It's hard to imagine that, years back, boats routinely passed through them on their way to and from Lake Erie. One set of these giant gates is partly open with a small gap in the middle.

I can't believe what I'm seeing. Joe has clambered over the rubble and now he's climbing the tall gate as well. It is only a couple feet wide, and there is Joe, walking along the top with no guardrail. When he gets to the gap between the gates, he hesitates. I'm sure he must realize that if he fell onto that concrete rubble below, he'd be dead. I'm thinking only a crazy person would do that.

"Geronimo!" he yells as he jumps across the gap then calmly continues to the opposite side of the stream where Walter and I are watching and waiting in disbelief. I'm thinking, *This guy really is nuts.* "Your turn," he mocks, knowing full well, me and Walter won't be following.

Joe directs us to an old railroad bridge a short distance upstream. This crossing looks a lot safer, but I'm still a bit nervous. The timbers supporting the rails are spaced about a foot apart, giving us a clear view of the stream and the ground below. I know the gap between the timbers is probably too narrow to fall through, but it looks awfully far to the bottom and Jackie could easily slip, so I snap on his leash.

"Hey, this is kind of fun," I tell Walter as we gingerly make our way across the long bridge.

"Yeah, as long as a train doesn't suddenly appear," he replies. He's got a point; the bridge is barely wide enough for a train. "If a train came, what would we do? Where would we go?" asks Walter. I must admit I never thought of that.

"I'm fairly certain trains don't use this bridge anymore," I assure Walter.

"Then how come the tracks are so shiny?" Walter shoots back. They don't look that shiny to me, but we keep our eyes and ears open and we quicken our pace across the weathered old timbers. I try not to look down at the rubble-strewn ground below.

■ ■ ■

"I was just starting to worry," Mom scolds as I walk in the door.

"Sorry, Mom, I know I'm late, but those Kowalski brothers sure like to hike, and they wanted to show me all sorts of neat things. And you would love the Burgoyne Bush. What beautiful woods, a bit like the old-growth forest near Woodland School."

"That's okay," says Mom, "I didn't fret too much; I knew you were in good hands with Walter and his big brother, Joe. They're such nice boys. You can tell us all about it over supper when your dad gets home."

Uh-oh, I'm thinking, *that could be awkward.* There is a lot to talk about, but I may just have to skip a few details.

SISTER JOSEPHINE

I just love St. Joseph's School. I can't say why exactly. In part, I suppose because it is small and intimate. There are only four classrooms, all much the same, one long wall dominated by windows with oodles of plants and flowers and artwork everywhere. The whole school is always spotless, and it smells nice. Of course all this does not just happen; it is lovingly created and maintained by the devoted Sisters of St. Joseph. I appreciate how hard our dear sisters work, and I do my best to earn their approval. I consider them super smart and a bit mystical as they swish around in their black robes.

After Sister Anna Maria, I thought there could never be another teacher quite as perfect, but it turns out Sister Josephine is great too. She teaches grades three and four, so I will only have her for one year. Sister Josephine is older than Sister Anna Maria, and not as pretty, but she is always jolly and quick to laugh. Some kids call her "Sister Jo." She doesn't seem to mind, but I shall call her Sister Josephine. I grow to really like my new Sister.

About once a month, Sister Josephine takes us on an outing—"field trips," she calls them. I don't know how much we learn from these field trips, but they are always fun. One in particular stands out.

It's early fall, that magical time when all the leaves are turning multiple shades of brown, yellow, and red. Fall is my favourite season and I was pleased to learn that others feel the same. We were nearing the end of a particularly beautiful afternoon when Sister Josephine declared that it is just too beautiful to be staying indoors. "Who would like to go for a hike through the woods tomorrow? she asks. Everyone cheers. Does anybody have an idea of where we should go?"

"Burgoyne Bush!" I shout without raising my arm for permission to speak. To my surprise, Sister Josephine agrees. Sister Josephine has never been to Burgoyne Bush, but she knows about it and is eager to see it for herself.

"And so, class, tomorrow bring a lunch and something to drink and we'll make a day of it," she suggests.

The next day is also crisp and sunny. The whole class follows as I lead the way. I neglected to tell Sister Josephine that we have to trespass across a private golf course where we could get kicked off if we are spotted. I also forgot to mention that we have to cross a creek where the water is knee-deep and will be ice-cold this time of year. Thankfully, there's a bridge. Mind you, it isn't much of a bridge.

It's actually a single log spanning the creek. My buddies and I have practiced our balancing skills to the point where we can cross without falling into the water—at least, most of the time.

For those not used to such things there are several long poles, conveniently left near the bridge, to assist hikers who don't trust their balancing skills. It is meant to be used like a long crutch, and I assumed that everybody would know how to use it.

"You just stick the pole in a firm spot on the bottom of the creek and inch along with your feet,". "Then you move the pole to a new position." That part is a bit tricky, but none of the kids have a problem, and neither does Sister Josephine. The whole class cheers as Sister Josephine, firmly clutching the pole, makes her way gingerly across without falling into the creek. I shudder to think how she would have managed with a soaking wet robe and no dry change of clothes.

Burgoyne Bush is even more beautiful than usual with all the trees wearing their fall coats. Clusters of crisp brown and yellow leaves are beginning to form a cosy blanket at their feet. Everybody is totally impressed, and a few ask Sister Josephine, "When can we come again?"

Strange question, I think. *I come here all the time, and I wouldn't think of asking anyone's permission.*

I boast to Sister Josephine that Burgoyne Bush could be equally beautiful in the spring when the spring flowers are in bloom. "You should see the trilliums in spring. Last year there were so many they formed a colourful carpet that covered the whole forest floor." I assure Sister Josephine that if we do another field trip in the spring, I'll try to find a less challenging route.

Sister Josephine is such a good sport. Another time, she takes us to Port Weller Beach, where we are free to spend the day splashing around and building sand castles. Of course Sister Josephine can't wear a swimsuit like the rest of us; she has to keep wrapped up in that suffocating, black robe, which must be super hot. Near the end of the day, her shoes are full of sand and she decides to take them off. A few of the girls pester her to remove her socks too, and to everyone's surprise, she does just that. Furthermore, she hitches up her long, black robe and strolls into the shallow water.

Everyone is staring—my goodness, what excitement. Nobody has ever seen our Sister's bare feet before, and now we are witnessing our very own Sister Josephine up to her ankles in water. I can't understand what all the fuss is about, but later I learn that such a thing is unheard of. A few even suggest that she could be in trouble if Sister Superior ever found out.

Oh, really! I think to myself. *What kind of nonsense was this when a person could get into trouble for walking ankle-deep in a nice, cooling lake?* I do know that this trivial indiscretion just endeared Sister Josephine all the more to those of us who loved and admired her.

WEAPONS OF DESTRUCTION

The Grenada movie theatre in downtown St. Catharines was my favourite place to be on a Saturday afternoon. Right after guitar lessons and a lunch of French fries, I would rush to watch a movie at the Grenada where there was sure to be a cowboy movie playing.

I would get totally lost in another world—a world of "cowboys and Indians," a world where horses were as important as the heroes who rode them. There was the Lone Ranger and his horse, Silver. There was Roy Rogers and his horse, Trigger. And my favourite, Gene Autry and his horse, Champ. I vowed, when I grew up, I would go out West and I would have my own horse and it would be an Appaloosa. On my horse, I would explore those wild frontiers I'd seen in the movies, and of course I would need a six-shooter for protection against bad guys.

For now, my buddies and I would have to make do with horses made from old wine barrels and toy cap guns that made a loud pop but didn't actually shoot anything. In the movies, all the good guys wore huge white cowboy hats. If a guy in the movie wore a black hat or dark clothes, you could be pretty sure he was a bad guy. Of course, none of us could afford a proper hat, so we all wore straw hats. That way nobody was a bad guy, and I suspect everyone considered themselves to be one of the good guys.

Over time, we outgrew these games, and when I was about eight years old, my attention turned to making things. I had watched my dad fixing things in his shop down the basement and learned what could be done with tools. It was understood that I could use his hand tools as long as I made sure not to lose them, but nothing was said about the power tools. I was careful to use these only when he wasn't around, but I was quite sure he wouldn't mind too much.

My buddies and I may have outgrown toy cap guns, but we were still very much interested in weapons, so we turned our attention to making "real" weapons—weapons that looked like the real thing or could send stuff flying. Being good boys, we seldom used them against each other and certainly not on animals, but practically anything else was fair game.

Wooden swords were a favourite. They were easy to make and were disposable, so when we engaged in sword fights, the main object was to destroy the other guy's sword. Sometimes things got a little out of hand, and there were occasional injuries, especially to our exposed knuckles.

Rummaging through the town garbage dump, I came across two items of great potential. One was a heavy-duty brass curtain rod, and the other was a taillight housing from an old car. With a heavy-duty hammer, I flattened the hollow brass rod over most of its length to form the blade and I attached the taillight housing near one end for a hand guard. The hand guard idea was great at protecting my knuckles, but this all-metal sword was heavy and just too unwieldy in a serious fight. Still, it was a great-looking weapon. It was the envy of all my buddies, and I was proud to wear it on my belt.

At the Grenada one Saturday they showed a movie with thousands of Indians on horseback galloping into battle against the US Cavalry.

The "Long Knives," as the soldiers were called, had rifles and swords, and even though they were outnumbered 100 to 1, the soldiers won. While most of my friends cheered for these 'brave' soldiers, I couldn't help but sympathize with the Indians, even if they were sometimes portrayed in a bad light. After all, they only had bows and arrows and short knives, which they used to scalp people. I really admired those bows and arrows and wondered if this was something we could make. It never occurred to us to buy factory-made ones, possibly because we didn't have the money—and besides, we should to be able to make our own just like the Indians.

A bit of futile scrounging around the neighbourhood convinced us that we would have to embark on another expedition to the Burgoyne Bush to locate the perfect materials. After a lot of trial and error, we learned that dry maple shoots made pretty good arrows, but they had to be perfectly straight. This was simple enough, but a strong bow with lots of spring was not so easy. After much experimentation, we found that if you started with a reasonably straight branch from a Hawthorn bush, shaped it just right with a pocket knife, let it dry for a week or two, and notched the ends before attaching the string, it made quite a decent bow. We never did learn how to fasten feathers to the arrows, so accuracy wasn't great, and we spent a lot of time retrieving the precious arrows. Quite a few were never found. It became clear why just a few Long Knives with their repeating rifles could defeat a whole tribe of Indians.

Not everything revolved around "cowboys and Indians." One Saturday afternoon, the movie playing downtown featured a tribe of African Bushmen, tracking and hunting lions with spears and only a handheld shield for protection. When we got home, my buddies and I wasted no time making spears from long sticks, and it was quite obvious that garbage can lids made good shields.

Since there were few lions in St. Catharines, my buddies and I prac-ticed on just about anything that could be construed as a wild animal. Metal garbage cans made good targets. They were about the same size as a lion, and when you hit one with your sharpened spear in the right place, it made a satisfying bonk, which to a young boy could quite easily be the death groans of some wild beast. My buddies and I thought this was great fun, and soon most of the garbage cans along the back lane were missing their lids and were bashed beyond belief. An unanticipated challenge to our hunting forays was when a home-owner would come running after us. But hey, this was just another threat you had to contend with when you hunted ferocious animals in the jungles of St. Catharines.

One Christmas, Santa gave me a set of darts. At first it was fun throwing darts at the little round target that came with the set, but they didn't work too well outdoors. I could see the potential, though, for something a little more robust.

Starting with a piece of broom handle, I ground one end on my dad's grinder until it fitted snugly into a short piece of water pipe which provided the needed weight. I then drove a big wood screw into the business end of the broom handle, expanding the wood and keeping the water pipe in place. Again using the grinder, I sharpened the head of the screw until it was as sharp as an ice pick. At the other end of the broom handle, I cut two slits with a hacksaw and, instead of feathers, two playing cards were folded at ninety degrees and glued in the slits.

This new dart travelled much farther than those puny commercial ones, and they were obviously going to be great fun. A few more pro-totypes to determine the right length of stick and a heavier weight at the front increased the range even further. This perfected dart was actually closer to a short spear but could be thrown with much more accuracy. With the two-inch steel screw sharpened to a fine point, it was no longer just a heavy-duty dart; it was now a deadly weapon. I was happy to make more for my buddies, provided they supplied the broomsticks. Now all we needed were some targets.

Telephone poles were our first targets. If you hit a pole off-centre, the dart would bounce off, so this did not count, but if you hit it near the centre, the dart would embed itself in the soft wood; only these would be counted as a kill. One day as we patrolled the back lanes, we spotted a new garage with no house nearby. My buddy Angelo threw his spear at the garage. It made a great thumping sound, and the point buried itself in the soft wood siding. Wow! Neat!

Over the following week, I made more spears until everyone in our little gang had their own, and of course we had to test them on that garage down the lane. Using a lump of coal, Pietro drew pictures of animals and faces on the back of this "deserted" garage. What a great time we had. At first the darts left only small holes, which we reasoned wouldn't really hurt the siding much, but we were getting more accurate, and we were throwing the darts with such force that the boards started splitting. We convinced ourselves that since there was no sign of an owner, it really didn't matter that we were totally smashing the whole back of this building. I guess we got carried away.

■ ■ ■

A few days later, our family was having supper when an agitated stranger came to our door. He screamed at my mom, telling her that some dirty, rotten kids had destroyed the back of his brand new garage and demanding to know if she knew anything about it. Uh-oh, I was afraid that this time I could be in real trouble. What would I say if my mom questioned me? I could not lie to her. Maybe because he was a stranger to the area, or perhaps because he was so obnoxious, my mom told him firmly that her son Jules was a good kid and would never do such a thing, if that's what he's suggesting. The stranger left fuming, and my mom never said another word about the incident. From now on we'll just have to be more careful about choosing our targets.

MY BUDDY ROLLY

It felt good to be back at St. Joseph's after the summer holidays. I was starting grade five, and Sister Julia would be my teacher for the next two years. True to schoolyard gossip, I soon learned that Sister Julia was a "bit different," but like the other sisters at St. Joseph's, she also has that Irish charm and sense of humour that I so admire and appreciate. I was sure everything would work out okay.

I can't believe how much everybody has grown over the holidays. It seems every kid has added an inch or two to their height except me. It feels a bit weird to think that I am the smallest kid in Sister Julia's room; even the girls are taller. Some of the boys call me "the runt," but they treat me okay, especially when they learn I can out-wrestle any of them.

Although I know most of the kids in our room, there are a few new faces. One in particular stands out and we learn that his name is Rolly Rougeau. He's a short, stocky, kid and a bit darker than most of the Italian boys I hang around with. But that's not what sets him apart. Rolly speaks with a strange accent, which sounds vaguely familiar. Sometimes it's hard to understand him. So one day I asked Rolly, "Tu parle Français" (you speak French)? His eyes lit up, and voilà, I became his translator and very soon, his best friend.

Rolly and his family come from a mining town in Northern Ontario—Kirkland Lake, he calls the place. Last year, Rolly's dad was injured in a mining accident and is now partially crippled. He can't work in the mines anymore. Exactly what brought them to St. Catharines? I'm not sure.

Through the summer, Mr. Rougeau has been building a small house near the outskirts of town; a shack, the neighbours call it. The family moves in before it is finished. Wall partitions, closets, and cupboards will come later. The place is an awful mess, with bedding, clothing, and kitchen stuff scattered everywhere. It gets even worse on rainy days when Rolly's mom hangs baby sister's diapers from the open rafters. To me they look like flags of surrender and add to the overall sense of chaos. The Rougeau family may be poor and a bit sloppy, but they are always cheery and make me feel welcome whenever I visit. I wonder what Rolly must think when he comes to my place where, despite all the people living in our house, everything is neat and tidy.

Rolly has never seen a fridge before. His family doesn't even own an icebox. He sees how wonderful a fridge can be when Mom offers him ice cream. To Rolly, a bathtub with hot running water is one of those luxuries he's never experienced and is in no hurry to try. The thing that impresses him most is our big Philco radio, which takes up a prominent corner of the living room. It's the fanciest piece of furniture in the whole house, and it's Mom's pride and joy. She plays it all the time, but on Saturday afternoons Rolly and I have the Philco to ourselves, and we listen to the adventures of the Lone Ranger and the Green Hornet. The fabulous music at the introduction is enough to get us both really excited. We turn up the volume until we can actually feel the sound vibrating in our bodies, or until someone in the house complains.

Mom sometimes speaks French when Rolly comes over, and even she has trouble understanding everything he says. "How come Rolly sounds so different?" I ask.

"That's because Rolly is half-breed, part Indian," she explains, "but never call him that. It's just not nice." Mom figures that Rolly probably grew up speaking Michif, a mix of French and Cree. She thinks that when Rolly started school in Kirkland Lake he was forced to switch from Michif to proper French, and so it shouldn't be too surprising that Rolly sometimes gets mixed up. Poor Rolly—now he's got to learn proper English, as well. No wonder he speaks with a strange accent and throws in words that don't make sense. A few mean kids tease him, but Rolly doesn't seem to mind; he's always happy and cheerful and he makes people laugh.

My Italian buddies all seem to like Rolly, and he soon becomes part of the gang, joining in our games and our regular hikes. It was on one of those hikes that Rolly brought along a slingshot his dad had made years before they came to St. Catharines. Rolly is a really good shot. He can shoot with amazing accuracy and much farther than we thought possible. All the boys are totally impressed. We all want a slingshot like Rolly's.

Slingshots aren't exactly new to us. Angelo and I made a couple slingshots last year, but they weren't very good. We sort of knew that the rubber just wasn't good enough. At the time, the only rubber we could find was from an old black inner tube we scrounged from the service garage on Facer. Now as we compare it to Rolly's red rubber, it's obvious that red rubber is much more elastic than black rubber.

As soon as we get home, Rolly and I approach his dad and ask where red rubber comes from, and how would we go about getting some. "Good luck with that," he tells us in a discouraging tone. He goes on to explain that even before the war, tire manufacturers were switching to synthetic rubber for tires and tubes. "All the decent rubber is reserved for army vehicles now, and what's left for regular cars is crap. The only place you'll find decent red rubber is on some old car, something at least ten or fifteen years old," he says with authority. "There's a war on, you know." Mr. Rougeau loves to talk.

I want to say, "*damn*," but we don't use that kind of language around adults, especially not your parents or your buddy's parents. "Maybe in some scrap yard?" suggests Rolly. Mr. Rougeau won't promise, but the next time he goes to the scrap yard he'll keep an eye out for a red inner tube.

Rolly explains to me how his dad is in the business of bringing dead cars back to life, so he visits the scrap yard quite often looking for parts. Rolly's dad tells us that when the war started, factories that were producing new cars were forced to switch to making war machinery. So now with no new cars available, back yard mechanics spend weekends fixing their old cars, hoping they'll outlast the war. My dad also fixes cars in his spare time but just for friends and relatives. He never charges them. Rolly's dad goes a step farther. He often starts with junk cars from the scrap yard, fixes them up, and gets them on the road again. It seems there are always customers ready to pay good money for a car that not so long ago was considered total junk. Rolly says his dad wants to build a proper garage one day and start a business fixing cars full time. Then he would make lots of money, and their family wouldn't be so poor anymore.

Rolly keeps pestering his dad to find us that precious red inner tube that we need to make proper slingshots. We know that because of the war, it won't be easy.

One day, Rolly invites me to his place and he pulls out a potato sack. He's smiling from ear to ear. I'm supposed to guess what he's got in that sack, so I put on a big show of surprise when he pulls out a beautiful red inner tube. I learn that over the weekend, Mr. Rougeau took Rolly to his favourite scrap yard and after a whole lot of searching; they found a junked 1928 Hudson. Mr. Rougeau figures this classy old car suffered a blowout from a really bad accident. "Maybe the blowout came first and that's what caused the crash," he wonders. In any case, both the tire and inner tube are made by Firestone, and Mr. Rougeau swears Firestone makes the best rubber. Rolly and I don't much care about all this. We're just eager to start making slingshots.

We carefully measure the overall area and count all the slingshots we can make with this new treasure. There seems to be enough rubber to accommodate everyone in our little gang, but we aren't about to give this precious stuff away. Instead, Rolly and I offer to make slingshots for everyone, and we're charging a quarter apiece. Everybody seems okay with this—I suspect, in part, because our buddies have very little free time. Italian parents keep their kids busy while Rolly and I have complete freedom to do whatever we want. Perhaps our buddies also recognize that Rolly and I are pretty good at making stuff. Now all we need are some good crotches.

. . .

The following weekend, we prepare for a hike to the Burgoyne Bush. We will be gone all day, and as usual, Mom is nervous about it. She is consoled by the fact Jackie is coming along. She knows what a tough, fierce, little scrapper Jackie can be. It's very unlikely anyone will give us any trouble with him around.

It takes a couple hours to reach the Burgoyne Bush, but it's worth it. The forest is as magical as ever, but this time our minds are totally focused on the hunt for the very best slingshot crotches in the whole world.

From hours of practice with those first crude models, we have a pretty good idea of what to look for. Anyone who has ever used a slingshot knows that you don't just grip the bottom branch of the crotch. You can get more force and better accuracy if you extend your thumb and forefinger high up on the two smaller branches, almost to where the rubber clamps onto the wood. For an amateur, this presents a hazard. As the stone comes flying from the pouch, it could smash your finger or your thumb. Ouch! For experienced shooters like us though, it's not a problem. So we look for narrow crotches with just the right angle and size to match our left hand. The type of wood is not too important, it's the size and shape that matters, and here in the Burgoyne Bush there's plenty to choose from. By the end of the day, we have at least a dozen perfect crotches, all we need to supply all our Italian buddies plus a few spare. There remains one more problem. Where will we get the leather to fashion the pouch?

It turns out our buddies have no trouble supplying us with old, worn-out boots. We make one or two pouches from each of the tongues and we throw away the rest. We found that good quality string, the kind used to wrap meat, works best to fasten the rubber to the crotch and to the leather pouch. If our moms don't have any on hand, well, the local butcher is glad to oblige.

The finished slingshots are a big hit. The Italian boys really appreciate them, and Rolly and I made a bit of money. These new weapons can shoot much farther and with greater accuracy then anything we've made before, and best of all, we don't have to spend hours making arrows. Natural stones are the ammunition of choice and they are quite plentiful at first. Over time we become more selective about the size and shape of each stone, and in no time we've used up every decent stone in the neighbourhood, including on our gravel driveway. What to do?

One day Rolly comes over all excited, his pockets bulging with beautiful round stones just the perfect size. Quite by accident, Rolly had discovered a fresh pile of gravel at a construction site near his house. After the workers leave for the day, Rolly and I fill a couple potato sacks and trundle them off in my little wagon. Now all we need is some way to carry a good supply when we're on the hunt.

The answer came when Rolly's parents took us to Port Dalhousie to take in the fun and games at Waterfront Park. I showed them where we used to live on Lakeport Road, but they weren't much interested.

It's Friday night and crowds of people are milling around taking in the sights, sounds, and smells of the busy circus midway. It's not uncommon to see young soldiers looking smart and fit in their Khaki uniforms and shiny black boots. I understand they are on leave and looking to have some fun while they can. A few are strolling hand in hand with their girlfriends. I wonder how long they have until they go back to the bloody war overseas.

There's a narrow lane of carnival games getting a lot of attention. A crowd has gathered to watch a muscular looking young soldier throwing balls at some target that looks, oh so easy. It took 3 bucks to win a silly "Cupie Doll" that his girlfriend just had to have. Rolly's Mom says you can buy the same thing at a store for a buck.

Not much of this interests me and Rolly. We have our sights set on another game, one with better odds and much better prizes. The fishing booth has been here since I was a little kid. I used to fish here sometimes, so I know how it works. Facing us are long tin troughs filled with dark, inky water. For a nickel you get a tiny fishing rod with a real hook tied to the end. The object is to drag your line along the bottom and try to snag a pretend fish, hiding in the dark blue depths. Each little wooden fish has a couple brass eyelets that your hook will eventually snag if you drag it back and forth long enough. Each fish also has a number painted on it which indicates the prize you've won. Some prizes are a bit cheesy, but you can keep adding points each time you catch a fish and over time you can win a better prize.

Rolly and I are interested in the neat army stuff on display. With a bit of luck you could win a helmet, a backpack, a deadly looking knife that can be used as a bayonet, all sorts of stuff but it's the ammunition pouches that grab our attention. They come in various sizes but just one colour: Khaki, just like everything army. Rolly's parents wait patiently while we continue fishing. Using the money we made selling slingshots, we are able to continue fishing until we have enough points to win those neat army pouches and web belts to match.

So now Rolly and I have the best slingshots, possibly in the whole world, we have a huge supply of near-perfect stones, and we have real army ammunition pouches that fit perfectly on our real army belts, now to test our deadly weapons. We can hardly wait. "Let's go on a practice run, right after supper tomorrow," Rolly suggests. We could go down those railroad tracks past my place."

It sounded like a good idea but after walking along the tracks for half an hour, we find nothing worth shooting at. Grapevines extend as far as we can see with sturdy high fences to keep people out. We shoot at the NO TRESPASSING signs but that's not much fun. Maybe we'll have to wait until tomorrow and find better hunting grounds. We're about to turn back when a huge, old barn looms into view. The long side of the barn lies parallel to the tracks and just in range of our slingshots. First, we walk the length of the barn to check if anyone lives here. We convince ourselves that this unpainted, decrepit old barn must be abandoned. How lucky!

We shoot at the weathervane on the roof, causing the rusty metal rooster to spin and to make weird noises. That's kind of fun for a while but it soon gets boring. What else can we shoot? There are dozens of windows the length of the barn, each with a set of smaller panes. We had no intention of targeting them, but they become irresistible. We each smash one just to see if we can. Rolly suggests a contest to see who will be the first to smash the next one. Of course it doesn't stop there. One by one, the small panes yield to our marksmanship, until, out of nowhere, a big vicious dog appears and charges towards us. Close behind, an angry old man is yelling and cursing in Italian.

We're running for our lives down the tracks with the big dog barking and catching up to us. We are absolutely terrified. I know enough Italian to understand the old guy isn't just cursing, he is commanding his dog to kill. Thank god we've used up most of the stones in our ammunition pouches, but our pockets are still full and they flop crazily back and forth sending stones flying in all directions. Rolly and I are good runners and we are just flying, but the big dog is catching up, barking furiously and nipping at our heels. I have no idea how close the old guy is, and I wonder which will be worse, the dog clamping his jaws around our throats or the old man beating us to death. In either case, I am convinced that Rolly and I are doomed.

We keep running, running, running to the point of total exhaustion. Finally, we just have to slow down. But wait? The big dog's barking doesn't sound so close anymore, and we can't hear the old Italian guy at all. A quick glance over my shoulder confirms that the dog has stopped running and the old guy is so far behind we can barely see him. Panting furiously, Rolly and I slow down to a fast walk, glancing back regularly in case the dog starts chasing again. Whew! What a relief; looks like we might survive after all.

"I have a question, says Rolly. How will we get home?"

The sun is setting. Soon it will be dark and we are miles from home. We don't dare go back the way we came, and the vineyards with their endless rows of grapes behind high fences don't look too inviting either.

"Let's keep walking along the tracks," I suggest; "we're bound to come to a road somewhere."

"And then what?" asks Rolly. "Do you have any idea where we'll end up?"

Not wanting to worry Rolly too much, I tell him, "Yeah, I think so," but I have no idea either. We keep walking.

"Hey, I think I see lights way up ahead," says Rolly. "That must the road you were talking about. What if the cops are waiting for us?"

Holy crap I never thought of that. "What if the old Italian guy is there with his dog?" We can't take that chance. It would be pretty stupid to be caught after all we've been through.

The vineyards finally give way to a peach orchid with just a puny low fence, so we leave the tracks and head blindly through the peach trees. We stop long enough to quench our thirst with the luscious, ripe peaches hanging low. By the dim light, we follow a line of trees, not knowing where it may lead. We continue walking until it is getting really dark. Reluctantly we must consider the possibility of spending the night in the peach orchard.

"What will our parents think? Do you suppose they'll call the cops? Then we could be in real big trouble," says Rolly. In the distance, we hear a dog barking. I'm pretty sure this isn't the same dog that was biting our heels a couple hours ago, but who's to say? This one could be just as vicious.

"That dog must belong to someone. How about we go in that direction?" I suggest. "At least it might get us out of this damn orchard."

"We really don't have much choice, Rolly agrees. "Let's try it." As we get closer to the barking, we see a dim light and speculate that this must be the dog owner's house.

"Let's not get any closer; I don't want to see another dog tonight," says Rolly. "Let's make a detour." We continue walking, walking,

walking. We stumble in the dark, trying to avoid branches that seem to jump out and whip us in the face.

Off in the distance, there's a mysterious dim light that keeps blinking on and off and moving in one direction. We finally realize that it must be a car, its headlights interrupted by a row of trees. We head in that direction, and sure enough, there's that road we've been hoping for. It's just a small backcountry lane, but my instincts tell me it's going in the right direction.

Finally, we come to an intersection. The sign says Carleton Street. Now I know where we are. It's the road we take when we go swimming at Lock Two on the canal. We stop for a breather then begin the long slog home.

Dad looks up from reading the paper and Mom scolds, "Young man, do you know what time it is? Where were you?"

"Rolly's parents took us to Port Dalhousie again, and I guess everyone lost track of the time," I offer.

Mom shakes her head. "Weren't you there last night?" She accuses.

"Yes, but Mrs. Rougeau wanted to take the cruise to Toronto like our family did last year," I brazenly lie. "It gets back to Port Dalhousie pretty late."

"I guess you can't blame those poor hicks from up north. They never seem to get enough of the bright lights and all the excitement going on at Port Dalhousie on a Saturday night. How could they afford such luxury?" she adds.

Dad returns to his paper and I hurry to bed. I've got to get up early before Sunday Mass so I can confess to Father Jacobowski. I do feel bad about lying to my parents. I know I have committed a sin—hopefully just a venial sin. I don't know what I should say about those broken windows. Father Jacobowski will give me at least twenty Hail Mary's and twenty Our Fathers for penance. Sure hope Rolly makes out okay.

THE WAR YEARS

Growing up in St. Catharines during the early forties, everyone was always aware of the war. Military casualties announced every day were a grim reminder, especially if it was someone local. We also felt sad for those loved ones left to mourn, especially for war widows and their children. For many, even if they were not directly involved in the fighting, it was a troubling and worrisome time.

Meanwhile, for plenty of others, it meant something else. For victims of the Great Depression, things were a lot better with plenty of jobs and new opportunities. Such was the case for our family and our small circle of friends and relations. Oh sure, there were still hardships, but compared to the misery of the great depression, the war years were good times.

No matter where you fitted in, there were constant reminders that Canada was at war. Talk of the war was part of everyday conversation. It was on the radio for what seemed like hours every day. News flashes interrupted regular programming with breaking news. I never quite understood exactly what they meant by that, but it sounded really important. And of course, news about the war filled newspapers and magazines.

The sisters of St. Joseph made sure that their students were also kept well informed. Starting in grade five, every kid was expected to have some understanding of the war and how it impacted every Canadian. Once a week, time was set aside to talk about the war and how it affected even us kids at school. At these sessions, Sister Julia would pick students at random and those chosen were expected to speak in front of the class and share what news had made an impression upon them during the past week. I was usually well prepared, and I didn't mind sharing what I had heard or read; in fact, I kind of liked when my name was picked.

I have my dad to thank for this. He was forever listening to the news, and I often joined him in front of the radio. Sister Julia also wanted us to read about the war. This was a bit problematic for me. No one in our house was much of a reader, so books and newspapers were a rare thing. I suppose they were considered a bit extravagant, and besides, everyone worked such long hours it didn't leave much time for reading.

One day, a copy of the *Toronto Star Weekly* appeared at our house, and I discovered that it had great coverage of the war with lots of photos. I told my dad I had to have a copy so that I could do my homework properly. He didn't question, and so every Saturday, he obligingly gave me a dime to buy the weekend edition of the *Toronto Star* from the corner store. There were always human-interest stories about the war, which I knew would be of interest to my classmates. Quite often, the story would include colour photos. I would clip them out and show the class, making my report a bit more interesting and my presentation a lot easier to remember.

To be honest, there was another reason I wanted that *Toronto Star*, something I admit was of greater interest to me. It was the comic section. My heroes lived within those colourful pages. There was Dick Tracy, the brilliant detective whose very survival relied upon pitting his keen intellect against all those criminals and bad guys. I was never quite sure whether he would overcome the latest evildoers. Sometimes it was painful waiting a week or more to find out how he could possibly prevail. Superman, on the other hand, had such powers that I didn't worry too much about him.

Mandrake the Magician was another of my heroes who could call upon his magical powers in worlds filled with evil forces, fire-breathing dragons, and other weird creatures.

Dad came to like the *Toronto Star*. He didn't much care for the comics, but whenever he was reading the paper and he began chuckling, you could be sure he was reading *Li'l Abner*. The stories all revolved around a hillbilly community called Dogpatch. According to

Dad, these stories were based on real-life people and they reminded him of quirky characters he came across while growing up in a place not unlike Dogpatch. Li'l Abner was also a hero of sorts. He was a simple-minded, charming hick who people tried to fool and take advantage of. Li'l Abner could be quite smart at times, and somehow, he would outwit those wicked city slickers who were up to no good.

At St. Joseph's, our Sisters did not condone the war, nor did they condemn it. They went along with all the war effort drives and made sure every student participated in some way.

Every room had a Red Cross donation box that sat on the wide windowsill. We were told the money was for medical supplies to treat wounded soldiers, and if we had any spare change, the Red Cross could sure use the money.

Then there were the War Savings Stamps and Victory Bonds. We were told that if ever we had extra money, this was the best way to save, much better than a piggy bank. War stamps could be bought from any store, or from your teacher for twenty-five cents each. The idea was simple and quite clever. Everybody was given a small booklet in which you could paste these stamps, and when you had filled a book, you would receive an official paper called a Victory Bond. We were assured that after the war, these certificates that cost four dollars in total could be redeemed for five dollars. What better way to learn about the power of interest earned on investment, and it felt good to know we had done our patriotic duty.

There were other ways to show your patriotism, like the tin drive, for example. We were told there was a shortage of tin, a vital metal, desperately needed for building aircraft for our gallant Royal Canadian Air Force. At the same time, there were tons of this precious metal being thrown in the garbage every day. How could that be? Well, we all know that cigarettes come in colourful, cardboard packages, but in addition to that, there was another layer of protection, a thin silver paper foil made of pure tin. Us kids were encouraged to rescue this precious tin whenever we could. Boys were good at this. We didn't mind rummaging through people's garbage, up and down the back lanes in our neighbourhood. Who knows what other treasures we might find besides that precious tin. If homeowners questioned or objected, we could honestly tell them, "There's a war on, you know. We're just doing our duty."

It didn't take long for hundreds of school kids to salvage every scrap of tin foil from the sidewalks, the streets, and hundreds of garbage cans. The more nervy amongst us would pester any smoker we came across to give us their foil even before they had finished their cigarettes.

We carefully shaped the foil into perfectly round balls and brought them to school. Rubber bands were also collected and wound into balls in the same way. It was easy to imagine that the rubber was needed for aircraft tires, but I never did find out what the tin was used for.

It was absolutely amazing to see the hundreds of balls of tin and rubber that accumulated in the basement of our school. Eventually, an army truck came to collect the stuff, and a soldier told us what a fine job we had done and to keep up the good work, and we felt good.

One day, a young woman dressed in a navy uniform came to our school to explain the vital role the Navy performs in protecting Canada's coasts and the many ships that cross the Atlantic Ocean every day. Sadly, sometimes a ship would get torpedoed by German submarines and people drowned.

"The Navy desperately needs lifejackets and they can only be made with milkweed pods," she said. *What?* Did I hear right? Milkweed pods are used to make lifejackets?

The young woman just happened to have one of those pods, which she opened to reveal a handful of soft white silky fibres. She went on to explain how it takes hundreds of these pods to fill just one life jacket, but a good life jacket could keep a sailor afloat for hours. Of course we all wanted to help. No sailor should be without a lifejacket.

Over the next few weeks, people called from all over the area to report milkweed locations and then volunteers gladly went out to pick them. One day, a farmer called to say he had millions of the pesky weeds on his farm, so our whole class was given the afternoon off to help. The farmer explained when the pods are left to ripen they burst open, sending thousands of seeds floating through the air. The fluffy seeds are carried by the wind, sometimes miles away. Eventually, the seeds land as if by parachute to start new plants. No wonder every farmer just hated milkweed.

Once again, we felt proud to be doing our bit for the war effort. And, who knows, maybe those pods we picked went on to save some poor sailor's life.

And then there was the aluminum drive, announced with great excitement on the radio. One of the movie theatres downtown was giving a free pass to anyone bringing in some item made of aluminum. Of course aluminum was required to build our fighter planes to fight the evil enemy, right? It seemed like a good idea, but where would we find scrap aluminum? My buddies and I spent hours poking around the city dump only to come up empty-handed. I pleaded with my mom to give me one of her pots. She refused, saying she needed all her pots and pans. On the day of the aluminum drive, I went downtown anyway. I'm not sure why, but maybe someone would have an extra pot to share.

Everyone had an aluminum pot as they stood in line to get their free pass, but nobody had a spare. I remember thinking: *Most of these pots appear to be in suspiciously good condition. Now why would anyone throw away such a good-looking utensil?*

Almost as exciting as the prospect of a free movie was the fun way of making your contribution. Next to the movie theatre was a narrow empty lot flanked on three sides by brick buildings with a fence at one end. At the back of the lot was a large billboard with freshly painted pictures of Hitler, Mussolini, and Hirohito.

Boys and young men eagerly threw their aluminum as hard as they could at the faces on the billboard. Some nervy guys jumped over the fence to retrieve their ammunition so they could have another throw. In less than an hour, the enemy faces no longer looked so evil, and there was a small mountain of aluminum piled against the fence. Probably enough to build a whole plane, I figured.

At last, the movie was set to begin, and everyone was welcomed inside whether they had brought an item or not. As my buddies and I walked home after the movie, it became clear that not all of them had asked their mom's permission for that aluminum pot. I was glad I got to see the movie without having to steal, and my mom still had all her pots.

An urgent bulletin came over the radio one day. "Enemy soldiers were spotted just outside the city. Are they part of a bigger force? Are they about to take over our country? Come out to Memorial Park next Sunday and watch our Canadian soldiers in action." Thank goodness the announcer was quick to explain that this was just a pretend invasion with pretend Nazis. Canadians could rest assured that our forces were on guard for us and would never let such a thing happen. Everyone was invited to come downtown to witness the mock battle, and there was to be a magnificent parade to follow.

I must say the show was impressive. There were soldiers all over the place, some hiding in doorways, behind cars, and just about any place that offered some cover. All the soldiers wore Canadian uniforms with the same insignia, but there was no doubt as to who the bad guys were. They were the ones with swastikas pinned on each arm and a white patch on their back.

Without warning there was a KABOOM, followed by a puff of white smoke, and then pandemonium as hundreds of soldiers started firing their rifles. One by one, we watched the guys with swastikas fall and others throwing up their hands in surrender. All too soon, the battle was over; the bad guys tore off their swastikas and assembled for the parade.

As my buddies scrambled to collect the blank cartridge shells, I had a different idea. I struck up a conversation with a friendly soldier and pleaded with him to give us some live blanks, and to my great surprise, he gave us each a live blank cartridge. What a treasure! We knew there had to be gunpowder in those blanks, and how we would deploy them occupied our collective imaginations for the rest of the day.

One of my buddies suggested we light a fire, toss in a cartridge, and run. We were so far away by the time it went off, the explosion sounded like a car engine backfiring. Nobody even bothered to look. Another buddy suggested we pry open a crimped cartridge with a screwdriver and make our own bomb by pouring the gunpowder into a tin can. But how would we set it off? One of the guys remembered seeing in a cowboy movie that you could make a thin trail of gunpowder away from the bomb and light it with a match; that would give us time to get back and stay safe. Sure enough this worked, but the expected mighty explosion turned out to be just a small pop, hardly worth the cost of two cartridges.

We had just one cartridge left. What could we do with it? It had to be more dramatic. I noticed the salvaged, spent cartridges we collected at the mock battle had a small circle of a different metal at one end, and each had a dent in the middle, while the ones the soldier gave us had a similar centre but no dent. It didn't take a great leap of imagination to figure out that this real cap, when hammered, probably set off the gunpowder that sends the bullet flying. Mine was the only remaining cartridge, and since I was the unelected leader of our little band, it was left up to me to come up with some way of detonating it. I had an idea, but how would I pull it off without blowing off our fingers?

Rummaging through my dad's tools and assorted nuts and bolts, I found one particular steel nut that fitted snugly around the cartridge and abutted beautifully around the rim. Using larger heavy-duty nuts stacked one on top the other, they served as a stand that supported the cartridge in a vertical position. Now, how to duplicate that dent on the cartridges normally fired by a rifle?

"We could use a nail and hammer it real hard," suggests Angelo.

"What would happen to the fingers holding the nail?" I ask. No one volunteered to try this method.

"We could hold the nail with a pair of pliers," another buddy suggests. That might work, but it also sounds pretty dangerous.

A flash of inspiration struck: What if I was to sharpen a nail on my dad's grinder to a real sharp point, just like on those heavy-duty darts we had perfected last summer? Perhaps I could tap the sharpened nail gently into the cap until it stood up on its own. Then, with fingers out of the way, one sharp blow with the hammer. Maybe that would work? A quick experiment with one of the previously emptied cartridges used to create our "bomb" proved the idea beautifully. With no gunpowder in the cartridge, we were rewarded with a sharp, harmless pop as the cap went off.

Now for the real thing. I set up the contraption on the sidewalk in front of our house. A gaggle of neighbourhood kids gathered round to see what we're up to. Angelo volunteered to hit the nail, but I let him know this was my cartridge, this was my hammer, and this was my idea, so I would deliver the blow.

KABOOM! My god, this was louder than that canon at Memorial Park last Sunday! There was a bright orange flash. The hammer flew from my hands. My ears were ringing like crazy. The whole apparatus disappeared. The heavy steel nuts, the cartridge shell, everything must have rocketed up to heaven. None of those heavy steel nuts or the cartridge shell was ever found.

The young kids all scattered. Curious neighbours came running and wanted to know what caused that loud explosion. "Oh, nothing," I replied as I retrieved the hammer which now had a big chunk gouged out of the handle. My friends and I laughed nervously as we hurried away from the scene, excited by what we had done but recognizing full well that we could all have been seriously injured, maybe even killed.

I sure hope Mom doesn't find out. She figures she's already ageing too fast, and she's not pleased with the way her hair is turning white.

SISTER JULIA

Sister Julia is the artsy one. She teaches grades five and six with a calm, casual style that gives her a kind of mysterious, brainy air. I get the impression there isn't a question Sister Julia cannot answer. I'm sure she did a fine job teaching us math, history, grammar, and other subjects, but what I will always remember is her determination to expose us to the finer arts.

Like Sister Josephine, Sister Julia also takes us on regular outings, only her idea of a field trip usually involves a museum, an art gallery, or a concert hall. I'm afraid most of this is lost on me. I don't much care for fine arts. Classical music, in particular, makes no sense to me. The more I heard the music of Beethoven, Bach, or Mozart, the more I disliked it.

Sister Julia isn't a classical snob, though. She also likes modern music, especially the big bands that are all the rage on the radio. This music is mainly meant for dancing, and as the music plays on the gramophone, Sister Julia can't help bouncing along to the music.

I don't suppose she would have been allowed to dance even if she wanted to. I don't dance either, but the sound of all those instruments playing together is just magical—all the more so when we learn the distinctive sounds of the various instruments as each play their particular part. I especially enjoy Glen Miller. He is kind of a hero because his band entertains our soldiers overseas.

Only our room has a gramophone. I don't know if it belongs to the school, or perhaps it is Sister Julia's personal property. I do know that everyone really enjoys our music lessons, when Sister Julia plays the latest hits circulating at the time. "We may not have musical instruments, but we have our voices," Sister Julia reminds us. Sister Julia writes the words on the blackboard and everyone is expected to sing along. From time to time, our class would put on a small concert for the whole school. It was mostly singing hit tunes that we had practiced while Sister Julia played the piano.

It is Sister Julia who introduces us to poetry. Like classical music, this is often a challenge for me, especially when we have to memorize poem after poem from some long-dead poet who routinely uses words and phrases unfamiliar to me. Even after Sister Julia gives us her interpretation of what the poet was trying to convey, it still doesn't do much for me. Chaucer, in particular, makes no sense at all. His writing may as well have been in Latin or Greek.

There is one little poem however, that intrigues me.

Life Is Just a Bowl of Cherries

Life is just a bowl of cherries
Don't make it serious, life's too mysterious
You work, you save, you worry so
But you can't take your dough when you go, go, go

Keep repeating, it's the berries
The strongest oak must fall
The sweet things in life to you were just loaned
So how can you lose what you never owned?

Life is just a bowl of cherries
So why not laugh at it all

The words are easy enough to understand, but the meaning? Less clear. The title especially makes little sense until Sister Julia gives us her interpretation. She passes around a bowl of ripe, sweet cherries. "Take one," she suggests, "but don't eat it just yet. Examine it closely. How would you describe the colour?" she asks.

"Dark red," a few respond.

"Like my mom's lipstick," offers one of the girls.

"Looks like dried blood," one boy blurts out. Everybody laughs.

186

"Who thinks the colour is beautiful?" Sister Julia asks. Of course we all agree. "Now look at the size of your cherry," she says. "It's small enough to pop into your mouth without biting into it, and yet it's large enough that having one at a time seems best. And, no peeling required. Now go ahead, pop that cherry into your mouth and bite down. Notice how the juice explodes and floods your taste buds with sweet, delicious nectar. "Cherries, aren't they beautiful? Aren't they delicious? Isn't a cherry the most wonderful fruit in the world? Perhaps the author of the poem chose the cherry as the perfect metaphor to describe cherished moments we live through each day, and when you have a full bowl, well, that's what is called 'life'—a bowl of cherries."

"What about the pits?" one of the kids asks.

"Good question," answers Sister Julia. "What do they represent to you? . . . Maybe the pits represent those little things in life that go wrong as we go about our daily business. And, what do we do about the pits? We simply spit them out and go on enjoying the rest. Right?" Everyone nods in agreement.

Remembering a lesson from Mr. Burton's farm, I offer another observation. "You know, if it wasn't for those pits, there would be no cherry trees." To my surprise, some kids don't know what I'm talking about. The lesson takes a detour, as Sister Julia has to explain about small seeds growing into big trees. Now our class wonders whether the author of the poem had this in mind too, and on it goes for each line of the poem.

Sister Julia has another lesson up her sleeve. She turns on the gramophone, and a bouncy little tune plays for a minute or so, and then *holy smokes!* A singer starts singing: "Life Is Just a Bowl of Cherries."

After the song, Sister Julia goes on to explain how poetry and music go hand in hand. Everyone agrees that when the poem is sung, it sounds much better, and the message becomes more powerful. And then, like a dim light slowly brightening, I begin to appreciate the wonders of poetry and music. Forever after, I shall listen for those rare songs where the music and the words fit so perfectly that the message comes across like magic and, sometimes, pure bliss.

CHAPTER 6
Brighton Avenue, 1943–1946

IRIS' BIRTHDAY

Before the war, St. Catharines Ontario was one of those single-industry towns with a big smoke-belching factory at its heart. It was called McKinnon's. They paid real good wages, and people who worked there were considered lucky. McKinnon's made mostly auto parts, but for the past year or so, they've been expanding like mad and converting to full scale production of war machinery. Thousands of workers from across Canada flooded into St. Catharines, eager to land one of those new jobs. Trouble was, they all needed a place to live.

Desperate people were willing to pay outlandish rents for modest accommodations, so when a large house in our neighbourhood came up for sale, Dad recognized the potential. It was spacious enough for our family and could accommodate a few renters as well. He bought the place even though it was way beyond our means.

With seven rooms, a full basement, veranda, and back porch, 13 Brighton was the biggest house on the street. The two-story house came with existing tenants, a Mr. and Mrs. O'Hara, who had a teenage boy named Sonny and a younger daughter named Iris. For the next several years, they lived upstairs in two small rooms and I got to know them quite well.

Mr. O'Hara was a steeplejack by trade and took great pride in his ability to perform any job at dizzying heights few would dare to climb. Mr. O'Hara told us whenever there was a super difficult job, he's the one they called. He often boasted that he was the best goddamn steeplejack in all of Ontario. No one dared to challenge his bold assertion.

Mr. O'Hara was also quick to let everyone know that he had no time for assholes and god help any who got in his way. It didn't matter how big the man or how tough, once he qualified as "an asshole who got in the way," he would get the crap beat out of him, and presumably would then become a better person.

During the week, Mr. O'Hara worked long hours, came home faithfully every evening, ate his supper, and we knew by his snoring that he fell asleep early.

Weekends were different. Saturday evenings, Mr. O'Hara would come home late, often bringing one or two drinking buddies. All brought booze and all smelled of smoke and stale beer. Mrs. O'Hara didn't seem to mind. She would join the men, and they would drink till dawn. At times the party became quite raucous, with Mr. O'Hara's garrulous voice drowning out all the others. He would sing sad Irish ballads and remind his guests that his daddy may have come from Dublin but he was a Canuck through and through and mighty proud of it.

There was lots of quarrelling and the occasional fight as Mr. O'Hara had to put one more asshole in his place. The muscular Mr. O'Hara had no qualms about throwing a previously invited guest down the steep stairs, and that was pretty much the end of the party.

Mrs. O'Hara was a stay-at-home, dutiful wife who kept her tiny apartment neat and clean. It seemed her main job was keeping her husband happy. She had a sad look about her, but it wasn't hard to imagine that she would have been quite pretty in her youth. And judging by random fits of laughter, audible through the whole house, she had a sense of humour too. Most days, though, she kept to herself and was so quiet that we sometimes wondered if she was home.

Mrs. O'Hara was not one to rock the boat. She was always meek and soft spoken, so it came as a shock late one night to hear her high-pitched voice screaming louder than her husband's.

"This isn't our goddamn house, you stupid bitch; have some consideration for the rest of the people trying to sleep." Despite closed doors, we could hear through the thin walls the sickening thump of bone on flesh, whimpers, sobs, and then silence.

The next morning, Mrs. O'Hara would go about her business as though nothing had happened. On one occasion, she wore dark sunglasses. We took this to mean: don't ask about the black eyes.

During the commotion Sonny would disappear, and by Sunday afternoon, Mr. O'Hara, now sobered up, would be in a rage demanding to know from some absent authority, "Where in hell is that goddamn kid? I'll wail the tar out of him when I catch him." And he would.

Mr. O'Hara would invariably find Sonny and forcibly drag him home. Iris told me how her dad would make Sonny take off his pants, lie face down on the bed, and accept his punishment in silence. Each time, Mr. O'Hara would add one more lash from the previous beating with his big black belt. Sonny once showed me his behind. It was covered with raw red welts and looked just awful.

I couldn't understand how Sonny never seemed to learn. "Why run away," I asked, "when your dad always finds you and beats you?" A couple months later, after he had healed and things seemed to be back to normal, Sonny would take off again. The horrific, ugly ritual would repeat. I often wonder what became of Sonny and can't help thinking that he faced a pretty grim future.

Iris was much like her mother, pleasant and pretty, but without the sadness. Mr. O'Hara would often tell Iris that she was his princess and that should anyone ever lay a hand on her, they would have to answer to him.

Iris' birthday was approaching, and Mr. O'Hara promised that Iris would have a party like she had never seen and to start inviting all her friends, as many as she wanted. After all, it would be her tenth birthday and this one was to be extra special.

It turned out only six kids showed up, each with a small gift for Iris. Mrs. O'Hara put them aside and told Iris she was not to open them until her dad came home. We all waited eagerly for the party to begin, but there was little sign that anything was about to happen. Mrs. O'Hara served everyone soft drinks and asked us to be patient. We would have to wait for Mr. O'Hara who was shopping for special treats and surprise presents for everyone. I thought to myself, *How neat!* Any party I had ever attended, only the birthday girl or birthday boy got presents. Mrs. O'Hara kept playing records on the gramophone and tried to interest us in some board games.

Time dragged, and every few minutes Iris would run downstairs and check to see if her dad was coming. I was getting pretty bored, so I went with her, and together we stood on the steps and stared down Brighton Avenue. One time, we ventured a little farther down the sidewalk, enough to see the streetcar on Facer Street, come to a stop, and sure enough, out stepped Mr. O'Hara.

He was carrying two large shopping bags and Iris ran to greet him. She must have noticed that her dad smelled of beer and sweat; it was Saturday, after all. She certainly didn't remind him that he was hours late. It was enough that he was home.

Suddenly the whole mood changed. This was some party with all the hot dogs you could eat, a huge birthday cake with ten candles and lots of nickels and dimes baked right in the cake. There were more kinds of ice cream than I knew existed, and everyone could eat as much as we liked. Everyone had party hats and whistles, horns, and tons of balloons.

Iris got the present she really wanted: a nurse's kit that included a white starched hat, a white apron, and a little metal box full of different pills that were actually candies. Iris just loved her stethoscope and never seemed to tire of listening to everybody's heartbeat.

As promised, everyone got a present, and Iris was very pleased with the gift my mom got for me to give. I can't remember what it was, but I do remember that we all had a great time, and I remember thinking: *Gee, maybe Mr. O'Hara wasn't such a bad guy after all.*

"Brighton Avenue"   Source: family photo

MRS. INGLIS

As the war progressed, more and more people were drawn to St. Catharines, all looking for work. They came from all over Ontario and beyond, some not knowing where they would live. Appeals went out over the radio to homeowners who might have a room to spare, urging them to take in a renter or two—after all, "there's a war on, you know," and it's everybody's duty to do their part.

With the recent arrival of baby brother Louis, we are now six (seven if you include my dog Jackie) in our growing family. Add to that our renters, the O'Hara family, and that makes ten people living in our house. Mom thinks that's enough. "We can't accommodate any more," she declares. Well, it seems when there's a war on, all sorts of things become possible.

It's not clear if it was patriotism or just a ploy on Dad's part to make some money, but without much consultation, Dad charges ahead with some pretty creative renovations. He partitions the second floor master bedroom to create two tiny rooms that he now calls an apartment. Mom and Dad and little brother Louis will have to sleep at one end of the kitchen, at least for now. The comfortable, spacious kitchen that Mom was so proud of is now part-bedroom. A partition will come later. Sisters Juliette and Alice share the remaining bedroom upstairs, and I shall sleep on a Toronto couch in the living room. The new apartment is put up for rent before the paint is dry.

A Mrs. Inglis is at the door within minutes of the ad appearing in the *St. Catharines Standard*, and she's pleased to learn that she is the first to respond. Of course she is eager to see the apartment. One glance at the rooms and she declares they will be just perfect for her and her three daughters.

"Whoa, wait a minute. Did you say three daughters?" Mom asks. She had pictured a single person occupying this limited space, two at the most. "How could four of you fit in this small space?" she asks. "And, are you aware that the kitchen has only a cold water tap and no proper stove, just a small hot plate?"

Before Mom can raise further objections, Mrs. Inglis starts to relate how her husband died recently and now she is a poor widow, totally dependent on her daughters to support her. They come from Bracebridge, a small town in mid Ontario where there is simply no work. Presently they are staying in a friend's basement. All three girls have jobs and they can afford the rent. "So when can we move in?" she asks.

Mrs. Inglis wastes no time filling us in on every detail of her family's life. We learn that the Inglis family are from proud British stock and they can trace their heritage back before the glory days of Queen Victoria. Many of the males in the family were involved with the military, and now her only son Merlin is overseas fighting Hitler's Huns.

Her eldest daughter Mary appears to be the gifted one in the family. She has just graduated from high school with top marks. "And she won an award for proficiency at the typewriter," her mother boasts. "And did you know Mary has a certificate in Pittman shorthand?" she asks.

Mary is one of those lucky people: smart, charming, and quite good-looking. I marvel at how her rather homely mother could have given birth to such an attractive young woman. Mary works in an office downtown and has a boyfriend who comes by once a week in his old Chevy.

Mabel, the rather quiet middle daughter, works at McKinnon's in the chain department, welding miles and miles of heavy-duty chain for the war effort. She's kind of plain and never wears makeup. She doesn't seem to care much about her appearance and she doesn't seem to have a social life. I overheard my mom tell one of my aunts that Mabel seems to like girls more than boys. I'm not sure what she means by that.

And then there's Maggie. "Her name is Margaret," Mrs. Inglis insists, but everyone continues to call her Maggie. Maggie has flaming red hair with contrasting snow-white skin. Her pale face is polka-dotted with rusty freckles. She just turned sixteen but could pass for younger if not for a hint of two tiny mounds hiding under her shirt. She is quick to smile and she laughs at just about anything even slightly amusing.

Mrs. Inglis wants Margaret to continue her schooling, but Maggie has a mind of her own. She quit before finishing grade ten and has no intention of going back. And so Mrs. Inglis continues to nag with monotonous regularity.

Maggie has no illusions about getting a fancy job like her sister Mary. She is happy working as a waitress in a greasy spoon downtown. "On a good day, I can make more money from tips than both my sisters earn," she boasts. Streetcar service along Facer Street is pretty good and stops about a block from our house, but Maggie saves her dime and gets a ride home almost every evening. The model of the car changes from time to time, and we take this to mean that Maggie has a new boyfriend.

I sometimes wish I could be Maggie's boyfriend, but I know I am too young. After all, Maggie is at least five years older than me, and I'm sure she regards me as just a kid, so I keep these fantasies to myself. I recognize the futility of these longings, but my mind conjures up all kinds of situations where I play the hero, saving Maggie from various dangers. Lately, there is one scenario that seems to reoccur with alarming regularity.

It starts with Maggie and I cruising around in my new convertible. All eyes turn to admire Maggie with her long flaming tresses flowing in the wind. Towards evening, we make our way to one of those swank roadhouses with the parking lot full of classy cars, and my cream-coloured Studebaker, with a black convertible top and oodles of chrome, outshines them all.

We dine at a romantic table for two overlooking beautiful Lake Ontario. In the background, Frank Sinatra is crooning romantic love songs and I am drowning in pure bliss at the thought of being alone with Maggie. We spend the evening dancing cheek to cheek and planning our future together. As the evening winds down, my fantasies take flight. My mind concocts various romantic scenarios, all ending up with Maggie in the nude and looking just gorgeous.

■ ■ ■

The Inglis family is barely settled in when Mom is invited for tea. I wasn't home at the time, but later I overheard Mom describe the occasion to a couple of my aunts. "Here we are, just the two of us, sitting in this tiny kitchen barely bigger than a closet. Belgian lace covers the steamer trunk they use as a table, and Mrs. Inglis has set out her heirloom silver tea set with real fancy cups and saucers. You'd think we were a couple of classy, rich ladies enjoying lunch together at some fancy restaurant in London." My aunts laugh and question how four women can manage to cook, eat, and sleep in this cramped space that used to be a single bedroom just a few weeks ago.

Mrs. Inglis makes her rounds, introducing herself to everyone and passing out English-style goodies. She apologizes for the store-bought cookies and goes on to relate how she would love to bake but recognizes that with only a hot plate, this is no longer possible. "Oh, how I miss that beautiful stove I had in Bracebridge," she says and goes on to describe how her "Findlay" was the centre of the household and how it had served her family so well for so many years.

Of course Mom felt obliged to offer the use of her stove. "It may not be a Findlay, and it's not a wood stove," she admits, "but you're welcome to use my plain electric stove any time." Little did Mom know how much her stove would be used from that day forward.

Mrs. Inglis was a great baker, a passionate baker, who spent her afternoons preparing fresh-baked treats for everyone in the household. It became almost a daily routine that endeared Mrs. Inglis to everyone—everyone except little brother Louis. He was barely two when one day he refused to thank Mrs. Inglis for a fresh-baked cookie. Mrs. Inglis was quite prepared to overlook this puzzling behaviour, but Mom kept insisting; still, my little brother stubbornly refused. Mom was plainly embarrassed and more than a little angry. She made it clear that Mrs. Inglis was not to offer Louis another cookie, or anything else for that matter, unless he said please and thank you. As far as I know, that never happened and little brother went without. Amazing!

Mom was equally generous with the use of her fridge, a big brand-new "Leonard" that Dad had bought a few weeks back. The O'Hara family and the Inglis family were each assigned a shelf for their exclusive use.

The manner in which we got this fabulous fridge is another story. There had been this large, nattily dressed man who appeared at our door while Mom was away. "Mr. Legal?" he demanded in a booming, authoritative voice. "Mr. Gabriel Legal?"

Dad immediately invited him in, not knowing what news this important-looking gentleman was about to reveal. For all he knew this might even be an undercover cop, and he wouldn't want the neighbours to hear. Dad went over in his mind if he could have broken the law in some way, and no, he couldn't think of anything lately, and it had been years since he and Uncle Midas were distilling wine into brandy.

The big guy sits himself down at our kitchen table and opens an official-looking briefcase. Dad is more puzzled than ever but waits nervously as our guest rifles through a bunch of papers. "Mr. Legal," he keeps repeating, "my researchers have been conducting an in-depth study in this area and they have concluded that no one on this street, indeed no one in this neighbourhood, owns a genuine, fully electric refrigerator. Furthermore, we have concluded that with your large household and your extensive mechanical knowledge you would make the perfect candidate to test our latest model."

"Does this mean we get a free refrigerator?" Dad asks with a straight face.

"Well . . . not exactly," says the salesman, reverting back to his briefcase to show Dad and me a picture of a lady in a fur parka standing next to an igloo and loading a fridge with groceries. "Even the Eskimos up north are buying them," he chuckles.

Dad is not amused. He just wants to know the price. I forget the exact cost, but I remember thinking that it sounded like a fortune, and it did to Mom too.

Whenever someone came to visit, the big white "Leonard" was the centre of attention, and Dad was happy to boast about its features. Whether they asked about the price or not Dad would repeat the salesman's final argument, the one that persuaded him to buy the "Leonard."

"Yes, it may be expensive," he admits, "but I figure the money we save from not having to buy ice will more than pay for this marvel of technology, and if you add up what we'll save from preventing food spoilage—why, that fridge will pay for itself in less than a year."

Mom is skeptical. She never allows food to spoil, but she is glad to be rid of the messy icebox and she is grateful for this modern appliance. Dad won't let her forget that we could never have afforded such luxury if it hadn't been for our renters. Mom can't quite understand the logic. "If that fridge is supposedly paying for itself, why do we need renters to pay for it?"

Now, with three families using the fridge and Mrs. Inglis using Mom's stove almost every day, there's a steady stream of traffic traipsing in and out of the reduced kitchen. "There is never a moment of privacy in this damned place," she quietly grumbles to no one in particular. One day I overheard her confide to my aunt: "You know, life was a whole lot simpler when it was just Gaby and me in that simple, one-room log cabin back in Manitoba." I have to wonder: *was it also a happier time before all us kids came along?*

COUNTRY COUSINS

Two young men dressed in lumberjack shirts and heavy breeches appear at our door one day. When they spot my mom, they let out boisterous whoops and take turns hugging and lifting her off her feet, and everyone is laughing so heartily it's like they've all lost their minds.

"This can't be Jules?" they shout as they turn their attention and hug me so hard I can barely breathe.

I vaguely remembered these cousins from Manitoba, but obviously they knew me well and started to relate stories from when my parents owned a general store in Ste. Geneviève where they would come to buy stuff and Mom pressed them into babysitting me.

Germain and Gabriel were brothers, in their early twenties, I would guess. They were Aunt Loretta's boys, Mom's older sister; the one everyone called La Vieille Belette (old weasel). Now there were two Gabys in the same house, and since my dad was older, people called this younger cousin Biel, and the name stuck.

Germain and Biel had a good winter cutting cordwood from along the Greater Water District rail line in Manitoba. They had saved a few bucks and decided to surprise Mom with their visit. They were planning to look for jobs in St. Catharines and wanted to work here until fall, if only they could find a place to stay. It was quite obvious that they were counting on living with us—for a little while, at least. Mom didn't seem the least concerned.

I thought the house was already full; just how many people could we accommodate? Just last month a neighbour had asked Mom if she could take in two young women from out west, "just for a month or so."

That meant sisters Juliette and Alice would have to give up their upstairs bedroom. They shall sleep on the Toronto couch that served as my bed in the living room, and I am happy to sleep in the open veranda on a narrow cot.

Mom creates a bedroom in the basement for her nephews. "Stay as long as you want," she tells them. There are now eighteen people living in our house. Luckily my country cousins don't bathe very often, so the line-up for the tub is still manageable.

Biel and Germain—the "Gauthier boys," most people called them—are such fun, always laughing and teasing and entertaining us with their stories. I never tire of listening to their adventures as hunters, trappers, and connoisseurs of home brew.

Both Biel and Germain are great storytellers. Each has their own favourite stories, and neither is allowed to tell the other's story. That would be like stealing. A lot of the stories revolve around spending the winter with a bunch of guys in some rough bush camp cutting cordwood. All the stories contain humour and plenty of colourful words, crude curses, and sacrilegious ones too. Biel and Germain are no followers of the Catholic faith and take great delight in ridiculing all things churchy. *"Maudit,"* (goddamn) is used liberally and sometimes lengthened to *"maudit criss."* And *"tabarnak"* is casually thrown in now and then, for no good reason that I can figure. A typical story might begin with Germain asking his brother, "Remember that winter of '39, remember that shithole camp we stayed in when we cut cordwood at Mile 53?"

And, Biel answers, *"Tabarnak!* Damn right I remember. That goddamn caboose was always cold, colder than a nun's tit!"

Germain continues, "Well, one morning we were sitting around having one last mug of coffee before setting off to work. Ti Pierre is getting dressed, and he can't find one of the insoles for his boots. Then Biel would interrupt to explain that Ti Pierre had the smelliest goddamn feet imaginable. Just how smelly? Well by the end of a hard day's work, no matter how cold it was, Ti Pierre's socks and felt insoles would be soaking with sweat. *Maudit criss!* It was enough to embarrass a skunk, and we had to smell that perfume all night long."

And as if he didn't already know, Biel asks his brother, "How was it that you found Ti Pierre's lost insole?"

Germain responds, "Well, you know me . . . I just love coffee, 'specially in the morning. I already had a couple mugs but so did everybody else. You know me . . . I hate to see anything go to waste, so I figure I may as well empty the pot. You know me . . . as I'm pouring the last of the coffee, a black hairy thing falls into my mug. *Merde, maudit criss, tabarnak,* it's a goddamn rat!"

Biel cuts in, "But it wasn't a rat."

Germain continues, "It was Ti Pierre's god-awful stinky felt insole. Ti Pierre had to admit that last night he hung his wet stuff above the stove because they didn't always dry where the rest of the crew hung theirs. It must have fallen into the open coffee pot. Well, you can be goddamn sure that was the last goddamn time he did that. And nobody felt sorry that he had to go to work that morning with one wet insole."

"Mind you," says Biel, "that insole didn't stink as bad as his other stuff, so it was suggested that Ti Pierre should boil his socks and insoles in coffee once in a while—but you better not use the same pot that you used last time, eh?"

Both brothers roar with laughter, and everyone is expected to join in. And when the laughter had died down, it was Biel's turn.

"Remember Emile Benoit, the big goofy guy whose nose was always running? Big Ben, we called him. Well, we were having soup one afternoon, Germain makes a good pot of soup, you know. Especially his pea soup, you gots to taste his pea soup. Well, us guys are sitting round the table enjoying our soup when one of the guys makes a small joke. Nobody's laughing, but Big Ben thinks it's hilarious and starts laughing and snorting like crazy. A big gob of green snot comes shooting out his nose like it came from a fire hose, and guess what? It lands right in the middle of his soup. Now everyone is laughing like crazy. When the laughing died down, Germain gets up to get another bowl for Big Ben. Germain always makes a huge pot, you know. Big Ben waves him away and continues sipping and slurping his soup with gusto. The rest of us are real quiet. Somehow Germain's soup didn't taste quite the same. After that, whenever Germain made pea soup, you could count on some guy making a remark: 'Looks mighty good, Germain, I just hope it's not snot soup.'"

Now it's okay for Germain to cut in. "Well, you know me . . . You know me," he repeats. "I tell the guys it may look like snot soup, it may taste like snot soup, but it's not snot soup."

Such was the good-natured humour that formed a big part of everyday life in those men-only bush camps.

It didn't take long for the Gauthier boys to find jobs. From their description of their workplace, it sounds just awful. It's a chrome-plating plant, and they have to wear heavy rubber aprons and rubber boots all day long to protect against toxic acids that permeate the building. They don't seem to mind. The pay is good, and they only have to work ten hours a day. Within a month, they earn enough for a new wardrobe and something else . . . Germain buys a violin from a pawnshop and Biel gets a guitar. Soon they are playing lively music like I never heard before. Mom does a little solo jig in the kitchen as other tenants come downstairs to see what the commotion is about.

Applause breaks out. The musicians don't need any coaxing to continue playing, and soon everyone is smiling and looking happy. Even our Ukrainian girls, Katie and Nellie, who are normally quite staid, are now tapping their feet in time to the lively music. After the performance, the girls announce that a Ukrainian picnic is planned for next Sunday and everyone is welcome. In particular, they want Germain and Biel to come. "And don't forget to bring your instruments," they insist.

The following Sunday after church, a few of Katie and Nellie's friends show up and we all pile in their cars and are transported to a remote wooded area along the Niagara escarpment. The setting feels a bit mysterious; there are no houses nearby and no orchards. A couple of colourful yellow and blue flags mark the driveway leading to what looks like a common woodlot.

As we proceed down the winding driveway, a scene unfolds that I could never have imagined. There must be a couple hundred people; mostly casually dressed folk, except for a group of pretty girls wearing bright red skirts and intricately embroidered white blouses with black velvet vests, traditional costumes from their homeland in the Ukraine. Older ladies have set up tables with large trays of exotic-smelling food.

Anyone passing by is urged to try some homemade borsch, holubtsi, perogies, and other dishes too difficult to pronounce.

"Eat, eat!" they urge.

All the food tastes great to me, some almost as good as my mom's. Beer flows freely, and a few of the boys are already drunk. An old bearded man is passing around samples of what he calls "vodka" from a gallon jug. Everyone uses the same shot glass. "Tastes a lot like the stuff we brew in Ross," declare the Gauthier boys.

Attention is now focusing around a large wooden platform decorated with blue and yellow ribbons. Costumed musicians appear with their instruments. Soon people are dancing, and the whole place comes alive.

And then, the moment we were waiting for: Biel and Germain are introduced and given the stage to themselves. As soon as they start playing it's obvious that people really like their lively music, especially the polkas, and couples rush to the platform to dance. By the end of the day, everyone is really happy, especially my cousins who never expected such a great reception. They even have an invitation to play at a wedding coming up later in the summer.

We saw less of our cousins after that wonderful Ukrainian picnic. I have to wonder, did they find girlfriends? But they loved Mom's cooking and so we could count on them joining our family for dinner just about every Sunday. Mom usually cooked a chicken potpie, and oh, how my cousins praised her for the delicious *"cipâte,"* as they called it. It reminded them of their mom's cooking, they said. Mom would modestly contend that it couldn't possibly compare to her older sister's. La Vieille Belette's *cipâte* usually included moose or deer meat. She might throw in some pork, rabbit, chicken, duck, or goose. God knows what else she put in that *cipâte*. Everybody is laughing; I'm not sure why, but rumour has it that La Vieille Belette was not above throwing in beaver, muskrat, perhaps a squirrel or two—actually, just about any critter she might get her hands on. Nobody dared ask what was in that *cipâte*.

One day the Gauthier boys came home with a bunch of live bunnies, and I must say they were really cute. Supposedly they were a gift for me and I could raise them as my pets. "What do you do with them?" I ask. "Can you play with them, take them for walks? Will we keep them in the house or let them roam around outside?"

Germain and Biel promised that they would build a special home just for the bunnies. They would also build a large pen so the bunnies could enjoy the outdoors too. The pen was made of two-by-fours and was about the size of a small room. Chicken wire was nailed to the outside of the frame. This clever "patent," as they called it, served a double purpose. It kept the bunnies from running away, and it protected them from cats and dogs. It was open at the bottom and could easily be moved by two people. The idea was that you could place the pen over a patch of nice, green grass until the bunnies had eaten everything within the pen and then it would be moved to a fresh spot. Once the whole yard was trimmed, fresh grass would have grown to replace the old stuff and the whole process would start all over again. Mom thought this was a great idea—especially since we didn't own a lawn mower, and our yard was getting pretty scruffy.

I soon tired of looking after the bunnies. It was a lot of work, feeding and watering and cleaning out their cages. Besides, I already had my dog Jackie. He was a whole lot more fun than those bunnies. And so, we all shared the chores and kept moving that damned pen all around the yard and our neighbour's yard as well. The bunnies quickly grew; one even had babies. Now what?

The problem kind of resolved itself. Whenever the bunnies were outside in their pen, one or two would mysteriously disappear and their numbers slowly dwindled. The feeling was that they must have crawled out from under the base of the pen and made their escape. I noticed that even when the pen was firmly placed over a perfectly flat spot, at least one would escape, never to be seen again.

My cousins observed that the bunnies had grown a lot these past few months and could quite possibly have jumped over the fencing.

"What's going to happen to them?" I ask with concern.

"Not to worry, Jules, rabbits are really smart," Biel assures me. "As you can see, there's plenty of grass everywhere so they won't go hungry, and rabbits can easily outrun any cat or dog. Hell, they can even outrun a greyhound. Don't you worry, Jules; they'll be just fine."

The last of the rabbits escaped just before Thanksgiving, and inwardly I was sort of happy. I could almost picture it, all those rabbits free and frolicking through the neighbourhood. Now, if they were as smart as Biel says, they might even have found each other and had a reunion. Who knows, maybe they found their way to the Burgoyne Bush, and that would be like rabbit heaven, I figure.

Each year, Mom puts on a big Thanksgiving dinner for all the relatives who followed our family to St. Catharines. All the ladies bring a dish, but it seems Mom's chicken potpie gets the most compliments. "This reminds me of those delicious *cipâtes* grandma Gauthier used to make," comments an aunt. "Where'd you get the rabbit?"

"That's not rabbit," Mom insists in a firm, almost angry tone. "This year I thought I'd be a little different." She goes on to explain that she was at the farmer's market last week and "you'd be surprised at how many types of chickens and turkeys they sell at that market. Oh, that must be the turkey you're tasting." Everyone is unusually quiet until another aunt changes the subject.

A sickening feeling of dread creeps into my gut and suddenly I don't feel hungry anymore. I never did find out what happened to all those rabbits, and I never asked. Just like I never asked about Santa Claus. It was just one of those things best left unsaid. That way, nobody has to admit to a lie, and nobody has to admit to how naive they were, and life just carries on.

BEST BATH EVER

There are now eighteen people living in our house, sometimes more, when yet another cousin from Manitoba comes for a "short visit." Amazingly, this diverse collection of people gets along pretty good. There is the odd complaint, but never anything serious. I do remember one continuing, vexing problem though, and how one day it brought about a delightful encounter that causes me to smile whenever I think back on it. It all revolved around our old, pathetic, hot water tank. It seems no matter how carefully bath times were scheduled; there was never enough hot water.

"Maybe the kids could all use the same bath water, one after another, starting with the youngest kid first," Dad suggests. "After all, that's what we did when I was growing up."

Ugh! I think to myself. *I would rather bathe in cold acid than use the same water as my sisters.*

Thankfully, Mom puts the kibosh to that idea. "We just have to be a little more creative," she says. "Maybe we could heat water on the stove and carry pails of hot water upstairs like we did when I was a girl. We even melted snow for our hair," she adds. How melting snow could help the situation isn't explained.

"And who is going to haul those dozens of heavy pails upstairs?" asks Dad without expecting an answer.

The topic is soon dropped. For my part, since I love to soak for long periods, I usually take my bath late in the evening after everyone has gone to bed, but that's not always convenient.

One Sunday afternoon, I come home from playing war games with my buddies. I'm covered in mud and I know my mom won't be happy. Bracing for a lecture, I'm ever so pleased to find she's not home. How lucky! Now if the bathroom is free, I might have time to clean up before she gets back. I rush upstairs and try the door. Great! It's not locked. Now if there's enough hot water, I might even have time for a quick bath. I lock the door behind me and get undressed. I am about to draw back the curtain which hides the old cast-iron tub when—holy smokes! It dawns on me: I am not alone.

From the exposed end of the tub, dainty white toes wriggle like they are waving hello. What to do? I'm about to tiptoe out the room, praying for anonymity, when a familiar voice croons, "I'll be out in a minute, Jules."

The calm, sweet voice belongs to Maggie, and she obviously is not troubled by my presence. "Could you pass me that towel?" she asks as her feet retreat and the curtain opens wide. My befuddled brain scrambles to make sense of this awkward scene, but now it instantly shifts gears and becomes totally engaged, greedily drinking in this vision of loveliness close enough to touch.

Until now I had only seen Maggie dressed in pants and loose shirt. I was only vaguely aware that her body was undergoing that metamorphic magic that transforms a young girl, seemingly overnight, into a voluptuous woman. How stupid of me not to see beyond the clothes. Now it is achingly obvious that she is indeed a young woman, a beautiful young woman, with pert small breasts, capped with dark oversized nipples. Curvy hips frame a mysterious little muff of red frizzy hair that perfectly matches the hair on her head. I glance up to try and fathom whether she might be angry with me, but no . . . There's that gorgeous smile which I take as permission to enjoy the moment. I feel that dreaded flush that turns my face crimson whenever I am embarrassed, but there is something else.

Maggie's green eyes dart downward. "Oh my; I see a little soldier standing at attention," she teases, and then bursts forth in that familiar, uninhibited laughter. Maggie quickly dries her hair and wraps the large white towel around her perfect naked body, and just like a stage curtain coming down too soon, the show is over. "I'm afraid I used up all the hot water," she laughs as she slips out the door. "Sorry!"

Without thinking, but still in a state of rapture, I find myself immersed in the tepid, sudsy water left by Maggie. And oh, it feels reeeal good.

MOTORING TO MANITOBA

The war is still grinding on through the summer of 1943, but things seem a little less urgent now. Is it a sense that our side is winning, or are people just getting used to a new reality? The war is a terrible tragedy for so many people, but for some it has brought a newfound prosperity, and yes, even security, especially for those who had been unemployed through the Great Depression. Everybody has a job now, and those twelve-hour shifts are winding down. Perhaps this is the time to enjoy a bit of leisure?

I wonder if that's how Dad saw things when he came home from work one day and announced it was time to visit relatives back in Manitoba. Mom sure got excited. This is something she has dreamed about for a long time. She has been banking most of the rent money so we have the cash, and Dad is able to take his first vacation since starting work at McKinnon's.

A number of relatives have joined us in St. Catharines since my parents led the way, others came for a short visit, but there are still plenty more we haven't seen since leaving Manitoba. There's a bunch of new nieces and nephews Mom has never seen, and she would like us kids to get acquainted with the rest of our large family.

Our family has also grown since our move out east. Sister Alice is five years old now, and little brother Louis is nearly three. They've never been to Manitoba. Mom is also longing to see her beloved parents. They are growing old and she longs to see them.

The train was pretty much the only mode of travel to Winnipeg, but when Dad found out the cost of fare for six people, he nearly had a fit. Sensing that Mom would not be deterred and always with an eye on expenses, Dad suggests another possibility.

"We could drive to Manitoba by car," he says. "The last leg of Canada's first coast-to-coast highway just opened last year, and cars can now travel through Northern Ontario along Highway #11 all the way to Winnipeg." At one time, Canadian motorists travelling west would have to detour through the US. However, since the start of the war, driving through the States is no longer an option. It's unlikely that Americans would sell their precious gas to Canadians, and of course, they would never accept Canadian gas coupons.

"You must be joking," Mom scoffs.

After a period of silence, Mom recognizes that Dad is indeed serious. A big argument follows with Mom pointing out the folly of such an idea.

"There's a war on, you know, and where are you going to get a car, and how about all the gas coupons it would take to drive to Manitoba and back? I told you we should have kept the Studebaker. We could have been saving coupons, and by now it might be possible."

What Mom won't admit is that if Dad hadn't sold the Studebaker, we could never have bought this big house on Brighton. She is well aware that the renters are adding considerably to our family finances, but I suspect she would gladly forego the rent money to have her privacy back.

Too bad Dad had to sell the Studebaker. That car was such a beauty, and it ran so quietly, so smoothly. It was the classiest car in the whole neighbourhood, and boy did I feel proud showing it off to all my buddies whose parents could never dream of owning such a car. When Dad bought it brand-new in 1941, I suspect he knew that this was the last year cars would be made in Canada, at least until after the war. He paid less than $1,000.00 for it, and one year later, sold it for more than double that amount.

"That's how we were able to afford this big house," he reminds Mom.

A couple weeks later, a tow truck deposits an old green car on our driveway.

"It's a 1934 Dodge," Dad tells me. "It was built the same year you were born. Got it from the scrap yard real cheap. The motor needs an overhaul, and the brakes and tires are worn, but other than that, it's still in pretty good shape."

Not nearly as classy as that '41 Studebaker, I think to myself, *but hey, I guess Dad knows what he's doing.*

Dad didn't tell me, but later I found out that he actually bought two cars from the scrap dealer. The other was supposedly for spare parts, but it serves another purpose. By registering it in my uncle's name, we qualify for extra gas coupons even though that car will never leave the scrap yard. Not exactly lawful, I suspect, so I keep this to myself.

Over the next couple months, Dad strips the old car apart piece by piece while I watch. I pass him tools and ask hundreds of questions. By the time he reassembles all the parts, I feel I have a pretty good understanding of how a car engine works. I have even more respect for Dad's ingenuity when he lets me push the start button and the heavy-duty inline six instantly roars to life. It is now purring smoothly in the driveway. I would love to go for a ride, but that shall have to wait for another day. All the wheels are off the car, and Dad has given up hope of getting new tires before our planned trip.

Once again, blame it on the war. All the tires that came with the car are pretty worn, and even counting those from its twin sitting in a scrap yard somewhere, there isn't much to choose from.

One Saturday morning, Dad and I haul a bunch of inner tubes to the tire shop down Facer Street. The existing, do-it-yourself cold patches are carefully removed and replaced with vulcanized hot patches. This is a magical process whereby the patching rubber is actually melted in place by burning a metal tray loaded with a mysterious white powder over the new patch; phosphorous, I think it's called. Plumes of acrid smoke permeate through the whole shop. It smells just awful.

We now have six black inner tubes decorated with twenty-eight bright red vulcanized patches, mostly round things but a few oval ones too. They look pretty impressive, but Dad still considers the tires and tubes to be the biggest worry for our planned trip to Winnipeg. It's a risk he is willing to take. As far as I'm concerned, it just adds to the sense of adventure.

Meanwhile, Mom has been busy packing. We shall be away at least a month, and she is finding it almost impossible to pack the necessities for six people. Dad won't entertain the idea of strapping a trunk or suitcase to the outside of the car as Mom has suggested; bad enough he was forced to attach a second spare when he realized how badly worn the tires were. At Mom's urging, Dad has built a wooden box to contain our food. At meal times, the box will serve as a picnic table. The rest of the time, it fits snugly between the front and rear seats and supports a makeshift bed which sister Alice and little brother Louis will use for napping.

We are finally on the road, and I can hardly contain my excitement. We shall be travelling north and west, mostly along Highway 11 for over 1,500 miles to Winnipeg, Manitoba. It's kind of neat knowing we are among the first to make this journey on a brand-new road.

It's taking forever to leave behind the familiar orchards and small farms, the factories and the warehouses that line the Queen Elizabeth. Traffic is heavy, and it seems everyone is passing us. Dad carries on at his own slow pace, ignoring the horns of impatient drivers. We go even slower as we creep along Yonge Street and through the canyons of Toronto.

Late afternoon, we're out of the big city, but where are the wild rivers, the blue lakes, and the endless forests that I thought would start right after Toronto? Hours go by, and at last we are in cottage country. It's all very nice, but it sure doesn't look like wilderness to me. There are lots of pretty lakes with cute little cabins and lots of boats of every description. The highway is lined with dozens of billboards and signs, and we read them all with interest for we are on the lookout for a place to stay overnight.

As we approach Gravenhurst, Dad spots a cluster of tiny, run-down cabins and decides this is where we will spend our first night. The proprietor informs Dad that each cabin has only one bed.

"The kids are happy to sleep on the floor," Dad tells him, "and no, we won't be needing supper."

I help Mom haul the food box to the crude little cabin, and we make do with ham sandwiches for supper.

Mom has spotted mouse droppings. She quietly sweeps them into a corner and is careful not to make a fuss. All night long, the mosquitoes are ferocious. Mom gets up to try to figure out where they're coming from. Only when day breaks does it become obvious: there's a big round hole in the wall where a stove pipe would normally connect to the outdoors. She stuffs a coat in the hole, and we are able to enjoy an hour or so of peace before we hit the road again.

We are leaving behind all the busy little lakes and the countless signs of civilization. The scenery is becoming more natural, and I'm getting excited to see true wilderness.

I am on the lookout for a certain glassy lake, a lake beautifully described in a poem we learned in school last year.

A White Tent Pitched by a Glassy Lake

A white tent pitched by a glassy lake,
Well under a shady tree,
Or by rippling rills from the grand old hills,
Is the summer home for me.
I fear no blaze of the noontide rays,
For the woodland glades are mine,
The fragrant air and that perfume rare,
The odour of forest pine.

A cooling plunge at the break of day,
A paddle, a row, or sail,
With always a fish for a mid-day dish,
And plenty of Adam's ale.
With rod or gun, or in hammock swung,
We glide through the pleasant days;
When darkness falls on our canvas walls,
We kindle the camp-fire's blaze.

From out the gloom sails the silv'ry moon,
O'er forests dark and still,
Now far, now near, ever sad and clear,
Comes the plaint of a whip-poor-will;
With song and laugh and with kindly chaff,
We startle the birds above,
Then rest tired heads on our cedar beds,
To dream of the ones we love.

The wild woods, the wild woods,
The wild woods give me;
The wild woods of Canada,
The boundless and free!

That poem really moves me. I vow that one day, I too will spend the summer living in a tent pitched by a lake. As we drive on, I am on the lookout for that perfect glassy lake with a shady tree. Of course spending a summer in a tent would be great, but my imagination carries me into another realm, an idyllic place where I would live the whole year all by myself.

I imagine a cozy little log cabin tucked in some remote corner of unspoiled wilderness. I would build my cabin with my own two hands, skilfully using just a few hand tools. Of course it would need a stone fireplace to keep warm in winter, which I would build with nearby stones. From the open porch, there's a clear view of a glorious waterfall that drops into a sheltered, cedar-fringed pool, just perfect for daily swims. Rippling waters gather from the pristine pool to feed a fast-flowing river before disappearing into the mysterious wilderness beyond.

My days would be filled hunting and fishing and exploring by canoe the countless rivers and lakes that go on forever. In winter months, I would craft fine wood furniture that I would sell to support my modest lifestyle.

"The Quints, the Quints!" Mom shouts, waking me from my daydreams. We are passing a giant billboard with pictures of the Dionne quintuplets, and I am reminded of all the fuss that swirled around them over the years. Apparently, they were the first quintuplets ever to survive their birth, and there were all sorts of souvenirs and products available for those who wished to be reminded of this miracle.

Mom saved box tops from Oxydol laundry soap and eventually got enough to exchange for five very special quintuplets spoons. Each of the spoons is shaped to look like one of the Dionne quints when they were toddlers, and each has their name embedded in the design. I chose Yvonne as my personal spoon because I thought she was the cutest. I suggest that I would like to meet Yvonne and her sisters, and Mom agrees that may be a good idea since we are so close to where they were born.

"Jules was born just one month before the Quints, you know," she reminds Dad.

Mom says they are living nearby in a specially built home where they can be viewed during certain hours. Sounds a bit like a zoo, but still, I would love to see them.

The Quints are the furthest thing from Dad's mind right now. He has detected a slight knocking sound coming from somewhere under the floorboards. He is relieved to find that the knocking stops when the car stops rolling. This tells him it's not the engine. He crawls under the old Dodge and quickly figures out it's the universal joint. He slathers on some butter and we proceed ever so slowly into North Bay.

"I'm sorry," says the garage mechanic as the car is hoisted towards the ceiling. "Normally I could have you back on the road in less than an hour, but we don't have a replacement part; there's a war on, you know."

The smell of gasoline draws everyone's attention to a steady drip coming from the gas tank.

"Oh, no!" the mechanic yells, "I'm afraid your gas tank is leaking."

Dad points out that it's the hoist that has punctured the gas tank. The mechanic disputes this. Another mechanic gets involved. The proprietor gets involved. This is going to take a whole lot longer than anyone had imagined, and it's getting late.

Finally, Mom intervenes. "Look! I noticed a hotel on the highway as we drove into town. Why don't we stay there for tonight, and you men will have all day tomorrow to fix the problem and sort things out."

The hotel is beautiful. It fronts onto a perfect sandy beach on Lake Nipissing, and I can't wait to go for a swim. Each of us has a bed, and there are no mosquitoes tonight.

Dad has left before we get up. Mom takes us to the beach and we spend a pleasant morning playing, swimming, and eating hotdogs. By early afternoon, Dad is back from the repair garage and is eager to be on the road. He explains how he had to go to a scrap yard and get a universal joint off a wrecked car and the gas tank had to be removed and steamed before it could be repaired.

I'm thinking this all sounds kind of interesting—maybe I should have gone with him instead of spending all that time at the beach. I'm thinking maybe now that the car is fixed and we're pressed for time, he'll pick up the pace; but no, we plod along at a steady forty-five miles per hour, and I am beginning to wonder if we shall ever get to Winnipeg.

As we press north, the tall, stately white pines slowly give way to seemingly endless forests of a tough-looking cousin, the jack pine. I notice they seem to thrive on bare rocks, sending their roots down through cracks to find the food and water they need. I especially admire their ability to cling to bare rock cliffs where no other plant stands a chance.

Dad explains that shortly after a forest fire, jack pines sprout like weeds because the heat has freed their seeds from compact cones tightly sealed from animals and other threats. My admiration for the jack pine grows as I equate them to people. Just like people, jack pines come in all shapes and sizes. Some are small and gnarly, but tough. Some are straight and tall and could be mistaken for a white pine except for their needles. The white pine has long, soft needles that grow in clusters, reminding me of a fancy overcoat designed to look stylish. Jack pine needles, on the other hand, are short and plain. The bark on the white pine is fairly smooth, while the bark of the jack pine is rough and gets rougher and flakier with age.

The sun is about to set as we approach Cochrane. There is enough light to see this is not your typical Southern Ontario town where sturdy brick buildings line the main streets, where sidewalks are cobblestone and flowers abound. The typical Southern Ontario town has an air of prosperity and orderliness that is hard to describe.

Here in Cochrane, all I see are crude, unpainted buildings, derelict machinery, and scrap cars strewn about. In stark contrast, the railway station looks mighty imposing, and there is a freshly painted fancy hotel across the street. I sense that Mom is hoping we spend the night at this elegant, comfortable-looking place. Instead we stop in front of what looks like an abandoned barn of a building. The only sign of life is a row of rough-looking old boys sitting on a weathered bench, smoking and drinking beer.

"You're not thinking of staying here?" Mom asks in a less than enthusiastic tone.

"I'm just going to ask where's a good place to stay," Dad assures her. I follow behind, getting out of the car quietly while the kids are sleeping.

The old guys are super friendly—jovial, even. They are all wearing heavy work boots except for one guy with regular shoes.

"Any other hotels around?" Dad asks.

"You're looking at a mighty fine place right here," says the guy with the shoes.

The rest of the old boys nod in agreement. "Used to be the best hotel in town," one offers.

"Still is, in my book," another chimes in.

"I've got a nice big room upstairs, big enough for you and the missus and this handsome young man," offers the man with the shoes. It takes me a few seconds to realize he is talking about me.

"I've got a couple more kids in the car," Dad explains. Before Dad can elaborate, the gentleman who by now I figure must be the owner, makes an offer Dad finds hard to resist. "You won't find a more peaceful place than right here," he says. "And I guarantee you won't find a better rate. I can put you up for seven bucks," he tells my dad, "and I guarantee, there's no bedbugs here." He makes it sound like all the other hotels in Cochrane are infested.

I remember mom talking about some pitiful relatives with lots of kids and they had bedbugs, and all the legs of the beds were sitting in cans of coal oil to prevent the bugs from climbing up. Ugh. Sensing that Dad is still not convinced, the proprietor makes one final pitch.

"I'll tell you what," he says. "Don't pay me now, and by morning if you're not happy you can just drive away." I guess that clinched the deal, because soon we are climbing the squeaky stairs to our room. After checking for bedbugs, Mom has to admit the room isn't so bad. That pervasive smell of smoke and stale beer I would learn was pretty standard wherever you went up North.

Come morning, Dad doesn't need any reminders to fill the gas tank before we continue along Highway #11. Even he is surprised to learn that just ahead is a 160-mile stretch that has no hotels, no stores, no garages, and no gas. Our jolly gas attendant seems to take great delight in reinforcing his message. "You better not have any breakdowns, especially between Hearst and Geraldton," he warns. "You could be stuck for weeks."

Now Mom is alarmed—what would she do with us kids if we were stranded along this rough new road with no shelter and little food? "What if we have to spend the night in the bush with the mosquitoes and the bears?" she asks. Dad just shrugs. Bears don't concern him, and besides, the mosquitoes can't be any worse than that first night near Gravenhurst.

"Look," he tells her, "sure there's not much traffic, but eventually someone will come along and give us a ride to the nearest train station, and if the car can't be fixed, well, we'll just have to leave it behind."

Wow! I can't believe what I'm hearing. Dad is quite prepared to abandon this great old car that he so lovingly restored. He goes on to assure my mom that all will be okay. I begin to fantasize what it might be like living in the bush, just like the Indian people that we've seen living in poor looking villages along the way.

Yeah! Let the car break down, I muse to myself, what a fabulous experience that would be. I'm sure my pals would be super impressed when they heard about our amazing adventure. I can just see the headlines in the *St. Catharines Standard*: "FAMILY SURVIVES ORDEAL IN NORTHERN WILDERNESS." I would be interviewed, and I would modestly explain that it really wasn't so bad. "You see, while Dad was busy trying to fix the car, I made a powerful bow and a quiver full of deadly arrows and went off hunting. Wild game was sparse, but I managed to bag a couple of rabbits, which we roasted over a fire for our supper."

As we plod along Highway #11, I keep adding to the fantasy to the point that I can well imagine writing a book—a book something like Robinson Crusoe—and it would become a bestseller, and I would be famous and make lots of money.

Dad concentrates on the driving while Mom and I pick out inviting places for our daily picnic lunch. There seems to be no shortage of beautiful, clear lakes and mysterious fast-flowing rivers. I can't help but wonder where those dark rivers come from—and where are they going? Oh, to have a birch bark canoe, and oh, to have the time to paddle and explore.

Kapuskasing is a super neat town. It is built along the shores of a beautiful lake, fed by a medium-sized river that we shall be crossing. Upon crossing the bridge, Dad stops so we can stretch our legs and have a look at the falls. Nearby, there's a small hydro generating station built especially for the town. Mom passes around cheese and crackers even though it's a bit early for lunch. Perhaps it is her way of preparing us for the long, lonely stretch that lies ahead.

I notice that the types of trees keep changing. Jack pines are fewer and far between now, while white spruce are more common.

"Why are they called 'white' when they are totally green?" I ask. Dad doesn't seem to know for sure and draws my attention to pockets of smaller spruce that look stunted and a bit sickly.

"Those are black spruce," he says, "and they seem to like swampy places. Now why do you suppose these are called black spruce?" he asks. "Don't they look green too?" I have to agree. Sometimes things don't make a whole lot of sense.

"Jack pine don't like to have their feet in the water," he explains. "Neither do white spruce."

"But Dad, aren't those white spruce over there, those that look like giant Christmas trees? How come their feet are in the water?"

"Those are tamarack," he corrects. "Tamarack don't mind having wet feet. We call them evergreens, but did you know that tamaracks lose their needles in the fall just like all the leafy trees in St. Catharines? Before they lose their needles, they turn a beautiful golden colour much like the silver birch."

I attempt to summarize. "So, let's see: jack pine and white spruce don't like wet feet, but tamarack and black spruce are happy with wet feet so they grow in wet places."

"And don't forget cedars; they also love wet places," Dad adds, "and you see that grove of trees over there that look like spruce? They are actually balsam fir."

This is just too much! For the first time, I realize that my dad is pretty smart, but he doesn't know everything. He doesn't seem to know why white pine and white spruce are called white when obviously they are green, and why black spruce are called black when they are also green. Why do we call tamaracks evergreens when they aren't green in the winter, and why do we call jack pine "Jack" when none of the other trees have human names? This is all kind of interesting, but it is also kind of boring. I think I'll have a nap.

I wake up as we approach Hearst and my parents are arguing. Dad wants to stay here overnight, and this time, it's Mom who is eager to carry on.

"Let's keep driving while the kids are sleeping," she insists. "It's still early." Dad points out a lone hotel along the main drag. "Looks pretty shabby to me," says Mom.

"It may be a long time before we see another," warns Dad. Rather than argue, Dad keeps driving ever-so-slowly through town, stopping only briefly to top up the gas tank.

Dad doesn't like to stop too often, but he gets the tank topped up at virtually every gas station along the way. "You never know how far to the next pump," he reasons. "The next town is Longlac. It's not that far, but will there be gas? And more critically, will there be a place to sleep?" On the map, Longlac looks no different than all the other rough little towns that we've passed through. The map doesn't indicate places to sleep. If there's no place to spend the night in Longlac, we could be in trouble.

I can almost feel Mom's disappointment as we slowly roll through the decrepit, dusty little village of Longlac. There's not a hotel in sight, and no gas station either. There doesn't seem to be much of anything. I suspect Mom is now regretting that we didn't stay in Hearst.

We pass by a large unpainted building that looks to be under construction. Mom spots a small sign above the door that reads: "CHAMBRES" (rooms). I would think that Mom would be relieved, but she is not impressed.

"There may not be another place to sleep for many miles," Dad reminds her. Before she can say any more, a lanky, muscular man in overalls comes running towards the car and, in tortured English, urges us to come inside. When Dad responds in French, the man's face lights up and he launches into an animated welcome that even my mom cannot resist.

As we enter, he introduces us to his ample wife who is breastfeeding a chubby, contented-looking baby. She is equally welcoming and asks when we last ate. "Ah, *mon dieu*," she declares, "you must be starving. You'll eat with us," she insists.

With those huge breasts, she could likely feed a whole family, I muse to myself. Thankfully, she points out that she just needs to throw some more meat and a few potatoes into the stew pot and there will be plenty for everybody.

After supper, a bunch of barefoot kids appear and invite me out to play. Everyone speaks French and I can converse with them, even though I barely speak French anymore. I shuck my shoes and eagerly join them in a complicated game of hide and seek that I have never played before. It seems half the kids in town have joined in, and everybody is running and yelling and laughing and having a great time. They think it's just hilarious that I have trouble running on the gravel roads in my bare feet. "But, what can you expect with such dainty white feet?" they tease. Not white enough for my mom, though, who insists that I wash my filthy feet before bedtime.

I am intrigued by the smoky kerosene lamp that lights up our bedroom. It creates weird, ever-changing shadows as people move about. The thin boards on just one side of the exposed stud wall offer scant privacy from members of our host family, but there are few mosquitoes and the fresh pine boards smell lovely and I don't mind sleeping on the floor.

The next morning there are at least ten kids crowded around the kitchen table and the heavy, round lady urges them to hurry and finish eating so their guests can have breakfast.

Our host enters noisily through the front door. "I found an almost-new tire for your car," he shouts, triumphantly, waving it above his head. Dad checks the numbers on the tire and smiles. With full bellies and a third tire strapped to the back of the car, we leave Longlac and wave goodbye to this big happy family who now seem related somehow.

Holy smokes, I can't believe it. Dad is zooming along at 50 mph, and I sense that there is both relief and excitement in the air. We are past the halfway mark, and the scenery is starting to improve. We leave behind miles of flat, swampy bush and are treated to a line of magnificent cliffs. They must be a couple hundred feet high and they seem to go on forever.

The view from the top must be awesome. How I would love to get closer, maybe even climb the jagged face. As we round a bend, it becomes apparent that someone has indeed climbed these impressive cliffs, but they weren't content to just enjoy the experience. They have, painted in huge white letters on the large uncluttered surface, "JESUS SAVES." This both puzzles and annoys me. Was this natural masterpiece not beautiful enough? Did the "artist" really think he was improving upon this wonder of nature, and what purpose did the message serve? Not something the Sisters of St. Joseph would approve of, I'll bet.

Nipigon! What a lovely-sounding name, and it perfectly suits this neat little forestry town nestled at the bottom of a gentle hill. Mom spots a hotdog stand, and it takes no coaxing for Dad to stop and we all enjoy hotdogs, French fries, and soft drinks. What a treat.

I notice the speedometer nudging 55; I guess Dad is no longer concerned about flats—not that he has ever shown any sign of worry. Nothing seems to bother him.

I used to think that no other lake could be as big as Lake Ontario, but we have been driving for hours and we still catch glimpses of this big beautiful lake, a lake so huge I cannot see across it no matter how hard I look. I guess it deserves to be called Superior; after all, it is the biggest of the Great Lakes and the highest in elevation. I idly compare the name to our Sister Mary Rudolf, who is also called Sister Superior. Even though she is quite short, there is no doubt who is the highest among all the sisters at St. Joseph's.

We leave Lake Superior at Port Arthur and continue on through its sister city, Fort William, through to Kakabeka Falls, our destination for the evening. Sister Juliette thinks the name is funny and keeps repeating, "Kakabeka, Kakabeka, Kakabeka."

The falls are absolutely magnificent. Of course they are not as grand as Niagara Falls, but they are almost as high and the setting is just gorgeous.

There is an intriguing legend told on a sign by the falls. It tells the story of an Indian Princess and how, many years ago, she saved her people from an advancing Sioux war party bent on murder. The story tells of her father, an Ojibwe chief, and his dilemma when he learned that a party of Sioux warriors were paddling down the Kaministiquia River towards their village. Fearing a massacre, he called upon his beautiful daughter, Princess Green Mantle, to use her wits and her charms to divert the Sioux. According to legend, she intercepted the approaching warriors and told them that she was escaping from evil people who had kept her as a prisoner. She persuades them to attack these wicked people who live downstream. Taking a position in the lead canoe, she urges them to follow her. Swiftly, they paddle with the current down the river. Faster, faster, she urges. With absolute terror, the Sioux warriors find themselves at the very precipice of the falls.

One after another, the canoes and their fearsome warriors plunge over the lip to their doom.

Judging by the swift current, the height of the falls and the rocks below, I can almost picture the scene in my mind. I close my eyes and I can hear the death moans of all those young men as they lay dying on those sharp rocks. And in the background, the sorrowful wails from Princess Green Mantle.

"Why couldn't the Ojibwe and the Sioux get along?" I ask Dad.

"If we knew that, there wouldn't be any more wars," he replies, "and the world would be a better place. All wars are dumb," he adds. He rarely talks about it, but I know Dad feels strongly that Canada should never have been involved in the First World War, and here we are fighting in another totally stupid European war.

I can't believe it; we are zipping along at 60 mph now. The road is proper gravel, a mix of sand and smooth stones. "Not like that crushed granite that went on for miles a ways back," says Dad. "Drive a little too fast, and that sharp-edged granite can slice through a tire like a knife through butter," he adds. Since we now have three spares and we've had no flats, Dad figures he can quit worrying about the tires. He also tells me that the engine is nicely "broken in," so he can go faster now. This puzzles me. I thought it was broken when it sat in our driveway in a thousand pieces.

Mom approves of this faster pace, and so do I. I am getting totally bored. All I see are mile after mile of jack pine with few lakes or hills to relieve the monotony. I remember very little of this stretch, but I do recall a smelly paper town called Dryden with a beautiful river running through it called the Wabigoon. And I remember another interesting lakeside town called Kenora with huge log rafts floating on a quiet bay.

At last, there's the sign Mom was watching for: "WELCOME TO MANITOBA!" I'm getting really excited, until Mom explains that we still have a ways to go before our final destination. Dad is quite willing to drive a few more hours to avoid another hotel, but Mom doesn't want to arrive in the dark when Uncle Romeo's family would most likely be in bed.

The sun is setting over the circular outline of West Hawk Lake. It cradles a crescent beach with pure white sand contrasting the dark still waters. Everyone is quiet as we drink in this picture-perfect scene that you might only see in colour postcards, the kind Mom has been mailing along the way. Dad turns off the engine and we coast slowly and ever so quietly down the hill and into a canopy of tall trees overhanging the road. I feel like we are in a magical tunnel that is dark and damp and cool and there is a lovely perfume in the air. We emerge to catch a final glimpse of the red sun disappearing over the horizon. I am selfishly pleased that there are no people in sight to spoil the scene. The beach looks so inviting; maybe I'll still be able to go for a swim before dark.

Just beyond the beach are nestled a dozen or so pretty, brown cabins with a type of siding that makes them look like real logs. How fitting to be spending our last night in a lakeside cabin just like we did on our first night near Gravenhurst, but the similarities only go so far. This attractive faux-log cabin has two tiny bedrooms with pine bunks for everyone and no mouse droppings. Mom is pleased she'll be able to cook up a meal in the small kitchen, and I can't wait to climb the steps to the upper bunk and dream my private dreams before I fall asleep.

It is not yet full light when Mom gently wakes me. Keeping one finger over her lips, she leads me outside to the front porch. Together we sit and watch a lazy mist rising from the cold water; the sun is not quite awake. A loon calls at the far end of the lake, and I feel a comforting sense of awe and well-being as we watch the orange glow transforming into a magnificent bright ball of fire. Everyone else is still sleeping, and I wonder why Mom chose not to disturb them. I don't ask, and I sense that this will remain our little secret.

After breakfast, while Mom and sister Juliette are busy with the younger kids, Dad and I have our daily ritual to perform. It is my job to wash the windows on the Dodge, paying particular attention to the windshield. This morning, they are dripping wet from overnight dew, but there are no bug smears, and since I finish early, I get to check the engine oil level. I like that Dad trusts me with this critical job. The tires, though, are his babies. He carefully checks the pressure of each tire, including the spares, and if one is down even a pound or two, it gets a few quick strokes from his trusty hand pump. He then applies spit with his finger to the end of each brass tube stem and watches for bubbles that would indicate a leaky air valve. I have yet to see a leak, but he never fails to do this test before screwing on the protective cap.

Dad marvels at how lucky we are that we have come all this way with worn old tires and patched-up tubes and not one flat. I prefer to believe that it was more likely due to his meticulous attention to detail and the painfully slow speed.

We are on the last leg of our journey, and this stretch is such a pleasure. The picturesque road winds around pretty lakes, beaver meadows, and a couple of lily ponds. At times, the road rises sharply, cresting a rocky ridge only to plunge down again to a low ravine where the fog has not yet lifted. Dad proudly admits that he was part of that small army of workers who pushed the TransCanada Highway eastward from Manitoba to Ontario during the 1920s.

He remembers vividly the heat, the flies, and those pesky mosquitoes that made life miserable for every worker and even more so for the poor horses. Horses? I didn't know they used horses to build roads. I pester Dad for details, and he goes on to describe the many road-building challenges and the ingenious machines developed to overcome them.

I try to picture all the labour-intensive, sweaty work that went into this cool, tidy road. It must have been quite a sight with hundreds of muscular men cutting through the dense bush with their axes. I can almost hear the noisy teamsters cursing and urging their straining horses through long, hot days of hauling countless tons of rock and gravel with their heavy wooden wagons.

"Home," at the end of a day, was a crude lakeside camp, quite often with a sandy beach where both men and horses would cool off and wash away the day's sweat. Dad chuckles as he remembers seeing some horses so eager to cool off they broke away from their handlers and galloped into the lake with full harness.

Just west of Caddy Lake is a horse cemetery. Mom and the kids aren't interested, so Dad and I walk together along a faint trail to a large clearing with a high fence. There's no sign, but Dad knows it all too well, since he did most of the excavating for the graves with his dragline.

"The fence is to keep out deer and other animals. There are hundreds of horses buried here, most died from anthrax," he explains. "The fear that this highly contagious disease could spread caused panic amongst workers, particularly those with horses."

I can just imagine how they must have felt. There was no known cure, so at the first sign of the deadly disease, a beloved horse would be shot and quickly buried. And that was usually the end of the teamster's job, as well. How horrible, how cruel!

As we pass the turnoff to Lake Brereton, Mom breaks the silence. "Remember when your dragline tipped over?" she reminds Dad.

Of course he remembers, but to this day, he is too embarrassed to talk about it. Apparently, he was "walking" the dragline over what looked like flat terrain when the ground suddenly gave way from under the tracks and the whole machine slowly keeled over. He wasn't hurt except for his pride, nor was the machine, but it attracted a lot of attention. Gawkers came by the dozen to observe the sight of the toppled dragline. For a lot of people, it was the first time they had ever seen such a machine. Mom speculates that this particular machine may have been one of the first draglines in Manitoba.

Turning south near the town of Whitemouth, we leave behind the rocky boreal forest. The land is now flat and sandy, but jack pines still dominate. Dad doesn't need a map; he remembers all the back roads and knows of a shortcut to Ross where most of the Gauthier clan live.

It would be an exaggeration to call this a road. It's just a rocky trail with willows growing on both sides and assorted weeds and shrubs brushing the underside of the car. Dad had used this trail for years and is shocked to learn that it ends in a marsh with cattails and bulrushes and water two feet deep: dramatic proof that the dry years of the thirties are over. There is no place to turn around, so Dad has to back up the car for what seems like at least a mile.

Mom says we'll be staying at Uncle Romeo's and Aunt Irene's farm for a while, and we'll meet lots of aunts and uncles and tons of cousins. Mom explains that although she has many brothers and sisters, Uncle Romeo is by far her favourite.

Dad also comes from a large family, the Legal's. Soon we shall all become part of one huge family with more uncles and aunts and cousins than we can imagine. We will also be visiting with our grandparents. For Alice and Louis, it shall be their first visit. I was only three when we moved from Manitoba, so I don't remember much. Sister Juliette doesn't remember anything at all.

As we turn into the Gauthier farmyard, we are greeted by a couple of big friendly dogs barking like crazy, pretending to be ferocious. Folks come pouring from the house, and we are overwhelmed with hugs and kisses. Cousin Leonard takes me aside and leads me to where he and I will be spending the next week.

Wow! I can't believe my eyes. This is fantastic. Tucked in a secluded corner of the yard and facing the Winnipeg Water District pipeline is a tent just like in the poem. It's not very white and It may not be "pitched under an old pine tree by a glassy lake," but I couldn't be happier. The two of us have this comfy tent all to ourselves, and Leonard is talking about horseback riding and swimming in the nude. He even has his own .22. Sounds like paradise to me; I want to stay here forever.

The following couple of weeks are filled with obligatory visits and dinners with newfound relatives from both the Gauthiers and the Legal's. The Legal clan are scattered around a nearby community called Ste. Geneviève, which is dominated by a small white church with a tall steeple. After mass, it becomes the place to meet and talk with neighbours and relatives, and on this beautiful Sunday morning, our family is the focus of attention. People keep asking if I remember them and then go on to relate events that might trigger a memory or two. Yes, I do remember a few things, but I am not good with names.

My grandparents look much the same as I remember them, but a bit older and a bit more stooped. Grandma Legal, in her sixties now, has snow-white hair and looks older than her years. She pays loving attention to all her grandchildren and wants to know more about our lives in St. Catharines. Mom is pleased to fill her in on the wonders of our modern city, shamelessly boasting about the mild climate, the beaches, the multitude of flowers and the lush fruit orchards all around St. Catharines.

"Sounds a lot like my beautiful home in Foucherans, France," says Grandma with a tone that betrays her sorrow over having to leave that idyllic paradise in Eastern France.

Grandpa Legal is a cheery old guy. He never talks about Brittany in Western France where he comes from. He tells me how pleased he is that I can still speak French, well aware that I struggle with the correct words. Still, he won't speak English. I'm told that Grandpa Legal can speak perfect English as well as Latin and Greek, and I have to wonder, *Does he ever get to use those languages?*

Meanwhile, Mom's parents are in their eighties and looking pitifully frail. Grandma Gauthier has lost that sharp, wise wit that made people laugh, and our once-invincible Grandpa Gauthier must use a wheelchair to get around. No one talks openly of their failing health, but whispers abound that their brief, vibrant role on this earthly stage is nearing the end.

Mom continues to put on a brave face, but I know she is grieving and trying her best to deny the likelihood of ever seeing her loving parents again. I'm sad too, but I'm glad I got to meet them, and we did communicate a little. Warm hugs and kisses all around as we say our goodbyes to grandparents, doting aunts and uncles, and numerous newfound cousins.

We end our Manitoba visit in St. Boniface, that charming, historic city that serves as the bastion of French culture in Western Canada. While most residents still speak French, English is spreading, and our relatives find they must also speak English at times.

We are warmly welcomed everywhere we go—more doting aunts and uncles, and more city cousins to meet and greet. And of course, it's understood we shall share a sumptuous meal together.

The Rowans, Aunt Geneviève and Uncle Alex, have allowed their home to become the place to stay when country relatives spend a day or two in the city. Some call it "Hotel Rowan." Their hospitality knows no bounds, and they would be insulted if our family didn't stay with them before we leave for St. Catharines.

Cousin Leo shows me around the neighbourhood and introduces me to his friends. All the boys are super friendly, and we have great fun exploring all sorts of neat places around St. Boniface. Leo tells me that just across the river is the City of Winnipeg, which is even bigger than St. Boniface. Tomorrow, we'll be going downtown to a movie at the Met.

From the start of our journey, it was understood that our family would be returning to St. Catharines by train. So why don't I feel more excited? Mind you, I am impressed just to be in this awesome, cavernous building known as the CNR Union Station. I remember being here before, but now it seems totally different.

Back when I was just a little kid, I remember clutching my mom's dress as we eagerly prepared to climb on board that train, knowing that soon we would be seeing my dad again. Today it seems everyone is a little sad, especially my mom. I notice her hiding tears. It breaks her heart to be leaving all her loved ones behind. I'm sad too, partly for the same reason, but something else is bothering me.

As we settle into our comfortable, private compartment, I pester my dad with a question I've asked before. "Dad, did you really have to sell our dear old Dodge? Wasn't it just the most wonderful car, carrying all of us those hundreds of miles to Manitoba without problems? Wouldn't it be perfectly okay to go back home the same way? And, when we got home, it could stay parked on our driveway, ready to take us any place we want to go."

Dad patiently explains we don't have enough gas coupons to get back, and besides, he is due back to work in a few days. "Travelling by car may be more fun, but it takes twice as long," he says.

I know he's right. He usually is. Mom has to admit this too from time to time. Wasn't Dad right to suggest this motor trip despite her initial objections? And, how many people thought he was just plain foolish to be taking our family halfway across Canada in an old car rescued from the scrap yard?

There were plenty of eager buyers for the old Dodge, such was the shortage of decent cars in Manitoba. Dad figures that he got way more money than he could ever get in St. Catharines. Mom is pleasantly surprised and even more surprised when Dad opts for us to travel back to St. Catharines first class.

The railway line closely follows our road trip from a few weeks back. I should be excited, but the sense of adventure is just not the same. I can't wait to get home.

Cigarette smoke permeates the whole train, adding to the heat and general misery. I'm glad Dad doesn't smoke, but he does have a nasty tobacco habit. Mom just hates it. I watch as he goes through the daily ritual. With a small pocketknife, he cuts a square from a brick of compressed tobacco labelled "Shamrock Chewing Tobacco" and chews it for a few minutes. Then he dips his finger into a small tin of Copenhagen snuff and deposits a pinch of ground tobacco behind his lower lip.

Maybe because I'm bored, I hear myself suggesting that I would like to try that. Dad is happy to oblige and cuts me a tiny piece of the Shamrock brick, and of course, I also have to try the Copenhagen snuff. Almost immediately, my head starts spinning and an unstoppable wave of nausea is building. The washroom is occupied, so I heave myself up onto the opening where the cars are coupled and I throw up like crazy. My vomit dribbles slowly down the side of the train and the wind carries the brown-coloured mess along the length of the railcar, displaying what I had for lunch.

By evening, I've seen enough of trees, and I'm tired of reading. I climb the narrow ladder into the foldaway bunk that our porter has prepared. I love the feel of the crisp white sheets and the air seems better now as I draw the curtains and retreat into my inner world.

My mind relives some of those days spent with cousin Leonard. What great times we had together. I particularly loved exploring the woods on horseback.

"These are actually work horses," Leonard reminds me. "They have a mind of their own, and they don't like to run." They absolutely refused to gallop, so we just had to walk most of the time. I did coax my horse to gallop just once, but having no saddle, I promptly fell off and my horse ran back to the barn without me. Leonard's horse didn't seem to mind carrying both of us the rest of the way home.

One day, we were riding down a faint trail through the bush behind his place, and I wanted to explore what looked like an animal trail. "Can we go down there, Len?"

Leonard warned, "There's a secret camp for young guys who don't want to go to war. Whenever the police come looking for them, they hide out. They stay in camp for a few days, eating mostly canned stuff and spending their time just lying around waiting until someone comes to tell them the coast is clear."

Apparently, very few eligible men from around these parts would willingly join the army. One exception was Dad's youngest brother, Uncle Albert. He joined the "Princess Patricia's Canadian Light Infantry" all on his own. So foreign was this idea to some locals that they didn't believe he was actually in the army. One day, he came home in full uniform. Even then, some skeptics speculated that he must have borrowed the uniform just to impress.

"So, how about this trail?" I asked Leonard.

"Can't go down there, either," he warned. "Our Grandpa Gauthier owns a secret home brew distillery hidden deep in the woods, and he would be mighty annoyed if we came anywhere near." Leonard could tell by the fresh hoof prints that there was probably someone there right now. "Nobody ever walks there," he told me. "Everybody working the still comes by horseback just to make it hard for RCMP sniffer dogs to find the still." I tried to imagine those gutsy guys distilling home brew by the gallon. It's a full-time job for some.

And what about those young guys living in the bush—sometimes for weeks—to escape conscription? "That can't be much fun," said Len. "They can't have a fire, they can't light a lantern; some won't even smoke, afraid that it might give them away. And no girlfriends, either," he added with a chuckle. I have to wonder, if I lived here and was old enough, would I be in one of those camps?

During our visit to Manitoba, I couldn't help but compare the two branches of my parent's families. Mom's family, the Gauthiers, are an exuberant clan, full of that "*joie de vivre*" that makes them great fun to be with. They work hard and they play hard. They are a creative bunch, always eager to try new things and to invent useful gadgets: "patents," they call them.

Celebrations typically include all the kids, and parties can go on until dawn. Conversations are often loud with plenty of jokes and good-natured teasing. Many of them play musical instruments, and it seems everybody loves to dance. There's always lots of great food, much of it from hunting and fishing. Of course, home brew is a natural part of all festivities. There is never any mention of religion, and some don't attend church at all.

The Legals are a bit more reserved. They are also hardworking but lean more towards cerebral things. The Legals love to read and have a high regard for education. Religion plays a big role in their lives, and everyone goes to church.

The Legals enjoy big family dinners where everyone loves to talk. They are more likely to keep up with the news, so they talk about the war and politics and just about any topic imaginable. They also ask lots of questions about life in St. Catharines and express how much they would love to visit, but there is always something that holds them back.

I sense that Mom is a typical Gauthier with all the typical Gauthier traits. Meanwhile, Dad does not seem to fit the Legal profile and has almost nothing in common with his brothers. As far as I know, he is the only one who left his family at such a young age. He certainly can't be accused of being overly cautious. He never talks about religion and only goes to church for weddings and funerals.

I don't consider myself a typical Gauthier, nor do I consider myself a typical Legal. I recognize that I have been shaped by the genetics of both my parents and their ancestors before them. I like that. I love and admire the rich culture that has shaped their personalities, and I wonder how much has been passed along to me.

Having moved away from Manitoba at an early age, I feel I don't really belong here. Do I belong in St. Catharines? I don't know. I just know that I love dearly all my newfound aunts and uncles and all my precious cousins, and I sense that they love me. Maybe that's all that really matters. I am content and happy, and I feel oh-so lucky.

"1934 Dodge"   Source: public domain

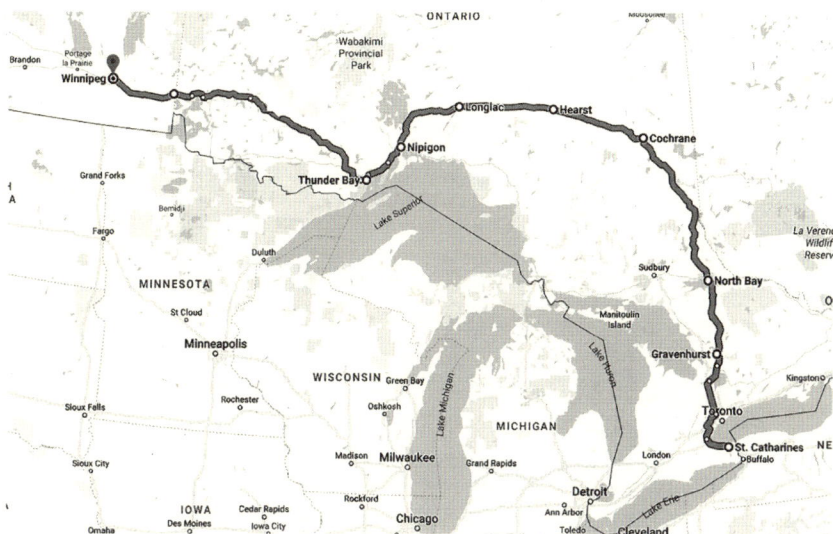

"Ontario road map"   By: Stephen Meehan

CATHOLICS AND PROTESTANTS

Ontario schoolchildren in the forties were either Catholic or Protestant, and the two seldom mixed. I was vaguely aware that Victoria school, just a few blocks down the street from St. Joseph's, was mainly for English Protestants, but they also took in the odd student who didn't fit these two main categories. St. Joseph's was exclusively Catholic and nearly all the students were either Italian, Polish, or Irish. Nobody called themselves Canadian in those days. Even if your grandparents had come to Canada many years ago, you still went by the racial origin of your parents, and so I was the only French kid until Rolly came along.

Generally, we got along pretty good with our Protestant neighbours. Occasionally we would meet one another on the street, and it was usually a friendly encounter. Still, the Sisters discouraged any formal contact. One time, a teacher from Victoria School suggested a baseball game between St. Joseph's and Victoria, and us boys were eager to take up the challenge. This supposedly radical idea was quickly shot down by Sister Superior. She explained we should not forget that all Protestants were Catholic at one time and they chose to leave the Holy Church of Rome. I was about to ask what this had to do with a baseball game, but one of the girls asked, "Sister, Sister, do Protestants go to heaven when they die?" Sister Mary Rudolf acknowledged that this was a very good question. Probably a better question than mine, I admit, so I kept my mouth shut.

"No one knows for sure," answered Sister Superior, "so we should not count on meeting Protestant friends in heaven. Meanwhile let us pray for them and hope that they see the error of their ways and return to the Holy Catholic Church."

Poor Protestants; is it any wonder that we grew up feeling somewhat superior and just a little wary of all things Protestant, and by extension, all things English?

At the start of grade six, a couple Indian kids from up north enrolled at St. Joseph's. To the Sisters' credit, they stressed that we should welcome these dark-skinned children with long black hair and make them feel at home.

Unfortunately, this message didn't get through to the Protestant kids, and soon these shy, swarthy outsiders were confronted with taunts and threats once they left the school ground. Things escalated and got real ugly after one of the Protestant kids was soundly beaten by the Indian boy they called Tonto.

The next day there were rumours flying that a gang from Victoria School had gathered somewhere beyond the schoolyard, waiting to get revenge. Naturally, we had to organize a group to escort our Catholic schoolmates home. It was amazing how quickly word spread. Our side quickly grew to include virtually every boy from St. Joseph's.

As we proceeded with our Indian friends, our small army grew ever larger as older brothers learned what was going on. Even some adults got caught up in the crusade. Many carried sticks and stones; a few had slingshots. Everyone was hollering and banging sticks on the pavement. We must have made quite a sight.

The Protestants were nowhere to be seen, and we congratulated ourselves for having scared them off. As we rounded a corner—Oh! Oh! There they were, an even bigger army of boys facing us across a large field. There was a lot of yelling, rocks started flying, and I have to admit, I was a bit scared. Slowly, each army advanced throwing stones, even though we were still beyond range of each other. Just when it started to look like someone could get hurt, police cars appeared, sirens wailing, and everyone scattered. I suspect we were all relieved as we made our way back to more familiar turf!

I was just a couple blocks from home when a gang of five boys from Victoria stopped me. At first, I naively thought they just wanted to make conversation, but they formed a circle around me, yelling and taunting and hitting me over the head with their sticks.

"Why didn't I just run when I first spotted them?" I agonized, but it was too late. Hoping to distract my tormenters long enough to make my escape, I began to yell.

From a nearby vegetable garden, a large barefoot woman in a sweaty dress was watching. She began cursing at the boys with every Italian profanity in her arsenal, spittle exploding from her mouth. At first the boys with the sticks seemed mildly amused and retorted with disrespectful language, calling her a fat "wop." Big mistake! Waving her short-handled hoe, this now ferocious mama came charging at the group like an angry bear protecting her cub. I am certain she could have thrashed all five of those dumb kids if they hadn't run like scared rabbits.

Obviously they didn't know that you don't mess with Italian women, particularly Italian mamas. I learned this basic truth first-hand when we first moved to 55 Concord, where most of our neighbours were Italian. Angelo became one of my best buddies and we were regularly at each other's homes. We played mostly outdoors, but when we smelled fresh baking, we could count on our moms to give us a sample, even when it wasn't yet suppertime. One day I was at Angelo's, and as we entered the kitchen, his mama asked him to do some minor chore.

Was it because his dad wasn't home? Or was it because I was there? Poor Angelo suffered a lapse in his thinking, and instead of complying, he made the mistake of sassing his mama. Without warning, Angelo's petite mom let fly with an open-handed smack across the side of his head that sent him sprawling across the kitchen floor. Note: *Never, ever sass an Italian mama.*

A couple weeks after the encounter with the Protestant boys, I was on my way to play evening baseball at St. Joseph's when I met four young boys I didn't recognize, walking down the back lane. Three were about my size with one a bit smaller. I didn't perceive them as a threat. I made what I thought was a friendly inquiry as to where they lived.

"None of your fucking business, Pope lover," the biggest one replied with venom in his voice. I must admit I was taken aback. After all, it wasn't that unusual to come across strange kids from another neighbourhood, and I felt I was just being friendly. Pope lover? What the heck does that mean? I had never heard such an expression. Sensing that any response at this time would only escalate into something uglier, I remained silent and carried on down the back lane, bracing for a possible attack.

Hearing the scuff of gravel behind me, I turned in time to deflect a charge from the biggest boy, and sent him crashing to the ground. Two of the other guys following close behind hesitated, perhaps reassessing the situation. Meanwhile, my brain was replaying that scene just a few weeks ago when I stood helpless while that gang of Protestant boys thumped me on the head with their sticks. I still had the lumps to remind me. Here I was only a hundred yards from home; how dare these punks attack me on my home turf? And then it dawned on me: The mouthy kid was one of those Protestant guys that had thumped me on my head with his stick. Now here he was with three other boys, his brothers, I suspect. Anger wells up in me like a pot about to boil. I can feel my whole body preparing for battle. Today, the "wrestling only" rule shall be put aside.

Before they could recover from seeing their leader lying in the dirt, dazed and confused and staring at his bleeding hands, I attacked the two guys closest with full ferocity. With fists flying and wrestling moves, I'm sure these boys had never seen, they were both knocked to the ground in seconds.

The smallest kid turned and tried to run from the scene. He may not have been a threat, but in that instant, I clearly remembered a piece of advice offered up by an older big brother on our block. Bruno, who had been in more than his share of fights, would regale us younger boys with stories of how he beat up anyone who gave him cause. "Always remember, guys," Bruno would stress, "If you're ever up against more than one attacker, take out the weakest one first. Show him no mercy, smash his face in; that way, you even the odds quicker, and if you're really brutal, you'll scare the shit out of the others."

I caught up to the innocent kid and slammed him to the ground like he was a rag doll. By now, the first guy (the one with the foul mouth) was back on his feet determined to try again, the other two following warily behind. The little kid just lay there whimpering. I grabbed him by the ankles and swung his limp body around like we were some crazy carousel. One by one, the trio toppled like bowling pins as they tried to get to me. The little kid was screaming his head off, his body smashing repeatedly into his brothers. I lost count of the revolutions we made and how many times his brothers were bowled over, but finally, I sensed they no longer had any fight left in them. I let go of the kid's ankles and he went flying face-first into the dirt, screaming ever louder.

I turned my attention to the pathetic-looking threesome and calmly asked, "Now, you Protestant bastards, have you had enough?" Silence! The gang retreated hastily down the lane, abandoning their little buddy. For a moment, just for a moment, I felt a twinge of pity as I watched the poor guy limping and crying and struggling to catch up.

I brushed myself off and joined my friends from St. Joseph's for our nightly game of baseball. As I stepped up to home plate for my turn at bat, I remember thinking, "You know, if ever we did get to play baseball against those Victoria boys, I don't think they'd stand a chance."

MY BUDDY BRIAN

Weapons at the ready, our hunting party is on the prowl to kill a wild beast and bring it back to the cave. Almost anything will do for we are desperate to save our tribe from starving to death. We come upon a mysterious, reed-lined swamp, and Hugo yells, "There's a crocodile!" and starts firing away with his weapon. We all join in, sending volley after volley across the swamp until the croc is dead. It flips over, its white belly facing up, legs twitching uselessly. Another one shows up, and we kill that one too.

All together we killed six crocs before reality finally takes over and I begin to feel remorse. In fact, we've killed six frogs with our slingshots, and the three of us feel guilty. One of the frogs that we thought was dead starts swimming slowly across the swamp, stroking with only one leg. It would be easy to pop him off, and maybe we should put him out of his misery, but now we all feel badly and just watch as he painfully tries to climb up onto the bank with his crippled leg dragging behind.

A couple boys, strangers to us, have been watching the massacre. One of the guys picks up a stick and smacks the crippled frog. I probably should be grateful, but I find myself objecting strongly and yelling self-righteously at him for killing the crippled frog. He does not take kindly to my yelling and approaches menacingly with his stick. "Who are you to yell at me after you wounded it, you little twerp," he spits.

"Drop that stick and I'll show you," I yell back at him. He drops the stick and the fight is on.

I sense that this will not be a vicious, no-holds-barred type of fight. My opponent is a bit bigger than me and is obviously a skilled wrestler. I suspect he is not out to hurt or maim, he just wants to put down this impudent kid and humiliate him in front of his friends. It is not my nature to hurt anybody either, but I don't intend to back down. He may be bigger and quite strong, but I am faster, so we are pretty evenly matched. I surprise him with a trick move and he goes down, but not for long. Now to my surprise, I am bowled over and a bit annoyed with myself. This is not going to be easy, but I am supremely confident I will prevail. The wrestling continues in an almost scripted fashion, each taking turns at dominating the other. I am using every move I have ever learned and exerting all my strength, but I cannot keep him down. I'm certain he is doing the same, and he refuses to yield. Fatigue is setting in. We are both moving slower and slower, like you see in the movies when some dramatic moment is portrayed in slow motion. The boys on both sides who have been silent spectators up to now move in and hold each of us back and we don't resist. My opponent's friend takes a hold of each of our arms and raises them. He shouts in an authoritative voice, "I declare this match a draw, now shake hands," and we grudgingly obey.

The next day, I am amazed to see my wrestling opponent arrive at my house on his bike. "Did you by any chance lose this?" he asks, holding out a pearl-handled pocketknife.

I recognize it immediately and accept it gratefully. "This was a present from my favourite uncle," I explain. I thank him and he just shrugs.

"My name is Brian Birch, would you like to go for a bike ride?"

"Why not," I reply. "My name is Jules Legal."

"I know," he says, "and you go to St. Joseph's." That summer, Brian Birch and I became the closest of buddies.

It seems a strange friendship; after all, it started with a fight, but more unlikely is the fact that we go to different schools. Brian goes to Victoria, so he must be Protestant, and of course, I attend St. Joseph's, where every student is Catholic.

When it comes to choosing friends, there isn't much mixing between Catholics and Protestants. Among Catholics, it might be okay to have a Protestant friend, but it's unheard of to have a Protestant as your buddy.

Brian may be Protestant, but he is also Irish. I find this puzzling because there is another Irish kid in my class at St. Joseph's called Glen, and he is Catholic. I thought all Irish people were Catholic.

Glen is a super athlete and a real nice guy, but every once in a while, he falls to the ground unconscious, foaming at the mouth, and thumping his head against the ground. Someone puts a jacket under his head and Sister Superior inserts a rubber eraser between his teeth.

"So he doesn't bite off his tongue," a knowing girl from grade eight tells us. "Glen's having an epileptic fit." It sure looks scary.

I ask my new friend Brian, "How come some Irish people are Catholic and some are Protestant?" Brian tells me his parents come from the North of Ireland, and he figures Glen's family probably came from the South. Weird!

During the summer, Brian and I ride our bikes all over our end of the city, following our whims and curiosity wherever they take us. We hear that a bunch of boys, Protestant and Catholic, are swimming regularly along the spillway below Lock Two on the Welland, and we decide to check it out. As we cross the Welland canal, just past the lift bridge, there's a sign: "NO TRESPASSING." It warns that it is extremely dangerous to swim along the spillway. Brian stops abruptly and won't go past the sign. I have no such hesitation. I reason, "Now that we're here, we just have to check it out. Brian, if you don't want to swim, well you don't have to." Then, I add, "Just think, Brian, what is it going to hurt if we ride down and take a look? Besides, if there was some good reason to keep people out, wouldn't they have put a gate across the road?"

Sure enough, down where the road ends at the spillway, a whole bunch of guys are swimming and to me it looks really cool. The scene reminds me of Tom Sawyer and his buddies swimming in their favourite hole along the Mississippi. It turns out we both know some of the guys, and they invite us to join them, and yes, Protestants and Catholics are in the water together. I like that, and so does Brian.

As a couple of guys clamber out of the water, Brian is totally shocked. "Wow, those guys are naked," he exclaims. "I never expected that."

"So what?" I tell him. "It's not like they're naked girls, now wouldn't that be neat?" Sensing this is too much for Brian, I don't share with him a private fantasy my imagination has just concocted of being at a beach where everyone is naked and gorgeous nude women are sunbathing and they don't seem to mind if guys stare at them. No, I'll just keep these thoughts to myself.

I strip and slide down the steep concrete riprap into the cooling waters, and oh, it feels so good. Eventually Brian does the same, keeping some distance and being careful not to expose any private parts. We soon discover that the bottom drops off quickly, and since neither of us knows how to swim, we must not venture more than a few feet from shore. Clearly we must learn to swim if we are to join the other guys playing at what looks like fun games in the deeper waters.

On our way home, I tell Brian about a school picnic I attended a while ago at Port Weller beach and suggest this might be a good place to learn swimming. Brian is familiar with the beach and quickly agrees. "We could pack a lunch and make a whole day of it," he suggests.

The next day Brian arrives at my house looking a bit sad. His parents have forbidden him to ride his bike on Niagara Street because there's too much traffic. Brian suggests we could walk to the beach. "How far can it be?"

That's actually a pretty long walk, at least three or four miles one way, but I reluctantly agree, "Let's try walking."

It's another sweltering day, it seems like we've been walking for miles when I spot a milk truck coming towards us and I stick out my thumb. To my surprise the driver stops and asks where we're headed. "Port Weller beach, eh? I'm going that way, hop on boys." We can scarcely believe our good fortune; I'm thinking we should be at the beach in no time, and I can almost feel that lovely refreshing water washing all the sweat away.

Uh-oh, the driver turns onto a side street, says he's got a couple of deliveries but it shouldn't take long. "You know, if you boys were to help me, we could get there that much faster," he says reassuringly. After a few deliveries, he doesn't bother getting out of the truck, leaving Brian and I to do all the legwork. "Just a couple more, a couple more," he keeps saying, and I'm regretting that we ever accepted the ride.

At one point, out of the guy's hearing, I suggest to Brian, "Let's just get the hell out of here."

Cautious Brian is hesitant. "But we don't know where we are, and all our stuff is still in the truck," he reminds me.

Hours go by, or so it seems, and I'm getting angrier with each delivery. I've had enough; I grab my bag and refuse to make any more deliveries.

"Okay, okay," the driver concedes. "No more deliveries."

Finally, we're at the beach turnoff, only a half mile or so to go! I can hardly wait. We should be there in a few minutes, but instead of turning down the lane leading to the beach, he makes a U-turn and orders us out of his truck.

"Bastard!" I scream as he drives away. Brian is calmer than me; I think I even heard him thank the driver. I am just furious, "After all that work, that asshole won't even drive us all the way," I grumble as we walk the last stretch to the beach.

Walking home is no fun either. After spending the morning delivering milk and playing along the beach most of the afternoon, we are exhausted. Brian won't consider hitchhiking, and we're dying of thirst. I vow I will never do that again.

The next day Brian says his parents would be okay with us riding our bikes to the beach as long as we stay on the side roads and avoid Niagara Street. Well, we tried the side streets, but we kept running into dead ends and it was taking forever. Finally, Brian recognizes the futility of it all and we take Niagara Street. I didn't ask Brian how he resolved things with his parents, but after all that nonsense, it seems this isn't an issue anymore.

Bikes are so much more efficient than walking, and they are such fun. In our neighbourhood, very few boys own their own bike. That is a luxury reserved for richer kids. I am riding my dad's bike, but I can only ride it when he's not using it. It's a double-bar heavy-duty CCM, and this is the first year I can reach the pedals. Last year, I learned to ride under bar, which was a real challenge. It's much the same for Brian except that his dad hardly ever uses his bike and he has no trouble reaching the pedals. So now Brian calls it his own bike and I start to refer to my dad's bike as mine too, and we are the envy of other kids.

Port Weller beach is great for swimming, unlike Port Dalhousie where the water is shallow for a long ways out. Here it gets deep quickly. At the far end of the beach is a small dock with a ladder, and this is where Brian and I will learn to swim. We walk a few feet out from the end of the dock where the water is waist-deep and attempt to dog-paddle back. At first, we each take turns, in case the other gets into trouble. It turns out easier than I expected. To keep afloat, you just have to remember to keep your lungs full of air, most of the time. When exhaling, do it quickly, then suck in a deep breath and hold it while kicking and stroking in a certain way. We practice various arm strokes and leg kicks, striving to increase our range. Each day we learn to swim a bit more efficiently, and each day we're able to swim a little farther. Brian is more cautious than me, but his competitive nature doesn't allow him to stand still. We are constantly trying to outdo each other. Who can jump the farthest off the dock? Who can dive the farthest, and who can swim underwater the longest? Our confidence level grows to the point that any thought of drowning now seems unlikely. It's time we paid another visit to the spillway at Lock Two.

The boys at the swim hole are welcoming. They invite us to participate in various water games, they teach us new swimming techniques and show us that Catholics and Protestant can play together. They also teach us something else. We learn that sometimes it's okay to steal.

It started out innocently enough. Several of us are on our way home and we are all hungry. We turn onto a barely visible path that eventually leads to a remote orchard where millions of gorgeous ripe peaches are hanging low, ready for picking. One of the guys assures us we can help ourselves because he knows the owner. "A distant relative," he says. "We have permission to eat all we want, just don't carry any home." We greedily bite into the ripest, most luscious peaches I have ever tasted, sweet, yellow juice running down our chins, our hands, even our elbows. We eat till we're stuffed. This becomes a daily ritual and Mom wonders why I can barely eat supper. I can't tell her because we have been sworn to secrecy; after all, we don't want the whole city to find out about this wonderful exclusive treasure.

A couple weeks later it's just Brian and me, and once again we turn down our secret path to our secret orchard when the owner suddenly appears. We are eager to thank him and tell him what fabulous peaches he grows. He asks where we get the nerve to steal his peaches. We explain the situation and assure him that we wouldn't dream of stealing. We offer our friend's name and the name of his distant relative. "That's total bullshit," he declares. "I'll let you off this time, but don't let me catch you here again."

I can't say this was the last time we stole fruit. If you were hungry or thirsty and there was a convenient orchard nearby with no fence, the temptation was just too great. But going forward, we would be a lot more careful.

That summer, Brian and I did all kinds of fun things together. We explored the Old Welland Canal, we hiked the Burgoyne Bush, and we taught ourselves to be pretty good swimmers. Best of all, we became really good buddies. I'd also like to believe that we learned something from each other. Wasn't it my influence that taught Brian to be more independent when dealing with parents? I believe he learned to be a little less uptight about things in general, and that swimming in the nude was a mighty fine thing. Meanwhile, Brian's scrupulous honesty and wholesome decency has taught me something new and important. Even though Sister Mary Rudolf would have us believe that Protestants are lost souls to be pitied and prayed for, I now know that Protestants can be real nice people too. And I'm quite certain that wherever I end up after this life on earth, Brian will be there too.

THE ROAD TO ARBAKKA

It is late winter, 1944 with no sign of spring. Canada is still at war with no sign of peace, and McKinnon's is busy as ever, cranking out all sorts of equipment for the war machine. The Forge Shop, where Dad works, is humming twenty-four hours a day, and there is always a shortage of workers. Dad has been working ten-hour days, six days a week. He doesn't often complain, but he doesn't hide the fact that he's getting sick of it.

Everyone thought the war would be over by now, and Dad was counting on finding another job, one that wasn't so noisy and so dirty. Even the air is filthy. Of course it would be great if he could find a job that was more suited to his skills, but he knows that isn't possible at this time. After all, "There's a war on, you know," and his was one of those jobs that was considered vital to the war effort. "You'd better have a real good reason if you want to quit your job," he was reminded whenever he mentioned it.

And then from out of the blue came a ray of hope that might just lead to what Dad was dreaming of. It started with an innocent comment from a relative in Manitoba. It was about last winter's heavy snowfall and all the rain they were getting. After years of drought, the rain was mostly welcomed, but pastures remained under water for weeks and haying was sometimes impossible. Dad sensed that this might be more than a passing thing. He dared to wonder if it might lead to job opportunities back in Manitoba.

Before the Depression, Dad had worked as a dragline operator with Vadeboncoeur Construction, a Manitoba company specializing in major earth-moving projects. The depression had halted all construction and drainage work, but now with full employment, maybe those stalled projects could start again. Letters were exchanged, and what had started out, as a hunch became a job offer. Vadeboncoeur Construction was back in business and Dad could start thinking seriously about getting back to the kind of work he loved best.

My parents don't argue much, but I sense that something is wrong, and I don't really want to know the reason. The details come out bit by bit as Mom shares her fears with various friends and relatives. I always thought Mom would welcome the idea of moving back to Manitoba, but ever since that visit last summer, it seems she has had a change of heart. St. Catharines is now her home.

I'm not sure where I stand. I like my life here in St. Catharines. I love school and all the sisters who teach at St. Joseph's. And I have to admit, I kind of like the idea that I've become the leader of a few good buddies—our little gang, we call it.

An official-looking letter arrived in the mail one day. Before Dad had a chance to open it, Mom knew what it was all about, and she was not happy. On the other hand, Dad was smiling ear to ear. His verbal resignation at McKinnon's had been refused, but he was quite sure this arranged letter would do the trick. It came directly from Mr. Vadeboncoeur, the owner and boss of the company.

The letter went on to explain how large areas of southeastern Manitoba were under water. Farms that had been dry a few years ago were reverting to swampy wasteland. Mr. Vadeboncoeur stressed that Mr. Legal's specialized skills were urgently needed in Manitoba to help save precious farmland. The letter ended with a reminder of the produce that would be lost if farms were left underwater. And what could be more important to the war effort than an abundant food supply? "There's a war on, you know," was the implied wisdom so often repeated.

Dad's crafty strategy paid off; within weeks, he was packing his little leather satchel and saying goodbye to all our friends and relatives who had followed his lead a few years before. Would they too return to Manitoba as job prospects back home improved? That was the question that would face countless others who had flooded into St. Catharines the last several years. What would they do when the war was over? Would there still be jobs for them after the war?

Without Dad around, things at home on Brighton Ave. are more hectic, but Mom is used to managing our busy household. She knows how to handle cranky renters, and she knows how to keep us kids in line. So nothing much has changed except I have noticed she spends less time worrying about me. Apart from a few chores, I can do pretty much anything that pops into my imagination as long as I'm home for supper. And now that I don't have to share the bike with Dad, I can go anywhere it will take me. I feel lucky and I recognize that few of my buddies enjoy such freedom. Still, I miss my dad.

Mom says we'll be seeing him soon and we'll be spending the summer holidays together. Dad hates writing letters, but he did send a short note to let Mom know that he has rented a house near his worksite. "It's on a small farm," he says, "not far from Arbakka." The train will only take you as far as Vita, but I'll be there to meet you."

"So how far is it from Winnipeg to Vita? How far is it from Vita to Arbakka?" I ask Mom. "Is Arbakka a town or a village, and why is it spelled with two Ks?" Mom doesn't seem to know.

"We'll find out soon enough," she says as we board the train for the long journey westward.

The first leg from St. Catharines to Toronto is totally boring, orchard after orchard and a couple small towns in between, so I let my mind wonder into a fantasy world. This comes real easy to a ten-year-old boy who thrives on comic books and cowboy movies.

What if Arbakka isn't a town, not even a village? What if Arbakka is actually the name of a huge cattle ranch? Yes, yes, I can picture it. There will be lots of cattle and lots of horses; I can just see myself galloping across the plains astride a wild, spirited horse chasing cows and buffalo and doing all the neat things cowboys do. Of course I'll be wearing a couple of revolvers for protection from wild animals, deadly rattlesnakes, and bad guys. Maybe l should pack a 30-30 Winchester pump-action rifle on one side of my silver studded saddle, just in case.

"Toronto, next stop! Next stop, Toronto!" shouts the conductor, rudely bringing me back to reality.

"Stay close," Mom warns as we huddle together on the platform while she tries to figure out where to catch our next train. Crowds of people are scurrying in all directions. Everything appears hopelessly confusing. Swells of smoke and hissing steam add to my sense of bewilderment. How will Mom manage with us four kids and our luggage? Last year on our train trip back from Manitoba, we must have faced the same thing, but then Dad was in charge and everything went so smoothly I barely noticed. Mom is waving wildly, trying to get the attention of a "Red Cap." And then, as though she had waved a magic wand, a cheery black man pushing a funny little wagon comes to our rescue and leads us out of the chaos to our sleek passenger coach.

Once aboard, the picture turns to one of tidy efficiency. The friendly porter in a starched white jacket shows us to our seats while explaining that at mealtime he will set up a table and bring us our food, then at night he shall transform our seats into a double-decker bed. I'm sure I must be the luckiest kid in the world as I climb the ladder to the upper berth and snuggle between the crisp white sheets. How easy it is to fall asleep listening to the faint *clickety-clack, clickety-clack* of steel wheels rolling over miles and miles of steel track.

I marvel at the monumental effort it must have taken to lay these endless tracks through the rock, the bush, and the muskeg. We stop briefly at rough mining camps and smoky lumber towns, where mailbags are exchanged. It seems there are always a couple passengers getting off and new ones getting on. *Where have they been?* I wonder. *Where are they going? What is it like living in these northern towns so isolated and alone in the vast wilderness?*

"Temagami, coming up," announces our conductor. "We'll be stopped for a while to load up on coal and water. Feel free to get off the train if you like, just be sure you hurry aboard when the whistle blows."

The station is an elegant-looking stone building, something you might expect to see in downtown Toronto. Indian people dressed in buckskins, some with feathered headdresses, are selling beaded moccasins, miniature tepees, toy birch bark canoes, and assorted trinkets.

This is all so exciting. I would love to see where these brown people live; probably along the rocky shores of that gorgeous blue lake we just passed, I figure. I can easily imagine idyllic villages where happy people live in tepees and paddle real birch bark canoes. I'm beginning to think it might be more fun to be an "Indian" than a "cowboy."

At last, we chug into Winnipeg where we are met by relatives who put us up for the night. Come morning, it's back on another train that will take us to Vita. "It's not very far," says Uncle Alex; a couple hours, he figures. Dad said he'll be there to meet us, and then it's on to Arbakka, that mysterious place that nobody seems to know anything about.

Now if Arbakka is in ranch country, I wonder: Will Dad be picking us up by stagecoach? I can imagine six lively horses, all black, pulling a beautiful stagecoach with big red wheels and shiny steel rims. I want to ride shotgun with the driver. Wow! That would be so much fun.

This shorter train is agonizingly slow. It barely gets up to speed when the whistle blows, indicating not necessarily another town but simply a crossing with a wooden siding where a bunch of shiny cans, about the size of fire hydrants, are the focus of attention.

"Cream cans," explains Wally, a friendly young man from the next seat over. Farmers send their full cans of cream to Vita where they churn it into butter. The creamery sends them a cheque, and for a lot of small farmers, that cream cheque is their only income."

"Tell me about Vita, Wally."

"It's the biggest town around these parts," he says. "There's a couple of churches, lots of stores, a hotel, and the only hospital for miles. 99 percent Ukrainian," he adds. I don't ask about the other 1 percent, and I don't bother asking him about Arbakka.

It is late afternoon when the conductor hollers, *"Vita, next stop! Next stop, Vita!"* We all press our noses against the window, eagerly watching for the sign that announces the town one mile before the station. With brakes squealing, the wheezing old engine comes to a stop and lets out one last gasp of steam and all becomes beautifully quiet.

But where's Dad? Here we are, Mom and us kids standing alone on the station platform with our luggage. *Just like in Toronto*, I'm thinking, *but no Red Caps here.*

The train is gone, a big white truck has hauled away all the cream cans, and now the station is nearly empty. A muddy old car pulls up. Looks like Dad's old Reo; could it be Dad? A lively fat man steps out and apologizes for being late.

"Your husband asked me to drive you to Arbakka," he says, without introducing himself or asking our names. "Unfortunately, it's been raining all week, and it'll be another week before the roads are passable. I can drive you to the hotel in town where you and the kids can stay until things dry up a little."

Everyone is devastated, sister Juliette starts crying, Alice and Louis are fussing, and we're all pretty hungry. Mom is clearly frustrated, and she's not about to accept this news without question. "There's got to be some way to get to Arbakka," she insists.

"Get in the car," growls the cranky fat man. He speeds past Petrowski's general store and splish-splashes down a muddy trail with deep water-filled ruts. We've gone less than a mile when the road disappears into a pond that could easily be called a lake. "This is the road to Arbakka," he explains. "I'll get stuck if we go any farther."

"I never doubted you," Mom explains. "I just thought we might hire someone with horses and a wagon."

The fat man is taken aback. "You mean you would ride in an open wagon with your young family all the way to Arbakka? It's at least ten miles, you know." I'm thinking, *Yes, yes, that would be great; maybe not quite as romantic as a horse-drawn stagecoach, but that would suit me just fine.*

He drops us off at a store in Vita, explaining our situation to Mr. Petrowski, the owner. Turns out that Mr. Petrowski knows Dad and his crew. "They buy all their groceries and supplies here," he says. He doesn't think Mom's idea is so crazy, and he has good news. A farmer he knows from near Arbakka is in town today, and he'll be coming by later to pick up groceries before heading home. "Maybe he'll give you a ride?"

"By the way, there's a restaurant at the other end of town if you want to wait there," suggests Mr. Petrowski. Mom doesn't want to miss the possibility of a ride. She buys a can of ham and a loaf of bread and makes sandwiches on the main counter. "This will be your supper," she gruffly tells us kids. We each get a soft drink and a chocolate bar for desert. It sounds like Mom is really upset. "Why isn't your Dad here?" she keeps repeating, knowing that only he can answer that question.

This is probably a good time to leave her alone, I'm thinking. "I promise, Mom, I won't go far." From the store's porch, I can see a church standing tall with three impressive copper domes. I see the hotel where we may yet have to stay for who knows how long. A few trucks are parked in front and teams of horses are hitched nearby. Nothing is moving except for a couple old cars splashing through the standing puddles on every road in town.

So, according to Wally, the friendly guy on the train, this is the biggest town around. Vita sure doesn't look like anything I had imagined. It looks nothing like those neat frontier towns you see in cowboy movies with elevated wooden sidewalks that let you walk in fancy cowboy boots even when the streets are muddy. Here in Vita, there are no sidewalks, period. It's mud, mud, mud everywhere, and I don't see anybody wearing cowboy boots. Sure hope Arbakka will be better than this.

I've pretty much given up on the idea of a stagecoach with six prancing horses to take us to Arbakka, but I'm still unprepared for what comes next. In front of the hotel, I can see an old man unhitching his team and slowly, ever so slowly, they inch their way towards Petrowski's. Finally, it dawns on me: Could this be our ride?

The driver is alone and looks pretty decrepit in his raggedy overalls, but he's a cheery old guy and of course he'd be happy to take us to Arbakka. Mr. Petrowski lets him know that we'll be going past Arbakka to the Andrusko farm. "That's miles out of my way," he protests. Mom offers him a ten-dollar bill, and that magically alters his mood. He briskly makes room between the empty cream cans and loads our luggage. Juliette and Alice rearrange the suitcases to form a makeshift bed while Mom and brother Lou ride up front. I feel I have to burn off pent-up energy, so I walk barefoot behind the creaky old wagon, jumping aboard when we come to the larger puddles flooding the trail.

King and Judy, the old guy calls his horses. They plod along only slightly faster than a turtle down the muddy trail. They look pathetic, shaggy and tired. I wonder how often they get groomed? And judging by their protruding ribs, I have to wonder if they get enough to eat? I feel kind of sorry for them.

We pass by seemingly endless swamps with tall green bulrushes and brown cattails. Stands of aspen and willows offer little relief from the boring scenery.

It's almost dark as we come to a crossing in the road. I see a small square building with a rough bench in front and a large sign advertising soft drinks. It must be some kind of store, but there's another smaller sign, that I can barely make out; "Arbakka Post Office," I think it reads. "So is this it?" I ask the old guy. "Is this Arbakka?" He just nods. I think he's falling asleep.

Good thing I didn't mention my fantasies of Arbakka being a cattle ranch with real cowboys and Dad picking us up by stagecoach. Sounds pretty silly now. Maybe the Andrusko farm will be more interesting, maybe there'll be kids my age and we will do fun things together, like cousin Leonard and I did last summer.

We continue on like this for hours, until it gets too dark to see. The poor old horses keep plodding along even slower than when we started. I must have dozed off, because suddenly, here's Dad, and he's with this friendly couple who welcomes us as though we are long-lost relatives. It becomes clear that my new world is looking just fine.

All the while, a mangy-looking dog is barking excitedly, causing the horses to fidget and stomp nervously. A sooty lantern gives off a soft yellow light and guides us to an unpainted house surrounded by rustling poplar trees. Ah yes, this will be home, at least for the next couple months, and I couldn't be happier.

■ ■ ■

Early light. I am awakened by sounds never heard in the city: roosters crowing, turkeys gobbling, and cows mooing. Mom and Dad are up, and it seems others are too. Stepping outside, it's as though I was transported into another world, or at least another country. I'm certain that every farm in the Ukraine must look exactly like this one.

The Andrusko farmyard is a neat cluster of fascinating buildings, all expertly built of logs except for a small one that stands apart from the others. It looks a bit quirky but quite pretty with whitewashed walls and bright blue trim. The matching door is built in two sections. The bottom half is closed, but I spot activity through the open upper half. Mrs. Andrusko waves me to come on in.

"This is our summer kitchen," she tells me. "This is where I do all the cooking and the canning during the summer months. It can get pretty hot in here with that wood stove, you know. At night we usually sleep in the house."

"You mean you have another house?"

"No, no," she laughs, "the house where your family is staying. That's our house."

"So where do you and Mr. Andrusko sleep?"

She points to a cot along one wall. "Pete sleeps over there and I sleep here." Her cot is so narrow and so short, it looks more like a bench, and I'm feeling kind of guilty. "No, no don't feel bad," she says. "Me and Pete, we don't have children of our own. It will be lots of fun to have your family with us for the summer."

Mr. Andrusko comes stomping in with two brimming pails of milk. He's about to pour one into a big round steel bowl on top of a strange-looking machine with a crank sticking out one side. "*Chekai, Chekai*," (wait, wait) she yells in a loud, sharp, voice. "I have to put the filter on the separator." Pete, it seems, is a bit slow. "*Ty Durnyi!*" (you fool) "*Ty Durnyi!*" she repeats. Mrs. Andrusko expertly ties what looks like a small bed sheet to the top of the steel bowl. Pete slowly empties the milk through the filter while trying to explain to me how a cream separator works.

"Just watch," he says. He begins turning the big crank, slowly at first, and as he picks up speed, a thin watery stream of milk comes pouring out of a spout into a pail on the floor. "For the pigs," Mr. Andrusko explains. "It's called skim milk." Meanwhile, from another, smaller spout, out pours a thick, rich-looking cream directly into one of those tin cans we saw from the train. This is fascinating; this is magic. I still don't know how the machine works, but I want to try turning that crank. It's a lot harder than it looks, and it takes a lot longer than I imagined.

Filling the big watering troughs from the dipping well is also fun at first, but after forty pails or so, it quickly loses its appeal. The one chore that's never any fun at all is cleaning manure from the barn.

I notice two healthy-looking horses grazing in the distance. "Do you sometimes ride those horses?"

"Oh no," says Mr. Andrusko, "those are strictly work horses. It would be too dangerous to even try."

I want to tell him that Cousin Leonard's horses are also work horses and they don't seem to mind having people ride them, but I sense it would be a waste of time.

Every Friday morning, after the farm chores, Mr. Andrusko opens a locked shed and lovingly dusts off his beautiful black buggy. Obviously it's only meant for light loads. It comes with a spring mounted leather seat just wide enough for two. *I'm thinking, with his frisky looking team I'll bet that rig can really fly. I'm sure Mr. Andrusko will offer me a ride,* but he takes off and disappears down the road without looking back.

Mom says he goes across the US border to shop for groceries. "Now why would he take you when he never takes Mrs. Andrusko?" she says. I sense there's more to the story, but she won't talk about it. I wonder if it's got something to do with Pete's drinking. Several times we've seen him come home after dark, staggering drunk—so drunk that Mrs. Andrusko has to unhitch the horses and remove their heavy harnesses.

Shortly after, the yelling begins. We can hear Mrs. Andrusko all the way from the summer kitchen to our house. It's probably just as well we don't understand Ukrainian.

I wonder what those poor horses did all day while Mr. Andrusko was drinking? Did they have to stand in the sun all those hours? Did they ever get a drink of water? That's not something Mr. Burton would ever do.

I don't much care for Mr. Andrusko. I don't want to follow him around like I did Mr. Burton, and I've been told there are no boys my age in the whole area. I can't imagine playing with my sisters, and little brother Lou is far too young. I guess I'll have to put aside my dreams of being a cowboy, but that's okay.

Tomorrow I'll lace up those beaded moccasins I bought in Temagami, and I'll wear my headband that I decorated with turkey feathers. I'll make a bow and a quiver of arrows and go hunting for game. I'll build a wigwam and sleep in it. I'll find a big birch tree that I can use to build a birch bark canoe and I'll paddle down the Roseau River. Oh yes! I'll live just like Chingachgook, -that brave warrior from my favourite book 'The Last of the Mohicans'. I may not have a good buddy to share these dreams but I know that this will be a fabulous summer filled with all kinds of neat adventures.

"Temagami train station"   Source: public domain

SISTER MARY RUDOLF

Sister Mary Rudolf teaches grades seven and eight while also serving as the school principal. All the nuns call her Sister Superior, and there is never any doubt she is the boss. She can be stern at times, but she has a soft side as well. She welcomes casual comments and interjections that liven up a sometimes-boring topic. Bubbling under her normally serious persona is a wicked sense of humour that bursts forth on a regular basis. She blames this on her Irish heritage. "We are here to learn," she reminds us, "but that doesn't mean we can't have a little fun too."

I thought I knew Sister Mary Rudolf fairly well; after all, I see her every day, and she often greets me by name. It seems she knows every kid by name, and she will quite often ask about their parents or siblings. She pays special attention to kids who may be struggling or those who are having problems at home. It wasn't until she became my teacher that I came to fully appreciate all her qualities.

It was in Sister Mary Rudolf's class where I learned that all our sisters belong to a particular religious order of nuns called "Sisters of St. Joseph." It was never clear in my mind whether they started St. Joseph's School, or was it a coincidence that the sister's order and the school were both named after St. Joseph? The Sisters of St. Joseph trace their proud heritage back hundreds of years. Our sisters are all of Irish decent, but their particular order originated in France. Somehow they are connected to the "Jesuits," and like the Jesuits, they have made education their main discipline.

The Sisters do their best to promote an environment that is perfect for learning while also stressing the importance of the arts and all things beautiful. Their passion permeates everything they do, and it trickles down to every pupil. In turn, they expect the best from each of us.

The Sisters of St. Joseph wear a style of habit much like any other religious order, but I've noticed something else. It wasn't obvious at first, but slowly it dawned on me just how fastidious our sisters are about their appearance. There is never a wrinkle marring the sweep of their black cotton habits. Their stiff white collars are always freshly starched. Their black shoes, when you can see them, are always polished to a bright shine, and their fingernails are carefully manicured. To me, they smell nice too, but that may just be the soap they use.

The sisters are always immaculate, but us boys can be a bit grubby at times. "Jules, when's the last time you had a haircut?" Sister Mary Rudolf might ask, in front of all the other kids. "If you kept your nails shorter, it would be a lot easier to keep them clean, you know."

And woe betides you if you were ever caught eating without washing your hands; now, that would be a sin. I was never quite sure if that qualified as a venial sin or maybe even a mortal sin.

The Sisters of St. Joseph lived by the old adage: Cleanliness is next to godliness. The sisters did their best to instil in us this important virtue, but they were not above calling in a professional to drive the message home.

The expert in this case is a trim-looking young woman dressed in a spotless white uniform with sparkling white teeth to match. She wears a funny little hat that indicates that she is a registered nurse. Sister Mary Rudolf has invited her to speak to the whole school and cautions that there may be a test at the end of the presentation.

Our prim young nurse quickly turns serious and launches into the importance of good hygiene. She rhymes off a seemingly endless list of diseases, describing how they can take over your body and cause severe pain and all sorts of misery.

"Want to see how we get these diseases?" she asks, as she opens a box full of large poster boards. "These are enlarged photos of real bugs and germs that live on our skin, in our hair, and under our fingernails, and they love to multiply and find new hosts to thrive on," she tells us. Wow! I've never seen such a collection of nasty-looking creatures.

Some have multiple legs and deadly-looking pinchers. "Although most are too small to see with the naked eye, they can make you sick, and some can even kill you." The young nurse seems to delight in repeating this line as she stresses the vital importance of good hygiene.

From the day I learned this, no matter how inconvenient, I knew I must wash my hands before eating. My inner voice nags, *How clean is this food? I wonder if the person who prepared this food washed their hands.* I find that if I'm hungry enough, I can, with some effort, override these fears, but the enjoyment is not the same. It's unlikely that I shall remember anything from the Catechism, but the fear of bugs and germs will remain with me forever.

The good Sisters of St. Joseph don't dwell much on sin and common human failings, but there is one vice in particular which they consider downright evil. There's not much mention of it in the Catechism, but addiction to gambling seems to have caught the Sisters' attention, and they are determined to prevent us from getting trapped in its sinister web.

The Sisters seem to know all about the gangs of pathetic young men who waste their time and money playing CRAPS in back alleys and getting into fights. They caution us not to go down that wicked path, and it pains them that some of their past students may already be sliding down that slippery slope.

Father Jacobowski has also been preaching about the evils of gambling at Sunday Mass. He tells the story of a family he knows, where the breadwinner has a good-paying job but routinely gambles away his pay cheque every Friday. The poor mother and her children are left to rely on charity to keep from starving. "And, it's not just men," he is quick to add. "There are housewives and mothers out there who spend their afternoons squandering their time and money at one of those illegal gambling dens while their husbands are at work."

None of these stories has much effect on me; they aren't part of my world. I must confess, Angelo and I watched from a distance one of those CRAP games that Sister Mary Rudolf talked about. Typically, there might be a dozen or more guys yelling and turning the air blue with their language. Onlookers placed bets while a couple of animated players made a huge production of throwing the dice. The noise was deafening as the participants cheered and cursed, and violence was never far away. It all looked kind of dumb, and I determined that I would never be sucked into these silly games.

I can't imagine any of my classmates getting caught up in this nonsense either, but Sister Mary Rudolf has good reason to be concerned. After school, she counsels a group of young men who have gambling problems, drinking problems, even some who've been in trouble with the police. It pains her that many of these young men were once her students at St. Joseph's.

And so, she has invited an odd-looking gentleman, who is supposedly an expert in mathematics. He will speak to us on the futility of gambling. He performs a few fascinating magic tricks, which gets everyone's attention. We all laugh and applaud while he smiles and bows. He puts aside his cape and top hat and gets down to business.

"I'm not here to entertain you," he declares. "How many of you believe that what you saw was real magic?" He waits a few seconds; nobody puts up their hand. "Of course you don't believe what your eyes told you was real, you kids are much too smart for that. Then how many of you can explain how I was able to fool you into seeing something that didn't make sense? My purpose here today is to show how those brilliant minds of yours can easily be fooled."

Our math expert launches into an explanation of how mathematical odds work and the difference between a person's perspective and the mathematical reality. He demonstrates by having one of the students flip a coin repeatedly after the class tries to predict whether it will land heads or tails. "In the gambling world, this would be called a bet," he tells us.

He keeps track of each "bet" on the blackboard. The class divides fairly evenly as each pupil bets on the next throw. The picture changes, however, when there is a string of just heads or just tails. To illustrate:

If a coin keeps landing on heads, there would be an increasing number of bets predicting that the next throw has to be tails even though the odds according to math are still fifty-fifty. One time, the coin lands on tails four times in a row. Now, every student is sure that the next throw has to be heads, the whole class is betting on it. Everyone holds their breath as the coin flips through the air and lands on . . . tails. Wow! The coin lands on tails again. That's five times in a row. The whole class is wrong. Now, this basic premise makes sense to me.

Our magician friend goes on to explain how professional gamblers use this simple fact to separate fools from their money. I don't intend to become a professional gambler, and I certainly do not want to be considered a fool, and so I vow that I will never, ever gamble. Period.

There was good reason why competitive sports wasn't big at St. Joseph's. For one thing, we didn't have a gym, so indoor sports were out of the question. Outdoor sports were also limited because the schoolyard was just too small. The space was made even smaller during school hours by that invisible line that kept boys and girls separate from each other.

Some of the guys pitched baseballs, others practiced Lacrosse drills, but it was considered too dangerous to actually play a game. I understand why Lacrosse games are prohibited; that hard ball, when thrown by a strong player could do serious harm. Why we couldn't play baseball I'll never understand. When we played after hours, girls sometimes joined us boys even though they weren't very good at the game.

Girls weren't bad at soccer, and Sister Superior allowed us to play against each other; we even played a few co-ed games and surprisingly that was kind of fun. One day a ball went through a neighbour's window, and that put an end to soccer.

One winter the school caretaker built us a skating rink in back of the school where us boys played hockey. The caretaker taught us the basic rules and acted as our coach. We weren't aware that our rink wasn't regulation size. When we went up against a school from a richer neighbourhood with a proper rink, we were in for a shock.

As we skated onto the regulation-size rink, I remember feeling totally embarrassed. Only our goalie had proper gear; the rest of us wore street clothes and hand-me-down skates. Protective gear consisted of cardboard stuffed into our stockings for shin pads. Meanwhile, the other team had slick-looking uniforms just like the "St. Catharines Saints." They even had proper, store-bought protective gear with shiny new skates and professional-looking gloves.

At half-time, the score stands at around thirty to zero. Our team scores a goal during the third period, and then surprisingly another. With a final score of forty-eight to two, a harsh reality is made clear: We do not belong in the same league.

Still the other team members are gracious and nobody sniggers. We all shake hands muttering, "Good game, good game," knowing full well it was unlikely that we shall ever play each other again. I'm just grateful we didn't get skunked.

Everybody knew we could never excel at sports, but there was one competition where Sister Mary Rudolf was determined that St. Joseph's would not be left behind. Starting in grade seven, everyone was taught formal debating. The basic rules were simple enough, and it was great fun. However, it soon became apparent that Sister Mary Rudolf had other ideas.

To her, debating was more than a game. This was an art form that required disciplined thinking, in-depth preparation, and plenty of practice: skills that not every student was willing to work at. Over time, the best debaters were singled out for advanced training. Classes were taught after school hours and attendance was optional. I didn't need any coaxing. This was something that really interested me, and unlike those music lessons, I didn't mind if it meant spending less time with my buddies.

Sister Mary Rudolf never did anything by half measures. She arranged for experienced debaters to demonstrate the finer points of debate and to evaluate our many practice debates at St. Joseph's.

Even Father Jacobowski got involved. He thought it would be useful for our debating team to understand the basics of critical thinking. Of course he was all too happy to explain how the study of logic went way back to Plato, Aristotle, and other Greek philosophers and how logic formed the basis of critical thinking.

Father Jacobowski went on to explain how Copernicus, an astronomer from Poland, used mainly critical thinking to prove that all the planets revolved around the sun and not around the earth as virtually everybody else believed at the time. I'm not sure how this helped in actual debating, but it gave us that extra edge of confidence when we rebutted some dubious points made by our opponents.

Our debating team went on to win every contest in our district. Sister Mary Rudolf was ever so pleased. She broke into tears as we received our first-place diplomas. As for our debating team? We all felt mighty good, and just a little superior to all our adversaries.

Seldom did a week go by without some outside expert being invited to St. Joseph's to share their knowledge, or sometimes simply to entertain. Sister Mary Rudolf was just great at mixing learning with fun. However, I remember one event that was organized purely for fun. It always took place on the last day of the school year, and every teacher and student was included.

It started with several public transit streetcars parking in front of our school on Facer Street. Once all were onboard, we were taken on a tour around our city, ending up at one of the prominent movie theatres. Popcorn and soft drinks were free, and we could have as much as we wanted.

The theatre showed a variety of cartoons and at least two good movies. The movie I remember best was called *The Bells of St. Mary's*. It told a charming story revolving around a Catholic school named St. Mary's, where the sisters looked very much like our own sisters.

Sister Benedict, portrayed in the movie by Ingrid Bergman, was Sister Superior. She was obviously in charge, just like our own Sister Mary Rudolf.

Of course the movie had to include a priest, Father O'Malley, who was played by the famous singer and actor Bing Crosby. I remember thinking: Wouldn't it be neat if our Father Jacobowski were more like Bing Crosby? But then, I don't suppose Bing Crosby could expound on Greek philosophy like our Father Jacobowski.

And I remember thinking our Sister Mary Rudolf may not be quite as glamorous as the famous Ingrid Bergman, but she doesn't need any lessons on how to run a school, nor how to motivate her pupils. She's just about the greatest teacher ever, I figure

GOING TO HELL

Religiosity was a casual thing in my family. The only time my parents went to church was to attend weddings or funerals, and the only apparent concession to their Roman Catholic upbringing was to abstain from eating meat on Fridays.

My religious education may very well have been non-existent but for the fact that the primary school system in Ontario during the forties was divided between Catholic and Protestant denominations. It naturally followed that when it came time for me to attend school in St. Catharines, I would be enrolled at St. Joseph's, the only Catholic school in the neighbourhood.

To me, the Sisters of St. Joseph were all wonderful teachers. I marvelled at how dedicated they were about everything they did, and how they made sure that all their students understood their lessons well.

The sisters created an overall environment that was a perfect blend of love and firm discipline. Their passion, mixed with an ever-present sense of humour, ensured that learning would be a joy for everyone.

For me, the one exception was catechism. I found it totally boring and completely detached from the world I lived in.

Once a week, our class was assigned several questions from the Catholic Catechism, along with prescribed answers that had to be memorized word for word. The following day, Sister Mary Rudolf would orally test us in what seemed like a random fashion. If you were chosen and couldn't answer correctly, you were in trouble.

One day I brazenly tried to fake the answer to a question that wasn't familiar to me.

"You didn't do yesterday's assignment, did you, Jules?" Sister Mary Rudolf accused. I had to sheepishly confess that she was right. "What, pray tell, was so important in your busy life that you couldn't take a few minutes to study yesterday's lesson?"

I knew better than to offer up some lame excuse. I knew very well that Sister Mary Rudolf, with her quirky sense of humour, was sure to turn my reply into a sarcastic comment and all the class would laugh. Better to just slink off to the cloakroom at the back of the room and wait with the other boys for our predictable punishment.

At the end of class, Sister Mary Rudolf would administer a single perfunctory smack with a hard rubber strap to each outstretched palm, and that was the end of it. The whole ritual struck me as mildly amusing, but I suspect poor Eddy didn't think it funny; he never seemed to have the right answers, and he would get the strap at least once a month. I can't say if it served much purpose, except perhaps to scare the girls into doing their homework. Girls never got the strap.

Every Sunday morning, we were obliged to attend mass where Father Jacobowski would drone on in Latin for what seemed like an eternity. I remember kneeling, then sitting, more kneeling, then standing, and on and on it would repeat. It was totally boring, but the exercise did serve to keep me from falling asleep.

Father Jacobowski would come to our school about once a month. He was always greeted with enthusiasm, for we knew he would regale us with stories from his native Poland. Each story contained lessons about the importance of honesty, hard work, compassion, and self-discipline; but the best part was when he would play the role of some historic figure from the past. Sometimes he would ask us to help with the performance.

The one I remember best was when Father Jacobowski donned a loose-fitting gown and proclaimed that we were in Athens. The year was 300 BC. He would play the role of Aristotle, whose style was to teach while walking. As his students, we were encouraged to ask meaningful questions about life as we followed him around the school. It was quite the scene.

Father Jacobowski loved telling stories and would often refer to the teachings of early Greek philosophers. Rarely did he mention religion. Philosophy was his thing. The minutiae of Catholic teachings were left entirely to the sisters. They did their best to inculcate us by repetitious rote, or by force if necessary. It was all so totally boring.

To me, those lessons from the Catechism were simply words that we were forced to memorize. I had never openly questioned any of the lessons, but one day Sister Mary Rudolf said something that grabbed my attention. That was the day we were introduced to sin.

We learned that there were two broad categories of sin. There was venial sin, and there was mortal sin. Just about everyone—except for saints—was bound to commit a venial sin from time to time, but not to worry; you could, with some effort, be returned to a state of grace. This stain on your soul could be expunged by confessing to Father Jacobowski, and he might order you to do ten Hail Mary's and ten Our Father's, and presto, your sins were gone.

But! If you should die with a venial sin on your soul before confessing it, you may have to spend some unspecified time in Purgatory. Your time in Purgatory depended on the nature of your sin and how many credits you may have accumulated throughout your life on earth.

Apparently, time in Purgatory could be almost as bad as hell, but eventually with penance, prayer, and, as I understood it, a measure of divine luck, yes, ultimately, you would still end up in heaven. Glorious heaven, where you would be reunited with your loved ones and your soul would float around in a state of bliss for all eternity.

"Sister, Sister?" I asked. "How about my pet fox terrier? What would heaven be like without my very best friend?" At first, it sounded rather hopeful that Jackie would be there too. Perhaps I should have left it there, but I carried on, "What about all the rest of the cats and dogs? What about all the wild animals? What about the farm animals we eat?" The answers were less clear, and then Sister Mary Rudolf abruptly changed the subject and went on to talk about mortal sin.

Now this was quite critical because, according to Catholic doctrine, if you should die with a mortal sin on your soul, you were doomed to burn in the fires of hell for all eternity. Having just burnt my finger with a match a couple days before, I tried to imagine what it must be like to have your whole body engulfed in flames forever and ever. Surely, hell was reserved exclusively for the most degenerate criminals who had committed some unspeakable evil deed, a sin so heinous that our innocent young minds could not begin to comprehend.

Remembering Aristotle's dictum to think for yourself and question everything, I raised my hand again and asked, "Sister, would you please give us a few examples of mortal sin?"

Sister Mary Rudolf began to rhyme off a list of horrific crimes—but wait a minute; did I hear our dear sister Mary Rudolf say that deliberately avoiding mass on Sunday was a mortal sin?

"Sister, how could that be?" I asked with obvious incredulity. Sister Mary Rudolf repeated in a firm, authoritative voice, "Yes, class, if you should die with a mortal sin on your soul, you are bound for hell."

Not quite satisfied with her answer, I offered up a hypothetical scenario: "Suppose next Sunday my parents decide to go on a family picnic and since they plan to leave early, we shall all miss mass. On the way, we are all killed in a terrible car accident. Would we go to hell?"

"No, Jules, if your intention was to go to mass but your parents insisted you accompany them on that picnic, you would be spared."

"But Sister, how about my parents, would they end up in hell?" I tried to imagine them burning in hell forever and not being there when I went to heaven. That would be awful. I wondered if my parents were aware of this terrible fate that hung over them.

"Sister, I have one more question. What if I really did want to go on that picnic and I died in that car accident. Would I go to hell?"

Sister Mary Rudolf looked a little flustered. After a long pause, she approached, put her arms around me, and whispered, "Jules, we would pray for you, but since you are a confirmed Catholic and can decide things for yourself, the Catechism is clear; you would most likely go to hell."

It took a while for me to process this shocking statement. *How could that be?* I asked myself. I was only eleven. I considered myself to be a pretty decent kid—not perfect, but not bad either. Oh sure, I may have stolen some fruit a few times and I may have lied to my mom once or twice, but I always confessed my sins to Father Jacobowski, and I always recited my Hail Marys and Our Fathers as penance. So now, if I chose to miss mass on a Sunday and died before the next confession, none of this would count and I would burn in the fires of hell forever?

How absurd! How totally ridiculous!

The seeds of doubt are now firmly planted. I suspect they've always been there, lying dormant somewhere in my wayward brain. From these seeds has emerged a hesitant little voice that persistently whispers in my ear. It asks awkward questions that I cannot answer. I try to brush it aside, but the little voice grows louder with each lesson from the Catechism and mocks irreverently whenever Sister Mary Rudolf speaks of God.

According to our dear Sister, there is only one true God, a kind, compassionate God, who loves us all, a God who is all-knowing and all-powerful. He created heaven and earth and every form of life upon it. My inner voice is shouting: *What about disease and death and car accidents? What about hell? Why did God with all his powers allow Satan to create hell? Who, pray tell, created Satan?*

The persistent voice continues: *And which God are we talking about, anyway? Is it God the Father? Is it God the Son, or is it God the Holy Ghost?* And yes, I listened carefully as Sister Mary Rudolf told the story about St. Patrick using a shamrock to explain the Holy Trinity to the pagans in Ireland. That cloverleaf didn't clarify a thing for me.

Of course I cannot repeat any of this to Sister Mary Rudolf, just like I couldn't tell my mom when I finally realized how silly it was to believe in Santa Claus. Mom figured it out soon enough. Maybe Sister Mary Rudolf will also figure out that I no longer accept all those unlikely tales and myths. I'm also having trouble believing all those miracles, like Jesus turning water into wine and feeding thousands of people with a few loaves of bread and a couple fish.

The final straw came around Easter, just before my twelfth birthday. Sister Mary Rudolf is talking about sin again. It seems that besides venial sin and mortal sin, there is yet another type of sin that I never heard of before. It's called the "original sin."

It all started with Adam and Eve. Adam ate some fruit he wasn't supposed to and thereby committed the first sin on earth. Since then, Adam's sin has been passed on to every descendent and is still with us to this day.

Catholics are lucky, because this original sin we were born with can be banished from your soul by "holy baptism." This is a ritual that can only be performed by a priest. He mumbles a couple of prayers in Latin and sprinkles the person—usually a baby—with holy water, and presto, that pesky original sin is gone.

New parents are urged to have their babies baptized soon after birth, just in case they should die prematurely. We certainly wouldn't want to take a chance, especially if the baby is sickly. It would be a tragedy if the baby died before baptism; who knows where it might end up with that dreaded original sin staining its soul.

This story is hard enough to swallow, but now Sister Mary Rudolf goes on to explain that we would still be stuck with this original sin if not for the love of Jesus. Jesus allowed himself to be nailed to a cross and then died a slow torturous death. This was called the crucifixion.

Somehow, this crucifixion was meant to appease God, Jesus' father, who was still angry because a long time ago Adam disobeyed him. God would be less angry now, and perhaps he might forgive that original sin, the one Adam committed when he ate that forbidden apple in the Garden of Eden. Wow! That sin sure caused a whole lot of trouble, didn't it?

Our dear Sister reminds us again and again that Jesus died on the cross because he loves us and we should pray and give thanks for his ultimate sacrifice. All this happened on "Good Friday." I would have called it "Bad Friday" or "Sad Friday." Oh, well.

Then as the story continues, his body was laid to rest in a tomb and a huge boulder was placed across the entrance. By Sunday, his body had disappeared. So obviously he ascended to heaven to join his heavenly father. Not just his spirit (or is it his soul?), but his mortal body too.

By the way, did Jesus have an earthly father, as well? Who knows? After all, wasn't Joseph married to his mother Mary? Did Jesus have two fathers? Does his heavenly father have a wife?

My inner voice is screaming. It's giving me a headache. The whole Catechism is so ridiculous I just want to throw it in the garbage, but I don't want to hurt Sister Mary Rudolf's feelings. How will I tell my parents I don't want to go to church anymore? I don't know where all this will lead, but one thing I do know for sure: *I am not going to hell.*

SONIA

"Saskatoon, Saskatchewan," I heard dimly as I sat daydreaming at the back of the grade seven class at St. Joseph's. Maybe it was the giggling that woke me enough to hear Sister Mary Rudolf finish her announcement. "And so, class, tomorrow, I want all of you to welcome this visitor from out west. We want this young lady to feel comfortable while she is far from home."

Who cares? I thought. *Just another one of those tedious people called girls.* Saskatoon, Saskatchewan, eh? Come to think of it, that does sound kind of funny; no wonder some of the kids were giggling.

But getting back to girls, what a pain they were. It seemed they couldn't do anything right, like building snow forts or having snowball fights. They could barely throw a snowball overhand, and when they tried, they couldn't hit anything, and if a girl ever got hurt, she would go crying to one of the Sisters. Meanwhile, if boys got hurt, they would just suck it up and keep on fighting.

St. Joseph's may have been co-ed, but we were kept apart in other ways. The entranceways, where we often hung out, were at opposite ends of the school. Carved in stone above one door was marked "GIRLS" and the other marked "BOYS." Even the grounds were separate. An invisible line designated by two posts divided the small playground down the middle. How unfair when all the girls ever did was skip rope and play hopscotch. They hardly used the play field at all. Meanwhile, us boys had to stick to our crowded section; and better not let that ball stray onto the girl's side too often, especially if one of the sisters was watching.

Yes sir, everybody knew that boys and girls were different. Maybe we weren't from different planets, but we may as well have been. There was absolutely no mixing at all, and that suited us boys just fine, especially if you had sisters attending the same school. Having to put up with them at home was bad enough; heaven forbid you had to deal with them at school, as well.

They were a pain in the classroom too, with the sisters pointing out how the girls always did their homework. They even studied for tests and exams, if you can believe that. Imagine doing schoolwork at home.

The next day, Sister Mary Rudolf left the room after warning us she would be right back. "Boys, you'd better behave, because the girls will take down the names of anyone who talks or fools around"—and they would, too. That's how sucky girls were.

When Sister Mary Rudolf came back, she was followed by this girl from Saskatoon, Saskatchewan. This time I was somewhat awake and paying attention, but I was totally unprepared for what happened next.

It was as though I was struck by lightning. My heart started pounding so loud I was quite sure everyone in the room could hear. I began sweating like mad and my brain went numb. Through the fog, I did hear Sister Mary Rudolf say, "Class, this is Sonia. She will be with us for the rest of the term. Sonia shall be a great addition to our school because through her, we will learn about life in Western Canada. Let us all give her a warm welcome."

As the two stood side by side, the contrast couldn't be starker; there was Sister Mary Rudolf in her black habit, with only her wizened, unsmiling face showing past the black shawl and starched white collar. The rest of her body was totally obscured within reams of black cotton. Sonia was taller with a clearly defined figure, exaggerated curves, and protrusions in all the right places. Sonia wore a brightly coloured skirt and an intricately embroidered white silk blouse, the likes of which had never been seen in St. Catharines. Sonia explained that just for today, she was wearing her traditional Ukrainian costume because Sister Mary Rudolf had asked her to. She went on to explain the significance of the patterns and colours, but I heard none of it. All I could think was, *This is not a girl. She must be a goddess, the most beautiful vision I have ever seen in my entire life*, and I wondered for a moment, *Could she possibly be from another planet, maybe a planet called "The Ukraine"?*

And then, and then, Sonia looked straight at me with her glorious, green eyes that struck me as being too divine to belong to a mere mortal. I was totally enthralled, lost in a state of rapture and ecstasy. I had never felt this way before, and I couldn't imagine anything more thrilling. And then, I swear, she winked at me. She winked at me with her left eye. It was like a blinding flash that stunned me into a barely conscious state. I don't know how long it lasted, but when I recovered, there was Sonia sitting just ahead of me in the next row. I remember thinking this must have been divinely planned.

For hours I would marvel at the way the sunlight glinted off her hair that flowed down past her waist. I likened them to strands of pure gold streaked with ever-changing hews of bright copper. From my vantage point, I could safely stare at Sonia while I remained invisible to her. Occasionally she did turn and our eyes would meet. She flashed that gorgeous smile that would turn my brain to mush. How I managed to finish the school term remains a mystery.

It turned out that Sonia had all sorts of attributes that separated her from the rest of the girls. After supper, when the whole school ground was available, a bunch of the boys would play baseball. One evening Sonia appeared and asked if she could join us. Wow! Could she play! She could hit, she could run, and most surprisingly, she could throw the ball overhand just like a boy and just as far. Imagine that!

After the game, Sonia asked whose ball this was, and I quickly volunteered that it was mine. She pointed out the stitching was unravelling and the leather cover would soon come off, if it wasn't repaired soon. She offered to take it home and fix it. The next day she handed it back to me, and I remember thinking, *This is not the same ball*. It was gleaming white with flawless red stitching binding the cover tighter than it had ever been, and there was no sign of where the threads began or ended. I remember thinking, *Only a genius could ever do such a thing*.

Sonia was full of surprises like that. Needless to say, that baseball never saw another game. It remained under my pillow for months.

Another time, Sonia brought little strips of clear cellulose to school. She called them love strips and claimed that with these strips she could tell if someone was in love, simply by placing one on the palm of your hand. If it curled downward you were cool, but if it curled upward it meant you were in love. She insisted on placing one on my hand.

That strip curled up faster than cheap bacon on a hot frying pan. I just stood there watching this silly cellulose strip curl ever tighter, too stupefied to utter a word. Sonia smiled and laughed as I melted into a pool of embarrassment.

Too soon, the school year was over and Sonia had to go back to Saskatoon. Meanwhile, if Dad has his way, we might be moving too—back to Manitoba. According to the big map of Canada on the wall, Manitoba is right next to Saskatchewan. Someday, I vowed, I would go to Saskatoon, Saskatchewan, and look for Sonia. I imagined that Sonia was probably waiting for me, and we'd get married and live happily ever after.

Years went by, and bit by bit, thoughts of my childhood heartthrob faded and life carried on. Eventually, I barely thought about Sonia; I even convinced myself that maybe it was better that way.

I may no longer be looking for my first crush. However, if by some miracle, I did bump into her, I would ask Sonia if she remembers those magic moments at St. Joseph's; the baseball games after school, those love strips. I would also thank her profusely for teaching me that girls are not such hopeless creatures after all. And I wonder, should I remind her about that baseball with the perfect red stitching? I may no longer keep it under my pillow, but I still cherish that ball and I shall treasure it for all time.

WAR'S END

Spring 1945: Everyone knows it's only a matter of time before that long, painful war shall end. Still, it came as a shock in late April when *The St. Catharines Standard* proclaimed in huge headlines that Mussolini, the wartime leader of Italy, had been captured and executed. His body, along with the bodies of his followers, were put on public display, hanging by their feet from a makeshift gallows. The photos made a grisly scene.

While some of our Italian neighbours cheered, others wept. We could only guess how each felt about the devastation this costly war had brought to their homeland and the gruesome way it ended. It became obvious that most of our Italian neighbours were relieved that the war was now over, but one family a few doors down the street from our place viewed this as an occasion to observe and pay homage.

The Magnifico's were a musical family. The parents who came from Italy before the war were reputed to be professional singers, while all four of their boys played musical instruments. On summer evenings, the boys would practice on their open veranda while strollers often stopped to listen and enjoy familiar songs from Italy.

Word got out that this coming evening was to be different, something very special, and everyone in the neighbourhood was invited.

Immediately after supper, neighbours started gathering in front of the Magnifico house, and soon there was a crowd of curious people filling the street, some bringing chairs.

The Magnifico family were magnificent. The boys weren't just practicing tonight. On this warm summer's evening, they played beautiful music, mostly Italian classics but some folk music as well. Music rarely heard on the radio.

And then, a hush; everything is strangely quiet. There is no announcement, but it seems everybody knows Mr. Magnifico is about to sing.

He starts with a soft, subdued voice that is pleasant enough, but without a microphone or amplifier he is barely audible. Slowly, as though somebody was cranking up the volume on our big Philco radio, Mr. Magnifico's voice fills the entire neighbourhood with the most beautiful, passionate singing I have ever heard. The background instruments are inconsequential now as Mr. Magnifico's powerful voice reaches full crescendo, his tenor vocal cords the only instrument required.

Tears creep down troubled faces. Is it the music? Is it the lyrics, or is it the deep emotions of the times? I guess I'll never really know. Even if I understood Italian, I doubt that I could fully appreciate the moment. I just know that this will remain one the most special moments that I shall cherish for all time.

The following week, Hitler's forces surrendered. That long, horrible, European war was finally over, and people of every background cheered and celebrated.

There was dancing in the streets. Noisy, colourful military parades blocked downtown streets practically every weekend. Sundays were reserved for quiet reflection, and prayers were offered up in every church.

Even though our family had little direct involvement in the war, Mom and our relatives got caught up in the excitement too. We are grateful that none of our relations or close friends were killed or seriously wounded, but we were all aware that there were many casualties and countless tragedies. One struck close to home.

It began rather ominously when a uniformed young man parked his bike outside our door and asked for Mrs. Inglis. Others gathered round, ready to offer support. They all know a telegram from 'Western Union' usually brings bad news. Mrs. Inglis signs the receipt with trembling hands, repeating, "Oh my, oh my, oh my," over and over again.

The telegram reads: "Merlin Richard Inglis wounded in action. Details to follow."

A couple weeks later, a long letter arrives informing Mrs. Inglis that her son is a patient in an English hospital, recovering from shrapnel wounds to his head. There appears to be little damage to his brain, the letter assures. He is slated for surgery to have a silver plate fitted to the hole in his skull. Doctors expect that he will, in time, make a full recovery. He shall be discharged in a few weeks and should be home by late summer.

We can only imagine the anguish Mrs. Inglis and her daughters are going through. Of course they are grateful that Merlin has survived the war, but at what cost?

Things are sombre throughout the house until, one evening, Mr. O'Hara comes home drunk and confronts Mrs. Inglis in the hallway.

"So, I hear your boy Merlin got himself shot in the head," he shouts in a voice loud enough for everyone in the house to hear.

Mrs. Inglis is clearly shaken, but her cultured good manners and British reserve have rendered her mute, at least for the moment.

"What the hell is he doing in the army, anyways?" bellows Mr. O'Hara. "Your kid is barely twenty. Can he even get into a pub? I'll bet he's still a virgin, for Christ's sake."

"And why aren't you in the army?" asks Mrs. Inglis.

"Why in god's hell should I be fighting your stupid, goddamned war?" replies Mr. O'Hara. "Hitler never harmed me or my family."

"It seems you Paddies would rather beat up your wives than fight for King and Country," she says in a calm controlled voice.

Mr. O'Hara is taken aback. His face reddens, and big veins along his neck are bulging and pulsating. What if one burst—now, wouldn't that be messy?

"I'm not Irish!" screams Mr. O'Hara, "so don't be calling me no goddamned Paddy. I'm a Canuck and proud of it. I don't need no lessons on patriotism from you, you arrogant POME bitch (product of mother England)."

"Spoken like a true Wog," shoots back Mrs. Inglis. "The Irish were never noted for their civility."

Mr. O'Hara is trembling with rage. He clenches his fists and mumbles something incoherent under his breath. He is clearly rattled and doesn't know what to say, or what to do. I sure hope he doesn't use those deadly fists on Mrs. Inglis.

Mrs. Inglis takes a step closer, clearly indicating that she is not intimidated. She's now employing a soft, condescending voice. "I would suggest, Mr. O'Hara, that you calm down before you suffer a stroke. We can't afford to lose any more brain cells, now, can we?"

Thankfully, Iris grabs her dad's hand and pulls him away. "Come, Dad, please, Mom has a lovely dinner waiting." And Mr. O'Hara follows meekly behind his little princess.

Wow, I think to myself, *that Mrs. Inglis is something else*. Looks to me like Mr. O'Hara has finally met his match. Things were kind of quiet around our house after that, and for a long time, nobody talked about the war.

THE CHERRY CAPER

We're coasting through the last days of school at St. Joseph's, and every kid is looking forward to the summer holidays—everyone except my good buddy Angelo. He is not happy at all. He has just turned thirteen, and his dad has arranged for Angelo to work at a farm all summer. It sounds like we won't be seeing much of each other.

"But just think of all the money you'll make," I tell Angelo. "You'll be able to buy your own bike, and we'll be able to explore all sorts of places together." Angelo would just love to own his own bike.

"Fat chance I'll get to keep any of it," says Angelo. He's probably right. Mr. DeLillo is a very stern man.

Sometimes I take Angelo for a ride on my dad's bike. I'm too short to reach the pedals while sitting on the seat, so I ride over-bar while Angelo sits on the seat. One day we discovered that the pedals are wide enough to accommodate two sets of feet. Now, instead of Angelo being just a passenger, we both pedal. It may not be the most comfortable, but boy can we move!

One of the richer kids in the neighbourhood just got a beautiful racer-type bike from his dad. How he loved to show it off, and how he delighted in challenging others to a bike race. Of course, he always won. And oh, how he laughed when Angelo and I challenged him to a race. Was he ever embarrassed when we beat him with my clunky, heavy-duty, double-bar CCM while Angelo and I felt real good.

I learned from younger brother Cice that Angelo got into some kind of trouble with the cops last summer, and that made Mr. DeLillo really, really angry. "That's why we moved out to the country, you know. My dad figures he's got to keep Angelo busy and away from bad people," says Cice. Neither of the brothers wants to talk about the troubles with the cops.

After my last visit to Angelo's, I kind of figured it had to be something like that. We had spent a pleasant afternoon, just Angelo and me, exploring their new acreage. We were on our way back to his house when Mr. DeLillo suddenly appeared. Without saying a word, he grabbed Angelo by his shirt collar and delivered a firm kick to Angelo's bum, letting loose a barrage of curses, all in Italian. Angelo started crying, desperately trying to tell his dad something. I wanted to run, but I was worried about Angelo, so I followed at a distance as we headed back to the house.

I had no idea what the heck was going on. Neither of us had done anything wrong, but every time Angelo tried to say something, Mr. DeLillo gave him another kick. As we approached the house, Angelo broke free and ran towards the house screaming and shouting in Italian. Mrs. DeLillo appeared on the porch and began yelling at her husband. Mr. DeLillo was promptly subdued. He was ever so sorry, and offered Angelo a quarter.

I was eager to get away from this nightmare when Mrs. DeLillo turned to me and spoke in English. I had no idea how much her English had improved. It wasn't perfect, but I understood she was really, really, sorry for what happened. She feels badly that her husband mistook me for that bad boy from the old neighbourhood who got Angelo in trouble last year. Now that he knows I am "that French kid" who lived down the street on Concord Avenue, Mr. DeLillo also feels badly. They invite me to stay for supper. I declined politely and pedalled quickly down the driveway, vowing never to return.

So, on the last day of school when Angelo invites me to come to his house, I'm a bit surprised. Angelo assures me his parents and little brother Cice are in Toronto attending a funeral and he has the house all to himself. Angelo has also invited the rest of the gang, telling each of us to keep it to ourselves. Everyone is curious, but Angelo won't say what he has in mind.

The next day, all the guys meet up at Angelo's house. He gives us a tour of the place and we are impressed. Things are a bit run-down, but knowing the DeLillo work ethic, they'll have things looking neat and tidy in no time.

Angelo starts telling us about a neighbour who lives down the road, and I sense that we are about to learn the main purpose of our visit. The story revolves around Mr. Moretti, who came from Italy many years ago. Sadly, his wife died shortly after arriving in Canada, and they had no kids, so the old guy has lived alone ever since. His modest house sits on a few acres that was likely a mixed farm with a few animals, some grapes, and a collection of fruit trees, but it looks like the place has been neglected for years. "The trees are mostly dead," says Angelo. "Wild shrubs and weeds have taken over the property."

"So how do you know all this?" Dino asks.

Angelo admits that he had a sneak peak around the property a couple weeks ago, when the old guy was away. "I spotted some old cherry trees, most are dead, but some are still bearing fruit." The cherries weren't quite ripe then, but Angelo figures they should be just about ready by now. He's certain the cherries will just rot if nobody picks them, so it wouldn't really be stealing if we were to take a few. The guys have questions, but all agree we must salvage at least some of this neglected treasure.

I love every kind of fruit. I especially like peaches that have ripened on the tree, but cherries are the crème de la crème. Everyone loves cherries. That's why cherry orchards are usually protected with better fences, and you don't often see them growing near busy roads.

"Here's the deal," says Angelo. "Mr. Moretti goes out every afternoon in his old truck, probably for lunch. He's usually gone for an hour or so, which should give us plenty of time to pick all the cherries we want. And remember guys, we have to be super quiet so we don't disturb the dog."

"*Dog*! What's this about a dog?" asks Rolly. I just know Rolly is reliving that time when the two of us were chased down the railroad tracks by another old Italian guy with his dog nipping at our heels. "Could it be the same old guy? Could this be the same dog?" Rolly asks.

"Don't worry, Rolly," Angelo assures him. "This dog is always chained up, but we don't want it barking and alerting the neighbours."

Angelo goes over the whole scenario and how everything should play out. He makes each of us confirm our assigned instructions. I'm thinking this seems vaguely familiar. It all sounds like a movie I saw a while ago at the Grenada. I have to wonder if Angelo saw the same movie. I don't ask. Right now, we have more serious things on our minds.

My job is to act as lookout. I will give the signal when all's clear and it's safe to enter the property. It is also my job to sound an emergency alarm should something go wrong. I hunker down in the tall weeds at a sharp bend across the road from Mr. Moretti's place. From my vantage point, I have a clear view of his driveway. I can also see where the boys plan to cross the fence onto his property.

I never dreamt that learning to sound like an owl would ever serve a purpose. Lots of guys can cup their hands a certain way and sound out a note or two. They may think they sound like an owl, but not many can play that particular five-note tune needed if you hope to have real owls answer you. There may not be an owl answering back today, but I'm confident it won't cause the dog to bark, and it will be the signal for my buddies to get on with the plan.

It is 1:00 in the afternoon. Just as Angelo predicted, a hunched old man appears at the gate leading from the property. I have never seen Mr. Moretti before, and I'm surprised at how decrepit he looks. There's no way he could ever climb those cherry trees. He probably can't climb a ladder, either. I idly wonder if Angelo ever thought of asking the old guy for those cherries. Oh well, too late for that now. Slowly, the ancient Ford half-ton creeps down the road, gears grinding as though it, too, is feeling its age. Time to sound out the owl song. "*Hwoo, hwoo . . . hwoo, hwoo, whoooo.*"

Angelo and Dino step out from the bushes. They approach the barbed-wire fence and grab the middle wires. Days before, Angelo had pulled the staples, so the wire strands spread apart easily while Rolly and Brian hop through. Then, reversing roles, the Italian boys step through and all four disappear into the shrubbery, all in less than a minute.

I am relieved at how smoothly Angelo's plan is working, and deep down I am also relieved that I didn't have to cross that fence. My pesky conscience is having an easier time being the lookout and not having to be picking—or is it stealing?—those cherries. Maybe that's why Angelo picked me to be lookout, but I prefer to believe it's because I can hoot like an owl and whistle really, really loud if there's trouble. Although Angelo taught me the basics of that high-pitched whistle, I have perfected it to the point that if I have to sound the alarm, I'm sure they'll be able to hear me from a mile away.

So far, so good. There is very little traffic on this country road, and nobody has seen us. I fully expect to see the guys coming back any time now. What's keeping them? Are the cherries so few and far between that it takes a long time to pick a decent amount, or are they so luscious and plentiful that the boys are reluctant to leave? And then I hear a familiar sound, and oh, oh! It's Mr. Moretti returning, earlier than expected. Damn! I let out three super loud blasts.

I hear twigs snapping. I can just picture the guys jumping out of the big old cherry trees. The dog starts barking. Then pandemonium, as the guys come charging out from the scrub. Mr. Moretti is cursing in Italian, the dog is barking like crazy, and it sounds like he must be off his chain. My buddy Rolly must be petrified.

According to plan, the guys disperse in different directions, disappearing into the dense woods across the road. I remain in hiding, and I get to see Mr. Moretti and his dog finally arrive at the scene where the boys have long since made their getaway. I can see him testing the loose strands of the fence. I can almost hear Mr. Moretti cursing under his breath and then shouting for his dog to quit barking.

Angelo, Dino, and Rolly are back at the house when I arrive; only one guy is missing. All are quiet and a bit anxious. Where is Brian? Is he still hiding? Did he get lost? Maybe he got caught. I dread to think what his parents would say if the cops caught him. The waiting is awful. And then, footsteps on the porch and blessed relief as we welcome Brian back.

I'm having trouble taking in this mix of emotions as my buddies gather close. We congratulate Angelo, handshakes and hugs all around. Dino does his little happy dance. Unabashed camaraderie and laughter flows freely as we relive the day's events. Angelo pores us each a glass of wine, and I'm thinking, *Oh boy! I sure hope Angelo knows what he's doing.* We all know that Mr. DeLillo makes wine by the barrel, so hopefully he won't miss five small glasses. I know his dad would not approve, but nobody questions; we just sip and enjoy the moment.

Everyone dumps their cherries into the big bowl in the middle of the kitchen table, and I'm reminded of one Sunday a couple years back when I was invited to Angelo's for dinner. Mrs. DeLillo had doled out her special spaghetti from this bowl, a precious heirloom whose story she delighted in sharing, with Angelo's help filling in the right English words. I shudder to think what would happen if somehow it got broken. Once again, I am struck by Angelo's amazing boldness.

The bowl is overflowing with luscious-looking cherries, and everyone is eager to dig in, but Angelo has something to say. With emotion in his voice, Angelo informs us he'll be going to a different school this coming fall, and we may not see each other very often, but he wants us to know we are his very bestest buddies and will remain bestest buddies for as long as we live. "And," adds Angelo with a flourish, "this brings us to the story about this bowl and why I chose to include it in our celebration this afternoon.

"A long time ago in a small village in sunny Italy, a young couple decided to marry. By all accounts it was a grand wedding, attended by everyone in the village. The newlyweds received many lovely gifts, but the most precious of all was a beautiful ceramic bowl, hand-painted by a famous artist who lived in the village. After performing the wedding ceremony, the priest blessed the bowl and proclaimed that from this day forward all who shared a meal from this bowl would become life-long friends. Never would there be an argument amongst them. That young couple was my grandfather and grandmother," says Angelo. "When they died, my Mama inherited the bowl, and when my parents decided to come to Canada, my dad had to build a special heavy-duty box to make sure the bowl wouldn't break during the long boat trip to Canada.

"For over a hundred years, this bowl has been reserved for special occasions," Angelo emphasizes, "and I just want you to know that nothing is more special than having you guys as my buddies." Angelo is tearing up. I'm thinking I should say something, but I find it awkward to digest all this mushy stuff. Everyone is quiet, thinking his own thoughts, when finally, Dino blurts out, "For Christ's sake, Angelo! It's just a friggin' bowl of cherries. Let's eat."

CHAPTER 7
Vita, 1946–1948

BACK TO MANITOBA

November 1945: Mom just got word that Dad is working with German prisoners of war, somewhere up north. It comes as no big surprise to her. This isn't the first time he's taken on a job in some remote place unfamiliar to her. She'll have to be patient and wait for a fuller explanation when Dad finds the time.

To me this all sounds so mysterious, a bit scary too. "I thought the war was over? Has Dad been arrested? Is he locked up with German prisoners?"

Mom has no idea what he's doing, and only a vague notion about the location. "Somewhere along Lake Superior," she says. She tries to assure me that all's well, and she expects that Dad should be home by Christmas.

I sure am relieved when, at last, Dad does come home, but it is soon obvious that things are not going well between my parents. They do their best to keep from arguing in front of us kids, but over the holidays it becomes clear there is a problem—a pretty serious one, I suspect.

Mom puts on a brave face, making sure that our family enjoys our usual family Christmas with lots of good food, lots of visiting with relatives, and lots of presents.

The presents this year are a little different, at least some of them. I find it kind of funny that my sisters Juliette and Alice and little brother Lou still believe in Santa. They have no idea that this year their presents were made by German prisoners. "Boy, Santa's elves sure make nice stuff these days," I tease as each opens their present. I try not to snicker. Mom gives me stern looks, and Dad just smiles.

"So, Dad, why didn't you come home last fall when your work in Arbakka was through for the season?"

"You gotta go with the flow, Joe; and you gotta follow the job, Bob," he says with a chuckle.

Now where did he get that silly line, I wonder? I'm not sure what he means exactly, but I don't particularly want to know. I guess that's a good enough explanation for now.

Dad brought home a photo of what appeared to be a mountain of logs. Tucked in between the neatly stacked piles is a familiar-looking machine.

"Is that your dragline?" I ask.

"No, but it could be a dragline, just like the one I used last summer," says Dad, "but this one's been equipped to hoist logs. See those big grappling hooks? They can grab a couple dozen logs at a time. That's the machine I've been using to load those logs onto railway cars; flatbeds, we call them." To me, the machine looks like a toy, sitting in the middle of those huge piles of logs. It's hard to imagine that all that wood was cut with handsaws and axes by prisoners.

"I guess it's one way to keep those German boys busy," chuckles Dad.

"Or from going stir-crazy," offers Mom.

"So where did all those neat toys come from? You know, the ones Santa brought?" I ask.

"I bought them," says Dad. As if that explained everything.

It took a lot of questioning, but over time I learned that certain prisoners enjoyed a measure of personal freedom. After their workday, they were free to roam around the camp, and those who spoke English could socialize with the locals. Dad became friends with one of the prisoners: Fritz, they called him. Dad saw no problem with joining Fritz and his buddies for a game of cards in their bunkhouse.

"It wasn't much different from the bush camps I used to work in," says Dad. "Young men playing cards, reading, and listening to music. They had it pretty good. Some preferred to pass the time making things, mostly stuff out of wood. Some of the boys were pretty smart and real talented. You know that little suitcase that Santa brought you?" says Dad, looking around to make sure the kids aren't listening. "That was made from a raw log with just a few hand tools. Even the hinges and the latches were made by hand from scrap tin. I thought you could use it to pack your stuff when you come to Stuartburn next summer."

"Stuartburn? What's this about Stuartburn?" Neither Mom nor Dad want to talk about it. I sense that I better not push it, at least not right now. Mom changes the topic.

"Did you know, Mrs. Inglis will be moving pretty soon?" she starts. "With the war over, she managed to find a proper apartment. Lord knows she sure could use more space. Five people when you count her son Merlin. I don't know how they all fit in that tiny space that was once our bedroom. Ridiculous!"

Mom figures that the O'Hara's will also be moving, and she can't wait to see Mr. O'Hara gone. "Everybody's fed up with his loud, violent behaviour. Just think," she says, "once they move out, we can finally have the house to ourselves, and the kids can each have their own bedroom. Maybe I could have my nice big kitchen back. Wouldn't it be great to live like a normal family again?"

Dad is strangely quiet. I suspect he's heard all this before and sees no point in restating his position. He figures we could also live like a normal family if we all moved to Manitoba, and besides, job prospects in his line of work are much better out west.

Meanwhile, Mom is not convinced. She's quite certain that with all his skills and experience, Dad should be able to find a good job right here in St. Catharines. She doesn't want to move. She has grown to really love St. Catharines. I love it here too, and I hate the thought of leaving all my good buddies behind. And so, the argument hangs and things are uncomfortably quiet during the rest of the holidays.

■ ■ ■

January 1946: It's back to school for me and my sisters, and it's back to the prison camp for Dad. The war may be over, but it's taking forever to process the prisoners before they can be returned to the "Fatherland." Meanwhile, they are forced to continue hacking away in the bush, and Dad keeps loading those flatbeds.

When Sister Mary Rudolf heard about Dad working with German war prisoners, she asked if I could share with the class what I knew about life in a prison camp. There wasn't a lot to tell, so I brought along my little wooden suitcase to show the class how some prisoners spent their spare time. I described how it was made from dozens of thin boards cut from a cedar log, and how the hinges and latches were made by hand from scrap tin. That part didn't seem to interest anybody. Oh well! I kinda like my little suitcase, and I'm grateful to Dad and his friend Fritz for the unusual gift.

The rest of the winter went by with no word from Dad and no visits either. Spring came and finally a short note to let us know that he was back in Manitoba, back with his precious dragline dredging his way through another swamp. This time the job is near Stuartburn, a small town west of Vita. "A real pretty place," he says, "with the Roseau River running through it. I'm sure you'll like it." There was no mention of moving back to Manitoba permanently, so I was quite sure this would be just a visit, much like the one to Arbakka last summer.

One day, Mom takes me aside and suggests I should build a crate for Jackie. "Remember how bad things went for poor Jackie when you left him with your friend Rolly last year? Well I found out from the railway company that Jackie can come on the train with us. Mind you, not in the passenger car. Jackie has to stay in a locked crate in the baggage car. He may not like the travel, but he'll spend a better summer than last year."

Oh, sure! Locked up in a crate for three days with only short visits to clean any mess he might make. I know he'll just hate it, but I guess it's better than leaving him behind. I know that we'll have lots of fun together when we get to Stuartburn.

School's out and here we are, Mom and us kids on the train again, headed west to see my dad. It's becoming quite familiar, riding the train, and pleasant enough, but it can get pretty boring at times—mile after mile of endless track and millions of green trees. The train stops for most small towns, but we're not always allowed to get off. I'll be glad when this trip is over.

Poor Jackie, I don't know what he's thinking. It must be a nightmare for him, alone in his cage not knowing what's going on.

Yesterday our porter came by to tell me that Jackie had made a mess in the baggage car. "Youse best come quick," he said. "It smells real bad. Best not feed him. I told you, no feed him."

"But he's got to eat something."

"I knows dat," said the kindly black man. "Me ask Massa conductor, he da boss."

It must seem odd for passengers seeing Jackie and me getting off the train, even when it's too short a stop for everyone else to get off. Jackie never misses an opportunity to leave his mark; sometimes he leaves more. Everybody smiles as they look on.

Dad was right. Stuartburn does look real pretty; it's a tiny, quirky little village with a lovely river running through it. It's a hot day, and kids are swimming and splashing around. There's a rope hanging from a big tree where boys swing out and drop into the water. Sure wish I could join them. If Dad doesn't come soon, I may just do that. I wonder if Mom packed my bathing suit?

A bright orange truck with an open wooden box appears, and sure enough, there's Dad. He's sporting an unfamiliar beard and smiling ear to ear. Everyone's super excited and everyone's super happy, though we don't quite know how to show it. Mom hops in front while us kids jump in the back.

I just love the feel of the wind blowing past my face as the truck speeds down the dusty trail. Jackie is trying to get my attention with his tail thumping and panting like crazy. I know what he's saying. "Let me out of here. Let me out of here," he's frantically telling me. I knock on the roof of the truck, and Dad stops in the middle of a farm field. Jackie has another quick pee. He's got to mark this new territory, after all. We all get out of the truck and watch as Jackie starts running, running like mad in wide circles around us. Everyone is laughing. "Doesn't he ever get tired?" asks little sister Alice.

We're all eager to see where Dad is taking us, and finally, as we round a bend in the road, there it is, a trim little house with a thatched roof. The walls are sparkling white with bright blue trim, tall trees all around. So this'll be our home for the next couple of months. Looks real nice to me. I wonder what Mom is thinking.

Gathered in front are a group of smiling people. "The Novotni family," says Dad. "They're the folks who own this place. It's the original homestead their grandparents built years ago when they first came from the Ukraine. Now they live in a bigger house down the road." Dad tries his best to introduce everyone.

The matriarch of the family offers up a big round loaf of bread on a fancy cloth. Her husband sprinkles salt on top and mumbles something in Ukrainian while all the kids look on in silence. We follow them into the house where more surprises await. There's a big table loaded with all kinds of food.

"Eat, eat!" orders the big bossy lady as she pulls apart the loaf and passes chunks of bread to each of us.

Her mob of kids is now allowed to talk, and they are full of questions. Unlike their parents, they speak English pretty good but with a funny accent. I bet they think we talk funny too.

The house is lovely with walls freshly whitewashed inside and out. It looks a bit like Mrs. Andrusko's summer kitchen in Arbakka but bigger. The floor looks the same, too: packed clay, shiny from years of food spills and thousands of bare feet. I must remind Mom that she's not to wash the floors. There are three rooms on the main floor, and upstairs there's a low sleeping loft with no partitions. It looks like an attic. I want to sleep in the far corner, behind the chimney. *At least there'll be a bit of privacy there*, I figure.

One Sunday, a couple of the Novotni kids appear at our door. "Mama wants you to come to our house," says the older girl.

"I'll lead the way," says the younger one. And so we follow, not knowing what to expect.

"I'll bet there's plenty of food," predicts Dad. "That seems to be the custom with Ukrainian people, and they're always super friendly."

The whole family takes us on a tour of their well-kept farm. They are particularly proud to show us the animals. I kind of like watching the cute little piglets, wandering freely around the farmyard but always sticking close to their big, fat mom. The chickens, too—they're also free to wander. It's so cute to watch the mother hen scratching up the dirt for her chicks to discover tasty treats.

"Baba and Gigi (gramma and grampa) used to live in your house," says a girl with long braids.

"Yeah, but, they're both dead now," says her younger brother.

I want to hear more, but we are interrupted by a god-awful racket outside. Jackie and the neighbour's dog are having a ferocious fight, and I'm worried sick. The other dog is twice Jackie's size, but I'll bet it was Jackie who started it. Mr. Novotni heaves a pail of cold water on them, and they stop fighting long enough for me to grab Jackie. I scold him mercilessly as I drag him home. He spends the rest of the day locked up in his crate licking his wounds. That should teach him. Stupid dog.

Summer days pass by pleasantly. I don't have my regular buddies to hang around with, but I always find something to do. Sometimes I walk to the Vadeboncoeur base camp. There's a comfy-looking caboose that Dad's fellow workers call home and a separate caboose serves as kitchen and living quarters for the cook. I keep hoping to see Dad, but he's never there. "He's way off in the swamps somewhere," says the cranky camp cook. Sure wish I had my bike; maybe I could visit him.

One super hot day, I decide to walk to Stuartburn and go for a swim, maybe swing over the river from that rope in the big tree. After a couple hours of steady walking, I gave up and came back home. Sure wish I had that bike. Just as the summer starts to get boring, a curious thing happens. The camp cook quit her job without notice. Mom was asked to fill in, at least until the boss can find a replacement. This means Mom has to get up way before dawn, walk a mile or so to the Vadeboncoeur camp, and cook breakfast for the work crew and come back home before everyone awakens. She asks if I would go with her. "To protect her from demons and ghosts," she says. Is Mom serious? Surely she doesn't believe in such things. She knows I'm not a believer, but who knows what dangers might be lurking in those woods. The dark doesn't usually bother me, but one morning we did have a bit of a scare.

We're on our way to the camp, this damp and foggy morning. It's super dark. Clouds cover the small crescent moon, and there are no stars. Mom tells me she hears footsteps and twigs snapping in the bush nearby. We stop walking. Silence. We continue. Wait a minute! I think I hear something too. Now I'm a bit nervous, but I won't admit it. Mom shines her flashlight where she thinks the sounds are coming from. Nothing. We walk a little faster, and now there's no doubt about it; we both hear distinct footsteps. They are close by, and we are really scared. "Somebody's following us," whispers Mom. We start running.

Who could be out there, and what do they want? And then a tiny sliver of moon peeks out from behind the clouds, and the mystery is solved. It's a farm horse staring back at us from behind the fence that separates the pasture from the road. We share a great laugh and we carry on.

Only years later did Mom choose to share the story with others. Everybody thought it was hilarious, and I felt kind of sheepish for being scared, scared of a farm horse.

It's nearing the end of August. School will be starting in two weeks, and nobody's talking about heading back to St. Catharines. Finally, one day Mom gathers us kids to break the news. Through her tears, she tells us we won't be going back. Not even to say goodbye to our friends and relatives. Dad and his work buddy Hector have formed a partnership and bought their own dragline. Dad says he will need every nickel to invest in this bold venture. "Going back to St. Catharines for a farewell visit is out of the question," he says. "It's just too costly."

Mom is totally devastated. Left behind is our big, beautiful house with all the comforts and conveniences. She was so looking forward to more peaceful times when all those pesky renters were gone, and how wonderful it would be when we could each have our own bedroom.

Dad says this new business will make lots of money. "We could be rich one day," he tells us. I sense that Mom is not convinced. She's heard it all before.

"Vita will be our new home," she tells us, "at least for a while. Meanwhile, be prepared, kids. It'll be nothing like St. Catharines. This hick town is at least fifty years behind the times. No electricity, no running water, no flush toilets, no telephone—they don't even have a bakery, for heaven's sake."

"But Mom, at least you'll have your privacy," I remind her.

She looks around at all of us and continues in a softer tone, "And maybe we'll have more time to do things together as a family," she says, her face betraying a slight smile.

"Yes, and Dad will be home every night, and there'll be nothing to argue about. Right?" I'm thinking maybe we'll grow to like this new place and things won't be so bad after all.

"Ukrainian pioneer house"   Source: public domain

SHEVCHENKO SCHOOL DAYS

I remember Vita from our trip to Arbakka last year. It had rained for days, and the roads were awash with giant puddles. Mud everywhere. The whole place looked gloomy. Today the sun is shining and the streets are dry; a bit dusty, even. How much cheerier everything appears. I love the sun.

Vita, as the name implies, is bustling with life. It serves as the business hub for south-eastern Manitoba, and today it appears busier than ever with cars and trucks zooming around and sweaty horses pulling wagons with wood-spoked wheels rimmed with steel.

The buildings are all trim and tidy, even those left unpainted since their construction. In time, they turn a silvery grey with brownish streaks, all on their own. I kind of like that look. They remind me of main streets in cowboy movies; especially those that have false square fronts and wooden sidewalks. Why the square fronts, I wonder, when it's obvious they all have peaked roofs?

There's a mix of stores that handle just about any day-to-day needs: groceries, hardware, clothing, even school supplies. Vita also has a drug store, a butcher shop, a restaurant, a blacksmith shop, and two automotive garages. Compared to St. Catharines, Vita looks like it belongs in another age, but I feel there's something charming about it too. I'm curious to know how things work in this town with no electricity, no running water, and no sewers. Most of all, I'm looking forward to meeting new people, especially boys my age; and who knows, maybe there's another Sonia out there.

Mom is grateful that there's a well-equipped hospital with a great reputation. It's by far the most important amenity in town, serving a diverse community scattered over a large district. They even make house calls.

Dr. Waldon is the unquestioned authority and appears to be the only medical doctor around. It seems there's nothing the good doctor cannot treat or fix. Since his arrival over twenty years ago, Dr. Waldon has delivered practically every baby born in the Vita hospital district. "Could be over a thousand," guessed one of the locals. He is regarded with such reverence that many would nominate him for Sainthood, if they could.

Having a hospital nearby was a comfort to Mom, but the main reason we moved from Stuartburn to Vita was the school. Like the hospital, Shevchenko School is unique. It is the only high school for miles around, and Dad is hoping that we'll live here for as long as the work holds out.

Dad was counting on renting a house in town, but none were available. He was sharing this dilemma with his friend, Mr. Petrowski, whose eyes lit up when he recognized an opportunity. "Hey, I've got this beautiful empty barn out back. Maybe it could be converted into a proper house for you and your family." And so it was arranged for this "beautiful" barn to be moved onto a vacant lot, and a gang of workers set about transforming the crude little building into a modest home.

The finished product doesn't look bad from a distance: small but solid, with a brick exterior. Up close, it becomes obvious that the bricks aren't real. The building is clad with thin panels made from wood pulp and coated with brick-coloured rectangles made to look like bricks. Of course, the faux bricks fool nobody. The interior walls are covered with a similar product, but without the rectangles. "Donnacona," they call it. Both are supposed to have near-miraculous insulation properties, and Dad is pleased that he had the foresight to incorporate these wonders of technology into this rushed renovation job. He assures Mom that our new home will be super easy to heat this coming winter.

School starts in a couple days, and all our personal stuff is still in St. Catharines. Nobody seems to know if we'll ever see any of it again. Right now, everything we own is packed in a couple suitcases and one large trunk. "At least it makes moving real simple," says Mom, but she wonders if she can find enough clean clothes to send us kids off to school.

The sun is shining, the air is crisp, and the sky is a brilliant blue as my sisters and I walk the short distance to Shevchenko School. As we approach, we see a mob of kids hurrying to form a line along the entranceway. Each extends a firm handshake and murmurs words of welcome. Everyone is smiling as we enter into another world. I think I'm going to like it here.

Shevchenko School looks nothing like St. Joseph's, especially the interior. There's not a flower in sight, no green ferns, no plants of any kind. And no pictures of saints anywhere. That lovely perfume that permeated St. Joseph's is also missing, but there is a fresh smell of new construction that seems to suit the place.

All the kids look clean and neat, no signs of poverty, and everyone is painfully polite. I don't hear any rowdy boys like my Italian buddies in St. Catharines. I kind of miss those guys. The girls catch my attention—so many pretty girls. A number of blonds, and a few real beauties, but no Sonia.

A loud buzzer gets everyone's attention, and just like at St. Joseph's, we assemble in the large foyer to sing "O Canada." We are greeted with a short speech by each of the teachers and then off to our classrooms. My sisters Juliette and Alice follow Miss Hanuschuk, who guides her flock to their large, airy classroom. Dressed in a flaming red suit, Miss Hanuschuk looks absolutely stunning. You'd think she was going to a party. No modest nuns swishing around in their black robes here.

Meanwhile my teacher, Mr. Probizanski, also stands out. He's a handsome young man, smartly dressed in a formal suit and tie. He wears stylish, rimless glasses, and his hair is combed just so. He's a hometown hero of sorts, especially to baseball fans who consider him to be the best ball pitcher in all of Manitoba. "You ought to see him in action," they say. I was to find out just how good a pitcher he was even before seeing him strut his stuff at a game.

On that first day, Mr. Probizanski was at the front of the room writing away at the blackboard, when suddenly he wheeled around and fired his piece of chalk with deadly accuracy at an unruly boy near the back of the room. I guess the kid felt certain that Mr. Probizanski couldn't possibly see him. It must have hurt when the chalk bounced off the kid's head, but I suspect what followed was more painful. The whole class erupted into good-natured laughter. "Welcome to Shevchenko," says Mr. Probizanski. Everyone laughs even harder.

"It's almost like Mr. Probizanski has eyes in the back of his head," I whisper to Billy, my desk mate. Billy suspects Mr. Probizanski uses his fancy glasses as mirrors so he can tell what's going on behind him. I don't plan to be fooling around, but it's nice to know that humour and laughter seem to be part of the overall atmosphere at Shevchenko.

Billy's a nervous, energetic kid, about my age. We don't have much in common, but because we sit together at these quirky double desks, we soon become good buddies. He invites me to his house after school. Billy's parents are surprisingly young. They speak good English, and they seem interested in all sorts of things. I am happy to answer their many questions, maybe in more detail than they bargained for.

By week's end I was invited to the homes of practically every boy in our room. The visits went much the same as in our Italian neighbourhood in St. Catharines. The first thing parents wanted to know was what nationality I was, and could I speak Ukrainian? And just like those Italian neighbours in St. Catharines, some of the parents needed their kid to translate.

I don't get to play with Billy much; it seems he's always busy working. Right after school, he rushes down to the train station on his beat-up old bike and picks up a huge stack of *Winnipeg Free Press* papers and delivers them to customers all over town. "It takes me a couple of hours," says Billy. "Summers are okay, but in winter I can't always use my bike when the snow's too deep, so I have to hurry before it gets too dark."

I know what he's talking about. Last week, Mom sent me to the store on one of those evenings when there was no moon; no starlight either, much like that scary night when Mom and I walked along the dark trail to the Vadeboncoeur camp and we convinced ourselves that somebody was following us.

"Take the flashlight," Mom suggests. This surprised me a bit. In St. Catharine's there are so many streetlights that it never gets dark. We didn't even own a flashlight. Stepping out the door, I could fully appreciate the need. Without a flashlight, you could easily get lost. Mind you, it didn't stop people from shopping or just going out for a stroll. There must have been dozens of people wandering the streets, exchanging hellos and laughing when they recognized a neighbour or a friend just by the sound of their voice.

With no hydro, all sorts of things become more complicated. You can't just flip a switch to turn on a light. Every evening I'm reminded, "Jules, it's getting dark out," and so another ritual begins. Somehow, it has become my job to light the gas lamps hanging from the rafters. They operate on white gas, and it's best to top them up every evening so they don't run out of fuel at an awkward time. Then they have to be pressurized with what looks like a bicycle tire pump. And if everything works right, the delicate mantles burst into life with the touch of a flaming match. It only takes about ten minutes and I don't mind, but sometimes I get annoyed at being interrupted when I'm busy with more interesting stuff. We have to put up with a loud hissing noise for the rest of the evening, but you get used to it. I must admit, it does give off quite a bright light—plenty of heat, too.

Not having running water is probably the worst of the inconveniences, especially since Mom doesn't trust the water from the shallow well close to our house. It's fine for washing hands and faces, and apparently, it's okay for that dreaded weekly bath.

Bath times are a real pain. The ordeal begins by hauling pails of water and slowly heating a few gallons on the wood stove. Then you pour it into a small tub where only a sponge bath is possible. And you can't just pull a drain plug to get rid of the wastewater. You've got to dump the stuff in a nearby ditch. I hate bath times.

For cooking and drinking water, Mom has arranged with a nearby neighbour to let us use their deep well. We're not the only ones. The waters are reputed to have healing powers, so others use it too.

Sister Juliette and I share the job of hauling hundreds of pails of water in our little wagon, or with our homemade sled in the winter. Juliette hates this job. "Just pretend we're a team of horses coming to the rescue of a band of lost pioneers, dying a slow death in the heat of the scorching dry deserts," I tell my sister. "Our water saves them and their horses, and we lead them on to greener pastures." Still she grumbles.

"What delicious water," says Dad, "the best I've ever tasted," as he samples our fresh delivery. "Must be at least a couple hundred feet deep, that well." I've heard the line before, but somehow it makes the job just a little less tedious.

Shevchenko School doesn't have a proper well, either. Early every morning, Mr. Chorney, our caretaker, hauls water from some mysterious source with his ancient truck. He patiently carries pail after pail to fill two giant earthen crocks at the back of the foyer. One crock is for drinking, the other for washing hands. Each has a small tap near the bottom, and there's an open pail below to catch the spills. There must be over a hundred glasses and cups, each different from one another, lined up row upon row on open shelves. "Bring your own cup," a student suggests. "You don't want to share someone else's germs, do you?" I have to wonder: *Has no one heard of disposable paper cups, or are they considered too expensive?*

Shevchenko School doesn't have proper flush toilets; in fact, there are no toilets at all. Instead, there are three modest outhouses, partially hidden amongst scrub poplar, some distance from the school. One is for boys, one is for girls, and one is strictly for teachers. The boy's outhouse gets very little use. It seems boys just go a little farther into the bush with no need for walls or roofs. Works just fine for me—smells better, too.

The school grounds are huge, at least triple what we had at St. Joseph's. There's a baseball diamond, but no one seems to play there. This surprises me, considering Mr. Probizanski's involvement in the game. Instead, the boys all seem to gravitate to soccer.

It's not a game we played at St. Joseph's; there just wasn't room, but here at Shevchenko, there's lots of space and there doesn't seem to be any limit to the number of players on each team. At times there must be thirty, forty, maybe more players running around like crazy, kicking the ball in all directions and sometimes through the goal posts.

Soccer is new to me, and I must confess I never did learn all the rules. I was a pretty good runner, so sometimes I got control of the ball but I didn't know what to do with it. I couldn't always recognize who was on my team, so I was just as likely to pass it to an opponent. Amazingly, no one chastised me, and the game just carried on. People in Vita are so polite. I would learn they can be pretty determined too.

Soccer's a game that can be played all year long and in just about any weather. Maybe that's why it's so popular. There was a ferocious winter storm just after Christmas that left over two feet of snow with drifts three to four feet deep in places. I was certain this would put an end to our soccer games, but no, all the boys gathered on the field as usual. Someone threw the ball into the snow where it promptly disappeared, and we began to play. We struggled to move faster than a walk and had to waddle slowly through the drifts. The ball kept getting lost, but gradually the snow got packed down and the pace quickened. By the end of the week, there wasn't a square foot of that field that wasn't packed hard by thousands of moccasined feet.

The cold didn't seem to be an issue, either. It didn't matter what the temperature was outside; every recess and right after lunch, all soccer players would simply pull up the hoods on our parkas and we'd be on the field in minutes. You could tell roughly how cold it was by the crunching sound our feet made on the hard-packed snow, and how much bounce there was to the ball.

One very still and crisp morning in late January, the thermometer outside read minus forty. Even at that temperature, our modest little house was warm and cozy. Dad was quick to credit the "Donnacona" he had selected for the wall panelling. Mom didn't say anything, but I heard her getting up during the night to feed both wood stoves with jack pine. I felt pretty good about the part I played in helping to harvest that wood. I wonder if poplar would have done the job.

It was good to see that just about every kid from out of town got a ride to school that morning. What a fascinating scene: big scruffy horses with their shaggy winter coats drawing a variety of colourful sleds, their heavy breathing creating clouds of frosty vapour that hung in the still air.

The sleds came in all sorts of shapes and colours, and they all looked hand-built. The cabs were mostly enclosed, with multiple small windows and a simple door. Some of the fancier models even had a full windshield like you'd find on a car. The ones that got everybody's envious attention were those with an actual wood stove burning merrily in the cab, keeping their passengers warm. They really stood out with their stovepipes poking through the roof, puffing smoke like giant cigarettes. How decadent.

In heartbreaking contrast, we watched helplessly as four pitiful kids approached the school, all shivering like crazy, the younger ones with white patches on their cheeks.

"Frostbite," Miss Hanuschuk declared. "Come with me." A few of us followed as she took the kids downstairs to the warm furnace room. Miss Hanuschuk quickly removed their outer clothing and moccasins to check their feet for frostbite. Someone brought hot chocolate.

Things got off to a slow start that morning, but we still sang "O Canada" and classes carried on as usual without fuss. Later we learned that Miss Hanuschuk was able to make arrangements with the kid's parents and their neighbours. Never again would those kids have to walk alone those four long miles in the bitter cold.

On another of those super cold mornings, my sisters and I hurried to school expecting a warm refuge only to find it was almost as cold inside. Someone said the furnace had broken down. "Don't worry," said Mr. Boychuk, our principal. Mr. Chorney will have it fixed in no time and everything will be back to normal real soon. Meanwhile, "Please be patient, and keep wearing your parkas." And so we did, for the whole day, and no one grumbled.

The next day the whole school was toasty warm, and everybody was smiling except Mr. Chorney. It was whispered that he had slept in, and the big wood-burning furnace had gone out during the night. Everyone took it in stride. Some found it kind of amusing, but nobody complained. This surprised me a bit, but I was beginning to recognize that hardly anyone ever complained about anything at Shevchenko.

"Could this be another Ukrainian trait?" I asked myself—or was I picking up my parents' habit of generalizing about cultures and their characteristics?

Mom and Dad were raised in a totally French Canadian environment. They seemed to delight in making observations about the many differences between their own culture and everything Ukrainian. Food, clothing, housing, entertainment, even religion, all were fair game. I got the impression they considered their French culture to be better in most ways, but acknowledged that there was much to be admired in the Ukrainian culture as well. Most definitely, each could learn from the other.

A fine example occurred one evening just before Christmas. Our family was walking home after an extravagant Ukrainian concert that featured strange, lively music, colourful costumes, and spirited dancing. We all enjoyed it very much, especially Mom. "Did you see those acrobatic moves the male dancers go through in their high boots and baggy pants? You'd never catch a French kid do anything like that. And the costumes; who in the French community has the time or the artistic talent to create such gorgeous costumes?"

Dad was fumbling in his pockets, trying to find the keys to our house. He seemed to be taking forever while the rest of us shivered.

"Nobody had locks on their doors where I grew up," Mom declared. I know what she's thinking. In her culture everybody was totally honest and trustworthy; there was never a need for locks.

Dad had his own biases. How he marvelled at the incredible work ethic of Ukrainian people, especially when compared with the English. "Just look at that lovely house," he would point out as we drove past another Ukrainian pioneer home. "That place could be fifty years old, and still it looks good. It's made of poplar sticks and mud, with grass for a roof, yet it's comfortable in summer and winter. Looks nice too, once it's whitewashed.

"Meanwhile, those early settlers coming from England, they made their first homes from sod. How stupid is that! One good rain would destroy them, and those greenhorns were left homeless. And some of the French weren't too bright either, throwing up half-ass log huts that leaked or rotted in no time when they didn't take the time to peel the logs. Those Ukrainian homes were way better. I don't understand why no one else builds houses like that."

I wonder if that's why Dad's family moved out of their first log home after just ten years, but I don't say anything.

Other times, Dad would shake his head and question why it took so long for Ukrainian farmers to get with the times and start using tractors instead of horses, trucks instead of wagons.

There was, however, one Ukrainian trait that really impressed Mom and Dad, and they shared it with everybody, "Ukrainian people are the most hospitable you'll ever meet, they declare."

"And the friendliest people in the whole world," I figure.

"Shevchenko school"   Source: Shevchenko school archives

"Ukrainian house-construction detail"   By: Gladys Legal

THE TROUBLE WITH RADIOS

I never dreamt that owning a decent radio could be considered a luxury. Oh, we have a radio all right, but with no hydro in town, we make do with a battery powered, little white thing and I am not impressed. Dad doesn't understand my grumbling. He considers the radio he bought to be just fine. "It has the very latest technology. See those tiny glass tubes? They pull radio waves out of the air and magically convert them into sound. This modern radio uses so little electricity it can operate for a whole year on just one large dry-cell battery," he boasts.

Oh sure, I think to myself, *maybe that battery will last a year if you're super stingy about how much you use it.*

Dad's not overly strict, but we get the message. You only turn the radio on when you need to, like listening to the news or something important. The sound is so crappy that I don't bother listening to music anymore. Mom still seems to get some satisfaction out of certain morning shows, and of course everybody still listens to Lux Theatre, every Sunday evening.

One day, I tell my friend Billy about my frustrations, not expecting a solution. He invites me to his house and turns on his radio. It sounds real good, not quite as good as our big old Philco in St. Catharines, but a heck of a lot better than Dad's little wonder box.

"You don't have to put up with that crap," Billy tells me. "There's a better way." Of course I'm all ears. "You go to the junkyard. You tell the boss that you're looking for a used car radio, and he'll let you roam around the yard till you find the one you want. You check to make sure it works and be prepared to haggle, and presto, you've got a radio with a much better sound than that piece of junk at your house."

"Sounds great, so what's the catch? Why doesn't everybody do that?" I ask.

"Because they're too damn cheap," says Billy. Then he admits that you need a full-sized car battery to operate the salvaged car radio, and somehow you have to charge the battery about once a week.

This leads to a long explanation of his other business. When he's not delivering papers, Billy's busy charging batteries in his dad's garage. It's a messy-looking setup with old car batteries all over the place and wires running everywhere. I'm impressed that Billy can tell when a battery is fully charged with a simple-looking glass thing he calls a hydrometer.

"Normally customers drop off their dead battery and exchange it for a charged one; but since not everybody has a vehicle, I deliver charged batteries to their homes and pick up the dead ones every weekend. Give me a hand next Saturday and I'll give you a tour of the town."

Of course Billy knows everyone in town, and he fills me in on all sorts of gossip. "Notice how all the nicer homes belong to store owners and the shabby ones belong to poor folks." Billy tells me he plans to build his own house one day, and his will be the finest house in town.

We pass by a trim little place with flowers everywhere. In front is parked an almost-new Cadillac. "What kind of business do these people run to be able to afford such a nice car?" I ask.

"A young widow lives here," says Billy. Her husband died a few years back. He was really old, and they had no kids, but she sure has lots of boyfriends." I think I know what he means.

On every street there's another bootlegger and another story. "Vita must be the home brew capital of Manitoba," I observe.

"Could be," says Billy, "but each one's a little different. See that fancy footbridge leading to that expensive-looking house? Mr. Kaponiuk keeps his stash of home brew under that bridge. He only sells the concentrated stuff, and only by the gallon, to customers who come at night and pick up however many gallons they've arranged for. That way the full-strength alcohol is never on his property. Wholesalers dilute it and add some other stuff and resell it to customers by the bottle . . . Don't stare," Billy whispers, "and don't ever look under that bridge—you never know who could be watching, and if any of that precious brew ever went missing there would be hell to pay."

At the other end of town, Billy points out a run-down old building that looks like it should be torn down. "Mr. Sawchuk owns this place," says Billy. "It may look like a regular store, but they hardly sell anything. Upstairs, that's where the action is. Men hang out there to gamble, to drink home brew by the glass, and to talk. Some stay the whole day.

"Everybody loves Mr. Sawchuk. He's so kind, always helping others. Everybody knows he financed the construction of our new school. Some say that he paid for the whole thing himself. Meanwhile, he lives alone out back and drives a beat-up old Chevy. I guess he just doesn't like to spend money on himself."

Mr. Bachynski, the local blacksmith, is another of those kindly men who is happiest when helping others, often fixing things for no charge. He lives in back of the shop with his elderly mother. When the big double doors are open, you know he's open for business, and men wander in and out on a regular basis. Billy marches in and proceeds to a dark corner of the shop and pees into a funnel mounted on the wall. Holy smokes, I've never seen anything like this.

"Go ahead," says Billy.

"This doesn't seem right," I protest. "We didn't ask Mr. Bachynski, and besides there's no privacy at all."

"Go!" says Billy. "Just go!"

The funnel is connected to a long horizontal pipe that leads outside to a shallow ditch along the front street. Through a small, smoke-blackened window, I can see my discharge dribbling down, and so can anyone else passing by. Weird!

"You know Marie from Mr. Boychuk's grade ten class?" asks Billy.

I don't really know her, but of course I've noticed her. Everybody notices her. "That gorgeous goddess of perfection all the boys drool over?"

"That's the one," says Billy. "She lives here. I saved her house for last. I just adore her. Try not to say anything stupid if she comes to the door."

"Do you ever talk to her, Billy?"

"Well, not yet; it's usually her mom or dad who comes to the door."

"What would you say if Marie did answer the door?" I ask.

"Maybe I could introduce you as my friend from out east and tell her you're thirsty. Maybe she'll give us a glass of water. You never know, she might invite us in for milk and cookies or something like that. Wouldn't that be awesome?"

Marie's dad appears. "Just leave the battery here, boys. The dead one's by the garage."

As we trudge back to his house, Billy counts the cash he's made today. "Six dollars and fifty cents," he says with an air of satisfaction. He's not about to share any of it, but he does invite me to the local drugstore for a treat. "Two cokes and two bars," Billy orders. We proceed to a booth overlooking the sidewalk. As we munch away on our Sweet Marie chocolate bars, we stare intently along the street. You never know when that other sweet Marie may come strolling by.

I've been attending Shevchenko for a couple weeks now, and I'm starting to feel badly that I still haven't spoken to this shy, awkward guy who sits at the back of the room and rarely says anything. I know his name is Stan Honta. I must approach him and find out what he's all about. He's a tall, bony kid with big feet and long, messy hair—not the sort that would appeal to girls. At least, I wouldn't think so. Still, everyone seems to like Stan.

Once in a while, something strikes Stan as funny and he bursts out with a hearty, goofy laugh. The rest of us find it kind of funny just watching, and we smile without knowing what the joke is about.

Everybody knows Stan is super smart, maybe even a genius, and we know that Mr. Probizanski regards Stan as really smart too.

Stan doesn't go out of his way to make friends, so it comes as a bit of a surprise when he approaches me one day. "I hear you're interested in radios," he says. "Come over to my house and I'll show you what I've got. Saturday morning would suit me. You know where I live?"

It's a long walk to Stan's place. I've passed by here before but never ventured down the long, winding driveway. It comes as a bit of a surprise to see this tall wooden tower with a windmill on top. The propeller is spinning merrily away and there's Stan busy working on a bunch of electrical stuff below the tower. "You build all this?" I ask. "Sure looks complicated."

"Not really," he says. "I salvaged the generator from a junk car, and I carved the propeller from a tree. The batteries are throwaways from a local garage in town. They're pretty weak, but good enough for my simple lighting system. I'll show you," says Stan, and I follow him inside.

I'm glad that earlier in the week Billy had told me that Stan lives alone with his grandfather. "Don't ask him about his parents," warns Billy. "Stan was told that his parents died in a car accident when he was young, but gossips tell a different story. There are whispers that Stan's mom ran off with another man, and shortly after his dad disappeared and nobody knows where he is."

I don't see Stan's grandfather, but I won't ask about him, either. There's a layer of dust over everything, but the house is neat enough. A naked bulb hangs from the ceiling in the kitchen. Stan pulls on a string and sure enough a nice bright light comes on. "Sure beats our gas pressure lantern," I tell Stan. "And no hissing." Another bulb hangs over what must have been the dining table, but Stan has put it to a different purpose. The whole table is covered with books, electrical stuff, and small tools: all things new and intriguing to me.

"This is my version of a radio," says Stan as he points to a board decorated with copper wire coils and a neat collection of mysterious-looking parts all connected together with thin coloured wires. He places what looks like a pair of earmuffs over my ears and fiddles with some thingamajig on the board. "Hear anything?"

And then, like magic, I hear music—not loud, but crystal clear. Sounds a whole lot better than that crappy radio at my house. "Keep listening," says Stan. "They might say where they're broadcasting from."

Sure enough, a deep male voice announces that the music is coming from Omaha, Nebraska. Holy smokes! I'm just blown away. "Where the heck is Omaha, Nebraska?"

"In the states," says Stan, "about a thousand miles, straight south of here."

I'd like to know how this amazing miracle works. Stan patiently tries to explain. It's mostly lost on me. I don't understand what radio waves are, never mind how they can travel a thousand miles. And how can those earphones convert radio waves into sound waves?

"No battery needed," Stan concludes with a hint of pride, "all you need is the right antenna, the right coils, and a special crystal. Maybe next week we can start building one for you," he offers.

At the supper table that evening, I try to explain all the wonders of the fascinating technology I've seen at Stan's place and how I'd like to build a crystal radio just like Stan's.

"Sounds like a lot of work," says Mom.

"Expensive too," adds Dad. He turns on the little white radio. The tiny tubes glow, and through the humming and the hissing, a crackling voice that sounds sort of human is reading the news of the day.

"Sure wish we had our old Philco," says Mom.

And I'm thinking, *Maybe I'll be visiting Stan quite often from now on.*

WINTER WOOD

Winter is approaching. Everybody knows the weather's going to turn real cold and there are preparations to make. "We'll need another stove," Mom reminds Dad. He's well aware but doesn't seem concerned. It's a simple matter of going to Smook Brothers General Store and picking up a stove, along with a bunch of stovepipes to connect to the chimney.

It's a flimsy, tin thing, the kind used in bush camps, trapper's cabins, and sometimes a regular home. A "box stove" most people call it even though it's oval shaped and doesn't look anything like a box. They're real cheap and are often thrown out after one or two seasons. Mom is familiar with this all-purpose heater, and she certainly knows all about Manitoba winters. She has stuffed ribbons of rags around all the windows and the thin door that separates winter's wrath from our living space. With two stoves and a good supply of wood, she knows it won't be a problem keeping this crude little place warm, no matter how cold and windy it may get.

It's a matter of survival to have enough seasoned wood on hand to last the winter. It's also a matter of pride for Mom and Dad. They talk about visiting friends and relatives who wore heavy sweaters and boots all winter to conserve fuel. They speak with pity about people they've known who ran out of wood and had to rely on neighbours to survive the winter. Mom grew up in a household where there was always lots of firewood and there was no scrimping on heat. "In our house you could walk around in your bare feet no matter how cold it was outside," Mom would boast. A subtle dig that her in-laws' house, wasn't always comfortable.

"It was always too damned hot in that Gauthier house," Dad shoots back.

"But you have to admit, it's always nice to come into a warm house after working outdoors all day," Mom insists.

Now it is up to Dad to make sure we have plenty of the right kind of fuel. A few locals are selling stove-length, split and seasoned poplar, door to door. The price is temptingly cheap, but Dad has other ideas. Sure, it would be easy enough to buy a few cords of dry poplar that makes the perfect fuel for the cook stove, but poplar burns quickly and doesn't throw much heat. It would require feeding the box stove several times during the night to keep our family from freezing. Besides, Dad just can't imagine why anyone would spend good money on wood when just a few miles to the north is a jack pine forest, just waiting to be harvested by anyone willing to make the effort. Jack pine, it seems, is the perfect fuel for an overnight fire.

So here we are, just Dad and me, headed for this mysterious forest called "The Sandilands," and I couldn't be more excited. It's mid-November: a cold, bright, sunny morning with just an inch or so of fresh snow covering the frozen ground. Smoke is rising lazily from every chimney as we leave our pretty little village. Along the main road leading north, we pass by the "Holy Trinity Church". With its tall, onion-shaped copper domes, it's easy to imagine that we could be in the Ukraine. The scene is kind of magical, and I'm thinking this picture would make a gorgeous Christmas card.

Our vehicle is an olive drab, one-ton truck that Dad bought from army surplus real cheap. It's so beat up; it looks like it's been through the war. I half expect to find bullet holes. It was built by General Motors around 1942, and unlike our beautiful 1939 GMC truck, this quirky, snub-nose vehicle has absolutely no frills or basic comforts. It doesn't even have proper side windows. Dad says it's just as well because the truck has no heater either and the windshield would frost up if it had side windows. I don't quite understand the connection, but Dad must know what he's talking about.

One important feature it does have is four-wheel drive, making it the ideal vehicle for hauling workers and drums of fuel to the drag-line no matter how bad the roads. Sometimes it must plough through swamps that have no roads at all. It will also be great for hauling the wood we plan to cut today—that is, if we don't freeze to death before we get to the woods.

About an hour out from Vita, we leave behind the charming Ukrainian farms with their neat, whitewashed homes and unpainted barns. The cows are all indoors, but a few horses still roam the pastures looking to scrounge the last remnants of green grass before all is buried under feet of snow. We drive through miles of scrub brush with bulrushes and cattails threatening to overtake what may once have been a decent road.

Finally, we emerge into another world. There is no snow here, and the ruts in the road reveal pure sand, much like you see at Port Dalhousie beach. "So this must be the Sandilands?" I ask, not really needing confirmation.

"I'm taking you on a strawberry shortcut," Dad tells me.

"What?" I know there can't be any strawberries this time of year. "What the heck is a strawberry shortcut?" I have to ask.

"You know when you're on a trip somewhere and instead of taking the most direct route to your destination you deliberately take a longer one in the hopes that you might come across a strawberry patch? That's what we call a strawberry shortcut."

But if you take a longer route, that's not a shortcut, I think to myself; *and of course, there are no strawberries to be found in November*. It takes me a while, but finally I see the humour in it and I smile; but Dad laughs and laughs, confirming my suspicions that his sense of humour and mine are a bit different.

"There's the entrance to that strawberry patch I was telling you about," he shouts and starts to chuckle all over again.

All I see is a "NO TRESPASSING" sign and a big hump blocking what must have been a road at one time. Dad stops the truck and shifts into four-wheel drive before we climb over the hump. I marvel at how easily the truck handles the steep climb and the menacing stones, which could easily rip the bottom out of most vehicles. I also smile at how blithely Dad ignores the "NO TRESPASSING" sign, just like us boys ignored the "NO TRESPASSING" sign below Lock Two on the Welland Canal where my buddies and I went swimming.

Nature is doing its best to reclaim what must have been a wide, well-groomed road at one time. This is great fun, and I sense that Dad is enjoying pushing his spunky old truck through the dense shrubbery and mowing down saplings thick as my arm.

We've been grinding our way ever-so-slowly through the brush for what seems like hours. My mind starts to wander. *This could easily be an animal trail in the dense jungles of Africa*, I tell myself. I am with Sir Henry Stanley, and together we are searching for Dr. Livingston, who has disappeared without a trace somewhere in this vast "dark continent." We are getting nowhere, and Sir Stanley is getting frustrated. He turns to me and asks if I have any idea of where we should be looking.

"Let's call up Tarzan," I suggest. Everybody knows that Tarzan communicates with the animals, and one of them just might know about Dr. Livingston.

"Splendid idea, Mr. Legal," replies Sir Stanley, "perhaps your friend Tarzan could arrange for a few elephants to transport our gear, I sense that our porters are becoming mightily fatigued."

The jungle ends abruptly, and I am brought back to reality as we emerge onto a broad, flat field. A high wooden fence lines both sides of a dirt track. Dad shifts into second gear, and we speed along at the breathtaking speed of twenty miles per hour. I'm getting anxious to see this strawberry patch.

The tawny fields turn into a magnificent forest of mature jack pine, appearing almost black in the low light. Interspersed among the pines are contrasting clusters of white birch. Without their leaves, I can see the younger branches transition from white to rich tones of brown and then to almost red towards the tips. The fallen leaves have created a bright yellow carpet, covering the entire forest floor. The beauty that surrounds us blows me away. A feeling of euphoria washes over me. I want to stay here forever.

"This is it!" Dad shouts, waking me from my reverie. "Not much different than when I last saw it over twenty years ago. I'm surprised the buildings are in such good shape; no sign of vandalism anywhere." Not a word about the wonderland we just passed through. I guess this is another one of those times when Dad and I see things a bit differently. I'll bet Mom would be just as enthralled as I am. Too bad she couldn't be here to experience this lovely oasis in this jumble of scrub bush.

So this is the strawberry patch. These clusters of buildings look like a ghost town—a ghost town you might see in cowboy movies. Some of the homes look quite liveable even though the windows are boarded up. The paint is faded, but most of the buildings still look pretty good. A dainty picket fence surrounds each house, framing small yards overgrown with wild shrubs and small trees. Scattered here and there are plants that look like they don't belong. Rows of caragana bushes that were probably a hedge at one time now look more like trees. On a smaller scale, little bunches of green shoots look like newly sprouted onions. "Chives," says Dad.

"What are those red things hanging from thorny bushes?"

"Rose hips," he explains.

"Hips? Did you say rose hips?" I ask. "Weird, this English language."

"It's not just the language; all English people are a bit odd," Dad figures, and then launches into the story behind this intriguing little ghost town.

"It was during the 1920s. A group of greenhorn Englishmen bought this huge parcel of land from the Crown, real cheap. They must have had friends in high places, was the common gossip. No one knew just what they planned to do with all this land; after all, it was mostly swamp and sand and gravel, pretty much useless for farming.

"And then a bunch of fancy-dressed folk started showing up at the train station in Vita, bringing with them all kinds of stuff: enough books to fill a town library, musical instruments, even a piano. Most importantly, they brought suitcases full of cash.

"A small army of tradesmen followed. There were carpenters, masons, blacksmiths, and all kinds of skilled workers. Most were from Ontario and would be going back when their work was done, leaving locals to do the menial stuff.

"As the plan unfolded, it became clear that these foreigners were determined to transform the wilderness into one huge, elegant country estate—or 'ranch,' as prairie people preferred to call such a farm. Some locals thought they were starting a religious commune, although not exactly like a Hutterite colony. In this model community, families would still enjoy their privacy, each in their own home, but their social life would revolve around the rather fancy communal hall where everyone would gather. Some called it the 'opera house.' The hall served as a school, a church, a library, and it was designed to accommodate all manner of learning and social activities."

Now that I know something about the history of this place, it seems less mysterious and I would love to poke around a little longer. I am particularly intrigued by the English architecture. Dad assures me there is still more to his strawberry patch and we'd best move on if we're going to cut some wood today.

Slowly we drive a short distance along a very pretty, leaf-covered lane, and there it is. It is absolutely formidable. It is by far the biggest barn I have ever seen. It looks almost new, painted spotless white with bright red trim. Even the fenced corals are impressive with their flawless white boards and fat cedar posts.

I've never seen so many windows on one building and none boarded up. Each window frames a half-dozen smaller panes, and all are intact. How tempting for boys with slingshots. I think back to that time Rolly and I shot out all the windows from that barn we thought was derelict. We take a peek inside through the windows, half expecting to see it full of horses. I figure this barn could easily handle a hundred horses, but it's empty now, scrupulously clean and tidy, no sign of manure anywhere. Of course my questions start pouring out, and Dad patiently tells what he remembers.

"Everybody knows that English people are dog lovers," he begins, "and plenty of them are horse fanciers too. Someone convinced these would-be ranchers that here in western Canada was a huge, unfulfilled market for horses. Promoters explained that all the dogs in Manitoba were mongrels and it followed that all Manitoba horses were mongrel too. Prairie horses were simply inferior, not really fit for the tough jobs required of them."

"The plan was to breed quality horses and sell them to eager Manitobans. When properly bred and properly trained, customers would come pounding on their barn door, so to speak."

"Most folks in the area believed the English were crazy; this bunch just a bit crazier than your typical Englishman. So a couple years later, nobody was too surprised when they began to pack up and leave. Some thought it was the 1929 financial crash that did them in. Some blamed it on the drought that was beginning to hit the western prairies." Dad has theories of his own. He remembers the gossip that swirled around at the time, and some of the stories still cause him to chuckle. He couldn't say if they were true, but he didn't find them too hard to believe.

One story has it that these would-be horse breeders only imported top-quality stock, mostly from the east. Some said they even brought in a stallion from England. That first spring, all seemed to be going well. The grass was green and lush, there was plenty of pasture for the horses, and all the mares were pregnant.

All was going well until early June, when the bug season began. These fancy horses might have experienced the odd mosquito where they came from, but they certainly weren't prepared for the Manitoba flies. One type of fly in particular, appropriately called the "horse fly," thrives all too well in southeastern Manitoba, and they are vicious. These flies can at times number in the billions, and they just love horses. They will bite relentlessly until the poor horse goes berserk. Some start running and won't stop until they collapse from exhaustion.

These eastern horses learned very quickly that the flies weren't nearly as bad inside the barn, and eventually they all refused to go outside. There may have been nice green grass close by, but these horses would rather starve. What to do? Locals will tell you, when Manitoba horses get hungry enough, they'll put up with the flies. Not these delicate beasts. They had to be fed hay and oats for months. Local farmers were happy to sell their stale hay, some even cut fresh grass to sell for a very good price. It was only a matter of time until the English realized they couldn't continue operating this way and everything started to fall apart.

Dad has another theory. He suspects the English were just a bit slow to figure out that by 1930 horses were pretty much obsolete. He recognized that tractors and trucks were taking over most of the heavy work, and when it came to travel, well, he much preferred a car.

Dad bought his first car, a Model T Ford, around 1920 when he was still a teenager. Oh, how farm people ridiculed those first cars, laughing and gloating every time a car broke down or got stuck in the mud. On occasion, he would remind yokels, "My car may sometimes need attention, but my 'T' doesn't eat much hay, and it absolutely hates oats."

Of course this invited horse and buggy folk to respond, "Well my horse never breaks down, and it doesn't burn much gas." The horse versus car argument sometimes got heated. Dad admits to such an occasion. He is not proud of it, but one time he lost his cool and ended an argument with the line: "Well, unlike your horses, my car doesn't piss and shit all over the goddamned place, period."

We're back on the road looking for a particular trail that Dad had spotted when travelling through here the year before. He coaxes the old truck deep into a dense forest of jack pine, brushing aside branches that appear to block the way in places. Finally, he stops the truck at a chaotic tangle of dead trees that look like they've been pushed over by some giant hand. "Must have been a powerful wind that swept through here," he says, "maybe a tornado."

"Why here?" I wonder. "It's all so messy."

"If we were cutting standing, live trees, they would be too green to burn properly, at least for this winter. It looks like these have been dead a couple years, which makes them just perfect for heating and won't plug up the chimney with soot.

"I'll start cutting, and you build a fire and make us some tea," he suggests. It may be a little early for lunch, but Dad recognizes the importance of keeping up fluid levels. "Never eat snow," he says. "It'll sap your strength and make you cold. You really shouldn't be drinking any cold liquids either," he adds.

Men working outdoors in the winter have known this for ages. I remember reading stories about *"coureurs des bois"* travelling great distances by snowshoe, and how they would stop every couple hours to boil tea. They would add a generous amount of honey or sugar and go all day without eating.

Much as I would like to fantasize and try reliving those days, we certainly won't be working all day without eating. Mom has baked fresh galettes. They may look like plain buns or biscuits, but these are loaded with pure lard. They are much more filling and can keep you going for hours. I just love them.

That's not all we'll be eating. We also brought along a couple rings of a traditional Ukrainian sausage. Kubasa, they call it.

When we first moved to Vita, one of our neighbours, Mrs. Storisiuk, brought over a loaf of home-baked bread along with a heaping pan of fried kubasa smothered in onions. It all tasted just great. Since that introduction, Mom has incorporated this versatile meat into much of her cooking, so we get to eat it quite regularly. I never get tired of it.

I know Dad would be quite happy to just cut off a chunk and chew into it, even though the kubasa is frozen stiff. I have other ideas. I suspend several pieces over the fire just like a *coureur de bois* would do with wild game. We each pick a freshly created stump for a seat and wolf down our galettes and roasted kubasa in silence. *Sure is good stuff,*

I'm thinking. *Now to wash down this hearty food with a leisurely mug of hot tea.*

Before I can finish, Dad jumps up, handing me the axe. "You can limb those logs over there," he says, "and start loading the wood onto the truck, we've only got a few hours of daylight left."

I am not used to seeing him in such a hurry. I sense that I'm about to learn a lesson. I've known for some time that when Dad is in working mode, he rarely stops. He doesn't rush, but he doesn't waste time either. Small talk, even simple observations or jokes—that's for another time. He doesn't tell me to hustle, but I know that's what he's implying, so I guess that's what I must do. All afternoon we work really hard, stopping occasionally for a quick drink of cool tea.

I love the job of trimming branches from the logs with my new lightweight axe. I'm getting pretty good at this; one stroke is usually all it takes. Hauling the eight-foot logs to the truck is something else. It's not so much the weight; I can handle that. It's the footing. It's just awful. I must watch carefully where to take each step. Despite my best efforts, too often I trip and fall in the tangled mess on the ground. *Focus, focus!* I tell myself. How come Dad never falls?

With his trusty, muscle-powered "Swede Saw," Dad is like a machine. I swear he can cut through a ten-inch jack pine in less than a minute. I'm having trouble trimming the branches as fast as he cuts the trees into logs. The really fat limbs are the problem. They can take several strokes, especially when the wood is bone dry and super hard. Dad will sometimes cut the bigger branches in a couple seconds with his new saw, and I recognize how much more efficient than an axe a Swede saw can be.

Dad bought the saw and two axes when we were at Smook's General Store getting our box stove. "I always thought lumberjacks used only axes to cut down trees?" I question.

"Well, that may have been the case at one time, but the Swedes changed all that. The old-fashioned wood frame bucksaw has been around for a long time," he says, "and they are still great for cutting logs into stove lengths, but they don't stand up to the rough handling they get in the bush. The 'Swede saw,' on the other hand, has a spring steel frame that is practically indestructible, and it keeps a constant tension on the blade. The Swedes really improved the blade, too. In the old days, you never knew when a blade might break, and it usually got dull before the end of the day. Used to be that you needed to bring a spare blade and a file when you went into the bush. This was all too much for some people, so they kept using an axe. Mind you, you can't beat a light, sharp axe when it comes to limbing." Dad got a second axe, a heavy thing with a longer handle, while we were at Smook Brothers. He designates it my axe, and it looks like I shall be doing all the splitting this winter.

The sun is setting, and now I see why Dad was in a hurry. He is determined that we shall bring home a full load—at least two chords, he tells me.

"How do we know when we have two chords?" I ask.

"Well, a chord measures four feet by four feet by eight feet, and the logs we cut today are mostly eight-footers. You measure it and do the math." It takes me a few minutes, and Dad is happy to learn that we have almost two and half chords.

"Now, that was a good day's work," he declares, "considering all the time we wasted at that strawberry patch, and not even a small basket of strawberries to show for it." He chuckles.

I can almost feel the poor old truck groaning. It's a heavy load, Dad admits, but he's not about to leave any of our precious wood behind. We proceed down the rough trail ever so slowly. There's a small creek coming up that has him worried. The ice held firm this morning when we crossed, but can it take our heavy load? He hesitates a moment as we approach. He decides we don't have much choice and guns the engine. The front wheels cross the creek and I breathe a sigh of relief, thinking we are safe, and then *splash*, and the trucks stops as suddenly as if we had hit a brick wall. Dad turns off the engine. He knows we're not going any place for a while. *But we have four-wheel drive*, I'm thinking. Of course Dad knows; there's no point even mentioning it.

How amazingly quiet it is. All I hear is a gentle rippling sound as the fast-moving water detours around the stuck wheels. Looking around, I can see in the fading light that the surrounding forest is beautiful— maybe not as dramatic as that magical place we saw earlier in the day, but I wouldn't mind spending the night here. We have lots of wood for a fire; we could even build a shelter. We have galettes galore and enough kubasa to last another day or two, and the creek water looks crystal clear. Heck, I bet we could survive comfortably out here for days—maybe weeks. Wouldn't that make for a neat adventure? The only bad thing is that Mom would be worrying like crazy, and I would miss school.

Dad emerges from under the truck. "Just checking to see if the driveshaft got bent," he says. He admits it could have happened if the truck had sunk any deeper, neglecting to add that we could've been stuck here for days had the damage been bad enough. The tough old truck appears to have survived the crash just fine.

"We're not out of the woods yet," I remind him. No response. I guess Dad doesn't appreciate my attempt at humour. I would have liked some assurance that things would be okay. I guess that's not his style.

"Alright, let's get busy," he orders. Dad disappears into the bush with his Swede saw to find a special tree from which he will fashion a lever to lift the truck. Apparently we have no jack—at least, not one that would work in this awkward spot. I'm left to unload the logs from the truck, all two and a half chords. It's almost dark and I'm getting worried. What if Dad gets lost? What if he gets injured and can't walk. What if he has a heart attack? I'm just about to shatter the still air with my powerful whistle when he appears, carrying a perfectly straight pine, about twelve feet long. It's roughly six inches in diameter and straight as a board. "It can't be green," he says, "because it would just bend; too dry and it could crack. Everything depends on that lever working perfectly, he tells me." So that's what took so long.

"Every lever needs a fulcrum," Dad explains as he goes about fashioning a log structure close to one wheel. "Now you build one for the other wheel." Meanwhile, with the axe, he scallops one end of his lever so it won't slip off the wheel hub. He positions it under the hub and applies his full weight, all 220 pounds, at the other end. Magically, the truck rises a few inches, and I must quickly shove small logs under the wheel. We do the same with the other wheel, repositioning the setup again and again, I don't know how many times. Finally, both wheels are above the surface of the ice and the truck can be moved onto solid ground.

The woods are in total darkness now as I stumble around in the dim reflection from the headlights. I suggest we come back for our logs tomorrow. Dad carries on as though he hasn't heard. Somehow I manage to be of some help until every last log is on the truck. After clambering awkwardly into the cab, I collapse from exhaustion and fall into a fitful sleep. I am vaguely aware of a cold breeze blowing through the absent windows and I'm trying desperately to suppress the pain.

The truck has been stopped for a while as I slowly wake and realize we're home. I've never been so cold and stiff in my entire life. Oh, the heat from that little box stove is going to feel good, and I'll bet Mom has a delicious hot meal waiting for us—but what's that noise I'm hearing? It's Dad unloading the truck. He doesn't have to say anything; of course I have to help him. After all, we'll be going for another load tomorrow, and it wouldn't do to start the day handling yesterday's wood.

As we finish supper, Mom serves up her famous *sucre à la crème* for dessert. "I hope you saved enough of that fresh cream to go with dessert tomorrow," says Dad. Everyone is waiting for him to explain. "Well, there was this shortcut with nice, lush strawberries, but we were too busy to pick any today. Maybe tomorrow Jules will pick some for us. Cream always goes nice with strawberries . . ." He chuckles.

Nobody is laughing. With puzzled looks, everyone is waiting for me to interpret what he's talking about. I shrug and hope they'll drop it. Dad may be the smartest, toughest man I know, but humour is certainly not one of his strong points.

I'm so tired and so sore, I just want to go to bed. I don't know how I'm going to manage tomorrow, even if we skip that strawberry patch.

"Holy Trinity Church"   By: George Penner

"1942 Army truck"   Source: public domain

HAPPY NEW YEAR

Christmas was a quiet affair that first winter in Vita. With no relatives or close friends nearby, it was just our family opening small gifts, and a chicken supper before going to bed. "Things will be different tomorrow," Mom promises. She has a plan.

We'll be going by jeep to Ross, Manitoba, where we'll be staying at Uncle Romeo's for the rest of the Christmas holiday. We've visited with them before, but never got a chance to see all the relatives that we lost touch with when we moved to St. Catharines. And of course Mom is worried about her parents who are getting old and quite frail.

Boxing Day: It seems like we've been on the road all day and everybody's getting cranky. Normally it would only take a couple hours from our house to Ross, but it's been snowing since early Christmas day and just about every road is closed. Dad had to take a much longer route that only he knows how to navigate. Now, here we are stranded in Thibaultville about eight miles from our destination.

Our family is huddled around a big pot-bellied stove in the general store, soaking up the glorious heat. How good it feels as life returns to our numbed bodies. I wonder if this is how turtles feel when you see them basking in the warm morning sun.

It was an uncomfortable ride in Dad's World War II jeep, with cold drafts creeping through cracks in the homemade cab. It has a heater of sorts, but as Mom says, "It puts out less heat than the breath from a sick puppy." The windshield keeps fogging up and needs constant scraping. Mom lets Dad know that she is not impressed. "Why did you ever buy this stupid thing in the first place?" she says. Dad knows that without the jeep's four-wheel drive, we'd likely be stuck somewhere along some remote road. He doesn't say anything; it would only lead to more aggravation. Mom is in a bad mood.

She didn't quite believe that the road to Ross is plugged with snow too deep even for our four-wheel drive. Dad obligingly drove a short distance down the unploughed road, nearly getting stuck in the process. "We're bound to run into drifts and deeper snow. There's no way I'm going to risk it," he says with finality and puts the Jeep into reverse.

What a huge disappointment, especially for Mom. She's been looking forward to this visit for months. In a few days, it will be New Years, the most important day of the year for the Gauthier clan, and it looks like our family will have to go back to Vita and ring in the New Year by ourselves.

We've been living in Vita for four months now, and the neighbours are very nice, but to Mom, it doesn't feel anything like home. Our place is small, warm, and cozy, but to her it's just a "converted chicken coop." She can't imagine ringing in the New Year without close relatives to help celebrate this special time.

We're still warming around the big wood stove, wondering where Mom has disappeared. Now she's back and flashing a big smile. "I've just sent a message to my brother Romeo," she says. "He should be picking us up in a couple hours." Wow! How did she accomplish that?

"I just phoned the storekeeper in Ross, and he'll pass along my message to your Uncle Romeo," she tells us.

"But your brother lives a mile from the store, and it'll be dark soon. How do you know Meo is even home?" Dad asks. "With all this new snow, I'm not sure if we can even make it back to Vita."

"Looks like it's turning into a blizzard out there," says the storekeeper. "You don't want to be on the road in this weather, especially after dark. You're welcome to spend the night in the store. We've got a spare couch, a couple of benches, and lots of blankets."

"My brother, Meo—he'll be here," says Mom with total confidence. And so we wait. I want to believe Mom, but that bench looks mighty inviting, and I'm getting awfully sleepy.

I'm not sure if it was the frigid gust or the noisy stomping of feet that awoke me. There's a man at the door in a bulky fur coat covered with snow. And now shrieks from Mom as she recognizes who it is.

She rushes to take his coat, and everybody is deliriously happy. Of course it's Uncle Romeo. She knew he was coming.

"No time to waste," he says, "it's wicked out there and soon it'll be dark."

We all pile into the rough open sled and cover up as best we can with an assortment of blankets and furry hides. The horses are wearing coats too—"not for warmth, but to keep them dry," says Uncle Meo. They get a quick snack of oats and we're off.

I like the faint sound from the tinny bells that tinkle to a regular beat. Oh, this is so exciting, so much more fun than that slow ride to Arbakka a couple years back, and so much more fun than that cold ride in the jeep.

I just love the horses. They've worked hard pulling that heavy sled eight miles through the deep snow. Now we are six more people, and yet they are willing to work ever harder. Uncle Meo slows their pace to a fast walk. "We mustn't push the horses too much. We'll be on the road at least a couple hours. We don't want them sweating."

Sweating? How could they be sweating while the rest of us are so cold? It's dark now, the wind hasn't let up, and snow is swirling all around. The ditches have blended together with the roadway, transforming into one wide swath of featureless snow. I wonder how the horses stay on track. There's not much point in straining. I know we're in good hands; may as well hunker down and try to keep from freezing. I suspect everybody's feeling some discomfort, but no one's complaining. I know for sure that Mom is totally happy and so am I.

"We're home; home sweet home"—at least, that's what Mom calls it when we arrive at the farm. She pats the horses and murmurs something to them as we unload the sled. She continues on with her brother to help unhitch the horses. Mom won't feel right until she sees the horses fed and watered before leaving them to rest in the warm barn.

Waiting patiently for us are Aunt Irene and cousins Jerry, Leonard, Evelyn and Mea, all smiling warmly, free with their hugs and kisses.

The cold is behind us now; time to eat. Everyone's famished. It was suppertime a few hours ago, but that doesn't seem to matter now.

"This is where I grew up," Mom reminds us. "Grandpa Gauthier built this house in 1906, a year before I was born." How well she remembers all the happy times she enjoyed as the youngest of the family; a spoiled brat, some called her. Oh, how she loved to be amongst her brothers and sisters and all the Gauthiers. She is determined to visit with as many as possible in the short time we have before returning to Vita.

I know we're going to have a good time, just like we did the last time we visited. Leonard is sixteen now, almost an adult, and he's expected to do a fair share of the work around the farm. "It's my job to clean the manure from the barn," he says as he hitches a skittish young horse to the stone boat. "What a shitty job," he jokes as we shovel cow poop and horse poop onto the stone boat and haul it away to the manure pile.

"Why do you call it a stone boat?" I ask.

Len patiently explains that every spring, stones sprout up in the fields, just like big mushrooms, and they play hell with machinery, so we dig them out, roll them onto the boat, and haul them away.

Like mushrooms? Sounds a bit farfetched to me, and why this crude sled is called a "boat" still puzzles me. "Now why are you shovelling snow onto the stone boat, Len?"

"Well, we wouldn't want those fancy moccasins of yours to get covered with cow shit, would we, my little cousin? Hop on and hang on tight," he says as the horse takes off. It's standing room only.

"But there's nothing to hang onto," I protest.

"That's the whole point," he says as we pick up speed. I wobble and stagger, desperately trying to keep balance and loosely clutching onto Leonard's coat. A couple hundred yards down the road I find myself rolling head over heels through the snow-filled ditch. Leonard waits patiently while I hurry to get onboard again. A few more tumbles and we're away. Wow! Now this is what I call fun.

The frisky horse speeds up to a fast trot, kicking up clumps of snow that fly at us like shrapnel, adding to the challenge of staying upright.

We're on our way to visit relatives a mile or so down the road, one of my mom's sisters and her family. Though we arrive unannounced, we both know we'll be greeted warmly and offered tasty food. "I just love your tourtière, the best I've ever tasted," I tell my aunt. I'm grateful she doesn't challenge me to name who rated second or third.

If we were a little older, we'd have to try uncle's home brewed whiskey. It's a common commodity in these parts, and there's ongoing competition to see who distils the best brew. It goes without saying that it takes a lot of sampling to determine the winner.

Before we leave, our cousins want to see Leonard riding that stone boat. Everybody is in awe as Leonard guides the willing horse through a bunch of fancy manoeuvres, sending the powdery snow flying in all directions and never losing his balance. One of our cousins (a knowing girl) likens Len to a Roman warrior charging into battle with his war chariot. So now the crude sled is dubbed "Leonard's Chariot," never to be called a stone boat again.

The rest of the week is spent visiting with favourite relatives. Sometimes we go to their homes and share a meal. Other times, they come to Uncle Romeo's. After the meal, men and women drift apart. Woman in the kitchen, cleaning up leftovers, looking after babies and sharing stories—gossip, the men call it. Meanwhile the men gather in the living room, smoking and sampling home brew. Virtually all their talk revolves around hunting, farming, or working in the bush. Kids can do pretty much anything they want. There are no rules. We can play outside with cousins, we can play indoor games or just hang out with the adults. Whatever your thing, you could count on lots of love, laughter, and good cheer. Such is the nature of the gregarious Gauthier clan.

There's an air of anticipation on the last day of the year—so many things to prepare for the festive evening ahead. Aunt Irene has a huge *cipâte* in the oven and the aroma from the kitchen is simply mouth-watering. "Supper this evening will be a simple one," she tells us. "Help yourselves when you're hungry."

Len and I begin our chores early, paying special attention to tidying the barn and making room for the guests' horses. Most will come by car or truck, but there are still a few who rely on horses for travel, especially in the winter. It's our job to make sure that they will be comfy too.

Mom tells me everyone coming tonight is an aunt, an uncle, or a cousin—everyone is related in some way. Some she hasn't seen since leaving Manitoba; others, we'll be meeting for the first time. As the guests arrive, we take their coats and pile them on the beds upstairs.

The big old house is filling up and the chatter is getting louder all the time. Older folk gravitate to the kitchen to play cards. Kids have been shooed upstairs where a quieter mood prevails. Some sit on the steps watching the adults acting younger than their years, all happy and laughing and drinking beer and home brew.

Musicians are tuning their instruments. That's the cue to move furniture from the living room and rearrange chairs along the walls to make room for dancing.

The fiddler plucks a few notes, then with exaggerated flair, he sweeps his bow across the strings and out pours beautiful music. A couple young ladies step out, shyly at first, and start dancing together. The accordion joins in, then the guitars, and soon the dance floor fills with dancers of every age. It all seems lively enough until the fiddler kicks into high gear, sweeping his bow faster and faster and grabbing everyone's attention. The dance floor clears. Old folks put down their cards. It's jigging time. All eyes are on a lovely young woman dressed in the fashion of a bygone age. Hands on hips and feet flying in perfect time to the music while making it all seem so easy. I am totally enthralled and I suspect others are too. Too soon, the jigging is over and a new form of dancing is about to begin.

I've never seen square dancing before; couples are moving around the floor in weird patterns, following instructions from a man with a very loud voice. I don't understand a word. Everyone seems to be having lots of fun, but to me it looks kinda boring. I best get some sleep. It's going to be a long day tomorrow.

All the beds are taken, but that carpet of coats strewn across the floor looks perfectly fine to me. The music, the stomping, and the laughter carries on while welcome sleep gently wraps me in a warm blanket of comfort and joy. I wonder how long the party will last?

It's early morning. The old house is quieter now. Women are busy frying eggs and salt pork. Men are outside hitching horses to sleds and pulling frozen cars that won't start. Some are standing by a lively fire waiting for pots of water to boil. It seems not every car owner has antifreeze in their radiators, so they drained them the night before. "Antifreeze for your radiator? Much too costly," they will tell you. "That's strictly for city folk, too lazy to drain their rads when they park the car. Besides, what better way to warm a frozen engine than with a fresh fill of boiling water?"

One of my uncles has built his own small fire, and I'm curious to know why. As the fire burns down, he recruits his boys to help push their Model T over the glowing embers where it will sit soaking up heat, just like we did around that stove in Thibaultville. No one's in a hurry.

The boys take turns cranking the engine over by hand. It all seems so futile. *That old engine will never start,* I tell myself. *It's just too darn cold.* But I was wrong. A little fiddling with the choke, a few more cranks, and the engine starts coughing and sputtering and everyone is cheering. What a sight they make as the family climbs aboard the open vehicle, all bundled up and singing merrily as they putt-putt-putt down the driveway.

The days flash by, and too soon we are headed for home. The roads are now passable, and some cousin has offered to drive us to Thibaultville in his old car.

The little jeep looks so forlorn buried in snow, but Dad doesn't have to fill the radiator with hot water, nor does he have to start a fire. The Jeep has glycol antifreeze and a new battery and starts right away without fuss. It's colder than ever in the drafty Jeep, but Mom doesn't complain as she dutifully scrapes the frosty windshield. The roads have been ploughed and everyone knows we'll be home real soon. School starts tomorrow, and I have a feeling that 1947 will be a very good year.

"Gauthier House"   Source: family photo

FIRST JOB

I miss my aunts and uncles and cousins in St. Catharines. I especially miss my close buddies. And of course I will never forget the dear sisters of St. Joseph's. As for the material stuff, the only thing I really miss is my bike. I guess somebody else has it now, and so I desperately want another bike.

I wouldn't think of asking Dad to buy me one. I know money's super tight in our family, and besides, it was kind of understood that if you wanted a bike of your own you had to earn it. Like Billy; he has his own bike, but he bought it himself with his paper route money and his battery charging business. Every boy in town who owns a bike most likely worked for it. So I spread the word on the off-chance that someone might be able to use a kid willing to work at pretty much anything during the summer holidays, anything that will get me a bike.

And then one day at the supper table, Dad casually mentions that his helper wants to take a break from his oiler's job for a couple weeks. "It's haying time and Ernie is needed on the farm. Would you by any chance know of a young man who could fill in while Ernie's away?" asks Dad.

"Absolutely," I replied, "and I can start tomorrow. How much does it pay?"

There followed a long period of silence. I guess Dad was taken aback. Mom just smiled. "You aren't serious?" she says. "You just turned thirteen. You're still a kid, you know."

"I was fourteen when I started my first job," says Dad. "Everybody told me I was too young, but somehow I managed, and it felt good knowing I could do a man's job."

Turning to me, Dad says, "So what makes you think you can handle the job?"

"Of course I can handle it," I tell him, without a clear idea what an oiler's job entails. "Didn't I help cut our winter wood, and didn't I saw it all into stove lengths and split it too? And didn't we work in the bush together when we made those pads for the dragline last winter?"

Whether this qualified me or not, Dad didn't say, he just wanted me to be aware that there would be a lot to learn and those twelve-hour shifts can be mighty long, especially the nights.

Mom may not like the idea, but she isn't about to stop me. If she harbours any misgivings, she keeps them to herself. She even helps me pick out proper work clothes and heavy-duty rubber work boots.

Getting ready for work that first Monday morning, I can hardly contain my excitement, and when Mom hands me my lunch bucket, I thought I might bust. It's the classic metal type, just like Dad's. It's black and comes with its own thermos fitted snugly in the lid.

The morning shift doesn't start till seven, but Dad and I are out the door by six. We've got to pick up fuel for the dragline, and then it's eight miles of rough slogging that only a high clearance, four-wheel drive vehicle can handle. You'd think this battered old army truck was specially designed for the job. Dad seems to delight in ploughing through the muck and the water-filled puddles along the way.

We pass by Dad's base camp without stopping. "Everyone's at the dragline preparing for the next shift," he says. "There'll be minor repairs and adjustments, oil levels to top up, and dozens of grease nipples to pump. Your job this morning will be filling the gas tank for the main engine. It's shameful how much fuel that old engine goes through in a day. It still works pretty good, but it's obsolete now. A modern diesel engine would use about half the fuel and wouldn't need nearly as much attention. Next year," he says, "next year that old 'Waukesha' has got to go."

We're near the machine—or at least as close as we can get. There's ankle-deep water all around. Time to try out my new boots. I follow Dad onto the back of the truck, and he tips the forty-five-gallon drum on its side like it was a toy. I guess he knows I can't do that yet. Not a good way to start. "Just roll it off the end," he says.

"Really? The truck box is over three feet off the ground and that drum is full of gasoline, and you want me to just roll it off the back end?"

"Unless you can think of some better way to unload," he says with a hint of impatience.

And so, with some trepidation, I follow orders. *Splash!* And now I'm left to wrestle the 400-pound drum the rest of the way to the machine. Rolling the drum over swamp grass goes easy enough, but as the water gets deeper, the drum begins to float and it's quite a struggle to shove, roll, push, and pull it along the rest of the way. Damn, now I'm going to need help to stand it up again. *And where's that manual fuel pump?* I wonder.

Operating the pump seems easy at first. You just push the handle back and forth at a steady clip until the tank is full. After pumping for almost half an hour, the tank's still not full. It feels like my arm is going to drop off, but I don't dare stop. Men are watching.

I can see that this job is going to be tougher than I thought. Where did I ever get the notion that this would be an easy way to make a few bucks? I can't wimp out now, though. I know the rest of the crew are keeping an eye on me, and of course I mustn't disappoint my dad.

Whew! It's nearly seven. The shift-change chores are complete, the night crew has left, and now it's just Dad and me and the dragline for the next twelve hours. Time to look around and take stock.

We're in the midst of a huge marsh—or, as the locals prefer to call it, a useless swamp, six-foot bulrushes all around. They go on as far as the eye can see. There's a pungent perfume in the air. "Crushed bulrushes," Dad explains. It seems pleasant enough at first, but it becomes obnoxious over time.

The big steel bucket is chewing a muddy channel through the lush green vegetation while clear water rushes into the new brown ditch. Too bad the roar of the machine drowns out the sound of rippling water. I love the sound of rippling water.

A casual observer might wonder: How does this forty-ton monster move in this mushy marsh? What keeps it from sinking out of sight in this smelly goop of decaying vegetation? The trick involves keeping a large bed of logs under the tracks at all times. It'll be my job to help manage these logs, which must be moved at regular intervals as the machine digs its way through the marsh.

It helps that the logs are bundled together with fat steel cables into units of four. Pads, we call them. Part of my job is hooking them up to the bucket with an S-hook. Then the operator swings the pad from one end of the machine to the other, in effect laying down a

337

fresh corduroy road. This allows the dragline to crawl forward a few more yards, and the digging continues. This exercise is repeated every twenty minutes or so.

The result is a wide, shallow ditch that will ultimately connect to the Roseau River. In time, the swamp will dry up, creating thousands of acres of new farmland. Dad is proud of his achievements, and farmers are happy too.

It's hard to believe that the timbers for the pads were beautiful trees not so long ago. Just last winter, Dad arranged to purchase a bunch of logs from a farmer not far from Vita. How he managed that is a mystery to me; Dad speaks no Ukrainian and the farmer barely speaks English. The old man looks to me like he could have stepped off the boat yesterday. His face is totally hidden behind a scraggly beard, and with his huge fur hat, it isn't clear where the beard ends and the hat begins.

Key to the whole operation is the old guy's team of horses. They're also big and shaggy and seem to understand Ukrainian. I marvel at how hard they work to snake these heavy logs through the rough bush and out to the road.

The whole scene is kind of weird, especially at lunchtime. The old guy reaches into a white pillowcase and pulls out a loaf of bread and a ring of kubasa. He doesn't need a lunch bucket or a thermos; talk about keeping things simple. He guzzles something from a gallon jug then offers Dad a swig. Dad figures there's enough brew to keep the stuff from freezing. Then the old guy pulls the bread apart and snaps off chunks of kubasa. "Eat, eat," he says as he offers me a piece with his leathery, grimy hands. I wonder when's the last time he washed them—*ugh*. Sister May Rudolf would not approve.

Such a contrast with the lunches Mom makes: perfectly prepared sandwiches with just the right condiments and always a dessert, sometimes a fruit, and of course a thermos of hot tea. Lunch breaks are always something I look forward to during those long shifts on the job.

I learn something new every day. One hot evening on the night shift, the mosquitoes were so thick the buzzing sounded like a small airplane. "Build me a smudge!" yells Dad from his perch at the dragline controls. I have no idea what he's talking about, and he isn't about to stop the machine to explain. "Just build a fire and cover it with swamp grass!" he yells. I guess I have to figure out the rest.

There's not a dry stick in sight. The nearest wood will have to come from that little poplar bluff several hundred yards away. And where do I build that fire with standing water everywhere? So many questions. Oh, and it better be upwind from the machine; the smoke wouldn't do much good if it drifted in the wrong direction.

Wow! I've never seen mosquitoes this bad. Got to light that fire quick, but I've got no paper. *Just pour gasoline on it*, a little voice tells me. And then as I strike the match, there's a mighty *SWOOOSH*, like a hushed explosion. I guess I used too much gas. Good thing Dad wasn't looking in this direction. How will I explain my singed eyebrows?

The smudge produces clouds of dark, smelly, smoke and does a pretty good job of driving the mosquitoes away. What a relief. Dad orders one every evening after that. Just part of the job, I guess.

I watch as Dad changes the recording disc on the time clock mounted at the back of the machine. "The clock records only the time the dragline is working," he says. "Everything else is dead time." Apparently, it's part of the oiler's job to keep dead time to a minimum. So when the machine slows down or comes to a halt, I'd better be ready with the emergency repair kit and a functioning flashlight. Every minute counts.

One day, I'm idly watching Dad making a minor repair. "Now if I had a twelve-inch crescent, I could finish adjusting this brake band," he says. I continue watching for a minute or two before realizing he actually wants that wrench, and so I amble off to fetch it. And then he says, "I should have asked for that crescent yesterday, and by now we'd be rolling again." I'm puzzled at first and then he says, "But you know, I probably won't need it tomorrow." Finally, I catch on and I run like mad. From then on, whenever there was a slow down or a break, I would picture myself like a surgeon's assistant, super alert to every demand, even anticipating in advance what instrument/tool may be required.

Not everything is needed in a huge hurry. A lot of errands can be handled while the machine is running. These are known as "gopher runs"—you know, go for some snacks, go for some water, go for some dry socks. No dawdling, though, it's always hustle, hustle, hustle. You never know when you might be needed for something real urgent.

It seems everybody finds the night shift long, but I don't mind those cool, dark nights. I spend most of the time inside the dragline cab, there's really no place else to go. It's awfully noisy, but there are fewer mosquitoes, and I can fall asleep on the steel floor with only a bag of rags for a pillow. When I hear the engine slow down, that's my signal to get up, and I better be quick about it. I rush outside and go through the routine of shifting pads so the machine can advance a few more yards. It takes less than ten minutes, and then it's back inside and I'm asleep in seconds.

Sometimes, though, sleep doesn't come easy, so I let my imagination run, and I pass the time concocting various adventures and dreaming of the places I might discover when I get my bike.

One of the first things I'll be looking for is a place to swim. It's been super hot lately, and yet nobody around Vita goes swimming. Unlike Stuartburn, Vita doesn't have a cooling river nearby, but there's no lack of water. All the ditches are brim-full of nice, clear water. I guess access is the problem. Dense willows line the banks of every ditch and stream, but I'm sure there's the makings of a fine swimming hole hidden somewhere. I will find that perfect place and clear an access path with my axe and create a cooling swim hole. Maybe, with a little help, I could build a park where people could picnic, have a wiener roast, or camp overnight. It would become the recreational hub for the whole town—a place to swim and cool off in this hot weather, and everyone will say, "How clever! Why didn't someone think of this before?"

And if I had a bike, I might visit that cute little blond who lives just out of town. I'm sure she'd be happy to go for a ride. Together we'd find a secret spot where we'll enjoy a romantic picnic and go swimming, just the two of us. And of course there would be no need for bathing suits.

"Nobody sells bikes in Vita. You got to go to Gooch's Bicycle Shop in Winnipeg," says Billy. "They've got hundreds of bikes in every size and colour and all kinds of neat stuff you can stick on your bike to give it that sexy look." I know I won't have enough money for a brand-new bike, but if I did, I would buy a CCM touring model. It would have twenty-six-inch wheels, maybe even whitewall tires. The frame would be a bit smaller than adult size, so I wouldn't have to stretch to reach the pedals. My dream bike would be midnight blue with silver pin striping. It would have chrome handle bars and a genuine leather seat. Oh, that would be beautiful. I might even get a headlight that has its own generator for travel at night. That would be so cool.

Ernie returns tomorrow. I'll be out of a job, but that's okay. This work is a little tougher than I expected, and I recognize there are some things I'm just not able to do yet, like tipping those 400-pound drums. Next year though, I'll be big enough and strong enough to do everything without help, and maybe Dad will hire me for the whole summer. Then I could make enough money to buy that dream bike. Meanwhile, I'm pretty sure I've earned enough to buy a pretty decent used bike, and there's still plenty of summer left to do lots of riding and exploring. I just know this is going to be a really good summer.

"One yard dragline"   Source: Public domain

BLUEBERRY HILL

A shabbily dressed Indian lady appears at our door one evening. Clinging close to her is a shy young girl, about five, whom we take to be her daughter. Mom doesn't ask what brought her to our house; she knows they would like some food. Sharing food with local Indians was a common practice where Mom grew up, and she was taught to be kind and respectful to all.

Mom switches to speaking French, and the surprised look on the woman's tired face turns into a broad smile. We learn that they are from the Roseau reserve some thirty-five miles to the west and they've been on the road for two days now. "A couple more good days should get us to Menisino, where we plan to pick blueberries," says the woman. "It's one way to make a little cash."

Mom invites them in for tea and galettes, but it takes some coaxing before the woman reluctantly accepts. They don't stay long. She has to get back to their camp at the other end of town. "My people will be waiting," she says.

I have long sensed that Mom had a soft spot for people in need. Dad is also a softy, but I don't think he would go so far as to give away practically everything in the pantry. It's a good thing we already had supper; she might have given that away too.

The next morning, we watch them go by; a pitiful caravan of scrawny horses pulling a motley collection of buggies and wagons loaded with gear. Only the old folk and a few small kids get to ride. The rest, about fifty souls I would guess, are walking behind, along with their skinny dogs. I've never seen such a sad sight. Four days to travel roughly sixty miles—meanwhile, a car or truck could cover that distance in about an hour.

Mom takes me to Petrowski's general store to help her carry the groceries we'll need to restock our pantry. Petrowski's is a good place to shop; it's also a good place to catch up on the latest gossip. The main topic today is that ragtag caravan that just passed through town. "Why are they so poor?" is the common question.

"Don't they have farms?"

"Don't they have jobs?"

"They're just lazy," declares a bent old lady.

I'm thinking, *How lazy can they be when they're willing to walk four days just to pick blueberries? How come nobody offers them a ride?*

Mom is strangely quiet.

"Everyone's predicting a bumper crop this year," says Mrs. Petrowski, trying to change the subject. "Those big fires they had around Piney a couple years back, bad for trees, good for blueberries." Mom nods in agreement.

"Blueberries are my favourite," says Mom. "I just love them in pies or jam or anything really. And the picking is fun too."

I've never tasted blueberries. They can't possibly be as good as cherries, but I wouldn't mind picking some. Trouble is the blueberries are miles from here and we don't have a car. There's Dad's jeep, but he needs it for work even on weekends.

"Well, we could walk there like the Indians," I suggest. Mom just laughs.

Mrs. Petrowski draws our attention to a notice on her bulletin board:

LARRY'S TRUCKING is offering transportation to
anyone interested in picking a bonanza of blueberries.
Meet at Petrowski's this Sunday 7:00 a.m.
Bring a lunch, and lots of containers. $1.50 per person.

Mrs. Petrowski explains that Larry is an ambitious young man who
recently bought a brand-new truck. His business is keeping the various
stores in Vita stocked with a variety of specialty items. He drives into
Winnipeg every day, picks up your order from any part of the city, and
then delivers the goods right to your door. "He'll provide the same
service for you too, you know. And he'll gladly take a passenger or two
in the front seat," adds Mrs. Petrowski, "Anything to make a buck."
She chuckles.

Early Sunday morning, sister Juliette and I are at Petrowski's with
our pails. Mom would love to be coming with us, but she has to stay
home with sister Alice and brother Lou. And we recently learned that
she is expecting another baby.

She didn't ask if we wanted to go. She just paid the three bucks and
we were going, period. After all, "Somebody has to pick those berries,
or they'll just rot in the bush," she reasons. "And Jules, make sure your
sister doesn't get lost; oh, and keep an eye out for bears."

People are gathering outside Petrowski's, and I'm thinking surely
not everybody here plans to ride in Larry's modest little truck; there
must be a dozen of us already. How can we all fit? Larry arrives on
time and sets up a makeshift set of steps in back of the truck. It's now
clear how he plans to fit us all in. There are no seats, not even benches.
It's standing room only, but at least there are ropes strung across the
top of the box so everyone has something to hang onto.

A few elderly people need help climbing aboard. How will they
make out when the truck starts bouncing over that washboard road,
I wonder?

There are twelve of us crammed into the snug space, all adults except for me and Juliette. *This isn't going to be much fun*, I'm thinking, as Larry closes the truck gate.

"Now we're going to find out how cattle feel when they get hauled off to market," says one of the pickers. Everybody laughs.

"We're all going to die," adds another in his deepest voice. More laughs.

"I wonder how many steaks they'll get out of Olga?"

"And how many kubasa rings from Mike?"

"As long as we don't end up as dog food," chimes in another. More laughs. And on it goes until a young woman starts singing a lively Ukrainian song. Others join in and everyone start clapping in rhythm. How lovely! The whole truck is transformed into a happy party. Maybe this ride won't be so bad after all.

There is a sombre moment as we approach the Indian encampment near Menisino; the same group that passed through Vita a few days before. Tall tepees covered with ratty-looking hides overlook a collection of wagons, buggies, and unfamiliar stuff. Hobbled horses graze nearby. Old folk are huddled around a smoky fire. They return our wave as we pass by. The tepees look so inviting, but what a messy setting—not what an Indian camp should look like, I figure.

As we approach the village of Piney, Larry turns onto a sandy, rutted track: a logging road, he calls it. He's driving much too fast for most of us and barely slows down around curves. Sharp bends are a real challenge as we struggle to keep our balance.

What a relief when Larry finally stops at a small clearing and we all pile out. Only now do I notice that most of the ladies are wearing long skirts and colourful babushkas. The younger ones look real pretty—a bit exotic, even.

Larry explains that he will sound the truck horn every fifteen minutes. "So never, never, never, stray beyond the sound of the horn or you might end up lost. But you won't be alone," he adds. "Some bear is going to come along and wonder how come you're picking his berries. If you hear three blasts of the horn, it means we're moving or it might be lunchtime. So come back to the truck as quick as you can."

I find picking blueberries can get really boring. It helps if you let your mind wander and dream of other things. I'm pretty good at that, so the morning goes by pleasantly despite a few mosquitoes. The islands of pine left by the fires are beautiful, and there are lots of blueberries. By noon, Juliette and me have picked a full pail. I thought we did real good—that is, until we got back to the truck and found out everybody else had picked way more than us. The trick, claimed veteran pickers, was to pick dirty. "Never mind the leaves and the twigs and the bugs, you can always get rid of those when you get home."

Meanwhile, the wiser ladies with their colourful babushkas and long skirts have a better idea. While sitting on the ground, they fashion a basket-like depression in their loose skirts and shovel in a handful of berries. A practiced flick sends the berries flying high in the air. Being heavier, the berries fall first, followed by everything else. A couple more flicks and magically all the debris ends up on top where nimble fingers quickly toss out the chaff. Wow! This is so neat. I wonder if I could do that? Mind you, I know I would look pretty silly in a long skirt so . . . maybe not.

Mom was ever so pleased with all the blueberries Juliette and I had picked. It took days to clean and can them, and the house got so hot and steamy from the wood stove, nobody could stand it. Mom says we probably have enough jam and preserves to last a couple years, so I don't think she'll be sending us out again. It wasn't a bad experience, but I'd rather not go next year.

I had almost forgotten the blueberry-picking venture until one Saturday evening the topic came up unexpectedly.

A bunch of us boys were hanging around the Vita community hall to take in the weekly movie. There was time for idle talk as we waited for the projectionist to set up his generator and related equipment. We were just young boys with simple boyhood interests, but occasionally, speculation about girls and sex would creep into the conversation.

"How do you know when a girl is interested, you know . . . interested and ready?" asks one of the guys. Everyone had a pretty good idea of what he was talking about, but no one rushed to answer. Instead all eyes came to focus on Boris.

Boris Stepaniuk was a big kid with a deep voice, almost an adult in our eyes. He was quite good-looking, and he knew it, always combing his hair and wiping invisible dust from his shoes. So when it came to girls and sex, Boris was sure to know more than the rest of us put together. And even if he didn't know, he could spin a pretty good yarn. Some called him Mr. BS—not to his face, of course; nobody wanted to light that short fuse.

Now, Boris was quite smart in lots of ways, but he hated school. Last winter, when his mother died, he willingly dropped out of school to look after his younger brothers and sisters while his dad spent time at the bootleggers. We suspected Boris led a pretty rough life, so we cut him slack and never teased or criticized him.

"Well you just have to look at them," says Boris. "If they've got big boobs and hips to match, that's a good start. Then you gotta pay attention to what they're wearing. The more skin, the better. But when it comes to girls, you never really know; girls can be pretty complicated. Last year, when I went picking blueberries, there were a few really cute ones. Sweet young things," Boris calls them. "They were all covered up, with no skin showing at all, yet they looked pretty sexy. But, you really don't want to hear the details?" Boris teases.

Holy smokes. I didn't know Boris went picking blueberries last summer. I might have asked a few questions, if only I had known. Of course we all want more details, even if some BS is thrown in.

"Well," Boris says, the same way he begins all his stories. "Well . . . We all know that babas (grandmas) like to wear babushkas and long skirts; after all, that's what they wore in the Ukraine for hundreds of years, right? So why would a 'sweet young thing' want to cover up and look like a baba?"

Fair question, I suppose, except I never compared those "sweet young things" to wrinkled old babas. To me, they're just pretty young ladies wearing colourful babushkas and long skirts. Here in Vita, there's no shortage of good-looking girls. To me, they always look good, no matter what they wear. So what the heck is Boris talking about, anyways?

"It's a matter of practicality," says Boris. "Us guys can always find a place to pee. Right? For women, not so easy. So whenever they go out, and they don't know if there will be proper facilities, what are they to do? Well... with those long, loose skirts they can just spread their legs and pee almost anywhere."

"Wow! I never knew that."

"For Christ's sake, Boris, we all know that," says one of the guys. "What's that got to do with girls and picking blueberries?"

"Well . . ." says Boris, "after lunch, I thought I'd take a little snooze, so I lay down in the grass and nodded off. And then something woke me. I don't know what. When I opened my eyes, there was this sweet young thing sorting and cleaning her blueberries, not ten feet away."

Boris didn't have to explain how Ukrainian ladies clean blueberries. Probably every girl learns this trick at an early age, I figure. Was Boris going to remind us that this was just another reason why Ukrainian ladies sometimes wear those long skirts?

By now the guys are getting impatient or excited, I'm not sure which. "Go on, go on," they urge.

"Well . . ." repeats Boris, "once my eyes got used to the low light, I could see she wasn't wearing underpants. And every time she flicked her skirt, I got a pretty good view. And after each flick, I noticed something else. After each flick, she flashed a little smile.

"I could have watched all afternoon," says Boris, "but now everyone goes back to picking, and so did my sweet young thing. I sort of followed from a distance. Eventually that distance got closer, and sometimes when the picking was good, we shared the same blueberry patch.

"I noticed the truck horn sounding faint and far away," Boris continues. "I look around to let her know we should be heading back, but she's gone. Just having a pee, I thought. Time goes by. What to do?"

At this point Boris pauses the story for what seems like an eternity.

"Well . . . I call out her name," resumes Boris, dragging out every detail. "I thought I heard an unfamiliar sound. Was it a bird? Was it an animal? Was it the truck horn? Was it my imagination? Or, was my sweet young thing in some kind of trouble?"

"So, what happened, Boris? Did you find her? Was she okay? Why don't you tell us her name?" These were all questions on everyone's mind.

"It took a while, but yes, eventually I found her, between the blueberry bushes. There she was, lying on her back, eyes half closed, bright blue skirt above her knees. A vision of loveliness."

"'Just resting,' she says softly. 'Come'."

Boris lowers his voice, to a point where we can barely hear him. "And that's when . . . that's when I lost it," he says with sad finality.

"What? Don't tell me you lost your temper!" says one of the guys. "What the hell's wrong with you? You idiot." The rest of us are quiet. And I'm wondering, *why on earth would Boris get angry at a time like that?*

"Guys, guys," Boris finally relents. "Guys, I should tell you, I didn't mind losing it, and I don't miss it one bit. Guys, the only thing I lost on that beautiful warm afternoon was my virginity."

Stunned silence. No one says a word, and Boris erupts into a fit of loud, rumbling laughter that just won't stop. He laughs better than Santa, I figure. Boris is the only one laughing, the rest are looking kind of sheepish. I suspect no one believes the story. It was all a load of BS, they'll say, but not to his face.

Still I can't dismiss the story altogether. Maybe there is some truth to it. After all, he's probably right about those long skirts. I'm left wondering, how did it really end?

And then I did an incredibly stupid thing. After Boris finally stopped laughing, I got his attention and timidly asked, "Boris, why didn't you tell me all this before I went picking blueberries just a couple weeks ago?"

Boris looks at me with a solemn, straight face. He puts one hand on my shoulder. "Because, my dear little friend, I just wasn't sure whether a lady killer like you could be trusted alone in the pines with all those sweet young things with long skirts and no underpants."

Now everybody is laughing like crazy. I realize I'm the butt of a pretty good joke, and yes, I feel totally embarrassed.

Come next year, though, I may just have to check out those blueberries. And who knows? Maybe I'll have my own story to tell.

THE SPEED QUEEN

It's a glum, overcast day, with patches of snow hiding in ditches and shadowy places. I'm shivering uncomfortably in the windowless army truck as I wait with Dad at the train station. We're expecting to take delivery of a major purchase that Dad had resisted for months. He understands the need for this expensive machine but worries that it may not be suitable once we move away from Vita.

It's a top-of-the-line washing machine called a "Speed Queen," and since there's no hydro in Vita, this model comes with a gasoline engine. It's safe to say there's not a woman in town who wouldn't be thrilled to own such a marvellous machine. Dad is hopeful Mom will be too, but he knows that may be expecting too much.

The washing machine story began a couple weeks back. I was lying awake in bed one morning when I overheard my parents arguing in hushed voices. Still, I could make out what they were talking about. The issue revolved around how long we would continue to live in Vita.

"Two years!" Mom said, firmly. "I bargained for two years, and pretty soon those two years will be up. I sure as hell don't want to be living in this dump a day longer. It was bad enough before baby

Anne came along. Just look at this place. Diapers and baby stuff everywhere. There's no place to move. And there's no privacy, even in our bedroom. How come we don't have a door on our bedroom?" Dad is awfully quiet. He knows by now that when Mom is angry, he's not likely to win any arguments.

"We've got five kids now," Mom continues, "and they've grown since we moved to this god-awful place. They all need space and a bit of privacy, and don't expect that you can just dump our family in another glorified chicken coop." Dad knows that when the two years are up, there's not a force on earth that will persuade her otherwise. Mom would love to return to St. Catharines, but it sounds like Winnipeg shall be the compromise.

No one can say that Mom didn't hold up her end of the bargain. From the day we moved to Vita, she has worked tirelessly, trying to make this primitive place into a decent home. And it wasn't easy with no electricity, no running water, not even a proper well. And there's that dreaded outhouse at the back of the property that everybody hates.

Even in town, everything is more complicated. Without hydro there's no refrigeration, so none of the stores carry dairy products. Oh sure, they sell a few packaged cheeses, but you can't buy a quart of milk, you can't buy cream, and worst of all—from my point of view, at least—you can't even get an ice cream cone. So Mom arranged to buy raw milk from a nearby farmer.

That seemed to work fine at first, until one day Mom decided to visit the farm at milking time. What she saw appalled her. She noticed the cow's udders were filthy, some splattered with manure, and no one took the time to wash them. Of course the milk wasn't pasteurized. How long before someone got sick, she wondered. Besides, the whole idea of having bits of manure in our milk disgusted her.

Rather than looking farther afield for a farmer with higher standards, Mom came up with a creative idea. Somehow, she managed to convince the farmer to sell her all the milk produced by one of his cows, and she would undertake to milk it herself. It was a proposal that puzzled the farmer, but if it meant one less cow to milk, well, how could he argue against that? Mom chose a cute-looking little cow with a mottled tan and white coat—part Jersey, she figured.

According to Mom, some cows are fussy about where they lie down while others are downright sloppy and will lie just about anywhere, even in their own poop. Meanwhile this little beauty seemed cleaner than the rest. Mabel, we called her. She must have wondered why she got her udder washed twice every day.

I'm sure this ritual didn't go unnoticed, and no doubt it gave the neighbours one more reason to gossip about that crazy French family from out east.

Despite her small size, Mabel produced more rich milk than we could possibly use. Mom had that figured out too. She ordered a cream separator from Eaton's and recruited us kids to operate this magical little machine. I must say it was pretty satisfying to see fresh, rich cream pouring out one spout and skim milk out the other as we turned the crank.

It's amazing how many uses there were for that cream. We slathered it over our desserts. Mom used it in her baking, and she often made trays of that delicious *sucre à la crème* fudge. I just love it. Let the cream sour a bit, and it's great over baked potatoes and perogies too. We even churned our own butter. Sometimes Mom tried making cottage cheese, but that didn't always turn out. Of course our new Miss Piggy was happy to take care of any leftovers whether it was skim milk, buttermilk, or anything, really—it was all scrumptious to her.

Mom couldn't understand why there was no bakery in town. "Unbelievable!" she would declare with disgust to anyone who would listen. "I'll bet there isn't a town in all of Ontario or Québec that doesn't have its own bakery." She would repeat her frustration whenever she found blue mould growing on the store-bought bread that she resorted to from time to time.

"Just cut those parts off," Dad suggests. "That's what we do in construction camps all the time." Mom doesn't bother to respond. She throws the whole loaf in with the rest of the leftovers destined for Miss Piggy and sets about baking her own.

She doesn't hide the fact that it's not a task she enjoys, so she bakes too many loaves at a time. Her bread is just wonderful the first day or two, but it soon gets hard. "Hard enough to qualify as building material," suggests Dad.

Mind you, there were ways to deal with this stiff-as-a-board bread. I found that toasting it on top the stove really helps, and if you add a spoon or two of bacon fat, well, that smartens it up real good.

Dessert was a well-established tradition in our family. We all looked forward to a sweet treat of some sort after every supper. Mom didn't always feel like baking, especially during those hot summer months, so a favourite alternative was to boil up another pot of *sucre à la crème*, but instead of turning it into fudge, it was kept hot in liquid form. You pour a generous amount of this super sweet sauce over a slice of that stale bread, and voila, you've got a great dessert and used up some of that rock-hard bread at the same time. When there was no *sucre à la crème*, I would sometimes soak a slice of Mom's bread in a saucer of fresh cream, then smother it with brown sugar and cinnamon. That worked pretty good, too.

Despite a complaint now and then, Mom took on these onerous chores with good humour, but there was one job that she positively hated, and that was washing clothes. And who could blame her? In St. Catharines, she always had a modern washing machine with wringer rollers to force water from the wet clothes. Here, she had to wash clothes the old-fashioned way.

Every Monday, Mom would start by heating up gallons and gallons of water on the wood stove, getting the house hot and humid as a jungle in the process. Then she would fill up two tin tubs and scrub the clothes over a corrugated washboard with strong, smelly soap. This was followed by a seemingly endless series of rinsing and wringing by hand before the clothes could be hung outside to dry. It took all day.

It was on one of those bleak Monday mornings that Mom straightened up from the washtub and held up her hands like a surgeon preparing for an operation. "Look at my hands," she says. "Just look at these ugly, scaly hands. It's all those dirty diapers, you know. I think that's what causing my eczema to flare up. Maybe you should be washing these diapers," she tells Dad, knowing full well that he would rather walk barefoot across broken glass.

Was it the fear of being pressed into such a task, or was he just being considerate? Without telling Mom, Dad ordered the most expensive washing machine in Eaton's catalogue. Perhaps it would keep Mom happy, at least until we moved.

The Speed Queen is up and running, and Dad is pleased with himself for making this tedious chore so much easier for Mom. Then one day he made the silly mistake of asking, "So how's it working?"

"It's still a pain in the ass," Mom insists. "There's the gas tank to fill, the engine doesn't always start, and on a gloomy day like today, it's miserable having to wash outdoors. Can't you put a pipe on the exhaust, so I could use it inside the house? Can't you make this noisy thing run more quietly?"

Dad crouches under the machine, examining the inner workings and trying to figure if he can convert this gas-powered Speed Queen so it will operate with an electric motor.

Now I know we'll be moving to Winnipeg, and probably real soon.

"Legal family"   Source: family photo

CHAPTER 8
St. Vital, 1948–1954

BIG SHOT BOOTLEGGERS

How promising the world looked that August day in 1948 when our family moved into our new home near Winnipeg. Mom couldn't be happier. It was such a contrast from that "converted chicken coop" to this lovely place in St. Vital. It's a big beautiful house with five rooms downstairs and three rooms upstairs, about the same size as our previous home in St. Catharines but newer and classier. The house sits on a rise facing St. Mary's Road, a comfortable distance from our closest neighbours. I'm sure it's the nicest house in the whole area. Oh yes, we have electricity now, running water, and a flush toilet too—and, best of all, no renters to share the space.

Much as Mom loves our new house, I think she's even more excited about the property. In the days of Louis Riel it was likely part of a self-contained farm that provided everything needed by a pioneering Métis family. The farms were typically long, narrow, river lots that fronted onto the Red River. More recently these farms were divided into smaller lots. Our portion includes twenty acres of prime agricultural soil—Red River gumbo, it's called—.

We learn that a few years ago the property supported a thriving market garden that grew tons of vegetables. Now there are ten acres of alfalfa, eight acres of wheat, and two acres accommodating the house, a vegetable garden, lots of leafy trees, and too much grass. Also included are a cute little barn and a generous size chicken coop.

When Mom first saw this idyllic property she almost swooned. She wanted this place so badly, she just had to have it. Dad recognized there was no chance of convincing her otherwise. It was way beyond our means, but off to the bank went my parents. Somehow they managed to secure a huge loan with minimal collateral.

Over the next few months there's a steady stream of visitors, mostly relatives, but some strangers I've never met before. Mom is in her glory, showing off our new home. It's safe to say, all are duly impressed with our new digs and of course they'd be happy to join us for supper. A few will stay overnight; we have the space now.

"How clever of Gaby to have started his own business," observed one such guest. "Does his dragline print money, like one of those printing presses at the mint?"

"Maybe you won the lottery and you're not telling us," suggests another.

"I never dreamed we'd have a 'Big Shot' in the family," teases another. Mom just laughs, not bothering to refute the silly notions.

Mom plans to convert our acreage into a small mixed farm with a couple of cows, a pig or two, and a whole flock of chickens. She knows that it will take time and money to fulfill these dreams and she knows that it will involve a whole lot of work. Dad is not about to help. In the summer months he's totally busy with his dragline business—besides, he's just not a farmer.

While Mom handled most of the work, she wasn't shy about cajoling and pressing us kids to help with various chores. We may grumble, but in the end we do her bidding. So while my sisters Juliette and Alice do most of the housework, Mom and I work the garden, cut the grass, and begin that model farm she dreams about.

Weekends we often spend working for some nearby market gardener. I hate the work; it's menial and the pay is lousy, but I know it helps pay for personal stuff, and it seems we can always use a little cash. Mom also likes the added bonus of being allowed to salvage damaged or stunted veggies.

One time we really struck pay dirt, if I can use that expression. It was late October; all the vegetable crops in the area were harvested— at least, they should have been. It had been raining for days, the soil was totally saturated, and one of the market gardeners we worked for had yet to finish digging up his carrots. No equipment could operate in this muck. Snow was in the forecast when he finally gave up the idea of salvaging what remained. And so reluctantly he offered free carrots to any of his workers willing to dig them by hand. Turns out only Mom took up the offer.

So here we were just the two of us in our raincoats and boots, rain coming down, up to our elbows in the freezing mud. We must have made a pitiful sight, Mom and me, like a couple of Chinese coolies, backs bent, slaving away in some flooded rice paddy. "I'd rather be one of those coolies," I complain. "At least my feet wouldn't be so cold, and the mud couldn't possibly be as sticky as this awful Manitoba gumbo."

Mom didn't see much point in grumbling. She just keeps working, remarking cheerily how lucky we are to be getting all these beautiful carrots for free. We must have dug up several hundred pounds. I can't imagine how we'll use them all, no matter how beautiful or tasty they might be.

Snow arrived early that first winter. Dad and I would have been in the Sandilands cutting our winter wood by now, but things are different here. Our new house is heated by a sophisticated hot water system with radiators in every room. The heat comes from a boiler with a complicated-looking furnace that burns only coal—tons and tons of expensive anthracite coal that must be delivered by truck and dumped in a special room we call a coal bin.

The coal supply is running low, but there's no mention of getting more and the house is getting kind of cold. "Just put on another sweater," says Mom. It reminds me of that cold day in Vita when the wood-fired furnace at school wasn't working. We had to wear our parkas, but that was just for one day; this has been going on for weeks now. Sometimes I wonder if it wasn't more comfortable in that crappy little shack in Vita. At least we never ran out of wood, it didn't cost us a dime, and it was always warm.

Later I found out that we were not only running low on coal, but we were also running low on cash. The last government cheque owing Dad's business hadn't arrived, and things were getting desperate. My parents were too proud to ask for help from friends or relatives, so the furnace was used sparingly and we had to wear sweaters and coats for weeks.

When that long-awaited cheque finally arrived, Dad did some quick arithmetic and concluded there wasn't enough cash to last the winter. And so without admitting there was a problem, my parents took our family into a kind of survival mode. We never went hungry, but our diet got pretty boring: potatoes and carrots at every meal, with store-bought food being a rare treat. Much of the time we ate what I would call "less-than-top-grade grub," purchased from the farmer's market downtown.

Every couple weeks, Dad takes me with him to check for bargains in the Old Market Square. Everything he buys has got to be cheap, and that means it's usually sold in bulk. It can get pretty heavy, so he brings me along to act as his mule—like the time he was looking to buy some fish direct from a local fisherman. "Much cheaper by the fifty-pound bag," the fisherman tells Dad. "Only nine cents a pound." So Dad bought two bags of frozen mullet along with a few other items.

Now we faced a two-hour ride by streetcar and bus. It annoys me that Dad's jeep remains parked in the back yard. "Too costly to keep it running," he says. So we spend half our day on public transit, and often it's standing-room only. What a huge waste of time.

Before we get home, the frozen fish starts to thaw and fellow passengers are sniffing the air. Dad seems blithely unconcerned and I am desperately hoping that I won't be recognized by a schoolmate.

I know I would be the butt of mean jokes at school that would carry on forever. It's bad enough that I'm routinely teased for being the only kid wearing moccasins to school.

Mom is not impressed. What is she to do with a hundred pounds of frozen fish, guts and heads included? "Mullet?" she mocks. "That's just a fancy name for suckers. They feed on the bottom of swampy waters. They don't taste very good, and they're full of bones." She scolds Dad mercilessly. "Didn't you notice the fish weren't cleaned? They don't fillet well, either. I'll have to scale them." Then comes the challenge of cooking the smelly fish. Mom tries frying, baking, boiling, adding all sorts of spices, and trying various recipes in a futile attempt to make them palatable. Nothing makes them tasty. Ugh! Everybody cheered when we ate the last of them.

Another time, Dad bought a couple of boxes of frozen pork. "Yes the farmer admits the price is cheap because the meat comes from a mature male pig, and yes if you have a fussy palette you might detect a slight difference in the taste. But," he quickly adds, "it's perfectly good meat, and some people actually prefer the taste."

"What nonsense," says Mom. "That boar was likely used for breeding, and who knows how old it was before losing its ability to perform. At home when I was a girl, we used to feed such meat to the dogs and the chickens." Still, Mom didn't throw it out. She used it mainly in her famous *cipâte*. With extra onions, garlic, and a few spices, no one detected the difference—or at least no one openly complained.

Meanwhile, Dad had what he thought was a brilliant idea for a home-based business. "We could be making lots of money," he says. Somehow I was dragged into this business without knowing what he had in mind.

It started innocently enough. I thought we were going to the farmer's market again, but instead, we continue up Main Street and down Selkirk Avenue to the Merchant's hotel. "Just picking up some brew for the holidays," says Dad.

We're cooling our heels in the hotel lobby when a well-dressed gentleman approaches. I've seen him before in Vita, but I don't know his name. He greets only Dad and doesn't even look at me. They disappear into the men-only beer parlour while I'm left waiting in the lobby.

Finally they return, and Dad tells me we're going for a ride. I still don't know what's going on. The well-dressed gentleman zooms around the neighbourhood, constantly checking his rear-view mirror before parking his classy Cadillac in a scruffy-looking back lane. He hands over two sturdy cardboard boxes. "Your streetcar stop is just around the corner," he says, and then quickly drives off.

Wow! Judging by the weight, there must be several gallons here. "Who's going to drink all this stuff," I ask as our streetcar trundles slowly along the tracks. Dad finally admits that he plans to sell some of the brew. "Holy smokes! That's called bootlegging, isn't it?"

We didn't talk much the rest of the way home. Dad seems unconcerned, but all sorts of thoughts are circulating though my mind. I keep hearing tinny, gurgling sounds as we bounce along with gallons of illegal brew on our laps. *Sure hope none of it leaks.* How would we explain the distinctive smell of concentrated home brew? That would be more embarrassing than the smelly fish of a few weeks back. And let's hope some undercover cop hasn't followed us. He could conceivably make an arrest at any moment, and we might end up in jail. Everybody knows the RCMP is cracking down on bootleggers.

It didn't take long for the word to get out. A steady stream of customers come knocking at our door, eager to buy a bottle or two of the diluted stuff for about half the price charged by the Manitoba Liquor Commission while Dad makes a healthy profit. Mom is real nervous. Could the next car coming down the driveway be the cops?

I hadn't planned to help transport the raw stuff Dad got from his friend with the Cadillac, but I must confess I volunteered to help with the bottling. It seems harmless enough. First Dad runs a series of tests, including smelling and sampling a small amount to determine the strength and quality of the original product. He then tells me what percentage of diluents to add, and I do the rest.

It starts with removing the labels from used bottles and giving them a good scrub. Sometimes when the empty liquor bottles have perfect labels, I just rinse them and fill them with the appropriate diluents. "Why not try to make it look like the real stuff?" says Dad. "It doesn't fool the buyer, but it looks better when serving guests." Rye whiskey always has an amber colour, so instead of using plain water I use strong tea to dilute the clear home brew. Pour the mixture into a bottle with a nice "rye whiskey" label and presto, it becomes a quality Canadian rye. Mix molasses as the diluent and pour it into a rum labelled bottle and it could pass for a fine Jamaican rum. Vodka bottles only need plain water. Now I feel that I'm part of the business, and I've got to admit it feels good to know that our financial situation has eased somewhat. Dad is not one to show emotion, but he's obviously quite pleased as he tallies up the profit. Within a few weeks, the stash is sold out and the Christmas season is just beginning. There's no stopping him now.

He orders a much larger amount of home brew, this time direct from distillers in Vita. The catch is they won't deliver such quantities. "You've got to come and pick it up in person," they tell him. Apparently getting caught in the transportation of such a large amount of home brew means your vehicle would be seized, plus you would likely end up in jail. Bootleggers are used to paying a fine from time to time but a jail sentence was something to be feared.

If Dad was afraid he certainly didn't show it, and he didn't object when I asked to accompany him to Vita. A regular yellow cab comes to our house and the driver needs to know where we're going. "To Vita," says Dad, "to visit a sick friend. It's about an hour and a half's drive." If the driver thought this unusual, he didn't let on as he reported to his dispatcher that he would be busy for the next several hours.

I'm alone in the back seat. It's dark out—nothing to see, and there's little conversation. It's a good time to have a nap. I awake just as we pull into Vita and Dad instructs the driver to stop at a crossroads just outside of town. Pleasant memories are racing through my mind. Just a few months ago, we lived here. I have friends here. Sure would be nice to visit with them. Mind you, I wouldn't want anyone to recognize me now. How would I explain what we're doing here? And so I pull my toque over my face while we wait by the side of the road. Snow is falling gently onto this pretty little town. In my wildest dreams I could never have imagined such a scene.

A vehicle pulls up and the transfer is made. Boxes and boxes fill the trunk. The driver says nothing. I wonder what he's thinking? He's probably guessed by now that there's no sick friend. Within minutes we're on the road back to Winnipeg. The ride home is awfully quiet, and I can only guess what is going through the cab driver's mind. And I'm thinking, *This sure beats riding for two hours on that damned streetcar.*

The next few weeks are completely crazy. It seems like half the people in St. Vital are knocking on our door, all wanting a bottle or two, sometimes more. And we get repeat customers, all impressed with the quality and the price. "It's every bit as good as the government stuff," they say. And Dad just smiles.

Mom is worried sick. She's certain the cops will be raiding our place any day now. She knows court costs and fines would be a financial disaster. We likely would lose the property and Dad could end up in jail. Maybe I would be charged too? Not much point in protesting; Dad pays no heed. And so the bootlegging carries on through the winter.

The coal bin is full now and the house is nice and warm. We get to eat more store-bought food and Dad just got his jeep running. Life is good. Sure hope we don't go to jail.

GROWING UP

Snow came early, the winter of 1949–1950 and continued well into April. Nobody could have predicted the hardships it would bring. And January was one of the coldest months on record, inflicting even more misery. It was during one of those cruel January blizzards that our beautiful little barn burnt down; "electrical fault," said the fire chief. Luckily, one of the neighbours spotted the fire in time to save Mom's precious little cow, Sophie. That barn was Sophie's home, and now she's forced to move to a cold, empty shed nearby. Poor Sophie! At least she didn't get burnt alive in that horrible fire.

I've never seen so much snow. I swear, I must spend every weekend shovelling tons and tons of the stuff just to keep the driveway clear. "It's got to be kept open for coal deliveries and other stuff, and yes, the sidewalk too," Mom insists. It can take a whole day to do a proper job and just a couple hours for nature to fill it in again.

Meanwhile, Dad's jeep is parked in a snowdrift behind the shed. If only it had a snow plough; it would make short work of this thankless job. When will it end?

Mom's been keeping the radio on all day lately. I'm not sure why; all they talk about are floods. "We could be next," she says. I find this hard to believe; yes, we've had lots of snow, but a few hot days around mid-April and it was gone. Oh sure, there was plenty of runoff, but by early May things were actually starting to dry up.

Reports of extra high waters in Fargo, Grand Forks, and Emerson caught my attention, but not enough to cause alarm. *They're still far away*, I tell myself, *and besides, it wouldn't be the first time that homes built in low-lying areas were in trouble.*

And now there are reports that whole towns along the Red River valley are drowning. Even in St. Vital, people are filling sand bags, building dikes, some preparing to leave their homes. Where will they go? It all seems so improbable.

The cold, muddy, waters came soon enough. It started with Kingston Crescent, Victoria Crescent, and properties along the Seine River. A few days later, we awoke to find shallow pools across St. Mary's road in front of our house.

Soldiers came by in their amphibious vehicles—"duck boats," they called them. "Time to leave, they order. Will you be needing help?"

"We'll be fine," Dad assures them. Like me, he's still not convinced that we'll have to leave our home but he alerts his younger brother Albert, just in case.

The army and the government appear to be well organized. They've even arranged for farm animals to be evacuated. Mom is relieved when a farmer from out of town comes by with a big truck. "I'm here to pick up your cow," he announces.

"She's pregnant you know?" Mom tells the farmer.

"I can tell," he says, "I own a dairy farm and some of our cows are pregnant too; she should fit right in."

Mom doesn't find it amusing. She worries and wonders if she'll ever see her little cow again, and "what's going to happen to her baby when she delivers?"

"Don't worry," the farmer assures Mom. "She'll be well looked after."

Dad has been accumulating an assortment of used machinery in the back yard. "Useless junk," Mom calls it, and there's a pile of squared timbers that Dad insists he'll need one day. We are about to anchor them down so they won't float away when it occurs to me that they could be put to another purpose. "These timbers would make a great raft," I suggest. "Something that might be useful should those predicted flood waters come."

"Great idea," says Dad as he goes about trying to elevate some of his better stuff. "You go ahead." A couple day's work and the timbers become an ark—maybe not as elaborate as Noah's, but I'm sure it will accommodate our family should the need arise. And now a part of me is looking forward to higher water levels to test it out.

We didn't have long to wait. Of course it floated nicely and everyone wants a ride. How neat to pole our way around the neighbourhood and offer rides to those still in their homes. And how convenient when we can pull up to the back porch and step into the house without getting our feet wet.

Good thing it was tied securely last night. The waters rose dramatically, and by late morning the basement flooded and yes, yes, we need Uncle Albert and his truck. "Please hurry." By the time he arrives the water is around two feet deep in front of our place. The ark comes in handy, ferrying everybody to the truck, along with a bunch of personal items. Destination: Ross Manitoba, where Mom's relatives have found a place for us to stay.

Dad and I lead the way in the jeep. It feels strange driving confidently through such deep water, while other vehicles sit stalled, awaiting their fate. Waves of water are thumping against the floorboards but the little jeep just keeps ploughing through. I guess it was designed for stuff like this. What a marvellous little machine. I compare it to a tough little burro, small and unremarkable but able to handle so many jobs.

It's taking forever to get out of the city. I'm wet and cold and feeling downright miserable, a bit like the time our family travelled from Vita to Thibaultville to visit relatives in Ross. At least the jeep had doors back then. I wonder where those doors disappeared?

It can't be much fun in Uncle Albert's truck either? Six people crammed into a small cab. They might be warm but I wouldn't trade places. There are long line-ups of cars, all trying to leave the city—up to 80,000 souls, according to the radio. And all those poor wild animals left behind. I try not to think of what fate has in store for them.

Everything is in darkness as we pull up to what looks like an abandoned building in Ross. Is this the right place? And then I notice a dim yellow light coming from a tiny window and a note that simply says, "WELCOME."

A wave of warm air sweeps over me as Dad opens the unlocked door, and how wonderful it is soaking up heat by the comforting stove. The rest of the family will be here shortly, and I am selfishly glad that, for the moment at least, I have the stove to myself. How come Dad isn't cold?

The scene quickly changes as Mom and the family arrive, followed by a bunch of relatives bringing hot food. The rustic cabin fills with loud voices and laughter as we feast together. Once again my world is looking just fine. I know I'll sleep well tonight.

The sound of a fire crackling, a whiff of sweet smoke, the smell of bacon frying and coffee perking on the stove; there's no better way to begin a new day. Mom is sitting by the stove alone in her thoughts, waiting and worrying.

I was told that our place of refuge would be an old log cabin that nobody has lived in for years. I'm expecting layers of dust and cobwebs everywhere. It's now plain to see that my preconceived notions were totally off-base. The place is spotless. I'm blown away by the precision craftsmanship. Ruler-straight logs, now mottled dark with age, perfectly fitted to one another. I'm left in awe of the original builder. "Who was he? When was it built?"

I know that Mom has a lot on her mind, but she seems willing to talk as we wait for the rest of the family. "I was just a young girl when Mr. Nielsen built this place," she tells me. "I remember his family and others who came from Denmark around the same time. None of them spoke French, and their English was hard to understand. They soon learned to speak our language, and more of us were learning English, so communication was never a problem. And you know, everybody got along just fine."

"So what happened to Mr. Nielsen?" I ask.

"Oh, he's still around. He's an old man now and lives alone in a tiny house just down the road. We'll pay him a visit tomorrow."

Mr. Nielsen is an interesting old guy: tall, wiry, and he walks with a confident air. He reminds me of Mr. Burton, and like Mr. Burton he loves to talk.

"What brought you to Canada?" I ask.

"Oh, I just love the Canadian wilderness," he says. "Especially in winter. Fall's a good time for hunting, but winter is best for trapping. With a good pair of snowshoes you can go places that are impossible in summer." He pulls down a well-worn pair, hanging against a wall. Of course he made them. He also shot the moose whose hide he used for the webbing. "Oh, I've lost track of how many pair I've made over the years." I'll bet Mr. Nielsen has hundreds of stories, and I just know he'll be glad to share a few.

I can see how a person could get used to living this carefree life: no school, no tedious chores, and nothing to worry about. I'm free to wake up when I please, go where I please, and do as I please. Most days I get together with a cousin or two and we become *coureurs des bois*. We explore the woods together, wishing we were born two hundred years ago.

Word has it that all the rural roads are passable again, and too soon my *coureur de bois* career is over. Dad is eager to finish overhauling his dragline, and I'm happy to tag along and try to be useful. We'll be working together until we return to our home in St. Vital. Sure hope it hasn't floated away.

It's a beautiful day. We are bouncing along a pot-holed road. We pass the lovely little church in Ste. Geneviève, and then Dad veers onto a muddy track. He stops at a small clearing surrounded by dense willows and sparse scrub poplar. There are pools of standing water everywhere. If he hadn't pointed it out, I doubt that I would have noticed anything unnatural about this particular place, but sure enough, there appears to be a low, rectangular mound of rotting wood that has yet to be absorbed by the saturated soil. The only indication of life comes from a chorus of noisy frogs, vigorously proclaiming their lust.

"This is where I was raised," Dad tells me. "This is all that remains of the log cabin your grandfather built in 1902, the year I was born." Holy smokes! I can't imagine anyone living in this "almost swamp." What brought them here? What were they thinking? Looks like Dad and I will have all kinds of things to talk about as we continue on our way to Vita.

My mind switches gears as we approach my familiar little town of Vita where we lived not long ago. Fresh memories awaken, good memories mostly, as we drive slowly down the main drag. It's been two years since we lived here, and precious little has changed. I wonder how much my buddies have changed? Have I changed? Will they recognize me? There'll be time enough to get reacquainted. Right now Dad is eager to get to his machine. He turns south past Petrowski's, and right away I notice something different.

"Hey, isn't this the road to Arbakka? It doesn't look anything like that primitive trail that was half underwater when we came from St. Catharines to spend the summer with you."

"Nope. This is the new road to Arbakka," says Dad. "Looks a bit different eh?" It finally dawns on me. This must be the project he's been working on for the past year. There's a wide, water-filled ditch now, and a dry roadway several feet above the surrounding swamps. "It'll take the rest of the summer to push it through to the Roseau River," he says.

I'm surprised that the provincial government saw fit to invest in this land of marginal farms and endless swamps. "Should people even be living here?" I ask in my innocence.

"Of course they should," says Dad. "People make a pretty good living here." Left unsaid is the fact that Dad's business wouldn't survive if it weren't for these kinds of projects.

We pull into one of those typical Ukrainian farmyards. Everything neat and tidy—a modest little house and a freshly whitewashed summer kitchen close by. Dad always likes to park his caboose in a friendly farmyard. "We'll meet the owners tomorrow," he says.

A big old dog comes running towards us, and I brace for the barking that will announce our presence. Instead he wags his tail. I guess he recognizes the jeep, and he wags ever harder when he recognizes Dad. Buster, they call him.

We pass by a few outbuildings, and way in the back I spot Dad's machine. It's mostly hidden in a dense cluster of young aspen, heavy with fat, dark, buds that are about to burst. Soon there'll be a gazillion bright green leaves that we know will tremble and whisper in the slightest breeze, just like they have for countless centuries. I love the subtle perfume that permeates the still air.

I doubt that Dad is interested in nature's wonders right now. His mind is totally focused on his precious machine, mute and immobile and in a thousand pieces. He pulls away a canvas tarp, revealing a pile of abstract parts. How he knows where each will fit and what purpose they all serve is a mystery to me. I've been appointed chief cook, so while Dad is busy taking inventory, I'll go check out our home away from home.

It's a quirky-looking orange caboose with a roof that resembles one of those covered wagons that pioneers used to cross the western plains—a pumpkin on wheels, some call it. The steel bunks look fine, but I'm a bit worried about the grub. I've done very little cooking, and I've never used a gas camp stove before. "Nothing fancy," Dad said when he gave me the job, "keep it simple." I know he's not fussy, and we both have good appetites, so I guess we won't go hungry. It's understood that I'll also be chief gopher—but who's going to pick up the groceries and stuff from town? Vita is several miles to the north.

It's bacon and eggs for breakfast, and we're out the door by seven. Dad boards the jeep on the passenger side; is this his way of telling me that I'm to drive, even though I don't yet have my driver's license? Hey, this could be fun.

We're headed for St. Malo to see a Mr. Martel about a new drum shaft for the dragline. "He's a genius, that man," says Dad. "There isn't a thing he can't make from raw steel. Factory parts for the old dragline are no longer available; we'd be in trouble if it wasn't for Mr. Martel."

"And," continues Dad, "did you know that Mr. Martel may be the only one in Manitoba who can take old-fashioned steel-wheeled tractors and convert them to rubber tires?"

"It's not something I ever thought about, but why would anybody want steel wheels?" I ask.

"At one time, all farm tractors had steel wheels," says Dad. "Rubber tires were considered too expensive. And then in the early thirties, rubber tires became the norm and pretty soon everybody had to have rubber. So, what do you do with a perfectly good tractor with steel wheels? Sure, if you've got lots of money you scrap the whole tractor and get a new one. Mr. Martel thinks that's awfully wasteful, *just change the wheels*,' he says, and so now it's a big part of his business."

"MARTEL'S MACHINE SHOP," reads the sign. Sure doesn't look like much from the outside, but as we enter I'm blown away by the bewildering collection of complicated-looking machinery. Mr. Martel takes us on a tour, explaining the function of each machine. I'm particularly intrigued by a worker operating a giant machine—a lathe, he calls it. Strips of steel, blue with heat, are peeling off a spinning chunk of metal like it was a piece of wood. I am totally impressed. What a thrill it must be, having that kind of power at your fingertips.

"This is the machine that made your new drum shaft," explains Mr. Martel as he carefully lifts the lid from the protective wooden crate. I try lifting one end.

"Holy smokes! It must weigh a couple hundred pounds."

"Closer to three hundred," corrects Mr. Martel.

"Wow, It's hard to imagine how a bar of steel this size could get bent," I comment. Dad thinks it happened last fall when the bucket hit a huge boulder.

"Before the operator could release the drag clutch, the drag cable snapped, and the machine wasn't the same after that, says Dad. The old Waukesha engine would likely have stalled, but the new diesel is so powerful it snapped that steel cable like it was a piece of twine and bent the drum shaft in the process."

We work well together, Dad and I. He doesn't teach exactly, but I watch closely and he answers all my questions. I've grown quite a lot since that first job. I can tip a full forty-five gallon drum now. I feel more useful, but oh my, there's so much to learn. We've been at it several weeks, and we're making good progress. "Another few days and we should be operational," says Dad. At the end of the day I'm so tired I can't stay awake long enough to listen to the news on the radio. I wonder what's going on in the outside world.

Buster is barking like crazy; there must be a visitor. A familiar car pulls up, and out steps my cousin Jerry, Uncle Romeo's oldest son. He's worked with my dad a couple summers now, and it's understood that he will again this year. I guess he wasn't expected quite this early.

Jerry brought word that Mom has paid a visit to our home in St. Vital. The floodwaters have receded but oh, what a mess. She wants us to come home ASAP.

"I've yet to visit with my buddies," I protest.

"Go," says Dad. "Jerry and I will finish up here. We'll leave Monday morning."

It's late on a Saturday afternoon in Vita. I spot my buddy Billy puttering in his dad's garage. He's busy with his battery business just like he was two years ago when I last saw him. Progress comes slowly, it seems, when there's still no hydropower.

"I knew you'd be coming," says Billy. Word travels fast in this close community where everybody seems to know everybody's business.

"My, how you've grown," says Billy's dad.

"You'll stay for supper?" his mom insists.

After supper, Billy and I spend the rest of the evening zooming around town in the jeep, visiting friends and reminiscing on the fun things we did together not so long ago.

"By the way, how's your sweet Marie?" I ask.

"She's married now," says Billy in a sad voice.

Damn! I shouldn't have asked.

Sunday morning, I'm back in Vita. All the guys are game for a swim as we pick them up from various parts of town. I notice the guys are all bigger now. There's no end of teasing and laughing as they pile into the jeep. This should be a fun day; everyone's in a jolly mood.

"Remember the times when we'd double up on our bikes so that every kid in town could come for a swim whether they had a bike or not." I remind my buddies.

"We still do that," says Stan. "There's still kids who don't have a bike, and nobody's got a vehicle, you know."

"And none of us has a rich Dad, either," adds another.

Damn! I stepped in it again.

The swimming hole that I had cleared a couple years earlier hasn't changed at all; it's a wide spot along a drainage ditch two miles east of town. The scrub willows, with their fresh, silvery leaves, provide a bit of privacy. Still, nobody owns a bathing suit.

The day slips by ever so pleasantly. We play a game of tag in fast-flowing, frigid water, then we dry and warm ourselves by the fire. I couldn't be happier. We roast kubasa over the fire and tear off hunks of delicious, crusty bread. My thoughts jump back to St. Catharines when my Italian buddies and I ripped off hunks of heavenly French bread from the bakery on Facer Street. "Hey, where did you guys get this fabulous French bread?" I ask.

"We have our own bakery now," one of the guys lets me know, "and by the way, that's Ukrainian rye you're eating." Oh no! Did I step in it again?

■ ■ ■

Mid-June: It's a beautiful sunny day, and St. Mary's Road is totally dry. I've never seen the trees so full and the grass so lush. From the road our house looks just fine. Mom doesn't think so.

"Did you see all the mud downstairs?" she says, "And did you know the septic system doesn't work?" And so, it's quickly decided that Mom needs me around the house more than I'm needed on the dragline. It's a good feeling, being needed, and so either way, I know I'll be busy doing stuff I don't particularly like.

What miserable work, scrubbing the basement walls. And it's no fun at all scooping up tons of smelly mud off the basement floor, one pail at a time. By the end of each day I'm thinking this is almost as bad as digging carrots in the rain, and I'm dreading the thought of having to work for some cheap market gardener again this summer.

"I can't find any structural damage to your house," says the insurance guy. "A couple more inches, and it would have been a disaster. You'll need a new septic system, though."

Mom is also grateful for another minor miracle. All her houseplants have survived. They're actually thriving. "How can that be?" she asks. "We've been away for over a month. Somebody must have watered them. Could one of the soldiers patrolling the area have a green thumb?" I guess we'll never know.

A big truck pulls into the driveway, the same one that took Sophie away, back in early May. Everyone gathers to welcome her home, as she is gently coaxed down the ramp. She's thinner now but still looks pretty good. "What happened to Sophie's calf?" Mom asks with obvious concern. The driver heads back up the ramp without answering. *Uh-oh, bad news?* I fear. He's in the truck for what seems like a long time and then emerges, carrying a tiny, perfect replica of Sophie. Our whole family is ever so excited and oh-so happy. I can't imagine a more wonderful scene. Everyone wants to pet the little calf. Sophie gets water and treats and a thorough brushing. I wonder what she's thinking? The two are put out to pasture, and immediately her little one is vigorously nudging her mom's distended udder, demanding supper. We all watch for the longest time, almost forgetting that it's our suppertime too.

"The frost should be out of the ground by now," announces Dad one morning. We all know that's his way of saying he's got to get back to his dragline. Before leaving he asks me to come with him to pick up some supplies from "Prairie Equipment," the company where he bought that new diesel engine for his old dragline.

I'm expecting another mule-type job, but no: Dad marches into the manager's office and I follow. They know each other, it seems. Another gentleman enters behind us and closes the door. There are introductions and handshakes all around, and the manager starts asking me a whole bunch of questions. It seems a bit odd. And then he tells me they've got an opening for a summer student willing to work with experienced mechanics repairing heavy earth-moving equipment. A brief description of the job follows, and then a familiar question: "So, do you think you can handle the job?" he asks.

I am flabbergasted. I can't believe my good fortune. "Of course I can handle it," I reply without knowing exactly what it's all about.

"We work nine-hour days, six days a week, and it pays seventy-five cents an hour," says the other guy. "See you at the Quonset, right after Dominion Day, July 2nd, 7:00 a.m. sharp." I do a quick mental calculation. Wow! I'll be making a fortune before heading back to school this September.

Despite the long, hard days, I really enjoy the job. I recognize that I'm working with a couple of professional mechanics that take great pride in their work. Their strong work ethic is much the same as Dad's, but comparing work habits only goes so far. These gentlemen are neat and tidy, and totally organized. Each owns a huge red tool cabinet with dozens of drawers containing every type of tool imaginable. And nobody touches the other's tools without permission.

Mornings begin with clean coveralls, a review of the day's work orders, a quick cup of coffee, and then it's on with the job. Breaks are brief, with no dawdling in between. Before leaving at the end of the day, the Quonset must be tidied up and the floors swept: all routines that appeal to me. However, I'm quite certain this isn't the kind of work I want to be doing for the rest of my life. I enjoyed working with my dad too, but we both know that I won't be following in his line of work either.

I've always known that every adult has to work at something, and every man has to have a proper job. So how do people end up stuck with a job they don't much like? Didn't they have a choice? So far I haven't come across any job that appeals to me. One thing I know for sure: I want to be able to choose the type of work I'll be doing, especially if it's to be for the rest of my life.

Meanwhile, I can't quite give up the idea of escaping into the wilderness and living the life of a *coureur de bois*. A persistent inner voice intrudes. *It's time to cast aside those silly boyhood fantasies*, it tells me. *You're all grown up now, better start thinking of how you're going to make a living.*

"I know, I know, but I can dream, can't I . . . ?"

FIRST CAR

She looked so forlorn, sitting quiet and alone at the back of the car lot. She appeared to list to one side: low tire pressure, I persuaded myself. It was a 1929 Model A Ford, and the sticker on the windshield said $50.00.

"I'll save you the trouble of towing it to the scrap yard," Dad tells the salesman. "Thirty bucks."

"Gimme forty," says the salesman, and wonder of wonders, I took possession of my first car. I know it's not drivable; at least not yet. We'll have to tow it home, but I couldn't be more excited.

During the fifties, it was every teen-age boy's dream to own a car of his own. Among the guys I hung out with, money was always tight, and nobody had parents who would let their teenage kid borrow the family vehicle—that is, if the family owned such a luxury. The odd kid with a good summer job might be able to buy a junk car or even an old beater, but keeping it on the road was the challenge. You had to have a bit of mechanical savvy, and you best prepare to spend most of your free time on maintenance and repairs. And of course there were always ongoing expenses like gas, oil, tires and replacement parts. Mobility was the obvious appeal, but there was more, a promise of a whole lot more.

Over the next several months, I spent every spare minute on this vintage vehicle that had been destined for the scrapheap. Dad warned me that it would need a valve job and piston rings, quite possibly a whole new engine. At least it has a pretty good body, no rust at all, so according to Dad the rest is all fixable. I have a suspicion this wouldn't have been his first choice, but since all the costs will be mine, he makes no move to change my mind.

"So why bother with such an old piece of junk?" people ask. There may be good reason why I wanted a Model A, but I couldn't put it into words. Lately, I was finding that not everything we do is for a logical reason. Take this girl who sits across from me in my homeroom at Glenlawn. Susanne is her name, but everybody calls her Suzy. She's a bit skinny, flat-chested, and not particularly good-looking, but I find her kind of attractive. Maybe it's her cheery independent air; maybe it's that "I-don't-give-a-damn" look that I find appealing. None of the guys in my class understand. They make nasty comments behind her back and chide me for defending her. In my mind, the Model A is a bit like Suzy, but I don't share such thoughts with these rude guys.

I thought Dad was going to help me with my restoration project, but he stays in the house, reading and playing cards: "charging my batteries," he says. He'll be off to his dragline when the weather gets warmer. Still, I'm grateful that he's available to answer questions whenever I'm stuck. Maybe it's his way of teaching me independence and to figure things out for myself. Mind you, he did come out to check the clearance between the pistons and the cylinders. "Pretty sloppy," he declares. "With new piston rings, you might be able to squeeze another season from that tired old engine." The valves are something else. There's no compromising here. "Keep grinding," he insists, as I laboriously rotate each valve back and forth by hand, hour after hour until they seat just perfectly.

"Now can we start it?" I ask as I torque down the last head bolt.

"Have you cleaned the carburetor? Have you checked the ignition coil and the condenser? And how about the points? Are they pitted and is the gap set correctly? You gotta do all that before you start the engine," says Dad. "And before you take it out on the road, you'll have to overhaul the brakes and the suspension system. You'll have to check the wheel bearings, make sure the transmission and the differential are topped up, and then there's the tires." Good lord! I had no idea it would be this much work. I've been working on just the engine for over a month now and was counting on driving before the end of summer.

Dad is finally satisfied. Time to see if it will run. I can hardly contain my excitement as I fill the gas tank and hook up the battery. And what a thrill it is when the engine obediently comes to life as if by magic. And what satisfaction to hear all four cylinders, firing in harmony, just like they're supposed to.

Dad's first words when I turn the engine off? "Sounds like you've got a leaky exhaust manifold. And you've got a loose connecting rod." Oh well, I know he generally approves.

Now that the engine is running smoothly, there's no stopping me. The hours of work and minor frustrations seem trivial now. I'm happy to spend every waking moment on my passion, sometimes past dark.

I can't wait any longer. We venture onto St. Mary's road my model A and me. It could use more power, but it handles nicely. And just as Dad predicted, the mechanical brakes don't work so good. I guess they'll need more attention? A wave of excitement washes over me as I imagine a new world unfolding before me. No more waiting for that crappy bus, no more waiting for that poky streetcar. The money that I earned last summer is nearly gone. A feeling of dread creeps over me as I begin to realize just how much it'll take to keep my new passion on the road. I've just got to get a job.

One of my classmates told me there might be an opening at Soubry's Hatchery where he works on weekends. A quick trip to the hatchery with my Model A, a five-minute interview, and the job is mine. Weekdays, my shift begins at 5:00 p.m.—just enough time for a quick bite after school before work begins. I'm home around 10:30; almost time for bed. I have no free time at all, but the pay's not bad and I just love my Model A.

At first my main job at Soubry's involved general cleaning and rotating eggs in the big walk-in incubators. "This is a very responsible job," the boss keeps reminding me. "If the temperature isn't carefully monitored, hundreds of chicks will die. If the eggs aren't rotated regularly, hundreds of chicks will die."

Things seemed simple enough at first, but he didn't tell me about the more gruesome details. They came soon enough when the incubated eggs started hatching. Most of the eggs magically transformed into cute little balls of yellow fluff that never stopped peeping. Trouble was, they didn't all turn out perfect. Some had defects like a bad leg or bulgy eyes. Culling, it was called, which meant they would be killed and chucked in a garbage bin. Then I learned that perfectly healthy chicks were also killed when they weren't the right sex.

"Leghorns make the best laying hens, but males aren't much good for eating," my boss tells me. "Nobody wants male leghorns."

It takes a trained eye to tell the difference. "Sexing" specialists they're called, and they come by, most evenings to perform their grim task. They don't say much, but when they speak, it's in another language—Japanese, I think. They sit at a long table, and I'm kept busy bringing them boxes of live chicks and the sorting begins. A quick glance at the chick's bum and the females are separated from the males. They are then placed in an open pen to feed and grow before being shipped to customers all over Manitoba. Meanwhile, the male chicks are killed and dumped in a garbage bin along with the defective ones.

Life can be harsh for farm animals. I try not to think about them too much. I don't want to know how innocent, cute little piggies can end up as delicious pork chops on your plate, and now it feels positively weird eating eggs. They are, after all, baby chicks that weren't incubated properly.

School is winding down, and so is the peak of the chick-hatching season. My job will soon be over, but I'm not too concerned. I've been assured I can return to Prairie Equipment, where I worked last summer. I also want to check out another job prospect that has come to my attention. It sounds impressive: "Assistant Brake Systems Specialist" with Ackland's Automotive. Again, the interview is short and pleasant. "When can you start?" asks the boss.

"Right after graduation," I tell him. He seems okay with that when I explain that I'll need a couple weeks to finish school.

As graduation approaches, I offer my nerdy friends a ride to the graduation party in my Model A. None of us has a girlfriend, so it seems natural enough. There's a parade being planned, with shiny cars and limousines all decked out with thousands of paper flowers. All those flowers seem kind of silly to us guys, but the Model A could use a facelift.

Every evening we go at it, weekends too, hammering out dents, smoothing body filler over rough spots, and then hours of sanding—hours and hours of sanding. I feel a bit like Tom Sawyer when he convinced his buddies to help him whitewash that board fence in exchange for small treasures—only I'm not going to charge for the privilege. I'm ever so grateful to my buddies for volunteering their time. The four of us work well together; everyone is super meticulous and intent on doing the best job possible. Finally we add a prime coat, a bit more sanding, and the two layers of high quality automotive paint, sprayed ever so carefully.

It's a sunny, Sunday afternoon; we all stand back to admire our handiwork. Wow! Everyone just loves the colour combination: a canary yellow body with shiny black fenders. It turned out better than we could have imagined. It had been a dull grey, which was quite typical for a Model A. When new, they only came in a few drab colours, as dictated by the Ford Motor Company. "We have totally transformed a frumpy old lady into a chic, saucy, young thing," observes one of my friends. "Henry Ford must be rolling over in his grave."

I'm thinking Suzy will also be looking great when she gets all dolled up for the grad, and I'm pleased that she has a date. I guess I'm not her only admirer. After graduation, I may just borrow her name and call my car "Suzy." I'm sure she wouldn't mind.

My buddies and I sure got our share of attention as we slowly putt-putted along the parade route. We wave to the crowd as we ride by, thinking we must look real cool, each wearing a suit and tie for the first time and sporting a boutonnière. The sight must be shocking to our classmates who have only seen us wearing less than stylish clothes, especially the girls—but are they impressed? Not likely! I suspect they are more interested in the car. Even without the paper flowers, my friends and I know that we are riding in the coolest-looking car in the whole parade, and it feels real good.

■ ■ ■

The following Monday, I report for my new job as "Assistant Brake Systems Specialist" with Ackland's Automotive. I learn that they are a well-known distributor of various specialized tools, auto parts, and safety equipment. It's also the go-to place for any brake related components. They sell mostly new stuff, but you can also get your worn brake drums and shoes refurbished and save money in the process.

"That's what this job is all about," explains Rob, my new boss. "It's all pretty straightforward except that the brake industry is undergoing a shift in technology right now. Since cars were invented, brake linings were always riveted to their shoes, now they are bonded with a special adhesive. This new method is supposed to double the life of regular brakes and eliminates that god-awful, ear-piercing, squealing you hear so often when brakes are applied on a hot day."

Rob seems a nice guy—in his early twenties, I would guess. He doesn't talk much, but we get along real good. Maybe I'll get to like being an "Assistant Brake System Specialist." Rob teaches me the critical steps required for bonding brake linings to brake shoes and all the safety tests required before any part can be added to general inventory. "This will become the main part of your job," he says, "but first, there's a fair bit of prep work required." He leads me to the back of the shop where a small mountain of worn brake shoes awaits, all with riveted linings. There are eight to ten rivets on each shoe, and there must be several hundred shoes. This is going to take a while.

And then the shoes have to be degreased, sanded, and painted: all jobs requiring a facemask. The mask keeps most of the dust from your lungs, but it does nothing to stop all the noxious smells in the air. There's the ever-present smell of carbon tet (carbon tetrachloride) from the degreasing tank. There's the overspray from painting and cleaning the spray gun. Everyone knows the stuff's bad for your health, but just *how* bad is never revealed.

The bonding ovens give off a continuous foul smell as the glue cooks and the ventilation fans just can't keep up. Then there's the abrasive dust generated whenever we use the industrial-size belt sander. Billions of particles fill the air. How much of it is asbestos?

One day Rob tells me that he plans to move on. I wasn't too surprised. "The job is yours if you want it," he says.

I can't believe what I'm hearing. "You mean I could be in charge of this shop? But I've only been here six weeks."

The manager confirms what Rob's been telling me. "And so, we are sorry that Rob will be leaving Ackland's at the end of this month, and we don't have a replacement. Rob tells me that you could take over his position. It comes with a generous pay raise," he adds. "Are you interested?"

Wow! This is incredible. I just turned seventeen, and I'm being offered this highly responsible job. "Chief Brake Systems Specialist"? The title sounds a bit silly, but I'm not about to object. All sorts of thoughts are swirling through my mind as I struggle to respond. Finally I ask the manager, "Could I run this past my parents? I'll have an answer by Monday."

Dad thinks this is a wonderful opportunity. He's seen the shop, all neat and tidy and filled with high-tech tools. "Sure wish I had been offered such a cushy job when I was your age," he says. "I'd still be working there."

Mom has a different take. "Give your head a shake," she says. "Breathing all that crap will get you a one-way ticket to the TB sanatorium down the road, besides you're already enrolled with that new technical school downtown."

Mom was right. I knew it the moment I entered the Manitoba Institute of Technology, and I quickly forget about Ackland's and the lofty title I passed up. MIT, as it's called, teaches all the trades, but the machine shop in particular is the most impressive. It occupies half the main floor. Huge windows facing South onto Portage Avenue gives it a bright, airy, atmosphere and lends a certain pride of place. It's chock-full of mysterious-looking machinery all spotless and perfectly arranged. I just know I'm going to love it here.

"This is where machinists are made," says Mr. Lane, the chief instructor. "During the coming year you will learn the fine art of crafting raw materials into virtually any mechanical component the human mind can imagine. And you will learn to make metal parts with such precision that dimensions are typically specified to the one-one thousandths of an inch (0.001")."

"You will learn about metals and their alloys—metallurgy, we call it. Each metal has unique properties, and each requires special tools and specific techniques to shape them into a finished product. And you'll learn how to heat treat high carbon steel alloys to the right hardness. You will learn about the strength of materials and how to calculate *'stress'* and *'strain.'* Included will be a short course in soldering, brazing, even a bit of welding. You'll also get an introduction to mechanical drafting, along with higher math, even an accounting course in case you start your own business.

"Once you've passed all the tests here at MIT, you must apprentice five years at a registered machine shop before you can qualify as a 'Journeyman Machinist'. Not all of you will make it. And," continues Mr. Lane, "if you're lucky and you work hard, then maybe, just maybe, after ten years or so, you might be able to call yourself a true machinist."

And so the journey begins. It all sounds a bit scary, but terribly exciting too. I feel a bit like when I started grade two with Sister Anna Marie. I'm ready to take on every challenge that Mr. Lane has to offer, and I am determined to become the best that I can be at every skill required.

The next several months are intense. There's plenty of academic work, and it's all stuff that interests me, but it's the hands-on skills that give me the most satisfaction. I find it positively thrilling learning to operate each new machine tool and practicing the specific tasks they were designed to perform. Mr. Lane reminds us that the MIT machine shop has over twenty different machine tools, but out in the real world, you will encounter many more. I appreciate his admission that he can only teach us the basics. It shall take years of persistent practice to be truly proficient at every skill.

Throughout the term, students are given drawings from which we are to fabricate a finished product (usually a hand tool of some sort). By April, a few of us have completed all the prescribed assignments and we are free to choose our own projects. How exciting! I know exactly the project I want to undertake.

The idea has been building for some time—ever since last summer when our ten acres of alfalfa was ready to be harvested. In previous years, it was just a matter of contracting with one of the local farmers to cut and bale the hay—a couple days' work with modern equipment.

This year, it seems, all were too busy. In the end, an old neighbour was cajoled into taking his team of horses out of retirement to cut and rake the hay the old-fashioned way, and a couple of cousins and I provided the muscle. The result was two large stacks of precious alfalfa hay. Sophie and her little calf will not go hungry this coming winter.

"Sure would be nice if we had our own tractor," I muse.

Dad quickly shoots down the idea. "Much too expensive for our small acreage," he says.

Now, what if I were to build a tractor? I ask myself. *I bet I could build a pretty good machine for less than $100.00, and it would be a great challenge.* Some of the key components are already sitting in the backyard, just rusting away. "A bunch of useless junk," says Mom. "One of these days I'm going to call a junk dealer to haul it all away."

Dad has been keeping a 1936, two-ton Ford truck that he got real cheap. "Just needs a differential," he says.

I remind Dad that his truck was submerged during the 1950 flood. For sure the engine will be seized, and the mechanical brakes will also be frozen with rust by now. "I sure could use that four-speed transmission, for my tractor," I tell him.

"Okay, okay, it's all yours," he finally concedes.

The other piece of junk that annoys Mom to no end is a 1931 Model A Ford that was involved in a serious accident. The body is totalled, but it's supposed to have a good engine. I bought it as a spare for my Model A, but since the original is still running pretty good, I plan to use what's left of this "piece of junk" for the heart of my tractor. Now what I need most is a good heavy-duty differential, and I think I know where to find one.

Spread under the high-voltage hydro lines crossing St. Mary's Rd. lies my favourite scrap yard. "It's not a scrap yard." Mr. Pearson insists. He points to a sign near the entry gate: "MIKE PEARSON'S, METAL & SALVAGE," it reads. I just love visiting Mr. Pearson and his neatly arranged collection of cars, trucks, assorted machinery, and multiple sheds full of mechanical parts of every description. I marvel at how

Mr. Pearson seems to know exactly what parts he has on hand and where to find them. He's a walking encyclopaedia on everything automotive. Mr. Pearson can keep you regaled for hours on the history of the various scrap vehicles when he's not too busy.

I explain my tractor project to Mr. Pearson, how I plan to use the motor and the frame from my junk Model A as a base and then marry up two transmissions in tandem to a heavy duty differential, and he immediately knows what I'm talking about. "Of course you'll need a good sturdy differential," he agrees. "The torque output from your second transmission will be tremendous; it could easily strip a regular two-ton truck differential. Do you know what a used differential like that would cost? Close to two hundred bucks," he says. My heart sinks. "Come with me," he says.

Parked at the back of the property is a monster of a car. I've never seen anything like it. It's a 1931 Lincoln Roadster with a V-12 engine. "Belonged to a famous bootlegger from the States." says Mr. Pearson. "Some idiot drove it to Winnipeg in the winter with water in the radiator. Of course it froze overnight and cracked the engine block beyond repair. The owner couldn't wait for a new engine so it ended up here. I've been meaning to fix it, but I'll probably never get around to it. Have a look at that beauty," he says as we crawl under the old Lincoln.

"Holy smokes, what a huge differential. It would be just perfect for my tractor, but what will it cost?"

"It's yours for fifteen bucks," says Mr. Pearson, "but you'll have to take it apart yourself." He throws in a couple of oversized wheels with matching bolt patterns and a decent set of used tires—all for free. I can't believe his generosity. I thank him profusely. "Just show me your tractor when you're done," he says. I really like Mr. Pearson.

It didn't take any coaxing to get brother Lou and his pal Jim involved. They volunteered to dismantle Dad's old truck, and they removed the crumpled body from my wrecked Model A. The young boys also helped to extricate the precious differential from Mr. Pearson's old Lincoln. They are only ten years old. I am totally impressed.

Our chaotic backyard grows ever messier, mechanical parts strewn everywhere. Time to start reassembling the key components. The Model A chassis becomes the main frame to which the drive train will be attached. The original motor and three-speed transmission are to be left intact. Then comes the four-speed transmission from Dad's truck. And finally Mr. Pearson's Lincoln differential—that precious differential. Each connection requires a special housing along with transitioning splined couplings, all parts I've custom fabricated at MIT. "Marrying them up" is the process of combining these separate, distinct components into one integrated unit.

The finished machine was a huge success. The two transmissions gave the tractor thirteen forward speeds and seven reverse: a wider range than any commercial tractor. In the lower gears it was ideal for ploughing or for excavating basements. At haying time it was great for mowing, raking, or hauling hay. Having retained the front spring suspension from the Model A, it worked pretty good as a road vehicle too. I once pushed it to over 50 mph down St. Mary's Road.

Dad never said much about my tractor, but he seemed pleased to see his derelict truck put to good use. The truck's four-speed transmission worked real well, and I converted the truck chassis into an all-purpose farm wagon, capable of hauling multi-ton loads. Components from seven different vehicles were incorporated in the overall project, and the cost was well below $100.00.

My fondest memory is of my newly finished tractor idling contently in the driveway, about to take on its first job. Hitched to the drawbar is my heavy-duty farm wagon loaded with hundreds of pounds of scrap iron. For the first time in years the yard is tidy, and Mom couldn't be happier. And of course I was thrilled to pieces as I hauled the load down St. Mary's Road. Destination: "MIKE PEARSON'S METAL & SALVAGE."

"1929 Model A Ford"   By: George Hopkins

"Jules' Tractor"   Source: family photo

MOMENTS TO REMEMBER

Dad surprised everybody when he pulled into the driveway in a brand-new 1952 Buick Road Master. What a big beautiful car. The curvaceous lines and the sheer size just exude luxury. It sports enough chrome to dazzle a movie star. And under that super long hood, you just know it's not hiding one of those puny six-cylinder, Chevy-type engines. No Sirree! This is a powerful, inline, straight-eight, with sixteen overhead valves. The extra long crankshaft is perfectly balanced so that it revs over at a low RPM with no vibration at all. And just like in the ads, you can place a glass of water on top the valve cover and there is barely a ripple as the big engine idles in serene silence.

The feature that really sets it apart is the revolutionary Dynaflow transmission. Torque is transmitted through twin turbines so that there is always a cushion of oil between the crankshaft and drive train. Acceleration is silky smooth; there's no telltale pause as the transmission shifts to another gear.

Visually, it's really impressive too—at least to my eye; the grill in particular. It looks a bit like the mouth of a giant whale with a multitude of shiny chrome teeth, ready to chew you to bits if you get too close. I just love that car. Best of all, it tells me that those years of penny-pinching may be coming to an end. Maybe now, our family can afford a few of the simple luxuries that others take for granted. Maybe we can all go to the beach this summer.

"How are you going to pay for that fancy toy?" asks Mom. "We still owe big time on the house, and payments on your new dragline will carry on for years." Dad just shrugs.

I kind of understand where he's coming from. Last year he bought a 1949 Meteor, the Canadian version of a Ford. It was partly to help a friend who was in financial trouble, and besides, it was about time that we had our own family vehicle.

Dad's business is doing pretty good, but he certainly doesn't need two cars. I am also doing pretty good. I have a steady job with a custom fabrication machine shop. Siemens Manufacturing, it's called. It's a small company that specializes in making aircraft parts. The hours are long, but the pay's not bad. I'm happy to take over the payments, and presto, the Meteor is mine. Needless to say I don't need two cars either, and there are ready customers for my Model A. Sorry, Suzy, hopefully your new owner will treat you kindly.

Over the past several years, cousin Leo and I have been seeing each quite regularly, even though we live several miles apart. Once I got my own car, we got together most weekends and became best friends. Others joined us, and we grew into a small group of like-minded guys who just enjoy hanging out together. Some call us a "gang," but we don't do anything bad. On a typical Saturday evening we might go to a movie or a drive-in or just cruise around, checking out places we've never been. The Meteor's flathead V8 may not be as smooth as Dad's straight-eight, but the compact engine is quite powerful and gobbles up the miles with no effort at all. This opens up another world for my buddies and I.

We think nothing of cruising to Lock Port for burgers and fries, or to the Half Moon for Footlong hot dogs, a forty-mile round trip. On a hot day, we may drive on past Bird's Hill to the Moose Nose gravel pit for a swim; sometimes we drive to Winnipeg Beach for a ride on the wooden roller coaster, a hundred-mile round trip.

It's a gorgeous, warm summer's evening, and we're cruising along Henderson Highway in the Meteor, the Red River in full view. All the windows are rolled down, the radio is on full volume, and the Mills Brothers are singing their hit song "Up a Lazy River." How perfect. One of the guys starts singing along, and the rest of us follow. We arrive at the Half Moon singing in our best voices. Of course this gets everyone's attention. They stare; a few are smiling, and we couldn't be happier. And so began a beautiful blending of voices and personalities that carried on for several glorious years.

We have a lot in common, us guys. We've all finished high school, and we all have jobs. Nobody talks about university; that's strictly for privileged kids with rich parents. Our parents aren't rich, but they aren't poor either. Everyone lives in their own home. Our dads all have jobs while our moms stay at home. Life is good.

You're bound to learn new things when you spend time with good buddies. I always knew that I enjoyed singing, but I considered this a private matter, something you only do when you're alone or with like-minded people. A bit like swimming in the nude. It feels good, but you have to be selective about where you practice this pleasure.

Our buddy, Rod, teaches us the lyrics to the latest tunes and introduces us to various singing styles. "If we're going to sing together," he says, "we should try to sound more professional, maybe like the Four Lads or the Four Aces or the Ink Spots," and he rhymes off a dozen other groups that are prominent on the music scene. And so we practice as we cruise around. Sometimes we just park in some quiet spot and sing our hearts out.

Meanwhile, cousin Leo thinks we should all be paying more attention to our appearance. "There's a new fashion going around," he says, "and if we want to impress the girls, we'll have to get with the times."

I have to admit this never entered my mind. I thought fashion was just for rich people or movie stars. "What's wrong with jeans and a T-shirt, as long as they're clean?"

Of course he's right, and now that we all have jobs, money is no longer an excuse. And so, on a beautiful spring day we find ourselves in the Daoust Tailor Shop to get measured up. This is a new experience for me. A week later, we're back, and I admit I'm feeling a bit nervous. Who are those giggly guys in the full-length mirrors with the classy-looking pants, wide at the knees and narrow at the ankles—"drapes," they're called? And they're wearing matching custom jackets; certainly not a style or colour I would have chosen. That was left to cousin Leo.

I've got to admit they look pretty cool. Black velvet, front and back, with a fine, black-and-white checked fabric for the sleeves. "You guys look awesome," says the tailor. Of course he would say that . . . but what will the girls think? And so now it's off to the shoe store. It wouldn't do to have these cool-looking duds and ratty-looking shoes. Heads turn as we stroll down Provencher Blvd. in our classy outfits.

"This calls for a celebration," says one of the guys. "Maybe we could try crashing a men-only beer parlour again."

"We just got kicked out of the Marion last month," says Les "Don't you remember, stupid? And the bouncer warned us, "You gots to be twenty-one years old, boys."

"Let's zoom down to the States," I suggest. "It's only a couple hours' drive, and I hear the pubs are a lot friendlier down there."

We're just outside of Grand Forks, North Dakota when we stop at an A&W drive-in for burgers and beer—root beer, that is. We may try for the real stuff later. A cute young lady on roller skates hangs a tray on each window and takes our orders. We emerge from the car to stretch our legs and almost immediately a few young people approach, curious to know the name of our group. I guess that makes sense—why else would five young guys be dressed in such classy outfits and be riding a classy-looking Meteor (not a car brand they're familiar with)? I guess the car does look pretty decent; it's midnight blue, polished to a high shine, and sporting whitewall tires.

We linger after the root beer and burgers, fielding questions, asking some of our own. A growing crowd of young people are convinced that we must be a singing group whose fame has not yet reached the United States, and they want to hear what we sound like. After some urging, we admit that we do sing together, but we haven't sold any records; at least not yet. We make lame excuses. Nobody wants to shatter the illusion. Leo explains that we don't do a cappella. It just wouldn't be right without our band, and that seems to satisfy their curiosity.

The charming little taverns across the Northern United States are so welcoming. The moment we walk through the door, everyone knows we are Canadian and they make us feel at home. We order beer and party on as though we belonged. After a few beers it becomes more natural to break into song as a familiar tune blares from the jukebox. Fellow patrons cheer us on and nobody ever asks our age.

We dare not drive back across the border in our less-than sober state, so we find a secluded spot and sleep in the open when weather permits. This becomes a pleasant ritual, a great way to spend summer weekends. It was on one of those occasions when we drank more than we should have and yet we brazenly bought more beer to take to our camp.

A sad love song is playing on the car radio. We sing along with subdued voices when I notice Remi is crying, tears streaming down his face. Remi's not usually one to show emotion. What's wrong?

"I just love youse guys," he blurts out, and proceeds to relate an embarrassing memory that comes to mind. "Remember last summer when we were crossing the border back into Manitoba?" asks Remi? "The customs guy asked if we were bringing back booze? I don't know what I was thinking when I answered, 'Yes . . . I got at least six bottles with me.' And how youse guys laughed when I told the customs guy they were all in my bladder. The customs guy didn't think it was funny. He kept us cooling our heels for over an hour. I had to be the smart-ass in the group, but youse guys didn't get mad at me." Everybody laughs all over again.

"And remember the time when we were approaching the border and we realized we still had a six-pack that wasn't touched?" says Les. "What to do? So we hid the beer by a culvert near the border and forgot about it. How long was it before someone remembered? A year perhaps, maybe two? Of course, we just had to find that beer and we had to drink it, even though it tasted kind of skunky. How cheap can you get?" More laughs.

"And remember when we thought we'd found the perfect place to camp, just outside Thief River Falls?" offers Leo. "Early in the morning we were awakened by voices and the sound of arrows whizzing past. Turns out the five of us were sleeping on the fairway of a private archery range, the bulls-eye target mere feet from where we slept. 'Good morning, boys,' the archers greeted. 'Sorry to be disturbing you.' They could have called the cops, but instead we enjoyed a pleasant exchange. They even wished us well as we picked up our empty beer bottles and went on our way. Minnesota people are so nice. Let's have another beer."

And so we kept drinking and listening to the radio, chiming in with our own version of a familiar song. And then someone remembers yet another story, and laughter echoes through the night. And what a surprise it was to see the sun rising when we hadn't slept at all. Where went the night?

■ ■ ■

It's a different Saturday night back in Winnipeg, and it's winter. It's too cold to be carousing the friendly pubs of our neighbours to the south. We've just enjoyed a John Wayne movie, and one of the guys suggests we try crashing a men-only beer parlour again. He's heard that the Transcona Hotel turns a blind eye to underage guys, and besides, we must look pretty cool with our long Panda coats and rakish fedoras.

A big burly waiter approaches. "You *boys* must be looking for your dad," he says. "He was here earlier with a few other '*men*,' but they left a long time ago. Sorry, '*boys*.'"

An even bigger waiter appears—or is he the bouncer? They escort us out into the cold. One turns to the other: "The nerve of those '*kids.*' They've got more balls than a brass monkey."

"Oh, they're harmless enough," says his partner. "They just think those clothes make them look like men." They laugh uproariously as they head back inside.

"We wouldn't like it in that smoky, noisy, men-only beer parlour anyway," I tell my buddies. "Just you wait until next summer. We'll have a good time, then . . . guys, we'll have a good time then." And we drive off looking for a place to park where we can practice that hot new song Rod has been raving about.

"Jules, Les, Remi, Leo"   By: Rod Vermette.

CHERRY PIE

It's early December 1953: Heavy snows have put a stop to dragline work, and Dad should be home by now. It's time for him to rest up after those gruelling long days; time for him to be playing solitaire, reading, and doing crossword puzzles at the kitchen table. We've haven't seen Dad since spring. He's sent a couple notes to tell us he's working somewhere west of Regina, Saskatchewan, dredging the headwaters of the city's municipal water system. "Buffalo Pound," they call it. We're expecting him home any day now. Instead, a letter arrives telling us that he's taken on another job that will likely carry on through most of the winter. In the letter, Dad invites me to join him at his new job. "It pays real good," he writes, "and with twelve- to fourteen-hour days, you could be making double what you earn now."

395

I had worked as an oiler for Dad on his dragline over several summers. I learned how to handle the long shifts, the hot days, the cold nights, and the hordes of mosquitoes. *At least there'll be no mosquitoes on this job*, I tell myself. I learned a lot, those early years, but the main lesson I took away was a simple one: I really don't much care for dragline work. It may be the kind of work Dad loves, but it's not for me.

Since our family moved to St. Vital, I've spent summers working at various jobs in the city, jobs more suited to my tastes and talents. The hours aren't nearly as long, so there's time to help Mom with chores around our little acreage, and on weekends I get to do fun things with my buddies.

I accept Dad's job offer without knowing all the details; I'm not sure why. I already have a decent job as a machinist making aircraft parts. The job is boring, and I plan to move on some day, but the real reason I'm ready to quit right now is the satisfaction there will be in telling my cranky boss what he can do with his crummy job.

And there's another reason—a more compelling one: a sense of family duty, you might call it. It began when Dad bought his new dragline a couple years back. He couldn't have known it was a bad time to be making such a major purchase. Drainage projects in Manitoba were drying up, so to speak, and he was forced to look further afield for work or forfeit his precious baby to the bank. And now for the first time he felt compelled to take on a winter job, just to make ends meet.

In his follow-up note, Dad says we'll be building a gravel mountain somewhere on the flat plains of South Saskatchewan. He also sent me a map showing how to get to the construction site. "Bring your sleeping bag," he suggests. "We'll be bunking in a caboose with a couple other guys."

I'm finding it a long, tedious drive across the wide, windswept prairie, with precious few signs of life. It's more pleasant in summer, I'm sure. I make a quick stop in Weyburn for supper, and then it's on to the work camp that will be home for the rest of the winter. Radville, the sign says as I turn south off Highway #13.

A disheartening sight unfolds as I approach the construction camp. Lining the long driveway is a collection of broken-down machinery and random garbage everywhere. A couple dogs—or are they coyotes?—are busy ripping apart bags of kitchen scraps, and now the wind is blowing the stuff all over the place.

Next to the cookhouse is a mysterious sheet of yellow ice, at least twenty feet across, and in the middle sits a crude little shack with a padlock on the door.

"Is that what I think it is?" I ask the guy in the office shack.

"Yep, we call it, 'The House of Pee.' There wasn't time to dig a proper hole, so the wee shack just sits above ground and gravity does the rest."

"So, why the padlock?" I ask, dreading the thought of even walking across this rink of frozen urine.

"Oh, me and you, we can't use the facilities. Them's just for the cookhouse crew. Girls only," he says with a wink. "Us boys have to make do with the big one."

"The big one?" I stupidly ask. "Where's that?"

He points towards the wide-open, treeless prairie and has a good laugh while I feel a bit foolish. "If you've got more serious business in mind, you go up the road a few hundred yards. You'll find an old caragana hedge that cuts the wind a little," the joker suggests. "Just be careful where you step."

Yuck! This is going to be worse than I imagined.

Nobody is answering the door at our designated quarters, so I let myself in. It's full of assorted tools, various supplies, and just plain junk. The smell of diesel fuel is overpowering. *This can't be the right place*, I tell myself. Nobody would ever live in such a messy, smelly place. As my eyes get used to the dark, I spot a few of Dad's personal items strewn across one end of a metal bunk. Damn! I guess this is the right place. It makes me sick to think of him living in such a stink hole.

The sun is setting, but there's enough light to take a quick tour of the gravel pit. It's huge, and it's not a pretty sight. I'm not sure what I was expecting. I just know it didn't match up with my vision of a gravel pit. The scene is something you might expect to find on the surface of the moon: a lifeless landscape with piles of rocks scattered here and there, mounds of sand and random trenches you wouldn't want to fall into. Not a tree, not a shrub, not a blade of grass in sight.

At the far end are a couple draglines and several stone crushers working in tandem to create gravel from the messy mix of sand and stones. Dozens of idling trucks are waiting to be loaded. I find Dad at the controls of a decrepit old dragline, labouring to bust up a thick crust of frozen overburden. *Where's his beautiful orange baby?* I wonder. I jump aboard and watch as he finishes his shift.

The noise from the giant stone crusher nearby is deafening as it busts up stones as big as a human head. Some of the stones appear about the same size and shape as a skull; even the colour is about right. Puffs of mist arising from the freshly disturbed depths add an air of mystery to the scene, causing my mind to speculate. What if this was the site of an ancient Indian burial ground? Would anybody spot a real skull, or would it end up in tiny pieces as part of the roadway somewhere in Saskatchewan? Would anyone care?

"Good to see you," I hear myself say as I extend an open hand.

"Yeah, glad you could come," says Dad as he finally recognizes my gesture and shakes my hand.

I believe this is the first time we ever shook hands, Dad and I. Should I give him a hug? Maybe not. A handshake is probably enough for him to handle right now.

"Let's grab some grub," he suggests, and I pretend I'm hungry even though I ate in Weyburn a little earlier.

"The food's real good," he tells me as we enter the cookhouse. Kate and her daughters do a mighty fine job, considering all the hungry mouths they have to fill. There's around forty guys here. They pop in at odd hours from seven in the morning until nine at night, seven days a week."

When Dad told me he was helping to build a mountain, I knew he wasn't talking about going into competition with the Rockies, but I had no idea of the scale of this project. I still can't fathom the volumes. "So, what's this about building a mountain?" I ask in my innocence. "Sounds simple enough. We'll be loading gravel onto trucks—piece of cake for a dragline, no? Then truckers haul the stuff a few miles to build this Mount Everest. So what's the problem?"

"Oh, there are problems all right, lots and lots of problems," Dad assures me as we make our way to the smelly bunkhouse. He lists the thousands of cubic yards of gravel the Saskatchewan government wants to stockpile along Highway #13 for next summer's construction season, but it doesn't mean much to me. Cubic yards mean everything to Dad. He knows the dragline has a one cubic yard bucket, and he knows how many buckets he can handle in a day. Factored into the equation are stops for refuelling, greasing, or for changing a cable. Of course that doesn't take into account a major breakdown which can takes days to repair. He knows how many yards a modern gravel crusher can handle when the going is good, but at this pit, the going is not so good. There's so much useless sand and way too many oversized rocks. He knows that a typical truck can handle five to ten cubic yards when the roads are decent, but the number of trips per day depends on many things. Broken axles and flat tires are common, almost routine. And the most critical question that no one can answer: How long will the frost last? One good thaw would turn this crappy road into mush and the season is over.

Dad was expecting to use his own dragline on this job. How simple it would have been to transport it by low-bed from Buffalo Pound to Radville when the weather was decent. He keeps telling the boss, Big Red, how his more modern P&H dragline with hydraulic controls could be loading almost double what this old machine can handle.

"Why can't the government just turn this mud trail into an all-weather road," I ask, "and then gravel could be hauled year-round?"

"Politics," was his response. And the snoring begins.

. . .

"Wake up, Jules," Dad announces cheerily. "It's a brand-new day." And I'm thinking, *Oh shit! What did I get myself into?* It's still dark out and freezing cold in this stinky bunkhouse. How I would love to remain cocooned in my snug sleeping bag, and I really could use a couple more hours' sleep.

Guys are stumbling from other bunkhouses, making their way to the cookhouse. Funny, how some skirt around the yellow rink while others saunter through it. I wonder if it says something about their personalities? And how about those ladies working in the cookhouse—what could they be thinking when they need to use the facilities? I try to block these thoughts from my mind as we sit down to eat.

I must say, Dad was right about one thing: the food is real good. Of course it has to be. Whether it's a lumber camp, a mining camp, or whatever kind of men's work camp, the food has to be good or workers will just walk away. It's not like they're super fussy; working guys will put up with all kinds of crap, but the grub has to be top-notch, and that means the cooks have to be top-notch too. I've heard of camps where unhappy workers will demand that the cook be fired. The boss had better find a replacement real quick. It's simply not negotiable. Everything will come to an abrupt halt, and the crew will disappear soon after if he should be stupid enough to hesitate. That's not very likely in this camp. Kate takes great pride in her culinary skills. She runs a tight ship, making sure that everyone is well fed and happy. Some of the young guys call her "Mama Kate." She doesn't seem to mind.

Big Red, the camp boss, and Kate are related somehow, and someone in the family operates a beef ranch nearby. A family operation, you might call it. Beef is on the menu pretty much every day. Whether it's steak, roasts, ribs, stews, or shepherd's pie, they all taste good to me. I never get tired of beef.

I feel much the same about desserts. Cakes, sweet buns, cookies, puddings: they're all good. My favourite is pie, and we get to enjoy this treat quite regularly. I figure there's no such thing as a bad pie, but some are better than others. A few of us guys make a point of expressing our appreciation to Mama Kate and her daughters, especially when a dish is particularly enjoyable, and of course there's always a broad smile in return.

One day I tell Kate how I particularly enjoyed her Saskatoon pie. "I can't take credit," she says. "My daughter Carol bakes all the pies. That's her specialty. So is Saskatoon pie your favourite?" she asks.

"Oh, I just love Saskatoon pie, but they're all so good. Now, if I really had to choose . . ." I hesitate for a moment, pretending I have to think about it. "Can she bake a cherry pie, Mama Kate, Mama Kate?" I sing the line from a song my buddies and I used to sing together; "Billy Boy," I think it's called.

"She can bake a cherry pie fast as a cat can wink an eye," Kate sings back, and then a big smile. "Burl Ives, right?"

The next day, to my amazement, there they were; beautiful, juicy, thick cherry pies with a lattice topping. Everyone raves about them, and Carol comes from the kitchen to take a bow.

Kate pulls me aside. "Since you're such a pie lover, I should tell you we don't have enough refrigeration in this place, so after two days any leftovers get thrown out. If you like, I'll put those two-day-old pies on a certain shelf before chucking them and you can pig out all you want." And so every once in a while, I'll eat a whole pie for breakfast, and you know I don't feel a bit guilty.

It was a challenge trying to make our crappy caboose a bit more liveable. I managed to find a home for the tons of stuff cluttering up the place. Then there was this freezing cold draft that blew unchallenged under the door. No one paid much attention until one morning after a blizzard; we had to shovel away a sizable drift so we could open the door. Now the place looks a bit tidier and it feels warmer, but with the drafts all sealed up, that god-awful diesel smell just gets worse.

It's obvious the smell is coming from the oil stove. There must be a leak somewhere. I clean the carburetor, refit all the connections, and still it leaks. To my horror I discover a crack near the burner that can't be fixed. Big Red promises a new stove, but who knows when he'll get around to it. All I can do is place a tray under the whole thing to collect the leaking oil. Oh well, at least it's no longer leaking on the wood floor. It still smells bad though. Sure hope it doesn't catch fire.

Dad and I share the bunkhouse with two other guys, weird old boys who never utter a word unless you ask a direct question. It seems they can't even respond to a "good morning" salutation. I find this mildly amusing—or perhaps annoying, I'm not sure which. I continue the ritual. I figure one morning they will get so pissed off with me they'll find it easier to say a simple "good morning," and who knows, they might just open up a little after that.

I wasn't expecting a "thank you" for the home improvements I had made, but I did expect some acknowledgement that the place was neater and warmer too. I got nothing. Maybe they didn't even notice.

Dad noticed, though, especially the coat hooks I made with big nails hammered onto a board that I attached to the wall. "Better than draping your clothes over the end of the bunk or throwing them on the floor," he says. Did he say anything about my other efforts? Not so far. Mind you, I'm used to that. I don't remember getting a compliment from my dad. It would have been nice to hear, "Well done, son," or "Good job, Jules," but I never heard any such thing. It just wasn't his style.

There was, however, one initiative that really pleased him, and he let me know it. It involved that most private of all rituals which no human on this planet can avoid. Some call it taking a dump, a number two, or serious business. Or if you're not into euphemisms, having a shit.

When that office clerk suggested that caragana hedge as the only refuge, I didn't believe him at first. How could you operate a camp of forty or so men and not have some kind of toilet facilities? It just seemed too primitive, downright cruel in winter. That was the reality, however, and just as expected, performing this act in the frigid open air with the likelihood of a poop buddy nearby was every bit as miserable as it sounds. Surely there has to be a better way.

A strategy that seemed to work for some of the boys with disciplined bowels was to drive the seven miles into town and have a meal at a local restaurant where you could use the facilities. Kate and her girls serve up better food than any Radville restaurant, so it was pretty hard to justify driving all that way and paying for a meal you could otherwise enjoy for free.

I was feeling that dreaded urge one day when I thought I'd take a drive around the neighbourhood and look for a better site. Almost any kind of wind break with a modicum of privacy would be better than that sparse caragana hedge, but trees around here are scarce as hen's teeth.

Something caught my eye as I passed by a lonely farmstead: a lovely setting on the crest of a ridge overlooking the broad prairie beyond. At first it looked like so many other farms in this harsh land. There was the usual assortment of unpainted sheds and rusting machinery strewn at random around the yard. It all looked so forlorn, so pitiful. *The folks who live here must be a tough breed*, I muse. *Why would they choose to live on top of this ridge where the cold wind blows pretty much non-stop? They may enjoy a fine view, but how do they keep warm in winter?*

And then it hit me. There's no smoke coming from the chimney. There are no tire tracks, and no footprints either. The house is abandoned. Looks like the barn is too. I wonder if the door is locked? Now wouldn't that make an excellent place for the business I have in mind. As I walk to the back of the property, I am greeted by an even greater gift. Tucked between two grain sheds stands a sturdy outhouse, a two-holer, intact except for the missing doors. A feeling of smug satisfaction sweeps over me. Maybe this cruel winter shall be bearable after all.

Dad was ever so pleased. "A genius idea," he called it. I wasn't going to tell anybody about this newfound luxury. I figure the guys in camp would fill it up in a few days, but Dad insists we share our good fortune with our jolly bunkmates, the two old guys who still won't say "good morning."

And did they ever express any appreciation? Nope. I guess that's just not in their vocabulary. Oh well, I know Dad and I are super happy, and what a magnificent view from the throne as we go about our business, our solitary serious business.

It was mid-January by the time Big Red finally recognized that his company wouldn't be able to fulfill the government contract. Mind you, it wasn't all, his fault. There was Christmas break when the whole camp shut down for a week, and shortly after, there was a most unfortunate accident that shut down operations for almost as long. I never did learn the details, but one of the truckers was involved in a tragic road accident that killed a young boy. Out of respect, Big Red shut everything down until after the funeral. Later I learned that the truck driver was so distraught he never returned to work.

The work schedule is way behind, and there will be a penalty to pay if that mountain isn't high enough by spring. Big Red puts aside his pride and asks Dad if he would go to Buffalo Pound and retrieve that fancy new dragline of his and put it to work ASAP.

It's 30 below the morning we leave camp, bright and sunny with very little wind, a good day to be on the road. How excited I am to embark on this adventure. It's bound to be a lot more fun than the everyday routine of keeping that decrepit old dragline oiled and operational. If Dad has any concerns or doubts about the challenges ahead, he keeps them to himself and tries less successfully to hide his amusement at my naive enthusiasm. I know it won't be easy, resuscitating that orange beauty hibernating in a lonely swamp somewhere near Buffalo Pound.

Draglines aren't meant to operate in the winter, especially when it still has summer weight oil and the greased joints will be frozen stiff. I have no doubt that Dad will know what to do, and I'm confident that I'll be up to the task, whatever that might be. I'm not looking for praise, but deep down I feel I have something to prove.

It's a pleasant enough drive from Radville to Elbow, where we'll be staying overnight. I can't say I'm overly impressed with the scenery though; two hundred miles, and it all looks the same to me. It's mostly flat with modest little mounds here and there. The locals call them hills. It gets pretty boring.

The towns in Saskatchewan all look much the same, with a wide main drag and unpretentious wood buildings seldom more than two stories. In stark contrast are the grain elevators, tall as skyscrapers, looking majestic in their solitude. You can spot them from miles away. They give even a modest village a look of prosperity.

Having been raised in Southern Ontario, I can't help making comparisons. The main street of any Ontario town, no matter how small, will always be paved, while Saskatchewan towns are mostly gravel. Seems awfully primitive to my mind, particularly when the road leading in and out of town is sometimes hard-topped. "Why can't they hard top through the town?" I ask.

"Different governments," says Dad, "provincial and municipal." Still totally weird.

"There it is," announces Dad, pointing to an open expanse of snow with tufts of low brush poking through in scattered patches. Ah yes, now I see it: A small orange dot on the horizon with what looks like a little stick pointing skyward at an angle. Hard to imagine that little stick is actually the sixty-foot steel boom.

We take a stroll towards the machine, "just to test things out," says Dad. *Hey, this isn't so bad*, I tell myself as we trudge through the shallow snow. It doesn't last. Those innocent-looking tufts are actually the tops of bushes almost two feet high, and then we encounter those gullies Dad was telling me about. Those dreaded gullies. "They're actually dried-up streams that feed the main swamp during heavy rains," he says. "Sure wouldn't want to tip the machine into one of these, would we?" It's late afternoon. "Nothing much we can do today," he says. "Let's see if we can get someone to give us a ride tomorrow."

We push on to Elbow. *A typical small town*, I'm thinking, except that it's perched on the banks of the mighty Saskatchewan River, which gives it more personality than most. I see one elevator and one brightly painted hotel. I guess that'll be home for tonight.

The proprietor remembers Dad, and we get a warm welcome. Of course he'd be happy to call around and see if someone would give us a ride across that swamp—a team of horses, perhaps, or maybe, just maybe, the blacksmith could be persuaded to give us a ride on his homemade snow machine. Wow! Now wouldn't that be exciting. It seems no matter where you go in Saskatchewan, everyone is super friendly and ready to offer a hand, even when you don't ask.

Our tiny room is a sparsely furnished thing, a cast-iron bed, a rickety wooden chair, and a tiny washstand with a fancy bowl and water pitcher. Somehow this looks vaguely familiar, and then I recall: Every time they depict a hotel room in a cowboy movie, it has to have a cast-iron bed, a chair, and that familiar washstand and bowl.

As I look around, I think I know why the room is so small. I suspect it once was a decent-sized room that could accommodate two beds. Apparently, at one time, it was considered quite normal for strangers to share a room, but we've become more civilized now, or maybe less desperate. That practice has passed into history, so the hotel management decided to throw up a half-ass partition down the middle. I smile inwardly as I recognize the distinctive panelling. Donnacona, they call it, the same stuff Dad used to partition our little house in Vita. It's made from paper pulp; "glorified cardboard," I call it. You could put your fist through it without bruising a knuckle. It was promoted as having near-magical insulating qualities, and many a conman made a good living selling this dubious product to naive customers looking to save on heat.

The bed is barely wide enough for two people. I'm not looking forward to sharing that saggy mattress with Dad. Of course Dad wouldn't consider booking two rooms. Oh no, that would be too extravagant. I think I'll sleep on the floor.

Down the hall is the community washroom. It serves all four rooms on the second floor, but since we're the only guests here tonight, that suits me just fine. I kind of admire the toilet. It's simply a big steel pipe poking through the floor with a conventional toilet seat mounted on top. When you have a dump, it takes a few seconds for the splash. Weird! A clever idea this big pipe; it doesn't need a flush system. It smells a bit, but you just crack the window a bit. I must say it's a whole lot better than at the King's Hotel in Radville, where guests are forced to make do with a five-gallon pail at the end of the hall. Gross! I wonder how many "kings" have stayed there overnight?

Next morning at breakfast, the hotel cook is incredulous as we explain our plan to walk to the dragline. He knows where it's parked. He shakes his head and mutters to himself as he prepares a huge pile of sandwiches for us to take on our little jaunt.

We don't talk much as we drive the ten miles or so towards the machine. I can better understand why nobody would give us a ride. It starts to make sense when we come up against those shrubs where the snow has drifted a couple feet deep. Less predictable are the gullies with sudden dips and holes where a machine could get stuck or a horse could stumble and break a leg. This is going to be rough.

It takes almost two hours to walk that long mile. I'm exhausted, and the day is just beginning. It would nice to rest a little, now that we're by the machine. There's no time for that, though. Dad is already busy checking things out. I best get busy too.

"Now all we have to do is start'er up and drive'er out of here," I joke. "Heck, we could be back in Radville for lunch." Silence. Either Dad hasn't heard me, or he doesn't appreciate my attempt at humour. I sense we won't be talking much today.

I soon learn that breathing life into this mechanical marvel when it has slept half the winter at temperatures down to minus 40 won't be so easy. Thankfully it's a balmy minus 24 this morning. I'm actually a bit too warm after that walk. No doubt that will change as the day wears on.

"You can start by making me a stove," says Dad. He waits a few minutes, finally realizing I have no idea what he's talking about. "Just punch a bunch of holes around the bottom of this pail. You soak a few rags with diesel and prop it under the transmission. The summer-weight transmission oil is thicker than molasses." Now, why didn't I know that?

To my surprise and frustration, the oil-soaked rags won't light. That certainly wouldn't be a problem in summer, I know. That's how I started smudges when the mosquitoes got really bad in those swamps around Vita. "Just soak a small rag in gasoline," Dad suggests impatiently.

Warming up the fuel lines with the blowtorch is my next assignment, and I'm pleased to realize I can use the same trick to light the reluctant blowtorch. And so the day goes, learning new skills and tricks and trying to be useful.

Meanwhile, Dad has started the small auxiliary gasoline motor that is built into the main Caterpillar diesel engine. I suspect he is feeling a bit smug right now. He had a choice when he ordered his machine a couple years back. He could go with the standard electric starter motor with a heavy-duty battery pack, or pay a bit more and opt for a gasoline starter motor. "The small gas engine serves two purposes," he proudly explains. "The hot exhaust gases are routed in such a way that they preheat the diesel's exhaust manifold, and then you engage a clutch and it cranks over the main engine. And no troublesome batteries," he adds with a smile.

I can better appreciate this critical feature after witnessing the rigmarole the gravel-crushing crew at the Radville worksite go through whenever they have to shut down the "Big Bad Buda"; the monster gravel crusher has to have a name, it seems. It must be a pain discon-necting the dozens of acid-coated battery connectors, then they've got to haul the heavy batteries down a steel ladder to the bunkhouse, the one they sleep in, just to keep the batteries warm. I had to smile when I noticed a small notch at the bottom of the bunkhouse door to accommodate the charger cables connected to a gasoline genera-tor purring outside through the night. "You got to keep those finicky batteries fully charged. What a pain in the ass," Dad smugly observes. "We could never start this machine if we had a battery type, electric starter motor."

Dad has been busy bleeding hydraulic lines and ensuring there are no air locks in the fuel system. Some of the rituals I don't understand, but now is not the time to be bothering him with questions.

All in all, things go slowly but smoothly. Warming that gummy transmission takes a lot longer than anticipated and it takes more time to go back to the half-ton for that special tool Dad just had to have.

The little auxiliary engine has been running at a fast idle for quite some time. Time to put it to work. I can almost feel its pain as it struggles to turn over the main engine, slowly at first and gradually it picks up speed. A few coughs, a pause, more coughs, and then a deep-throated rumble as the big Cat comes to life. The whole dragline shakes, just like a dog after a swim in a cold lake. I couldn't be happier, but Dad's not cheering. He's kicking himself for neglecting to fill the main fuel tank last fall. He hopes we'll have enough diesel oil, but he's not sure.

The big diesel is running smoothly now, the shaking has smoothed out to a steady vibration, and all the hydraulic clutches and brakes are operating beautifully. It's time to roll.

"Start the lighting plant," Dad commands. "It'll soon be dark."

This should be easy enough; I do that every evening back at the job site in Radville. "Why won't this generator start?" Dad narrows down the problem to a cracked ignition coil. It's not something we can fix right now. It's getting colder and the wind is picking up as the feeble sun sets in a blustery haze. No lighting plant means no lights to steer by. "We have a problem," Dad admits. What to do?

For the first time on our venture, I sense that Dad is worried. As daylight disappears, it will be impossible to manoeuvre this clumsy giant between the drifts and avoid those dreaded gullies. And if we get to the road, do we risk the possibility that a vehicle could smash into this immovable pile of steel in the dark? Now that would be a real disaster.

The alternatives are not great either. In less than an hour, it'll be too dark to see where we're going. Do we park the machine and wait for daybreak? Of course we'd have to keep the engine running the whole time. We mustn't let the machine cool down, not after all that work. And how long will the fuel last? Meanwhile one of us would have to contact the low-bed driver who shall be waiting at the rendezvous at dawn.

"Come on, Dad, let's just go," I insist. "You drive, and I'll walk ahead and direct you with a flashlight." At full speed the dragline travels about a half-mile per hour, so there's time to zigzag on foot and find a way. Luckily, I have two flashlights. As one dims from the cold, I replace it with another that I keep next to my body.

The temperature is dropping fast, but I barely feel the cold. I am totally focused as I trudge back and forth trying to avoid the deepest drifts and those treacherous gullies. We're making progress, but it's taking so long; it's been several hours, and I'm running out of steam. Just ahead, I detect a shallow depression that appears perfectly straight and goes on forever. *You dummy!* I tell myself. *That's the ditch that parallels the road.*

"We made it! We made it!" I shout. Now to find the truck; it can't be far.

Dad doesn't quite share my exuberance as we climb into the pickup. He is so frozen he can barely move, and I'm so exhausted I can barely move. We eat the rest of our frozen sandwiches in silence and slowly, ever so slowly, life returns to our bodies. We still have miles to go, but the worst is over and I'm feeling totally confident—a bit cocky, even. *The rest should be easy*, I tell myself, *a piece of cake*.

Dad is happy to let me drive the cold, ponderous machine while he follows in the warm pickup. He offers to spell me after a while, but I refuse. I know for certain I would promptly fall asleep at the wheel of the pickup and that would not be good. We carry on through the night, hoping we won't meet any cars or trucks or the police.

Our destination: a ranch that boasts a heavy-duty ramp designed for loading cattle onto trucks. "The ramp works well for draglines too," Dad assures me. That's where he took delivery of his machine last spring.

"And the low-bed will meet us at dawn," I say, repeating the obvious.

On the crest of a low hill, Dad calls me into the truck—to thaw out, I'm guessing, but no, he has a proposition to make. "Two more miles to go," he says, "four hours if we stick to the road. Or, would you like to take a shortcut across this field to our right?" he asks. "We could save some time, and we're running short on time."

"And fuel," I needlessly remind him. And then it dawns on me. "Wait a minute; how will the pickup handle the deep snow?"

"Oh, I won't be following you in the pickup," he says rather casually. "I'll be taking the road to the farm, and I'll wait for you by the ramp."

My mind is befuddled. I can't believe what I'm hearing. I ask Dad to repeat his plan.

"Well, if we stick to the road, it continues for another mile or so, then it turns right, goes another mile, and voila: we're at the farm with the ramp."

"Aha, I get it. The roads form a ninety-degree right angle, and the shortcut would be the hypotenuse of an isosceles triangle. I can calculate the length of the shortcut," I offer.

"Never mind," he says. I guess Dad's not too interested in geometry. "Can you take the machine the rest of the way by yourself? I've pretty much had it," he admits.

I am utterly flabbergasted. I can hardly believe it. Dad is asking me to drive his precious machine across this snow-covered field in the dark all by myself. Wow! I'm excited beyond words.

"There's a creek to the north," Dad warns. "If you see it, you'll know you've gone too far north. Don't get too close; there may be gullies. And if you come to a big ditch, you'll know you've gone too far west. I don't think it's steep enough to tip the machine over, but don't try it. And by the way, if you run out of fuel, stay with the machine. We'll get to you when there's light."

As I watch the pickup disappear down the road, I imagine the tail-lights drawing one leg of that isosceles triangle. There won't be another reference until I get to that creek or the ditch. Of course there'll be the lights from the pickup at the farm eventually, but I won't see them for a couple hours at least. I must position the machine at forty-five degrees to that imaginary line and just plough ahead—a shot in the dark, you might call it. Thank goodness there are no more gullies and no deep snowdrifts; just a foot or so of pristine white stuff with wheat stubble poking through in places.

All sorts of thoughts are running through my mind as the machine inches its way along the hypotenuse. According to Mr. Pythagoras, the distance should be 1.4 miles, which means it should take approximately three hours. That's providing there aren't too many corrections required along the way.

There's no moon tonight, not even stars; they're hidden by low clouds, making ambient light really faint. Visibility extends maybe a hundred yards, but there's no way to tell for sure. Everything is totally white, white, white.

I imagine that I'm on a giant spaceship floating through the cosmos, not knowing how far to the next planet or some faraway star. *Patience, patience*, I tell myself. *Eventually, something will show up.* I pass the time, shuffling back and forth from the controls to the back of the machine where the engine throws off a bit of precious heat. Must be getting colder outside. Maybe the clouds will dissipate? "Let there be light," I shout out loud, just to hear a sound other than the monotonous drone of the engine. Helps to keep me awake too, I figure. I don't dare sit; I'd be asleep in a flash. I've been awake for over twenty hours now; got to hang in a bit longer. I wonder if a person can fall asleep while standing upright?

Two hours pass. The thrill of piloting this big hunk of steel is starting to wear thin. I slide open the cab's steel door for better visibility and stare into the void. Nothing. I'm tempted to jump to the ground and exercise a bit. At a half-mile per hour, it's unlikely the machine would outpace me. A little inner voice cuts in. *What if you trip in a gopher hole and you break a leg, Jules? Happens often enough with horses, you know. And then you couldn't get back in to drive, and who knows where Dad's precious machine would end up? And who knows where you would end up, Jules? Most likely they'd find your frozen body in the spring.* I have to admit, that would be pretty awkward. Let's just close the door and carry on.

Stare long enough at something, and your mind starts playing tricks. I think that's what's going on right now. Off to my right there's a faint grey band along what could be the horizon. I stare in the opposite direction. Nothing. Back to the other side. Over time, the grey band gets darker. Back and forth I stare until there's no doubt. That grey band must be the creek Dad warned about.

My mind has now substituted my spaceship for an ancient sailing galleon from centuries past, and I am Magellan the mariner-explorer, and I'm determined to be the first human to cross the Pacific.

Those aren't willows I'm seeing off to starboard; those are palm trees indicating a low-lying Pacific island. I'll bet it's inhabited by hostile cannibals. We don't want to mess with those guys. "Eyes peeled, Helmsman! What say ye?" I shout. "Tack to port, ten degrees. Steady as she goes, mate, steady as she goes."

"Ahoy, captain," my first mate shouts from the crow's nest. "There's a faint light to port, four degrees. Looks like the Southern Cross star."

But it's not the Southern Cross, and I'm not Magellan. I'm just a kid who has piloted forty tons of steel across a frozen wheat field in Saskatchewan in the middle of the night. It's got to be at least minus 30 out there, and not much warmer in this semi-open cab. I've been alone in the dark for over three hours, and I'm super pleased with how everything turned out.

As I approach triumphantly, towards the pickup I can see Dad directing the low-bed truck to the ramp. My part is done, and I'm happy to let him take over the controls to do the loading. "See you in Radville," confirms the low bed driver.

"So, how'd it go?" asks Dad as we follow the low bed in our pickup.

"Just like Pythagoras hypothesized," I want to tell him, but that would be a smart-ass thing to say. "Nothing to it . . . piece of cake."

Dad chuckles and says no more.

∎ ∎ ∎

The early morning radio gal seems to delight in telling us that it's minus 34 degrees in Moosejaw with light winds; a typical January day in Saskatchewan. "Do you suppose we can stop for breakfast in Moosejaw, Dad? I'm starving."

We pass a sign announcing "EYEBROW." *Another weird name for a town*, I'm thinking, as I start to nod off. I'm awake enough to recognize that Dad has turned off the highway. He stops in front of what looks like a derelict building with a faded sign reading "CHARLIE'S KITCHEN."

"It's not yet seven, the place can't be open," I protest.

"Come on," says Dad. "You said you were hungry." He pounds away at the back door until a dishevelled Chinese gentleman appears in a ratty nightgown and bare feet. He rubs the sleep from his eyes and then a big smile of recognition as he greets Dad like some long-lost brother.

"The usual," says Dad, "only triple everything."

I can't believe the scene. Here we are, just Dad and me, sitting in a freezing cold Chinese restaurant with our parkas on, waiting for our breakfast. Meanwhile, Charlie's in the kitchen chopping wood for the stove, still in his nightgown. At least he's wearing slippers now. This will take a while, but I guess nobody's in a hurry.

"So how did you get to know Charlie?" I ask.

"Last summer I used to eat here pretty regular," Dad explains. "Charlie's a great old guy. His father came from China to help build the railway back around 1880. When it was finished, there were no jobs to be found so he started a restaurant. Later he went back to China and brought back a wife and together they had Charlie. Charlie took over the business when his parents passed away. I guess he's been here ever since."

I look around and try to imagine what this place looked like when it was new. It may have been fine for the times, but that was decades ago. It doesn't look like much has changed since—not the leatherette-covered booths, not the curtains, not even the paint.

Charlie never married. He has no relatives and few friends. "How does he cope," I wonder out loud, "living in this cold, bleak place, unable to fit into the local culture? God, it must be lonely!"

"Oh, Charlie does alright," Dad assures me. "He gets to talk with lots of people, and once a year he goes back to China for a month."

And now comes the food: plate after plate of exotic dishes, and they smell just heavenly. It looks like there's enough to feed a caboose full of hungry lumberjacks. We can't eat all this; there must be a mistake? But then Dad invites Charley to join us, and the three of us have no trouble putting it all away.

I notice Dad tipping Charlie with a two-dollar bill. "Way to go, Dad," I tell him as we waddle back to the pick up. "Maybe now Charlie will forgive you for waking him up at such a god-awful hour." Dad can be considerate at times.

A cold wind is picking up, blowing swirling wisps of icy snow across the highway, and it's minus 36 degrees. I hate the wind. I dread the thought of being stuck on some lonely road at a time like this, especially at night. "It happens often enough," says Dad. "You just need a minor mechanical problem, a flat tire, or maybe you run out of gas. If someone doesn't come along pretty soon, you die." It's a rare day in these parts when there isn't a stiff breeze blowing. Just add a bit of snow and presto, you've got a blizzard. Visibility fades to nil. So it comes as no surprise to hear of another highway death in Saskatchewan. I hate the wind.

It comes as a pleasant surprise when I learn that Dad has booked a room at the Empire Hotel. It's the classier of the two hotels in Radville. It comes with separate beds and a tub, and you don't have to go down the hall to some crappy public toilet either. *Yes*, I'm thinking, *Dad can be considerate at times.* I've never been here before, so I follow without question as he enters the men-only beer parlour. It seems natural enough, even though I'm below the legal age. "Two beers," he tells the waiter. "No! Make that four."

You know, we never did talk much about that whole marvellous adventure that winter in Saskatchewan, but nobody had to tell me; I wasn't a kid anymore.

Acknowledgements

Writing a book about my youth seemed simple enough at first. Little did I suspect that it would become a minor Odyssey, maybe not as epic as Homer's poetic tales, but daunting enough. Early on it became clear that I would need a co-pilot. Naturally I turned to my confidante, my life mate, Gladys Legal who became my main editor and my ultimate critic. Together we would turn my digital scribbles into something that resembled a book.

The journey began about ten years ago in a creative writing class where our teacher, Sharon Melnicer, maintained that we all have the ability to write. "We are all writers," she would insist and some of us actually believed her. As the lessons progressed it became obvious that every writer also needs advisors and honest critics. My daughter Paula, who had heard the stories multiple times before, encouraged me to write them down for posterity while another daughter, Louise, read every line, correcting mistakes and making helpful suggestions. Diane Little and Donna Goodman, both retired teachers, seemed willing to correct mistakes and point out flaws just as they had done a million times before with their former students.

When I had questions about family history, I turned to my cousins, Len Gauthier, Marcel Gauthier, Leo Rowan and Gerry Pelletier. All contributed as informal historians. I also took inspiration from Blandine Dornez and her daughter Claudette who wrote a charming account about everyday life in early Ste. Geneviève. There was also

Gilbert Legal who wrote a humorous personal memoir from another perspective. And then there is Cathy Pelletier who writes regularly in the Thorold News, a local paper in the Niagara region owned and operated by her and her husband. Thank you all dear cousins.

Delving into unfamiliar territory, I also leaned upon trusted friends that I considered expert in their field. Marcel Ritchot was my advisor in the use of French words, French phrases and yes, curse words too. When I wanted to throw in a few Ukrainian words for effect I turned to Wilma Sotas and Bohdan Grabbish for their version of the phonetic translation. Stephen Meehan, another dear friend, played a vital role in designing the book cover. He also restored damaged yet precious old photos, a few dating back over 100 years.

Finally a professional editor, Adrianne Winfield was retained and her expertise and attention to detail brought the manuscript to another level.

How I would have loved to also thank my Mom and several favourite aunts. Whenever they got together much of their time was spent, relating stories, exchanging opinions and telling jokes. Gossip some would call it but I just loved listening in. Even when they must have known that I was within earshot, their chatter continued unabated and I took copious mental notes. Sadly they are no longer with us but as you may have noticed, their voices permeate throughout the book.

Disclaimer

Through the editing and revision process a few readers expressed discomfort when the descriptor "Indian" was used to identify First Nations people. I wish to assure readers that any reference to Indian people was always written in a respectful context, never was it meant as a pejorative. Furthermore the terms "First Nations", "Aboriginals", "Indigenous", "Natives" were never heard during the era described. The historical value of the book would be compromised if the term "Indian" were replaced with any of these more modern terms.

Readers may find the language somewhat crude or risqué at times. I can attest that a lot of boys and yes some adults too, used unrefined language that some would consider offensive. It was just part of their persona. I cleaned up much of the crude talk that prevailed at the time but it didn't feel right to expunge all such language. I can only hope that I haven't offended anyone.

About the Author

Jules Legal is a Canadian writer who has lived an exciting and multifaceted life. After graduating from the Manitoba Institute of Technology, his education and pursuit of knowledge persisted for four decades, largely in the fields of science and technology. His professional life began in 1955 at the Manitoba Cancer Treatment and Research Foundation, where he devoted thirty-five years inventing, designing, and developing a variety of medical instruments and equipment, many of which were dedicated to the diagnosis and treatment of cancer. He then spent fifteen years working for the University of Pittsburgh's Rehab Engineering Department, designing devices for people with disabilities. Jules has also dabbled in politics, environmental activism, union activism, urban planning, architecture and woodworking. Leisure pursuits involved extensive travel and annual wilderness canoe trips where he and his buddies imagined themselves to be carefree, Coureurs des Bois, exploring the countless streams and lakes of Manitoba and Ontario. Born from a long line of storytellers, he was inspired to share the story of his own upbringing, as told in the pages of *A Bowl of Cherries*, his first publication. Jules currently resides with his partner Gladys in a timber truss home they built on the outskirts of Winnipeg, and together they share four amazing daughters and many precious grandchildren.

Printed in Canada